HISTORICAL DICTIONARIES OF
INTERNATIONAL ORGANIZATIONS SERIES
Edited by Jon Woronoff

1. *European Community,* by Desmond Dinan. 1993
2. *International Monetary Fund,* by Norman K. Humphreys. 1993
3. *International Organizations in Sub-Saharan Africa,* by Mark W. DeLancey and Terry M. Mays. 1994
4. *European Organizations,* by Derek W. Urwin. 1994
5. *International Tribunals,* by Boleslaw Adam Boczek. 1994
6. *International Food Agencies: FAO, WFP, WFC, IFAD,* by Ross B. Talbot. 1994
7. *Refugee and Disaster Relief Organizations,* by Robert F. Gorman. 1994
8. *United Nations,* by A. LeRoy Bennett. 1995
9. *Multinational Peacekeeping,* by Terry Mays. 1996
10. *Aid and Development Organizations,* by Guy Arnold. 1996
11. *World Bank,* by Anne C. M. Salda. 1997
12. *Human Rights and Humanitarian Organizations,* by Robert F. Gorman and Edward S. Mihalkanin. 1997
13. *United Nations Educational, Scientific and Cultural Organization (UNESCO),* by Seth Spaulding and Lin Lin. 1997
14. *Inter-American Organizations,* by Larman C. Wilson and David W. Dent. 1997
15. *World Health Organization,* by Kelley Lee. 1998
16. *International Organizations,* by Michael G. Schechter. 1998
17. *International Monetary Fund,* Second Edition, by Norman K. Humphreys. 1999
18. *Refugee and Disaster Relief Organizations,* Second Edition, by Robert F. Gorman. 2000
19. *Arab and Islamic Organizations,* by Frank A. Clements. 2001
20. *Asian-Pacific Organizations,* by Derek McDougall. 2001

Historical Dictionary of Arab and Islamic Organizations

Frank A. Clements

Historical Dictionaries of International Organizations, No. 19

The Scarecrow Press, Inc.
Lanham, Maryland, and London
2001

SCARECROW PRESS, INC.

Published in the United States of America
by Scarecrow Press, Inc.
4720 Boston Way, Lanham, Maryland 20706
www.scarecrowpress.com

4 Pleydell Gardens, Folkestone
Kent CT20 2DN, England

British Library Cataloguing-in-Publication Information Available

Library of Congress Cataloging-in-Publication Data
Clements, Frank, 1942–
    Historical dictionary of Arab and Islamic organizations / Frank A. Clements.
        p. cm. — (Historical dictionaries of international organizations ; no. 19)
    Includes bibliographical references.
    ISBN 0-8108-3977-6 (alk. paper)
        1. Arab countries—Dictionaries. 2. Islamic countries—Dictionaries. I. Title.
    II. Historical dictionaries of international organizations series ; no. 19.
    DS36.55 .C57 2001
    909'.0974927—dc21   00-052644

⊖™ The paper used in this publication meets the minimum requirements of
American National Standard for Information Sciences—Permanence of
Paper for Printed Library Materials, ANSI/NISO Z39.48-1992.
Manufactured in the United States of America.

Contents

Editor's Foreword

In few places is the word *unity* spoken with such fervor and sought so ardently as in the Arab world and the wider circle of Islamic countries. This is not hard to understand. The Arab heritage runs extremely deep and Islam is an exceedingly powerful unifying force. Yet, when considering the region, one finds disappointingly few concrete achievements despite the countless dreams and schemes. More strikingly, there are not even that many quite ordinary international organizations such as can be found in greater profusion in other parts of the world with far less common interests and traditions.

This paradox is certainly easier to grasp after reading the *Historical Dictionary of Arab and Islamic Organizations*. For it does what it should do, namely shows that along with the underlying sources of unity there are also sources of division. Moreover, all too often, excessive demands for unity have prevented more modest projects that could have paved the way to greater unity in a more distant future. This can be accomplished at several levels. First, that of the various countries, many of which have not achieved national unity and yet press for much greater unity. Second, that of the many bodies and organizations, which are forging practical links, but perhaps not fast enough for impatient observers. And third, that of the underlying forces, including Arab nationalism, pan-Arabism, and, most notably, Islam itself, whose expectations are so hard to fulfill.

Thus, unlike the other volumes in the series of Historical Dictionaries of International Organizations, this volume focuses not only on the organizations as such but also, and sometimes even more so, on key countries in the region. Further entries present the leaders, whether kings and emirs, politicians, ideologues, or activists, who dominate the debate and shape the actions. And others, also fairly numerous, explain the underlying forces generating deeper unity. This is done in the Dictionary. The broader background is presented in the Introduction. The Chronology traces the various trends and highlights crucial events. And the bibliography provides an abundance of further sources on the many aspects of unity and organization.

The author of this volume, Frank A. Clements, had been preparing for this task long before he ever began. He studied the Arab world back in the 1960s. In the 1970s he wrote a book on Arab nationalism and another on Saudi Arabia. In the 1980s he worked as a consultant in

Arab countries and produced further books on Oman, Kuwait, and the United Arab Emirates. This was followed in the 1990s by books on Arab regional organizations and the Israeli Secret Services. Some of these books dealt with political, economic, and social situations; others were bibliographies. The knowledge accumulated in this way has served Mr. Clements well in this historical dictionary, which combines substantive information on the countries and organizations with a comprehensive bibliography.

Jon Woronoff
Series Editor

Abbreviations and Acronyms

AACO	Arab Air Carriers Organization
AAEA	Arab Atomic Energy Authority
AAHO	Afro-Asian Housing Organization
AAPSO	Afro-Asian Peoples' Solidarity Organization
AASTMT	Arab Academy for Science, Technology, and Marine Transport
AAWA	Afro-Asian Writers' Association
ABC	Arab Banking Corporation
ACAC	Arab Civil Aviation Council
ACADI	Arab Center for Agricultural Documentation and Information
ACC	Arab Cooperation Council
ACM	Arab Common Market
ADB	African Development Bank
ADF	Arab Deterrent Force
ADF	African Development Fund
AFAED	Abu Dhabi Fund for Arab Economic Development
AFESD	Arab Fund for Economic and Social Development
AFPMCW	Arab Federation of Petroleum, Mining, and Chemicals Workers
AFRASEC	Afro-Asian Organization for Economic Cooperation
AGFUND	Arab Gulf Program for the United Nations Development Organizations
AHC	Arab Higher Committee
AICP	Association of Islamic Charitable Projects
AIPU	Arab Inter-Parliamentary Union
AKF	Aga Khan Foundation
AL	Arab League
ALECSO	Arab League Educational, Cultural, and Scientific Organization
ALO	Arab Labour Organization
AMF	Arab Monetary Fund
AMR	Association of Muslim Researchers
AMSE	Association of Muslim Scientists and Engineers
AMSS	Association of Muslim Social Scientists
ANM	Arab National Movement
AOAD	Arab Organization for Agricultural Development
AOHR	Arab Organization for Human Rights
AOI	Arab Organization for Industrialization
API	Arab Planning Institute

ARABSAT	Arab Satellite Communication Organization
ARADO	Arab Administrative Development Organization
ARAMCO	Arabian American Oil Company
ASBU	Arab States Broadcasting Union
ASCA	Arab Society of Certified Accountants
ATFP	Arab Trade Financing Program
ATO	Arab Towns Organization
ATU	Arab Telecommunications Union
ATU	Arab Tourism Union
AUDI	Arab Urban Development Institute
AWSA	Arab Women's Solidarity Association
BNLF	Bahrain National Liberation Front
BSP	Ba'ath Socialist Party
CAEU	Council of Arab Economic Unity
CEDARE	Center for Environment and Development in the Arab Region and Europe
CENTO	Central Treaty Organization
CIE	Council on Islamic Education
DRY	Democratic Republic of Yemen
ECO	Economic Cooperation Organization
ECOSOC	Economic and Social Council of the United Nations
ESCWA	United Nations Economic and Social Commission for Western Asia
EU	European Union
FAO	Food and Agriculture Organization
FIOE	Federation of Islamic Organizations in Europe
FIS	Front Islamique de Salut
FLN	Front de Libération Nationale
FNC	Federal National Council (United Arab Emirates)
FROLINAT	Front de Libération Nationale du Tchad
GAA	General Armistice Agreements, 1949
GCC	Gulf Cooperation Council
GIC	Gulf Investment Corporation
GOIC	Gulf Organization for Industrial Consultancy
GPC	General People's Congress (Yemen)

GRF	Global Relief Foundation
HAMAS	Harakay al-Muqawama al-Islami
IAIGC	Inter-Arab Investment Guarantee Corporation
IANA	Islamic Assembly of North America
IAP	Islamic Association for Palestine
IARA	Islamic African Relief Agency
IAS	Islamic Academy of Science
ICARDA	International Center for Agricultural Research in the Dry Areas
ICATU	International Confederation of Arab Trade Unions
ICC	Islamic Chamber of Commerce
ICD	Ibn Khaldun Center for Development
ICDT	Islamic Center for the Development of Trade
ICIRC	Islamic Committee for the International Red Crescent
ICO	Islamic Conference Organization
ICPICH	International Commission for the Preservation of Islamic Cultural Heritage
ICS	Islamic Call Society
IDB	Islamic Development Bank
IFSTD	Islamic Foundation for Science, Technology, and Development
IHRC	Islamic Human Rights Commission
IIFSO	International Islamic Federation of Student Organizations
IIIM	International Institute of Islamic Medicine
IIIT	International Institute of Islamic Thought
IINA	International Islamic News Agency
IIO	International Islamic Organization
IIRO	International Islamic Relief Organization
IIT	Islamic Institute of Technology
IIUI	International Islamic University Islamabad
IIUM	International Islamic University Malaysia
IJ	Islamic Jihad
IMAN	International Muslimah Artists Network
IMF	International Monetary Fund
INWRDAM	Inter-Islamic Network on Water Resources Development and Management
IOR-ARC	Indian Ocean Rim - Association for Regional Cooperation

IPPF	International Planned Parenthood Federation
IRCICA	Research Centre for Islamic History, Art, and Culture
IRF	Islamic Research Foundation
ISESCO	Islamic Educational, Scientific, and Cultural Organization
ISF	Islamic Solidarity Fund
ISTAD	Islamic Foundation for Science, Technology, and Development
IUN	Islamic University of Niger
IUU	Islamic University in Uganda
JDECT	Joint Defense and Economic Cooperation Treaty
KAR	Kurdish Autonomous Region
KDP	Kurdish Democratic Party (Partiya Demoktata Kurditane)
KDPI	Kurdish Democratic Party of Iran
KFAED	Kuwait Fund for Arab Economic Development
KFF	King Faisal Foundation
LNM	Lebanese National Movement
MAC	Mixed Armistice Commission
MB	Muslim Brotherhood
MEDO	Middle East Defense Organization
MEDRC	Middle East Desalination Research Center
MENA	Middle East News Agency
MFO	Multinational Force and Observers
MINURSO	United Nations Mission for the Referendum in Western Sahara
MNFI	Multinational Forces I
MNFII	Multinational Forces II
MNS	Middle East Neurosurgical Society
MWL	Muslim Women's League
MWL	Muslim World League
NDP	National Democratic Party
NGOs	Nongovernmental Organizations
NLF	National Front for the Liberation of South Yemen
NLP	National Liberal Party (Lebanon)
NLSY	National Front for the Liberation of South Yemen

OAPEC	Organization of Arab Petroleum Exporting Countries
OAU	Organization of African Unity
ODD	Observer Detachment Damascus
OGB	Observer Group Beirut
OGE	Observer Group Egypt
OGG	Observer Group Golan
OGL	Observer Group Lebanon
OIC	Organization of the Islamic Conference
OICC	Organization of Islamic Capitals and Cities
OIRAP	Organization of the Islamic Revolution in the Arabian Peninsula
OISA	Organization of Islamic Shipowners Association
OPEC	Organization of Petroleum Exporting Countries
PDPA	People's Democratic Party of Afghanistan
PDRY	People's Democratic Republic of Yemen
PFLOAG	Popular Front for the Liberation of the Occupied Arab Gulf
PFLOAG	Popular Front for the Liberation of Oman and the Arab Gulf
PFLP	Popular Front for the Liberation of Palestine
PKK	Kurdish Workers' Party
PLO	Palestine Liberation Organization
PNA	Palestinian National Authority
PNC	Palestinian National Council
PPA	Parti du Peuple d'Algérie
PPS	Parti Populaire Syrien
PSP	Progressive Socialist Party (Lebanon)
PUK	Patriotic Union of Kurdistan
RAITNET	Regional Arab Information Technology Network
RCC	Revolutionary Command Council
RITSEC	Regional Information Technology and Software Engineering Center
SASF	Symbolic Arab Security Force
SFD	Saudi Fund for Development
SSNP	Syrian Social Nationalist Party
UAB	Union of Arab Banks

UAE	United Arab Emirates
UAJ	Union of Arab Jurists
UAM	Union of the Arab Maghreb
UAR	United Arab Republic
UNDOF	United Nations Disengagement Observer Force
UNDP	United Nations Development Program
UNEFI	United Nations Emergency Force I
UNEFII	United Nations Emergency Force II
UNESCO	United Nations Educational, Scientific, and Cultural Organization
UNESOB	United Nations Economic and Social Office in Beirut
UNGCI	United Nations Guard Contingent in Iraq
UNHCR	United Nations High Commission for Refugees
UNIFIL	United Nations Interim Force in Lebanon
UNIIMOG	United Nations Iraq-Iran Military Observer Group
UNIKOM	United Nations Iraq-Kuwait Military Observer Mission
UNOGIL	United Nations Observation Group in Lebanon
UNRPR	United Nations Relief for Palestinian Refugees
UNRWA	United Nations Relief and Works Agency
UNSCOM	United Nations Special Commission on Iraq
UNSCOP	United Nations Special Commission on Palestine
UNSDNP	United Nations Sustainable Development Networking Program
UNTSO	United Nations Truce Supervision Organization
UNYOM	United Nations Yemen Observation Mission
USAID-WBG	United States Agency for International Development: West Bank and Gaza Mission
USTMA	Union Syndicale des Travailleurs du Maghreb Arabe
WAMY	World Association of Muslim Youth
WCIC	World Council of Islamic Call
WMC	World Muslim Congress
YAR	Yemen Arab Republic
YIG	Islamic Yemeni Islah Group
YSP	Yemen Socialist Party

Chronology

ca. 570-632   Life of Muhammad.

658   Split between Khariji and Ibadhi.

661   Ali assassinated.

681   Hussein, son of Caliph Ali, killed at Karbala.

750   Umayyad Caliphate ends.

751   Abbasid Caliphate Shi'i Islamic sect established.

932   Sunni Caliph in Baghdad subjugated, Fatamid Caliphate established in Cairo.

1710   Al-Sabah arrive in Kuwait.

1745   Wahhabism adopted by Al-Sauds.

ca. 1750 Bani Yas arrive in Abu Dhabi.

1783   Al-Khalifa arrive in Bahrain.

1830   French begin conquest of Algeria.

1911   Negotiations between Sherif Hussein of Mecca and Great Britain.

1916   Arab Revolt against Turkey declared.

1917   Balfour Declaration on Jewish National Home.

1919   Afghanistan gains independence from Great Britain. Wafd Party founded in Egypt.

1920   **10 August:** Treaty of Sèvres between Allies and Ottoman Empire.

1922   **December:** Uqayr Conference establishes neutral zone between Kuwait and Saudi Arabia and between Iraq and Kuwait.

1923   **23 July:** Treaty of Lausanne between Allies and Turkey.

1924   Hedjaz captured by Ibn Saud.

1928   Muslim Brotherhood founded in Egypt.

1929   **March:** Ikhwan troops defeated by Ibn Saud.

1932   Iraq becomes independent. Kingdom of Saudi Arabia established by Ibn Saud. Syrian Social Nationalist Party founded.

1937   Peel Commission on Palestine.

1939   London Round Table Conference on Palestine.

1941   Lebanon and Syria gain independence.

1944   **25 September–7 October:** Alexandria Conference of Arab States. **March:** Arab League founded.

1944   **2 December:** Arab Boycott of Israel begins.

1945   Jordan becomes independent.

1947   Arab Ba'ath Party established. **15 May:** United Nations Special Committee on Palestine formed.

1948   **14 May:** Outbreak of first Arab-Israeli War. Israel established. **December:** United Nations Relief and Works Agency for Palestine established.

1952   Arab National Movement founded. **22 July:** Free Officers coup in Egypt.

1953   Arab Ba'ath Socialist Party founded. **June:** Muhammad Neguib becomes President of Egypt.

1954   **March:** Ba'ath Party founded in Damascus. **1 November:** Front de Libération Nationale begins operations in Algeria.

1955   **24 February:** Baghdad Pact signed.

1956   Abdul Gamal Nasser becomes President of Egypt. **26 July:** Egypt nationalizes Suez Canal. **26 October:** Israel invades Sinai.

1958   Arab League Joint Defense and Economic Cooperation Treaty signed. **1 February:** United Arab Republic established. **July:** Outbreak of Lebanese Civil War. **14 July:** Abd al-Karin Qasim seizes power in Iraq. **14 July:** King Faisal II of Iraq assassinated, Prime Minister of Iraq, Nuri Al-Said assassinated.

1960   **September:** Organization of Petroleum Exporting Countries (OPEC) established.

1961   **19 June:** Kuwait gains independence. Kuwait Fund for Arab Economic Development established. **12 August:** Arab League force sent to Kuwait. **September:** United Arab Republic dissolved.

1962   Al-Fath founded by exiled Palestinians. Muslim World League founded. **3 July:** Algeria gains independence. **September:** Outbreak of Yemen Civil War.

1963   Ba'ath Party seizes power in Syria. **February:** Abdul Salem Arif becomes President of Iraq. **24 May:** Organization of African Unity (OAU) founded.

1964   **March:** Palestine Liberation Organization (PLO) founded. **May:** Palestinian National Charter convened. **13 August:** Arab Common Market established.

1967   People's Republic of South Yemen established. **5 June:** Outbreak of third Arab-Israeli War. **29 August–3 September:** Khartoum Arab Summit.

1968   **January:** Organization of Arab Exporting Countries (OAPEC) established. **September:** Popular Front for the Liberation of the Occupied Arab Gulf founded.

1969   **August:** Arson attack on al-Aqsa Mosque in Jerusalem. **29 August:** King Muhammad Idris al-Sanusi of Libya overthrown in coup led by Muammar Qaddafi. **3 November:** Cairo Agreement signed between Lebanon and Palestine Liberation Organization (PLO).

1970   **23 July:** Coup in Oman. Sultan Qaboos bin Said assumes power. **September:** International Islamic Organization founded. **28 September:** Death of President Abdul Gamal Nasser. Anwar Sadat becomes President of Egypt.

1971   Abu Dhabi Fund for Arab Economic Development founded. Black September founded. Popular Front for the Liberation of Oman and the Arab Gulf founded. **March:** Hafiz Assad becomes President of Syria. **May:** Organization of the Islamic Conference established. **December:** Federation of United Arab Emirates established.

1972   Islamic Call Society founded.

1973   Arab Fund for Economic and Social Development becomes operational. Polisario resistance movement formed in Western Sahara. **30 June:** Arab Bank for Economic Development in Africa established. **6 October:** Outbreak of fourth Arab-Israeli War. **17 October:** OAPEC oil embargo begins. **December:** Islamic Development Bank founded. **23 December:** Middle East Peace Conference in Geneva.

1973-1974   Arab oil embargo.

1974   Saudi Fund for Development established. **February:** Second Islamic Summit Conference in Lahore. **25 October:** Rabat Arab Summit recognizes PLO as sole representative of Palestinians.

1975   Arab Fund for Technical Assistance to Africa founded. Islamic Development Bank opened. **6 March:** Algiers Accord between Iraq and Iran. **13 July:** Treaty of Frontier and Good Neighborly Relations (Iraq-Iran). **31 October:** Moroccan troops enter Western Sahara.

1976   **28 January:** OPEC Fund for International Development established. **26 February:** Spain withdraws from Western Sahara. **27 February:** Sahawari Democratic Republic formed in exile. **April:** Arab Monetary Fund established. **8 June:** Arab Deterrent Force for Lebanon established. **6 October:** Riyadh Arab Summit on Lebanese Civil War. **25-26 October:** Cairo Summit Conference—agrees to provide funding for Arab Deterrent Force, Lebanon.

1977   **November:** President Anwar Sadat addresses Israeli Knesset.

1978   International Islamic Relief Organization founded. **July:** Arab Socialist Union (Egypt) dissolved. **18 September:** Camp David Accords signed. **25 November:** Baghdad Summit.

1979   **February:** Iranian Revolution. **26 March:** Egyptian-Israeli Peace Treaty signed. **April:** Islamic Republic established in Iran. **July:** African Economic Community established by OAU in Lagos. Saddam Hussein becomes President of Iraq. **1 November:** Attack on Grand Mosque in Mecca by Al-Utaiba.

1980-1988   Iraq-Iran War.

1981   **25-28 January:** Third Islamic Summit Conference. **25 May:** Gulf Cooperation Council established. **6 October:** President Anwar Sadat assassinated. **7 October:** Hosni Mubarak becomes President of Egypt.

1982 **3 June:** Israeli invasion of Lebanon. Hizbullah established in Lebanon. **August:** Second Conference for Islamic Mission in Tripoli. World Islamic Call founded. **13 September:** Bashir Gemayel assassinated in Lebanon. **16-18 September:** Massacre of Palestinian refugees in Shabra and Shatilla refugee camps, Beirut.

1984   **February:** Fourth Islamic Summit Conference. **November:** Rapid Deployment Force set up by Gulf Cooperation Council. **13 December:** Treaty of Oujda (Libya-Morocco).

1987   **December:** Hamas founded by Sheikh Ahmed Yasin.

1988   **February:** Chemical weapons used against Kurds by Iraq at Helabjh.

1989   Union of Arab Maghreb formed. **February:** Arab Cooperation Council founded. **15 February:** Soviet forces withdraw from Afghanistan. **3 June:** Death of Ayatollah Khomeini of Iran. **30 September–22 October:** Lebanese National Reconciliation Charter negotiated at Taif, Saudi Arabia.

1990   **22 May:** Republic of Yemen formed. **2 August:** Iraqi invasion of Kuwait.

1991 **16 January:** First Congress of the Popular Pan-Arab Islamic Congress in Khartoum. Outbreak of second Gulf War. **22 May:** Lebanese-Syrian Treaty of Brotherhood signed. **30 October:** Middle East Peace Conference in Madrid.

1992 **28 April:** Islamic Republic of Afghanistan established. **25 February:** World Trade Center in New York bombed. **9 September:** Oslo Accord signed. **13 September:** Declaration of Principles signed by Israel and PLO.

1994 **May:** Israeli Defense Forces withdraw from Jericho and part of Gaza Strip. Palestinian National Authority established in Gaza Strip. **4 May:** Israel-PLO economic agreement signed in Paris. **25 July:** Peace Treaty signed by Israel and Jordan.

1995 **28 September:** Israeli-Palestinian agreement on further Israeli West Bank withdrawal. **4 November:** Israeli Prime Minister Yitzhak Rabin assassinated.

1997 **March:** Indian Ocean Rim Association for Regional Cooperation established. **17 November:** Massacre of tourists at Luxor, Egypt by Islamic fundamentalists.

1998 **7 August:** Bombing of U.S. Embassies in Nairobi, Kenya, and Dar es Salaam, Tanzania.

1999 **7 February:** Death of King Hussein of Jordan. **15 March:** Turkish Kurd leader Abdullah Ocalan kidnapped in Nairobi, Kenya. **29 June:** Abdullah Ocalan sentence to death. Sentence suspended pending an appeal to European Court of Justice.

2000 **10 June:** Death of President Hafiz Assad of Syria. **July:** Israeli-Palestinian peace talks at Camp David collapse over future of Jerusalem.

Introduction

The Arab world has always been a significant area in world history being the cradle of civilization and the birthplace of three of the world's great religions. In terms of Islam, expansion of the religion throughout the Arabian Peninsula occurred between A.D. 632-661 and was then spread by merchants, traders, and mystics to Africa, Southeast Asia, Central Asia, Spain, Portugal, and southern Italy. The Arab world is rightly regarded as the heartland of Islam because of the holy cities of Mecca and Medina, but the majority of Muslims are now to be found in Africa and Asia. Islam has also grown significantly in Europe and the United States. It is the majority religion in more than 48 countries and is a significant minority in others.

At the end of the twentieth and beginning of the twenty-first century the Arab world has continued to play a prominent role in world affairs with the enduring influence of religion, the discovery and impact of oil, the question of Israel and Palestine, and, more recently, the Islamic revival movement and Islamic fundamentalism. All of these factors have involved the superpowers in the region, with cold war rivalries being fought by proxy resulting in decades of instability. In the second half of the twentieth century the dominant factor was the significance of the region to the world oil market, resulting in the area assuming strategic significance for the oil-consuming nations, and to the oil producers the significance of oil revenues to their socio-economic development was the feature of the period. The influx of oil wealth also enabled the oil-producing states to wield an influence in Islamic organizations and play a role in international relations not merited by their size or population. Islam has also continued to develop and grow in importance in Africa and Asia, particularly in those countries where it is the dominant religion, such as Nigeria, Sudan, Pakistan, Malaysia, and former republics of the Soviet Union in Central Asia. Islam has also been a major factor in nationalist struggles and resistance movements in several states, particularly Afghanistan, Kashmir, and those in Central Asia.

As a result, the Arab world and the Islamic community have a significant presence in international organizations and have generated their own organizations designed to serve the interests of Islam. However, this role is often difficult for outsiders to understand without an understanding of the situation in Islamic states in terms of economics, society, and especially the impact of Islam. In this context it

1

is essential to understand that one of the basic beliefs in Islam is that all Muslims are regarded as belonging to a single community; this has found expression in many of the organizations established to serve the Islamic community, regardless of nationality, and also conditions the behavior of Muslim states in broader international organizations such as the United Nations.

As the Arab world is the heartland of Islam, the largest geographical coverage of this work relates to these countries with an area of some 3.1 square kilometers and a population of some 110 million. However, only states which have a major Islamic influence, economic significance, or a role in Islamic organizations and international relations have been included. In this context coverage is limited to Bahrain, Egypt, Iraq, Jordan, Kuwait, Lebanon, Saudi Arabia, Syria, United Arab Emirates, and Algeria in the Maghreb. Israel has also been included as a geographical part of the Arab world and because of the significance of the Palestinian question and the role of the United Nations as a peacekeeper between Israel and the Arab states. The common link between these states is their Arab origins and Islam, but the states are different in political terms, with Egypt, Iraq, and Syria being primarily secular and radical while Saudi Arabia and the Gulf States are conservative and Islamic in nature. Coverage is also given to some of the notable political figures, such as Gamal Abdul Nasser, who have played an important role in the process of political development in the region by promoting unity through the concept of Pan-Arabism, as illustrated by the creation of the United Arab Republic between Egypt and Syria in 1958.

Although Islam is a common unifying factor, it can also be divisive in terms of the nature of the dominant sect. The area is largely dominated by Sunni Muslims, who also form the majority throughout the world, except for Bahrain and Iraq which have Shi'i majorities and with Lebanon being almost equally divided between the two sects. The religious composition causes strains where the ruling elites come from the minority sect, such as in Bahrain and Iraq. However, several states have significant Shi'i minorities which can lead to tensions given the differences between the two branches of Islam, the fervor of the Shi'i populations, and their tendency toward a more militant expression of Islam. These differences have also led to differences in development, with secularism in some states and political development into Arab socialist states such as the Arab socialism of Egypt and the Ba'ath Parties in Iraq and Syria. This is contrasted by Saudi Arabia, which regards itself as totally Islamic in terms of government and the legal system.

Islam has been crucial in the creation of Saudi Arabia, with the militant arm of the Wahhabi movement having provided the armed tribesmen, which enabled Ibn Saud to gain control of territories outside of the Nejd to create the Kingdom of Saudi Arabia. The conquest of the Hedjaz in 1924 led to Ibn Saud gaining control over the holy cities of Mecca and Medina and achieving a major role in Islam through being protector of the holy places and host to the annual pilgrimage or *hajj*.

Saudi Arabia regards itself as the leader of the Islamic world because of these factors and is a fundamentalist state with its government being based on totally Islamic principles and its legal system on total adherence to *Sharia* law. This adherence to Islam has led to Saudi Arabia founding the Organization of the Islamic Conference (OIC) as a vehicle for unifying Muslim states worldwide with the pursuit of common objectives in terms of politics and economics. However, even within Saudi Arabia there are Muslims who regard the regime as corrupt and not adhering to the real principles of Islam, which has led to unrest and actions such as the attack on the Grand Mosque in November 1979. Saudi Arabia represents the majority Sunni Muslims but there are a number of other Islamic sects throughout the Arab world, such as the Shi'i, the second largest sect, the Ibadhis, and the Twelver Shias and these are also reflected within the dictionary.

On the edge of the Arab world is the Islamic Republic of Iran, which has had a major impact on the development of Shi'i Islam through the Islamic Revolution of 1979 against the Shah of Iran led by Ayatollah Khomeini. Iran does not figure highly in the area of Islamic organizations but it has had a major impact on international relations, particularly in respect of the West, support for fundamentalist movements in Lebanon through Hizbullah, and for Islamic resistance movements in Afghanistan. The policies of the state have also led to instability in the area through territorial claims to offshore islands in the Arabian Gulf and Khomeini's avowed intention to export the Iranian revolution. This is particularly significant in Arab countries with Shi'i majorities and Sunni political elites, countries with significant Shi'i minorities, and even in Saudi Arabia, particularly during the pilgrimage or *hajj*.

Algeria has also been included as an Arab Maghreb state largely because of its significance to the region, its role in the Union of the Arab Maghreb (UAM), links with Africa, the struggle against colonialism, and problems with Islamic fundamentalism as represented by the Front Islamique de Salut. Although Libya as a state has been excluded, its leader Muammar al-Qaddafi has been included because of his role within the Arab world and Africa seeking regional unity, his views on the development of Islam, and his missionary role through the Islamic Call Society.

The Turkish Republic is included as a major Muslim country but its main significance is through its predecessor, the Ottoman Empire, which did much to mold the Middle East and had a major role in Islam through the institution of the Caliphate. However, the declaration of the republic on 29 October 1923 led Turkey down the secular path, which has meant that it has stayed out of a number of Islamic organizations, though in the last two decades there has been a rise in the influence of Islam in Turkish politics and society.

Afghanistan has also been included largely because of its recent history and the role of Islamic fundamentalism, as represented by the resistance to the occupation by the Soviet Union, the rise of the Taleban, and the declaration of an Islamic Republic. Its impact in the wider Islamic world is significant because of the support from other Muslim states such as Iran and Pakistan and the participation, on an individual basis, of fighters from Islamic countries and individuals such as Usama bin Laden. Other Islamic states, especially in Africa, the former Soviet republics of Central Asia, the Indian subcontinent, and Asia, are not dealt with individually but are represented through their involvement in Islamic, regional, and international organizations such as the Organization of the Islamic Conference, the Muslim World League, and Islamic education through Islamic universities in Islamabad, Malaysia, Niger, and Uganda.

The Arab and Islamic community has generated a large number of organizations, some of which address regional concerns while others are concerned with the Islamic community at large. In the Arab world the major historical concern since the demise of the Ottoman Empire has been the concept of Arab unity, which has found expression through movements such as Pan-Arabism and Pan-Islamism. Expressions of this desire have been manifested through the short-lived United Arab Republic (UAR) (1958-1961) between Egypt and Syria, the Confederation of Republics between Egypt, Libya, and Syria in

1971, and the Arab Islamic Republic between Libya and Tunisia in 1974, both of which were planned but never implemented, and Greater Syria, which was a long-term goal of President Hafiz Assad. The Links with Islamic Africa are illustrated by the never implemented Afro-Arab Union between Algeria and Morocco, the Organization of African Unity (OAU), and the Union of the Arab Maghreb (UAM) between Algeria, Libya, Mauritania, and Tunisia.

Further links in the Arab world were designed to cope with the creation of Israel and its encroachment on surrounding Arab territory as a result of a series of Arab-Israeli Wars from 1948 onwards. One of the main organizations is the Arab League, which is an outward sign of unity against Israel and through its specialist agencies such as the Special Bureau for Boycotting Israel. In Palestinian terms, opposition has been expressed through the Palestine Liberation Organization (PLO) and various militant radical splinter groups, such as Black September, which received support from some radical Arab governments, such as Syria.

In economic areas one of the most significant of the bodies established is the Organization of Arab Petroleum Exporting Countries (OAPEC), founded in 1968 to look after the interests of the oil-producing states. However, in 1973, it adopted an overtly political agenda with the imposition of an oil embargo following the Arab defeat in the 1973 Arab-Israeli War; this, coupled with a price rise set by the Organization of Petroleum Exporting Countries (OPEC), led to an unprecedented increase in revenues for the oil-producing states. A number of organizations were established to share this wealth for the benefit of development programs in other Arab non-oil states, primarily through the Abu Dhabi Fund for Arab Economic Development, Kuwait Fund for Arab Economic Development, Saudi Development Fund, and the Arab Fund for Social and Economic Development. Their activities were later expanded to target Islamic communities throughout the world but especially in Africa. Development programs in Africa have also been assisted through the Arab Bank for Economic Development in Africa and similar organizations. Another major player in the Islamic community is the Islamic Development Bank, which is a specialized organ of the OIC.

A further group of organizations are those identified with other sectors of activity such as health, education, trade, and technical expertise. Some of these are specialized agencies of umbrella organizations such as the Arab League Educational, Scientific and

Cultural Organization and the OIC with specialized organs, such as the Islamic Center for the Development of Trade and the Islamic Chamber of Commerce. In other sectors of activity organizations have also been established linking trades and professions such as the International Confederation of Arab Trade Unions, Union of Arab Jurists, International Commission for the Preservation of Islamic Cultural Heritage, and a number of other professional bodies, including the Islamic Academy of Sciences and the Association of Muslim Researchers. The rights of individuals within Islamic society are also protected by the Islamic Human Rights Commission and the Arab Organization for Human Rights.

At the same time the Arab states and other Islamic countries joined many international organizations such as the United Nations (UN) and its specialized agencies in which they play a prominent role. Their role in the UN has largely been dominated by Israel and the question of Palestine. This aspect is covered by the various UN peacekeeping forces that operate in the region and by the UN Relief and Works Agency (UNRWA), which caters to the needs of large numbers of Palestinian refugees in the Gaza Strip, Jordan, and Lebanon. Islamic states are also involved with the World Bank, largely as recipients, and with the International Monetary Fund, for which Saudi Arabia is a major contributor.

At the regional level a number of organizations have been set up, largely in the socio-economic sectors, though some have adopted political or security agendas. In this respect the two main regional groupings are the Gulf Cooperation Council (GCC) in the Arabian Peninsula and the UAM, both of which seem to be successful ventures, though largely at the economic level. The GCC is beginning to develop a security role, mainly in response to the perceived threat from Iran and the Gulf War of 1990-1991, whereas the UAM is largely a response to the economic threat posed by the European Union. In Africa the Islamic states are members of the OAU, in which they play a prominent role; on an interregional basis, the Indian Ocean Rim Association for Regional Cooperation is a good example of an economic grouping. A number of unification attempts have been made since World War II, which have been short-lived, such as the UAR, or never implemented, such as the Afro-Arab Union. Some state-to-state unification attempts have been successful with the main examples being the United Arab Emirates and the unification of the two Yemens.

On a wider front there have been dreams of Arab unity based on a single Arab state, or at least federations which would encompass most of the Arab world with its roots in the original Islamic Empire, but all attempts to date have never made progress. There are also historical aspirations for unification through concepts such as Greater Syria and Greater Morocco, but these show little signs of coming to fruition, though Morocco still has aspirations for the integration of Western Sahara into the Kingdom. Calls are also being made for Islamic unity; this aspiration can partly be found in organizations such as the Muslim World League and the OIC, with their various specialized agencies. However, success in this area is doubtful due to the fact that Islam itself is not united, being divided into two main branches, Sunni and Shi'I, and a number of other smaller Islamic sects. A further block to this concept of unity is the fact that independence has brought with it the concept of statehood, sovereignty, and vested interests among the political elites. Some states such as Egypt, Iraq, and Syria are governed by radical socialist regimes while Saudi Arabia and the Arab Gulf States are conservative, patriarchal states which would hinder attempts at unity. In economic terms there are vast differences between the oil-rich states, which are sparsely populated and the heavily populated states (such as Egypt) with differing systems of economy, wealth distribution, and societal structures, all of which militate against unity.

Any real drive for Islamic unity comes from fundamentalist movements, which are primarily opposed to the conservative regimes in the largely Sunni-dominated states. In the Arab world, much of this activity has been sponsored by Iran through its support for Hizbullah, Hamas, and Islamic Jihad. However, some fundamentalist groups are spontaneous and operate in only one country, such as the Front Islamique de Salut in Algeria while others, such as the Muslim Brotherhood (MB), have proliferated and operate in a number of states. However, even the MB does not consistently operate across frontiers. In Egypt, the organization operates outside of the existing political structures; in Jordan, it functions within the system; and in Syria, it has been brutally suppressed. The situation is further complicated by the presence in some states of significant minorities, some of whom have their own aspirations for unity or independence, such as the Kurds in Iraq, Syria, and Turkey. All of these factors militate against the concept of political unity amongst the Islamic community, though the underlying concept of a single Muslim community with common beliefs should not be underestimated, as it can be a force for unity of purpose, especially at an international level.

The successes of the various Arab and Islamic organizations are modest despite the strength of the links provided by Islam. Broader pan-Arab or pan-Islamic movements have been unsuccessful due to the inherent resistance of the ruling elites and the differences between conservative Islamic states and radical secular states. This has resulted in clashes between states and with fundamentalist movements, which has made resistance to unity even stronger. However, it is impossible to consider the region without an understanding of the Arab and Islamic organizations and other relationships, such as tribal loyalties, which often predate contemporary political structures.

The Dictionary

A

ABD AL-WAHHAB, MUHAMMAD IBN (1703-1792). Abd al-Wahhab was the founder of the Wahhabi (q.v.) movement that aimed to return to pure Islam (q.v.) as practiced by the Prophet, and he preached against all heresy and unbelief. His followers were known as the *Ikhwan* (q.v.) (Brethren), or the *Muwahhidun* (Unitarians). Abd al-Wahhab was firmly opposed to any innovation, and was against the decoration of mosques and the setting up of any intermediary between God and man. Abd al-Wahhab settled in al-Dar'iyya, later Riyadh, in 1744, and his theories were accepted by Ibn Saud (q.v.) who used the *Ikhwan* as his army to extend his control throughout the Nejd, which eventually led to the creation of Saudi Arabia (q.v.).

ABDUL MAQUID, ESMAT (1923-   ). Esmat Abdul Maquid is a lawyer and diplomat who served as Egypt's (q.v.) chief representative to the United Nations (q.v.) from 1972-1983, becoming Egypt's Foreign Minister and Deputy Prime Minister in 1984. In 1991, he was unanimously elected Secretary-General of the Arab League (q.v.), which reinforced Egypt's restoration as leader of the Arab world after the period of ostracization following the signing of the Camp David Accords in 1978.

ABDUL RAHMAN, OMAR (1938-   ). Omar Abdul Rahman is an Egyptian Islamic leader. Born into a peasant family, he went blind as a small child. Abdul Rahman was educated in local religious schools before attending Azhar University, obtaining his doctorate in 1965. He then became a lecturer in Islamic studies at the Azhar campus at Fahyum in the Nile Delta.

Abdul Rahman became prayer leader of the local mosque and began a career of opposition to successive Egyptian governments, delivering sermons critical of President Gamal Abdul Nasser (q.v.) and his ideology of Arab Socialism (q.v.). His criticism grew after the 1967 Arab-Israeli War, resulting in his arrest in 1968 and expulsion from the university. But he continued to criticize the government, especially over its policies on religious trusts and Islam (q.v.). Following the death of Nasser in September 1970, he was again arrested due to his instructions to the faithful not to pray for the soul of Nasser, whom he considered an atheist. He was released in May 1971 as part of a general amnesty decreed by President Anwar Sadat (q.v.).

Abdul Rahman returned to teaching at the University of Asyut in southern Egypt (q.v.) but left at the end of 1971 to teach in Saudi Arabia (q.v.), remaining there until 1978, though still in contact with Islamist activists in Egypt. On his return, he became professor of Islamic studies at Asyut University and continued to attack the government over the signing of the Camp David Accords (q.v.) and Sadat's policy of economic liberalization which, he believed, had led to moral and material corruption. On 6 October 1981, Sadat was assassinated by Islamic militants. Abdul Rahman was arrested as a suspect, being charged with issuing a *fatwa* (religious decree) for Sadat's assassination. He was released due to lack of evidence.

Abdul Rahman was denied reinstatement at Asyut University and he settled at Fahyum from where he continued his attacks on the government, now headed by President Hosni Mubarak (q.v.). He was arrested in 1984 for preaching a subversive sermon but found not guilty. His opposition to the regime continued with tours of the country campaigning for Egypt to be governed according to the *Sharia* (q.v.), and became an inspirational source for the fundamentalist organizations *Gamaat al-Islamiya* and *al Jihad al-Islami*. Abdul Rahman was placed under house arrest and prevented from speaking in public, but he still issued a *fatwa* encouraging the faithful to capture weapons from the police, or the military, to launch a jihad (q.v.) against the secular government.

In 1989 Abdul Rahman left Egypt, ostensibly to go on the *hajj* (q.v.), but he went to Khartoum and thence to Europe, Pakistan, and Afghanistan. Despite being on the prohibited list, he obtained a tourist visa from the United States embassy in Khartoum. Once in America, he ran a mosque in Brooklyn popular with Egyptian, Sudanese, and Yemeni immigrants. Abdul Rahman obtained an immigrant visa and moved to New Jersey, from where thousands of tapes of his sermons were despatched to Egypt.

In February 1993, the World Trade Center in New York was bombed. Abdul Rahman was arrested as a suspect, being found guilty in 1995.

ABU DHABI. *See* **ABU DHABI FUND FOR ARAB ECONOMIC DEVELOPMENT; UNITED ARAB EMIRATES ZAID IBN SULTAN AL-NAHAYYAN;**

ABU DHABI FUND FOR ARAB ECONOMIC DEVELOPMENT (AFAED). This organization is important because of its regional significance to Arab States and to other Islamic countries in receipt of aid. The AFAED was established by charter in 1971 and became operational in 1974, being largely inspired by the Kuwait Fund for Arab Economic Development (KFAED) (q.v.), which had been operating for some 10 years.

The main function of the AFAED was to extend economic assistance to Arab countries in the form of loans at favorable rates to carefully evaluated projects, primarily in the Arab World but also in some Asian and African countries. The AFAED is seen as a means of providing economic assistance beyond the borders of Abu Dhabi (q.v.) and discharging its obligations to less economically favored Arab neighbors. However, it is also a realization that Abu Dhabi's oil wealth is a political and diplomatic lever, if carefully managed.

The AFAED is managed by a Board of Directors which provides policy guidelines, while day-to-day operations are controlled by a General Manager, advised by a group of experts. The regulations issued by the Emir of Abu Dhabi gave the Fund freedom to determine the forms of assistance to be granted, provided that they were compatible with the goals of the fund. As such the fund has to meet only three operational conditions:

- that the fund's contribution to any single project should not exceed 10 percent of the fund's capital.
- that the fund's contribution to any single project should not exceed 50 percent of the total cost of the project.
- that the project to which the fund is giving assistance should not be in conflict with the economic interests of Abu Dhabi, or any other Arab country.

The first two conditions were designed to safeguard the capital of the fund while the final condition was a political reminder that the fund's activities must be in the interests of the Arab region in general, and Abu Dhabi in particular.

The management structure of the AFAED reflects the political considerations of the fund, as the Board of Directors is largely composed of Cabinet Ministers, including the Minister of Foreign Affairs. However, the fund's image had begun to change in the 1980s, largely as a result of reports from technical experts who asserted that political considerations should not affect the fund's activities. As a result technical considerations have assumed greater importance and, since the fund has gained in professional status, relieved political pressure on the Board of Directors and allowed decisions to be defended on the basis of technical criteria and professional expertise.

Infrastructure investment is the largest recipient of funds and this has been justified by the fund managers, who stressed that an adequate economic infrastructure was essential to any nation if it was to develop successfully. The policy is largely an expression of the traditional approach to aid funding which has been adopted by most of the international agencies, though in an international context the Abu Dhabi Fund is relatively small in terms of capital.

The AFAED has been one of the most generous funds in provision of per capita aid, and although oil price declines have reduced the amounts available, assistance has continued from funds replenished by repayment of loans. The Gulf War (q.v.) of 1990-1991 led to political considerations again coming to the fore with aid being withheld from countries that supported Iraq (q.v.). *See also* **United Arab Emirates**

ACADEMY OF THE ARABIC LANGUAGE. Founded in 1932 and based at Cairo, Egypt (q.v.). The publication program includes the *Review* (two per annum), biographical details of members, and books on the reviving of the Arab heritage and lexicons and dictionaries of terminology in science and technology. It also houses a library of some 60,000 volumes available to members of the academy.

AFGHANI, JAMAL AL-DIN AL- (ca. 1838-1890). Jamal Al-Din Al-Afghani must be regarded as one of the most influential and charismatic thinkers in the nineteenth-century Islamic world, through his extensive writings on anti-imperialism and strengthening of the self. Afghani was born and raised in northwest Iran (q.v.) and received his higher education in the Shi'i shrine cities of Iraq (q.v.). In about 1897, Afghani went to India before beginning his travels to Mecca (q.v.), the Levant, Iran, and Afghanistan (q.v.), becoming a counsellor to the Afghan Emir, and then being expelled by his pro-British successor. After a brief stop in India, Afghani went to Istanbul, where he resided between 1869 and 1871, entering the Council of Higher Education and lecturing at the new university. A public lecture at the university caused him problems with the religious leaders in Istanbul and he was expelled to Cairo.

It was while in Cairo from 1871 to 1879 that Afghani did his most important work through educating and inspiring a group of young thinkers and activists, many of whom became extremely active in later Egyptian political and intellectual life. In the late 1870s, he encouraged his followers, both Egyptian and Syrian, to engage in politics and to found newspapers, some of which published his lectures. Afghani was expelled from Egypt (q.v.) in 1879, returned to India via Iran, and stayed in the south-central state of Hyderabad, which was ruled by a Muslim prince. Here he wrote some of his most important pan-Islamic articles and a treatise on the *Refutation of the Materialists.*

In 1883, Afghani went to Paris and, using funds supplied by Wilfrid Blunt and a Tunisian general, founded the newspaper *Al-Urwa Al-Wutlqa* (The Firmest Bond), which continued until 1885. The newspaper was circulated as a free publication throughout the Muslim world and primarily published critiques of British policies in Egypt, Sudan, and elsewhere in the Muslim world. In 1885, Afghani went to London and joined Blunt in a campaign to negotiate British withdrawal from Egypt and Sudan. This was the only occasion on which he cooperated with the British, acquiring the unjustified reputation of being a British agent.

Afghani then went to Russia, but his plotting against the British came to nothing. He moved between Russia and Iran, and while in Iran he attacked concessions to Europeans, especially the tobacco concession to Great Britain, which resulted in Afghani being forced to flee to Iraq. Afghani continued to fight the tobacco concession in 1891 and 1892, but following an invitation to Istanbul by Sultan Abdul Hamid II, he was forbidden to write or speak publicly. He died of cancer in 1897.

Afghani is known primarily as a pan-Islamist, but this only really applies to his activities post-1883. His writings and lectures were primarily concerned with awakening and strengthening the Muslim world against Western encroachment, primarily by Britain, and sometimes advocated political reform, or local nationalism, and sometimes a pan-Islamic approach. Afghani was a charismatic orator and teacher and is for many a model figure of modern Islam (q.v.), largely due to the fact that he voiced many of the ideas in vogue with politically minded Muslims. *See also* **Ottoman Empire**

AFGHANISTAN. Afghanistan emerged as a political entity in 1747 under Ahmed Shah Durrani, who created an empire stretching from Khurasan to Kashmir and Punjab, and from the Oxus River to the Indian Ocean, with its capital at Qandchar. The capital was shifted to Kabul during the reign of Timur Shah (1773-1793) but by the turn of the nineteenth century the Durrani empire had declined due to internal struggles over the succession. During the years 1800-1880, Afghanistan became a battleground between Great Britain and Russia over the control of central Asia, eventually emerging as a buffer state with its borders having been determined by the two powers. Britain controlled Afghanistan's foreign affairs and successfully resisted two uprisings aimed at ending its control between 1838-1842 and 1878-1880.

Britain provided support for Emir Abd al-Rahman of the Barakzai Pakhtun clan to consolidate central rule, which was achieved by brutal suppression of other tribal and rural leaders. This period saw the founding of a modern state that became fully independent of Great Britain in 1919. During the rest of the early part of the century, power changed in Afghanistan but eventually returned to the Barakzai clan with the reign of Muhammad Nadir (1929-1933). Nadir was assassinated in 1933, and was succeeded by his son Mohammed Zahir who ruled from 1933 to 1973, a reign characterized by the consolidation of family power, a cautious approach toward modernization, and a xenophobic foreign policy.

The last decade of Zahir's rule saw an experiment in democracy that failed largely due to interference by his family and friends in the democratic process and his failure to sign legislation to legalize political parties. It was during this period that the Communist Party and Islamic opposition movements were formed, agitating both the government and each other. In July 1973, Sardar Muhammas Duad, the former prime minister and cousin and brother-in-law of the king, overthrew the monarchy in a military coup backed by the pro-Soviet Parcham wing of the Communist Party. Daud became president of the Republic of Afghanistan from 1973 to 1978, imposing autocratic rule and persecuted his perceived enemies mainly within the Islamic movements. However, on assuming power Daud distanced himself from his communist supporters, relying on his old power networks. As a result, he was ousted and killed in a communist coup in April 1978.

The new president was Nur Muhammad Taraki, the head of the People's Democratic Party of Afghanistan (PDPA), who became leader of the revolutionary council and prime minister. The republic was renamed the Democratic Republic of Afghanistan, the constitution was abolished, and all opposition movements were banned. However, by July 1978, the coalition of two factions of the PDPA fell apart. Supported by the Soviet government, Taraki attempted to establish a Marxist state, but by spring of 1979 a nationwide rebellion had begun, led by Islamic opposition groups and Muslim religious leaders. The government reacted brutally, particularly in the rural areas, and thousands of Afghanis fled to Iran (q.v.) and Pakistan, estimated by the United Nations (q.v.) as ultimately numbering some 5.7 million, forming the world's largest refugee population.

In September 1979, Hafizullah Amin, Deputy Prime Minister and Minister of Foreign Affairs, killed President Taraki and assumed his duties. However, at Christmas 1979, the Soviets invaded Afghanistan with 80,000 troops and Amin was killed and replaced by Babrak Karmal, head of the Parcham, as head of state. Soviet intervention led to increased factionalism within the political parties that resulted in riots and strikes in the main cities and turned anti-communist riots into a jihad (q.v.) for the cause of Islam and national liberation. During the period 1980 to 1986, Karmal tried to consolidate his power, reduce factional strife, and promote national unity, but his attempts ended in failure and he was replaced by Dr. Najibullah Ahmadzai, former head of the state security services. Ahmadzai adopted a policy of unilateral cease-fires, offers of negotiation, power sharing with his opponents, and the formation of a coalition government of national unity. A new constitution, adopted in 1987, allowed the formation of a multiparty political system, which won some support from his leftist opponents, but the seven-party alliance of Islamic freedom fighters, called *mojahedin*, the Islamic Unity of Afghan Mojahedin, remained defiant, calling for unconditional Soviet withdrawal and the abolition of communist rule.

The Soviet troops failed to achieve a military victory and the mojahedin enjoyed increasing military and financial support from outside from 1984 to 1988. These factors led to the signing of the Geneva accords on 14 April 1988 under the auspices of the United Nations and called for the withdrawal of 120,000 Soviet troops, a move completed by 15 February 1989. The collapse of the Soviet Union ended all military and financial support to the Afghan regime and Najibullah's forces began to defect in increasing numbers to the Islamic forces. On 16 April 1992, Najibullah was ousted from power and Kabul was surrounded by a coalition of Islamic forces led by Ahmed Shah Mas'ud. A 50-member Interim Council of the Islamic resistance groups was formed in Peshawar and despatched to Kabul to assume power from the communists. On 28 April 1992, the Islamic State of Afghanistan was declared.

However, the new state was controlled by the Taleban, the (so-called) religious students, who enjoyed considerable support from Pakistan and mounted a large military force. Thus Afghanistan was again beset by factional strife along sectarian, ethnic, and regional lines, which has severely hampered the repatriation of refugees, reconstruction, and the return of law and order. The main conflict was between the Taleban government based in Kabul and the tribes of northwestern Afghanistan led by Mas'ud, but after protracted fighting the central authority extended its control to over 90 percent of the country, restricting Mas'ud to small footholds in the north of the country. On 14 March 1999, following United Nations-mediated talks the warring factions agreed to share power and to work out a permanent cease-fire. The two groups agreed to have a shared executive, a shared legislation, and a shared judiciary and to an exchange of prisoners. The regime in Afghanistan is still not generally recognized, except by Pakistan, Saudi Arabia (q.v.), and the United Arab Emirates (q.v.).

AFLAQ, MICHEL (1910-1989). Michel Aflaq was born into a Greek Orthodox family in Damascus, Syria (q.v.), and educated at the University of Sorbonne, Paris, where he developed left-wing tendencies. On his return to Damascus in 1934, he became a history teacher at a prestigious secondary school. In 1940, with a fellow teacher, Salah al-Din Bitar, he established a study circle called the *Movement of Arab Renaissance* (Ba'ath in Arabic). The circle published pamphlets and papers promoting revolutionary socialist Arab Nationalism (q.v.) committed to achieving Arab unity. Once France left Syria in 1946, Aflaq and Bitar secured a license for the group, which then merged with another political faction, led by Zaki Arsuzi. The merged body became known as the Arab Ba'ath Party in April 1947 and Aflaq was elected a senior member of the executive committee of four. In August 1949, following a coup, he was made Minister of Education, but he resigned three months later having failed to win a seat in the general election. Aflaq fled Syria in 1952 to escape arrest by the regime of Colonel Adib Shishkali. In 1953 he merged his party with the Arab Socialist Party of Akram Hourani to form the Arab Ba'ath Socialist Party (q.v.), remaining a Secretary-General of the new body.

The ruling Ba'ath party seized power in March 1963 in Syria but was divided into two factions, a moderate civilian wing and a radical military wing. Aflaq identified with the moderate faction, and when the military assumed power in February 1966, he left for Lebanon (q.v.). However, he retained his position as Secretary of the National (i.e., all Arab) command of the Ba'ath, although he left for Brazil in 1967. In July 1968, there was a successful coup by the Ba'ath Party in Baghdad and Aflaq was invited back to Iraq (q.v.) to assume its leadership.

In September 1970, Aflaq left Baghdad in disgust at the regime's failure to support Palestinian commandos in their struggle with Jordanian troops. The rift with Baghdad lasted until 1974 when he returned to Iraq to lead the party's national command. Although the Iraqi regime regularly published his writings, he played no role in determining state policies and practices. During the Iraq-Iran War (q.v.), Aflaq was attacked by Iran (q.v.), which wished to exploit his Christianity to portray Iraq as a state that had deviated from Islam (q.v.). After his death in 1989, the Iraqi media announced that Aflaq had converted to Islam before his demise.

AFRICAN DEVELOPMENT FUND (ADF). The African Development Fund was established by the African Development Bank (ADB) at its annual meeting in 1972 and came into being on 30 June 1973. The Fund provides concessional loans for the purposes of :

- assisting the African Development Bank with the economic and social development of its African members
- promotion of cooperation, including regional and subregional cooperation and increased international trade among its members

The fund utilizes the complete facilities of the African Development Bank to carry out its functions and the President of the ADB is also ex-officio president of the fund and chairman of its Board of Directors.

Membership of the fund comprises the 53 regional members of the African Development Bank and 24 state participants, including Kuwait and Saudi Arabia (qq.v.). The Board of Governors of the fund has the Governors and Alternate Governors of the African Development Bank as ex-officio members, with each state member not represented within the ADB able to appoint a Governor and Alternate Governor to the fund. The fFund's Board of Directors consists of 12 Directors, six of whom are designated from regional members of the bank and six selected by the state participants.

AFRO-ARAB SUMMIT CONFERENCE. This conference was held in Cairo, Egypt (q.v.), in March 1974. The major agenda item was Arab aid to African states in view of the problems that the large price increases in oil were causing to the oil-importing states. The summit was attended by the leaders of 60 states, six national liberation movements, and 18 other organizations.

AFRO-ASIAN HOUSING ORGANIZATION (AAHO). The Afro-Asian Housing Organization was founded on 12 December 1965 and has its headquarters in Cairo, Egypt (q.v.). The aim of the AAHO is to advance cooperation between Africa and Asia in matters of housing, urban planning, and related areas. The day-to-day operation of the organization is in the hands of a secretary-general reporting to an Executive Committee, which meets annually and a General Assembly, which meets every two years. Algeria (q.v.), Egypt, Libya (q.v.), and Sudan are members of the AAHO.

AFRO-ASIAN ORGANIZATION FOR ECONOMIC COOPERATION (AFRASEC). The organization was founded in Cairo in 1958 as a means of promoting cooperation among member states but also to promote Egypt's (q.v.) influence in Africa south of the Sahara. Annual conferences were held but the body is now inactive.

AFRO-ASIAN PEOPLES' SOLIDARITY ORGANIZATION (AAPSO). The Afro-Asian Peoples' Solidarity Organization was established on 26 December 1957 by President Gamal Abdul Nasser of Egypt (qq.v.) as a vehicle for his attempts to maintain his position of leadership among the new and emerging states of Africa and Asia. The organization was supposed to be a nonaligned group but this was rather spoilt by Nasser allowing membership to the People's Republic of China and the Soviet Union, with these two states vying for leadership of the new states. AAPSO is a nongovernmental organization which can be joined by political parties and movements, and national committees have been established in member countries. The organization exists to further the struggle for independence and development of the peoples of Asia and Africa and to promote disarmament and worldwide peace. AAPSO is run by a secretary-general answerable to the president; there is an annual meeting of the governing bureau and irregular conferences. AAPSO has affiliated organizations, such as the Afro-Asian Writers' Association (q.v.).

AFRO-ASIAN WRITERS' ASSOCIATION (AAWA). The Afro-Asian Writers' Association was established by the Afro-Asian Peoples' Solidarity Organization (q.v.) in 1958. The membership is made up of national associations of writers and its headquarters is in Cairo, Egypt (q.v.). The AAWA has a publication program in English, French, and Arabic designed to promote Afro-Asian literature.

AGA KHAN FOUNDATION (AKF). The foundation was established in 1967 by His Highness the Aga Khan, 49th Imam (q.v.) of the Shi'i (q.v.) Imami Ismaili (q.v.) Muslims. Its objectives are to promote social development through philanthropic activities in the developing world and it is committed to assisting in the struggle against hunger, disease and illiteracy throughout the world. The AKF uses its human, physical, and financial resources to:

- innovate with new ideas
- promote "grassroots" development concepts
- assist with organizational and managerial structures
- promote practical technologies that have broad value and utility in resolving generic problems of development primarily in Africa and Asia

 The head office of the AKF is in Geneva, Switzerland. It is governed by a Board of Directors chaired by the Aga Khan. The Board reviews policy and management matters, meets three times a year, and liases with worldwide national committees in 11 countries, mainly in Africa and Asia. It controls a budget of $50 million drawn from its own assets and national and international donations.

 The AKF works with a number of governmental and intergovernmental agencies and with nongovernmental organizations (NGOs) in cofunding partnerships through 30 international, national, private, and public development agencies. The priority action areas of the AKF are in health care systems, education and rural development, and income generation to alleviate poverty. In the education sector, emphasis is laid on early child care and development. Among its projects are the Aga Khan University and the Aga Khan University Hospital, both in Karachi, Pakistan, and the Aga Khan Health Services, which promote social development in Bangladesh, India, Kenya, and Pakistan.

ALAWIS. The Alawis are followers of Ali and the term came into vogue in Syria during the French mandate. They are an offshoot of the Twelver Shi'i (q.v.) sharing their belief that Imam Ali, cousin and son-in-law of the Prophet Muhammad, was the legitimate heir but deprived of his inheritance by the first three Caliphs. Ali is held in higher esteem than any other of the prophets mentioned in the Quran, and the Alawis follow certain Christian rituals, such as Christmas and Epiphany, and some Zoroastrian rituals. The Alawis have seven pillars, which are the five of the Sunni (q.v.) sect together with jihad (q.v.) (holy struggle) and *waliya* (devotion to the Imam Ali family and hatred of their adversaries). Present-day Alawis are to be found in the mountainous region in Syria (q.v.) around Latakia and constitute 12-15 percent of the national population. The most renowned Alawi politician is President Hafiz Assad of Syria (qq.v.).

ALEXANDRIA CONFERENCE OF ARAB STATES. This meeting of Arab states was held in Alexandria, Egypt (q.v.), from 25 September to 7 October 1944 and was attended by representatives of Egypt, Iraq, Jordan, Lebanon, Saudi Arabia, Syria, Yemen, and Palestinian Arabs (qq.v.). The outcome of the meeting was the Alexandria Protocol which was signed on 7 October 1944 and committed the signatories to the establishment of the Arab League (AL) (q.v.). Special resolutions were also passed which supported Lebanese independence and the political aspirations of the Palestinian Arabs, later embodied into the charter of the AL.

ALGERIA. Algeria is a North African state which was Berber until largely Arabized between the eighth to eleventh centuries. The population of Algeria is about 30 million with 45 percent living in the urban areas and the growth rate being 3.2 percent per annum, causing the government to tentatively promote family planning. The bulk of the population are Sunni (q.v.) Muslims, but there are significant elements of the Ibadhi (q.v.) sect in the Sahara, who enjoy a degree of religious autonomy. At one time there was a long-standing Jewish community but they left Algeria at independence. Turkish and Moorish elements have long since been assimilated into the community. However, in the 1970s a militant Islamic tendency had developed, largely inspired by the Muslim Brotherhood (q.v.) and the 1979 Islamic Revolution in Iran (q.v.).

Algeria was part of the Ottoman Empire (q.v.) from 1516 until 1830 but control was tenuous and, in effect, it was still an autonomous state. The French began their conquest of Algeria in 1830 but faced resistance from the indigenous population, particularly between 1832 and 1847, under the leadership of Sheikh Abd al-Qadir, until his arrest in 1847. Further rebellions broke out in 1857, 1864, and 1871. However, tribal cohesion was undermined by French land reforms, which enabled the best arable land to be bought by European settlers, thus consolidating the French hold over the country.

Algerian nationalism began to emerge again during World War I when Muslims were conscripted into the French army. Three distinct tendencies developed: French-educated nationals seeking equal rights for Muslims but still under French rule, Abdel Hamid Ben Badis and the association of 'Ulama strongly opposed to any process of assimilation, and the separatists led by Messali Hadj, which drew support from the labor migrants in France. The French government, under pressure from the settler lobby, refused to concede on the assimilation issue, which strengthened the position of the separatists, though the Parti du Peuple d'Algerie (PPA) was banned in September 1939.

During World War II, France was defeated in 1940 and partially controlled by Germany, but the democratic ideals espoused by the Allies encouraged the nationalists to continue to press for self-determination, a move taken up by Ferhat Abbas, former leader of the assimilationist movement. However, France was not prepared to give up Algeria; on 8 May 1948, an abortive uprising by the banned PPA was put down with over 8,000 Muslim deaths. This divided the nationalist movement into two factions, those who favored a legalistic strategy through elections, and the supporters of Messali Hadj who adhered to a revolutionary vision. The paramilitary wing of the PPA was discovered in 1950 and effectively disbanded, but a small band of activists evaded capture, and on 1 November 1954 launched an armed struggle under the Front de Libération Nationale (FLN). The FLN forces, largely stationed in Morocco and Tunisia, were infiltrated into Algeria whenever possible. This can be seen as an early manifestation of inter-Arab/Maghreb unity.

The war in Algeria was a bitter struggle and the situation was not capable of resolution by successive French governments. Eventually the Algerian war brought the demise of the Fourth Republic and the return to power of General de Gaulle, but it took the new President three years to neutralize opposition within the army to his Algerian policy. It was not until 1961 that serious negotiations with the FLN government in exile based in Tunis got underway. These discussions led to the Evian agreements and a cease-fire on 18 March 1962, though the agreements were opposed by dissident army officers and settlers under the Organisation de l'Armée Secrète. Such was the distrust between the two communities that when independence came on 3 July 1962, most of the Europeans fled the country leaving behind a chaotic situation in the infrastructure and the economy.

Peace did not come with independence, as a power struggle ensued within the FLN, from which Ahmed Ben Bella emerged victorious, being backed by the armies on the Tunisian and Moroccan borders under Colonel Houari Boumedienne. However, Ben Bella's election as

President did not prevent the struggle continuing and Boumedienne seized power in a military coup on 19 June 1965. A further abortive coup was mounted by another military faction in December 1967, but this was put down and a period of political stability followed.

The first four years of this settled period saw the development of an infrastructure at national, regional, and local levels and the recruitment of a socialist element into the FLN in order to mobilize the population and to control the expanding bureaucracy. However, on the eve of the Party Congress in December 1978 Boumedienne fell ill and died, with the result that a struggle began to determine the succession.

In January 1979 the struggle for succession was won by Colonel Chadli Bendjedid with the support of the army and his candidature was endorsed by the reopened Congress, which confirmed the true role of the army in Algerian politics. It took until 1981 for Chadli to assert his authority and to remove Boumedienne supporters from the government, but opposition came from the Berberists and the radical Islamic movement. Berber opposition was largely a result of the government's refusal to recognize the Berber language and culture, and was marked by a series of strikes and demonstrations during March-April 1980, but the unrest was contained. Islamic radicalism was tolerated until 1982, when the government clamped down on the movement, arresting many of its leaders.

The world economic recession at the beginning of the 1980s forced Algeria to alter its economic policies to cope with the collapse in oil prices. This led to a retreat from the ambitious industrialization program, the pursuit of a more cautious hydrocarbon policy, and a positive attitude toward the public sector. Problems with the sprawling bureaucracy were also tackled by breaking up public corporations and state farms into smaller units to facilitate proper accountability and to reduce corruption.

Foreign policies were also affected by these changes and Algeria began to seek closer relations with the West while loosening ties with the communist bloc. Improved relations with the United States resulted from Algeria's mediations in the U.S.-Tehran hostage crisis, and close ties were established with Tunisia. Chadli was reelected president for a further term in 1984 and attempts were made to heal old wounds by rehabilitating victims of wartime purges and inviting political opponents to return home. Some did, but ex-President Ahmed Ben Alla, who had been released from confinement in 1980, remained in exile and formed the Mouvement pour la Démocratie en Algérie in May 1984.

Further adverse economic conditions led to domestic unrest. In July 1989, the government was forced to lift the ban on new political parties, resulting in 50 legal parties being formed within a year. Political parties were permitted provided that they were not externally funded or based solely on religious, regional, or professional interests. During the early 1990s, the Front Islamique de Salut (FIS) gained public support with an infrastructure based on a network of mosques and Islamic groupings. The FIS received a great deal of support from the urban poor who depended upon the organization for grassroots welfare services and social justice based on *Sharia* (q.v.) law. Elections were due to be held in June 1991 but were delayed as a result of protests over the new electoral law, which banned campaigning in mosques and constituency alterations, which favored the FLN. Further restrictions were imposed, with a state of siege being declared, curfews imposed, and FIS leaders arrested.

The general and presidential elections were eventually held on 26 December 1991 and contested by 59 political parties. In the first round, the FIS won 188 of the 231 seats and the FLN was pushed into third place with only 15 seats. The Assembly was dissolved on 4 January 1992 and President Chadli resigned on 11 January under pressure from the army, which would not countenance an accommodation with the FIS. An interim High Council of State, headed by Mohammed Boudiof, was formed on 14 January and the second round of elections scheduled for 16 January. These were cancelled when the army took over control of key installations in the major urban areas. Violent clashes between the FIS and the authorities broke out in February 1992 and a state of emergency was declared.

The FIS was dissolved and split into different armed groups who since 1992 have carried out attacks on government installations, key economic targets, politicians, intellectuals, foreigners, and members of the security forces. Liamine Zeroual was appointed president on 31 January 1995 to oversee the transitional period before new elections were held.

The elections were held on 16 November 1995 and President Zeroual won 60 percent of the vote in a poll with a 75 percent turn out. A referendum, which many observers felt was rigged, was held on the constitution in 1996 resulting in a ban on overtly religious parties and increased powers for the President. In June 1997, multiparty legislative elections were held which were won by the National Democratic Rally, which holds the majority of the seats with the FLN.

A cease-fire was declared by the armed wing of FIS in October 1997 but a splinter group called the Islamic Armed Group continued to carry out violent attacks. However, there is evidence that some of the attacks are by militias backed by the security forces. In seven years of internal strife, it is estimated by Amnesty International that 80,000 people have died.

In September 1998, President Zeroual announced that he was cutting short his period in office by 18 months and calling presidential elections. The new elections were held in April 1999, but they were surrounded in controversy as the bulk of the candidates withdrew accusing the army of vote rigging in the first round. This left Abdelaziz Bouteflika, the army's favored candidate, as the only contender. His election was confirmed and he was sworn in as president on 27 April 1999. Bouteflika proclaimed an amnesty for Islamists not guilty of murder, rape, or other serious crimes. Contrary to expectations, thousands of Islamists surrendered to the authorities, but many still remain in hiding and deaths still occur. Economic problems are still overshadowed by continuing instability, which the recent elections have not solved as there has been no lifting of the state of emergency, troops have not been returned to barracks, and reconciliation remains a distant prospect. *See also* **Islamic Fundamentalism**

ALGERIAN-MOROCCAN BORDER DISPUTE. The conflict between Algeria (q.v.) and Morocco had been ongoing for a number of years but in 1963 it degenerated into open warfare. The Arab League (q.v.) attempted to reconcile the problem but this failed and, while King Hassan of Morocco preferred bilateral negotiations, Prime Minister Ben Bella of Algeria preferred to use the Organization of African Unity (OAU) (q.v.) as a mediator. The OAU intervened under the chairmanship of Emperor Haile Selassie of Ethiopia and convened a meeting in Mali in 1965 with both leaders to discuss the situation. The meeting led to the declaration of a cease-fire and agreement for the OAU to set up an investigating commission. Under the guidance of the commission the border was adjusted over the next four years and the dispute came to a final resolution in January 1969.

ARAB ACADEMY FOR SCIENCE, TECHNOLOGY, AND MARINE TRANSPORT (AASTMT). The AASTMT was founded in 1972 as a specialized organization under the Arab League (q.v.) as the Arab Maritime Transport Academy based in Alexandria, Egypt (q.v.). Due to an expansion of the academy's programs, the Economic and Social

Council of the Arab League agreed in 1975 to change its name to the Arab Academy for Science, Technology, and Marine Transport.

The AAST takes students from Arab states, Africa, and Europe, sponsored by companies and institutions, or at their own expense, and offers courses leading to bachelor's or master's degrees, diplomas, or certificates of competency for deck officers and marine engineers. The educational facilities consist of Colleges of Marine Transport, Engineering and Technology, and Management and Technology, together with an Advanced Management Institute, and an International Secondary School.

The academy also houses a Maritime Research and Consultancy Center, which operates in the areas of technical research, systems analysis, computer science, and maritime economics and management. A specialist training facility is also available, divided into three distinct entities: the Institute of Productivity and Total Quality, Port's Training Institute, and an Integrated Simulations Complex.

The academy publishes *Marine Research Bulletin* (monthly) and the *Journal of the Arab Academy for Science, Technology, and Marine Transport* (twice a year).

ARAB ACADEMY OF DAMASCUS. It was established in June 1919 as a center for Arabic linguistics and studies in literature and the humanities, modelled on the Academie Française. The primary objective of the government of the new Kingdom of Syria (q.v.) was to ensure that Arabic became the language of the administration, the armed forces, high culture, and education within the country. As part of its program the academy mounted a series of public lectures on cultural subjects and oversaw a collection of manuscripts and books which had been collected by Sheikh Tahir al-Jaza'iri in the late nineteenth century.

Due to financial constraints the academy was closed in the summer of 1920 but was reopened in September 1920 with financial support from the French mandatory authority. However, the financial support from the French High Commissioner limited its ability to be a forum for open debate or to become a catalyst for Arab nationalist sentiment. The academy did produce a literary journal, *Majalla al-Majma al-Ilmi al-Arabi,* and a series of critical editions of works by prominent Arab authors.

In June 1923, the academy was incorporated into the University of Damascus and relaunched as a research institute for the study of formal Arabic language. Throughout the 1930s, 1940s, and 1950s, the institute held a number of international festivals celebrating Arabic literature and included among its corresponding members a number of celebrated Western scholars, including Carl Brockelmann and Snouck Hurgronje.

ARAB ADMINISTRATIVE DEVELOPMENT ORGANIZATION (ARADO). It was founded in 1961 as the Arab Organization of Administrative Science and based in Heliopolis, Cairo, Egypt (q.v.), becoming operational in 1969. ARADO is active in administrative development providing, training, consultancy, research, information, and documentation. It also promotes Arab cooperation in administrative sciences and coordinates a Network of Administrative Information for member states. The ARADO maintains a research library of some 20,000 volumes and 380 periodicals and publishes the *Arab Journal of Administration* (biannual), *Management Newsletter* (quarterly), research reports, and training manuals.

ARAB-AFRICAN UNION. On 13 December 1984, the governments of Libya and Morocco concluded the Treaty of Oujda, which called for a federation of the two states, but with each retaining their own sovereignty. The federation was officially known as the *Arab-African Union*, but was short of Muammar Qaddafi's (q.v.) objective of full and integral Arab unity. The treaty established a joint presidency, which alone had decision-making powers, a rotating permanent secretariat, a joint legislature, a court of justice, and various advisory councils. The treaty called for common approaches in foreign policy and for cooperation in economic, social, and political matters, but either state was able to enter into pacts with third parties without the agreement of the other party to the treaty.

One article of the treaty was a pact against aggression against one party, which was in effect a mutual defense agreement. The objective of the federation was greater Maghreb and Arab unity and the union could be joined by a third party, provided both signatories agreed. Referendums were held in Morocco on 31 August 1984 and in Libya (q.v.) on the following day and secured overwhelming endorsement of the treaty. Both countries gained from the agreement as it reduced Libya's diplomatic isolation and struck a blow for Arab unity, while Moroccan isolation because of the war in Western Sahara (q.v.) was also reduced.

Morocco also felt that the union provided for Libyan recognition of its claim to the Western Sahara, as Libya had agreed not to support the Polisario if Morocco refrained from interference in Chad. Morocco was also promised Libyan financial support and guarantees that Libya would no longer aid enemies of the monarchy. The treaty also demonstrated Morocco's independence from the United States and, as a result, bolstered King Hassan's domestic political position.

However, the Arab-African Union was not built on firm foundations, as the political positions of the two signatories were diametrically opposed. This was manifested by the difficulties faced by the advisory councils and commissions in trying to translate treaty provisions into functioning administrative bodies. The attempts to make the agreement function lasted until 29 August 1986, when it was abrogated by Morocco using joint Libyan-Syrian criticism of King Hassan's meeting with Israeli Prime Minister Shimon Peres as a pretext.

ARAB AIR CARRIERS ORGANIZATION (AACO). The Arab Air Carriers Organization was founded in 1965, and is one of the oldest tools of pan-Arab cooperation established under the auspices of the Arab League (q.v.). The declared mission of the AACO is to provide a framework for the development of cooperation among Arab airlines and to further their common interests through service excellence. The AACO also assists member airlines in developing technical and economic performance, rationalizing costs and enhancing revenues, and representing and defending its members' interests. The AACO also operates a regional training center in Amman, Jordan (q.v.), which operates in collaboration with the American University of Beirut. It has a membership of 18 Arab carriers and publishes a monthly statistical bulletin and occasional papers on research in aviation in the Arab world.

ARAB ATOMIC ENERGY AUTHORITY (AAEA). The AAEA was founded in 1988 and is based in Tunis, Tunisia. Its objectives are to coordinate research into the peaceful uses of atomic energy. The AAEA publishes *The Atom and Development* (quarterly), and other monographs in the field of nuclear science and its applications in industry, biology, medicine, agriculture, and seawater desalination.

ARAB AUTHORITY FOR AGRICULTURAL INVESTMENT AND DEVELOPMENT. The Arab Authority for Agricultural Investment and Development was founded in 1977 with the objective of promoting agricultural development in the Arab world to ensure food security in the region. The authority is based in Khartoum, Sudan, due to its potential for agricultural development. Six companies were established in the country in 1981 to deal with poultry, starch and glucose, dairy products, and vegetables, with a further two being founded in the following year to process oilseeds and to rehabilitate the Agadi State Farm. The member states are Algeria, Egypt, Iraq, Kuwait (qq.v.), Mauritania, Morocco, Qatar, Saudi Arabia (q.v.), Somalia, Syria (q.v.), and the United Arab Emirates (q.v.). It has an operating capital of $500 million.

ARAB BA'ATH SOCIALIST PARTY. *See* **BA'ATH SOCIALIST PARTY**

ARAB BANK FOR ECONOMIC DEVELOPMENT IN AFRICA. The Arab Bank for Economic Development in Africa (Banque Arabe pour le Developpement Economique en Afrique) was founded by the Arab League (AL) (q.v.) in November 1973, beginning operations in early 1975. The main objective of the bank is to provide financial assistance to Africa's economic development through provision of all, or part, of the financing required for development projects, and through the provision of technical assistance. In order to be eligible, countries must be members of the Organization of African Unity (q.v.) but they do not have to be members of the AL.

The bank is controlled by a Board of Governors, which is composed of the finance ministers of the AL and meets annually to review activities and to determine the finance available for the coming year. Only the Governors can increase the capital available to the bank. The operation of the bank is in the hands of the Board of Directors which meets three times a year to recommend policy to the Governors, to implement their decisions, and to act as the bank's executive. The Board of Directors consists of a chairman appointed by the Board of Governors for a five-year term and 11 other members, seven of which are permanent seats allocated to the largest shareholding countries, while the remaining four seats are appointments made by the Governors for a four-year term.

Loans are mainly made on concessional terms for development projects, with the percentage of finance varying with the size of the project. The bank also encourages Arab investment in Africa and provides technical assistance. The African countries themselves, through their development plans, determine sectoral distribution of approved finance.

The bank funds infrastructural, industrial, and agricultural projects and provides technical assistance to African countries faced with increasing energy costs. The main funding for the bank comes from Kuwait, Libya, Saudi Arabia, and the United Arab Emirates (qq.v.), but

African states have been critical of the fairness of allocations, as priority has been given to African Muslim states.

ARAB BANKING CORPORATION (ABC). The Arab Banking Corporation was founded in 1980 by the governments of Kuwait, Libya, and the United Arab Emirates (qq.v.) as a joint venture operation with an operating capital of $1 billion. The ABC was founded in order to increase Arab banking activities that had been hindered by comparatively small capital structures. At the end of 1989, the authorized capital was increased to $1.5 billion and in 1990 its shares were listed on the Bahrain (q.v.) and Paris stock exchanges.

The ABC has followed a strategy of diversified growth and developed a widespread network of branches, representative offices, subsidiaries, and affiliates in over 30 countries around the world. The ABC's branches focus principally on wholesale commercial and corporate banking and trade finance services. Its subsidiaries concentrate on opportunities in domestic retail and merchant banking sectors, with its affiliates offering specialized financial services. The prime aim of the corporation is to put the oil-generated wealth to productive use, and it has a special commitment to the Arabian Gulf region, with its headquarters in Bahrain.

ARAB BOYCOTT. The Arab boycott was instituted by the Arab League (AL) (q.v.) on 2 December 1945 as a measure of economic warfare against Israel (q.v.). Initially, the boycott called on all Arab states to prohibit the purchase of goods produced by Palestinian Jews in order to prevent the realization of Zionist political aims. However, following the creation of the State of Israel in 1948 and the displacement of hundreds of thousands of Palestinian Arabs, the terms of the boycott were expanded with the objective of undermining the viability of the new state. The boycott barred Arab states, companies, and individuals from buying or selling to Israel any goods or services, and prohibited other commercial or financial relationships with the Jewish state. In 1950, a secondary boycott was imposed, which extended the prohibitions to dealings with companies anywhere in the world that contributed to Israel's economic or military strength. A tertiary boycott extended the prohibitions to individuals and organizations regarded as supportive of Israel. A Central Boycott Office was set up in Damascus, Syria (q.v.), in 1951 to administer the boycott activities and to maintain a register of boycotted companies. By 1976 it had blacklisted 6,300 firms from 96 countries, but the rulings were only advisory and many Arab states ignored the secondary and tertiary boycotts, or followed them selectively.

In 1982 the Federation of Israeli Chambers of Commerce estimated that the boycott had succeeded in reducing exports by 10 percent and inward investment by 15 percent, representing a cumulative loss of $45 billion. Reactions to the boycott from outside the Arab world ranged from outrage and legal counteractions in the United States and some European countries, to reluctance on the part of Japan and South Korea to deal with Israel in case of offending Arab countries.

The AL solidarity in the boycott was destroyed in 1979 when Egypt (q.v.) withdrew from the agreement following its peace treaty with Israel, and Jordan (q.v.) took similar action following its signing of a peace treaty with Israel in 1994. Other members of the AL opened some degree of contact with Israel following the Gulf War (q.v.) and the Oslo Accord agreement between Israel and the Palestine Liberation Organization (q.v.). In February 1995, trade representatives from Egypt, Israel, Jordan, the United States, and the Palestinians signed the Taba declaration advocating the end of the boycott in the interests of free and open markets. *See also* **Special Bureau for Boycotting Israel**

ARAB BUREAU OF EDUCATION FOR THE GULF STATES. The Arab Bureau of Education for the Gulf States was founded in 1975 with a membership of Bahrain, Iraq, Kuwait, Oman (qq.v.), Qatar, Saudi Arabia (q.v.), and the United Arab Emirates (q.v.). The bureau acts primarily as a clearinghouse for information and a coordinator of educational activity in the member states. Among its activities the bureau promotes educational research relevant to the region, organizes exchange programs for staff and students from member states' universities, and promotes training courses. The bureau is closely involved with the Arabian Gulf University, which was opened in 1982 in Bahrain. It publishes *Risalat Ul-Khalef al-Arabi* (quarterly) and *Arab Gulf Journal of Scientific Research* (twice a year).

ARAB CENTER FOR AGRICULTURAL DOCUMENTATION. *See* **ARAB ORGANIZATION FOR AGRICULTURAL DEVELOPMENT**

ARAB CENTER FOR CONSULTANCY AND AGRICULTURAL PROJECTS. *See* **ARAB ORGANIZATION FOR AGRICULTURAL DEVELOPMENT**

ARAB CENTER FOR ENERGY STUDIES. *See* **ORGANIZATION OF ARAB PETROLEUM EXPORTING COUNTRIES**

ARAB CENTER FOR INFORMATION AND EARLY WARNING. *See* **ARAB ORGANIZATION FOR AGRICULTURAL DEVELOPMENT**

ARAB CENTER FOR THE STUDY OF DRY REGIONS AND ARID TERRITORIES. This is a specialized agency of the Arab League (q.v.) founded in 1968 and based in Damascus, Syria (q.v.). The center is responsible for the provision of training courses and the holding of conferences. It is divided into five main divisions: Animal Resources, Meteorological Studies, Plant Studies, Soil Science, and Water Resources, with each division undertaking regional research and development programs and publishing an annual technical report. The center also provides a forum for the exchange of information among Arab scientists.

ARAB CIVIL AVIATION COUNCIL (ACAC). This is a specialized agency of the Arab League (q.v.) founded in 1965, based in Rabat, Morocco, which began operations in 1967. The ACAC exists to develop the principles, techniques, and economics of air transport within the Arab world and to liase with the International Civil Aviation Organization (ICAO). Attempts are also made to standardize laws and regulations and technical terminology, and to coordinate Arab air rates. Among the publications of the ACAC are *Air Transport Activities in Arab Countries, Lexicon of Civil Aviation Terminology* (in Arabic), and *Unified Air Law for Arab States* (in Arabic and English).

ARAB COMMON MARKET (ACM). The Arab Common Market resolution of 13 August 1964, passed by the Council of Arab Economic Unity (CAEU) (q.v.), sought to establish regional economic integration among the states that had signed the Economic Unity Agreement of 6 June 1962. Members of the ACM are Egypt, Iraq, Jordan, Libya (qq.v.), Mauritania, Syria (q.v.), and Yemen (q.v.), and the implementation of the organization is controlled by the CAEU. Customs duties and other taxes on trade between the member states were eliminated in annual stages and abolished in 1971. The second phase was to be a full customs union, the removal of all restrictions on trade between members including quotas, and restrictions on residence, employment, and transport were to be abolished. However, the trading of national products or rights to residence between members has not yet been freed of all restrictions.

The CAEU has taken a number of measures to further the development of the Arab Common Market, as follows:

- introduction of flexible membership for the least developed Arab states of Mauritania, Somalia, Sudan, and Yemen
- approval in principle of a fund to compensate the least developed countries for financial losses resulting from membership in the ACM
- approval of legal, technical, and administrative preparations for unification of tariffs levied on imports from non-member countries
- formation of a committee of ministerial deputies to deal with problems in the application of market rulings and to promote the activities of the ACM
- adoption of unified customs legislation and of an integrated program aimed at enhancing trade between member states and expanding members' productive capacity

ARAB COOPERATION COUNCIL (ACC). The Arab Cooperation Council was formed in February 1989 in Baghdad, and had a membership of Egypt, Iraq, Jordan, and North Yemen (qq.v.), being those countries outside of the Gulf Cooperation Council (q.v.) which had aided Iraq during the war with Iran (q.v.) (1980-1988). The ACC decided to concentrate on cooperation in economic and nonmilitary fields, with the February 1990 summit deciding to work toward an end to Jewish emigration to Palestine and the Occupied Territories. The ACC collapsed in 1990 following the Iraqi invasion of Kuwait (q.v.) and Egypt's decision to join the allied coalition. *See also* **Iraq-Iran War**

ARAB DETERRENT FORCE (ADF). The ADF was the peacekeeping force created by the Arab League (AL) (q.v.), adopted at the Riyadh Conference (q.v.) to keep the peace in Lebanon (q.v.) from October 1976 to July 1982 and replace the Symbolic Arab Security Force (q.v.). The initial mandate was for a six-month period, but was renewed by the AL at six-month intervals. The ADF drew troops from Libya, Saudi Arabia, South Yemen (q.v.), Sudan, Syria, and the United Arab Emirates (qq.v.), with a total force of 30,0000. The Arabian Gulf States provided the bulk of the funding for the force, with Kuwait (q.v.) and Saudi Arabia each paying 20 percent of the costs, and the United Arab

Emirates and Qatar contributing 15 percent and 10 percent, respectively. The ADF was deployed across Lebanon, but was prevented from entering southern Lebanon by the presence of Israeli forces and eastern Beirut by Christian forces.

The ADF presence in Lebanon was also complicated by the deployment of the United Nations Interim Force in Lebanon (UNIFIL) (q.v.) in March 1978, with Syria regarding the force as a challenge to the Arab League's mission. The ADF gradually weakened with the withdrawal of troops by member states who questioned the wisdom of continuing participation with the civil war showing no signs of abating. Libya was the first to withdraw troops in December 1977, followed by Sudan in February 1979, Saudi Arabia in March 1979, and the United Arab Emirates in April 1979. The ADF was involved in 1979 in operations against Maronite irregulars, but by this time the force was drawn only from Syria. Further clashes with the Maronite militia in April 1980 at Zahla were largely successful, but prompted Israeli intervention.

Israel (q.v.) invaded Lebanon in June 1982, and in September 1982 the Lebanese government requested the termination of the ADF's mandate at the Fez Summit Conference. Although the mandate was terminated, the conference did not order the withdrawal of Syrian troops, who remained and engaged in an undeclared war with Israel. Despite withdrawal of their forces, the Arab Gulf States had continued to fund the operation, but refused to fund the continued presence of Syrian troops once the ADF mandate was terminated.

ARAB ENGINEERING COMPANY. A joint undertaking under the auspices of the Organization of Arab Petroleum Exporting Countries (q.v.), which was founded in 1981 and based in Abu Dhabi (q.v.). The aim of the company is to give support to national engineering firms through the provision of expert assistance, to train Arab engineers, and to organize a common operational base. The company has an authorized capital of $20 million.

ARAB FEDERATION OF PETROLEUM, MINING, AND CHEMICALS WORKERS (AFPMCW). The AFPMCW was formed in 1961 and is based in Tripoli, Libya (q.v.). The main objectives of the federation are the establishment of proper industrial relations policies and procedures for the guidance of affiliated unions, and the establishment of trade unions in countries where they do not exist within the relevant industries. It publishes *Arab Petroleum* (monthly in Arabic, English, and French editions), specialized reports, and statistics.

ARAB FEDERATION OF TEXTILE WORKERS. Based in Damascus, Syria (q.v.) with membership from eight affiliated trade unions.

ARAB FUND FOR ECONOMIC AND SOCIAL DEVELOPMENT (AFESD). The AFESD was established by the Arab League (q.v.) in 1969, becoming operative in 1973. The fund has 21 countries as members, together with the Palestine Liberation Organization (q.v.), and was founded in an attempt to deploy capital to foster economic integration among the member states. The organization is run by a Board of Governors appointed by the member states and is regarded as the General Assembly of the fund with full powers. Delegated powers are administered by the Board of Directors who are responsible for the activities of the fund and who are elected from the member states by the Governors for a two-year term. The Directors are six in number and are chosen because of their experience and competence, serving for a period of two years.

The fund participates in the financing of economic and social development projects in member states through:

- Financing economic projects of an investment character through soft loans to governments, and to public or private organizations and institutions. Preference is given to economic projects of benefit to Arab peoples and to joint Arab projects.

- Encouraging, directly or indirectly, the investment of public and private capital to ensure the growth of the Arab economy

- Provision of technical expertise and assistance in various fields of economic development

The fund also cooperates with other Arab organizations such as the Arab Monetary Fund and the Organization of Arab Petroleum Exporting Countries (qq.v.) in the preparation of regional studies and conferences. It also acts as a Secretariat for the Coordination Group of Arab National and Regional Development Institutions.

Funding is primarily in the areas of infrastructural and development projects such as railroads, sewerage and water supply facilities, fertilizer plants, and agricultural programs. In the objective of fostering economic and Arab integration, three schemes have been funded. The first was the development of the Pan-Arab Communications Network through the Arab communications satellite. The second was the Arab Organization for Industrialization (q.v.), but funding was terminated as a result of the internal troubles following Egypt's (q.v.) signing of the Camp David Accords (q.v.) in 1979. Lastly the Fund established the Arab Authority for Agricultural Investment and Development (q.v.) to promote sugar and grain production in Sudan to provide a source for import substitution. No profit has been returned on any of these investments, but they are regarded as a necessary means of providing regional food security. The whole process can only survive for as long as the oil-producing states continue to provide funding.

The authorized capital of the fund is set at 800 million Kuwaiti dinars and it may borrow twice the amount of its capital. Additional borrowing may be authorized by the Board of Governors but, to date, the power has not been used.

ARAB FUND FOR TECHNICAL ASSISTANCE TO AFRICAN COUNTRIES. The fund was established in 1975 by the Arab League (q.v.) to provide technical assistance for development projects in Africa. This is carried out through the provision of African and Arab experts, scholarships for African personnel, and training and finance for technical studies.

ARAB GULF PROGRAM FOR THE UNITED NATIONS DEVELOPMENT ORGANIZATIONS (AGFUND). AGFUND was established in 1981 and is based in Riyadh, Saudi Arabia (q.v.), with a membership of Bahrain, Iraq, Kuwait, Oman (qq.v.), Qatar, Saudi Arabia, and the United Arab Emirates (qq.v.). The fund exists to provide grants, not exceeding 50 percent of project costs, for projects in mother and child care undertaken by the United Nations (q.v.), Arab non-governmental organizations, and other international bodies, and to coordinate assistance by the nations of the Arabian Gulf. AGFUND had provided assistance to some 119 countries between 1981 and 1996.

ARAB INDUSTRIAL DEVELOPMENT AND MINING ORGANIZATION. This specialized agency of the Arab League (q.v.) was formed in 1990, based in Rabat, Morocco. It conducts sectoral studies and surveys on the situation and prospects for Arab industry, and assists member states with national surveys. The organization also provides consultancy and training services. The organization is a merger of the Arab Industrial Development Organization, Arab Organization for Mineral Resources, and Arab Organization for Standardization and

Metrology. The organization is headed by a 13-member Executive Council and has a High Consultative Committee of Standardization, a High Committee of Mineral Resources, and a Coordination Committee for Arab Industrial Research Centers. A Ministerial Council of ministers of member states with responsibility for industry meets every two years. Its publications include reports and studies, a bulletin, and the *Journal of Arab Industrial Development* (in Arabic).

ARAB INSTITUTE FOR FORESTRY AND RESEARCH. *See* **ARAB ORGANIZATION FOR AGRICULTURAL DEVELOPMENT**

ARAB INTER-PARLIAMENTARY UNION (AIPU). The AIPU was founded in 1974, following the October 1973 Arab-Israeli War, and marked the atmosphere of solidarity prevailing at that time in the Arab world. It is based in Damascus, Syria (q.v.), and has a membership, drawn from 19 countries of parliamentarians representing their respective assemblies. Its main objectives are to allow representatives of the different Arab member parliaments to meet, coordinate activities, and promote democratic values in Arab countries. The AIPU operates a rotating presidency and is run by a General Secretariat.

ARAB IRON AND STEEL UNION. The Arab Iron and Steel Union was formed in 1972 and is based in Algiers, Algeria (q.v.). The main aim of the union is to develop commercial and technical aspects of Arab steel production through assisting commercialization of production in Arab markets by guaranteeing them high-quality materials and intermediary products. The union also organizes training sessions and provides information to members on new developments in the industry. It has a membership of 71 producers from 14 Arab countries but many of them are small producers. It publishes *Arab Steel Review* (monthly), *Information Bulletin* (fortnightly), and an annual *Directory of Producers.*

ARAB ISLAMIC REPUBLIC. In 1972, Libya (q.v.) had attempted to reach agreement for a union with Tunisia, and in January 1974 Muammar Qaddafi (q.v.) tried again at a meeting with President Habib Bourguiba of Tunisia on the Tunisian island of Djerba. Agreement was reached in one meeting to create an Arab Islamic Republic with a single constitution, a single army, and the same legislative, executive, and judicial powers. However, no real planning had gone into these negotiations, and senior members of the Tunisian government were astounded at Bourguiba's acceptance of the agreement. At the time of the

Djerba meeting the Tunisian Prime Minister was abroad, but on his return the Tunisian Foreign Minister was dismissed and the pact allowed to lapse. Libya made a further attempt to revive the pact in November 1974 but this was also unsuccessful.

ARAB LABOUR ORGANIZATION (ALO). A specialized agency of the Arab League (q.v.), it was established in 1965 to foster cooperation between member states to deal with labor problems. Among the areas covered are the unification of labor legislation and working conditions. The ALO also conducts research programs, mounts training courses, and provides technical assistance to member states in areas such as social insurance and in-house training. The ALO has a tripartite membership of government, employers, and workers. The publication program includes research reports, a monthly bulletin, and a quarterly *Arab Labour Review.*

ARAB LEAGUE (AL). The AL, formally known as the League of Arab States, was founded in March 1945 as a voluntary association of Arab states with the objective of strengthening ties and coordinating policies and activities directed toward the common good of the Arab nations. A Council consisting of representatives from all of the member states, including Palestine (q.v.), each with a single vote, controls the AL. In terms of the decision-making process, unanimous decisions are binding on all member states whereas majority decisions are only binding on those states which voted for them. Representatives of the member states in rotation chair the Council, and emergency sessions can be held at the request of any two member states.

The Council has 16 committees attached to it covering a variety of specialized activities including culture, economics, communications, legal affairs, politics, oil, health, human rights, social affairs, and information.

The administration and financial management of the league are the responsibility of the General Secretariat, which is headed by a secretary-general who is appointed by the Council by a two-thirds majority for a five-year period. The Secretariat carries out the decisions of the Council and provides financial and administrative services for the organization including the 16 committees attached to the Council. The secretary-general has the rank of ambassador and, subject to the approval of the Council, appoints the assistant secretaries who carry the rank of ministers plenipotentiary.

As a complement to the initial Charter of the League, the member states entered into a Treaty of Joint Defense and Economic Cooperation in 1950 and established a number of specialist groups in this area.

- *Arab Unified Military Command*
  - formed in 1964 to coordinate policies for the liberation of Palestine
- *Economic Council*
  - formed in 1953 to coordinate the economic policies of member states; composed of ministers of economic affairs or their nominees
- *Joint Defense Council*
  - oversees implementation of aspects of the treaty concerned with common defense. Composed of foreign and defense ministers, with decisions taken by a two-thirds majority, binding on all
- *Permanent Military Commission*
  - founded in 1958 to draw up plans for submission to the Joint Defense Council and staffed by representatives of army general staffs

In June 1976, the Joint Defense Council established a Symbolic Arab Security Force (SASF) (q.v.) primarily to oversee attempts to stop hostilities in Lebanon (q.v.) and thereafter to maintain the peace. The costs of the force were to be met by all members of the League, though the oil-producing states contributed 65 percent of the total. This was replaced by the Arab Deterrent Force (ADF) in October 1976 and the forces' mandate ended in 1982.

The Arab League also maintains external relations throughout the world through a network of Arab League Information Offices with the prime task of coordinating work among the Arab embassies abroad. The AL also publishes a monthly journal of Arab Affairs, *Sh'oun Arabiyya,* and an information bulletin in Arabic and English.

The league also has a number of specialized agencies, to which all member states belong, and these constitute an integral part of the organization. These are: Arab Academy for Science, Technology, and Marine Transport; Arab Administrative Development Organization; Arab Bank for Economic Development in Africa; Arab Center for the Study of Dry Regions and Arid Territories; Arab Civil Aviation Council; Arab Fund for Economic and Social Development; Arab Fund for Technical Assistance to African Countries; Arab Industrial Development Organization; Arab Labour Organization; Arab League Educational, Cultural, and Scientific Organization; Arab Organization for Agricultural Development; Arab Organization for Industrialization; Arab Organization for Social Defense against Crime; Arab Organization for Standards and Measures; Arab Organization of Administrative Sciences; Arab Postal Union; Arab Satellite Communication Organization; Arab States Broadcasting Union; Arab Telecommunications Union; the Inter-Arab Investment Guarantee Corporation; and Special Bureau for Boycotting Israel (qq.v.).

ARAB LEAGUE EDUCATIONAL, CULTURAL, AND SCIENTIFIC ORGANIZATION (ALECSO). This is a specialized organization within the Arab League (q.v.), which was founded in 1964 with the objective of promoting the intellectual unity of Arab countries by means of education and the raising of cultural standards. In addition, the organization seeks to encourage participation in technical development and to train experts to research into Arab civilization. Each state is required to submit annual reports on education, cultural matters, and science. The ALECSO has a permanent delegation at the United Nations Educational, Scientific, and Cultural Organization (UNESCO) to act on behalf of those Arab states that are not members of that body. The organization has an excellent record in the field of information dissemination training programs and the provision of specialist advice and technical services. The bulk of the publication program takes the form of technical and specialist reports to the decision-making committees of the Arab League or to national governments. However, the following are also published under the ALECSO remit: *Arab Journal of Culture, Arab Journal of Science, Arab Bulletin of Publications, Arab Magazine for Information Scientists,* and *Statistical Yearbook.*

Four other institutions operate within the ALECSO. They are: Arab Literacy and Adult Education Organization, Arab Manuscript Institute, Institute of Arab Research and Studies, and Permanent Bureau for Arabization.

ARAB LEAGUE FORCE IN KUWAIT. In 1961, Iraq (q.v.) had threatened to invade Kuwait (q.v.) and a small number of British troops had been sent to counter this threat. On 20 July 1961, the Arab League (q.v.) passed a resolution calling for the withdrawal of British troops from Kuwait while, at the same time, offering support to guarantee the independence of the new state. However, the same resolution also stated that the Arab League would support a decision by Kuwait to voluntarily merge with Iraq (q.v.). The delegations from Iraq walked out of the meeting and preparations went ahead for the organization of a peacekeeping force. The Arab League signed an agreement on 12 August 1961 to establish the force of some 3,300 troops with contributions from Jordan, Saudi Arabia (qq.v.), Sudan, Tunisia, and the United Arab Emirates (q.v.) while Libya and Lebanon (qq.v.) declined to send contingents.

ARAB LITERACY AND ADULT EDUCATION ORGANIZATION. This specialized unit within the Arab League Educational, Cultural, and Scientific Organization (ALECSO) (q.v.) was founded in 1966 to assist member states in the drive to improve literacy standards. Its main activities are the establishment and development of national institutions for literacy and adult education; assistance with the formulation of national plans; mounting of regional training courses, seminars, and conferences; coordination of research work; granting of scholarships; and provision of technical assistance. It publishes *The Education of the Masses* (twice a year).

ARAB MANUSCRIPT INSTITUTE. A section of the Arab League Educational, Cultural, and Scientific Organization (ALECSO) (q.v.) founded in 1946 to provide photographic records and catalogs of Arabic manuscripts. It publishes the *Journal of the Institute of Manuscripts.*

ARAB MARITIME PETROLEUM TRANSPORT COMPANY. This is a joint undertaking under the auspices of the Organization of Arab Petroleum Exporting Countries (OAPEC) (q.v.) which was founded in 1973 and based in Kuwait (q.v.) with membership from Algeria, Bahrain, Iraq, Kuwait, Libya (qq.v.), Qatar, Saudi Arabia, and the United Arab Emirates (qq.v.). The company was set up to increase Arab participation in the tanker transport industry through the transport of crude oil, gas, refined products, and petrochemicals. It has an authorized capital of $200 million.

ARAB MILITARY INDUSTRIES ORGANIZATION. This organization was established in 1975 in an endeavor to create a joint military productive capacity for the Gulf States and Egypt (q.v.). The intention was to use the industrial capacity of Egypt backed by funds from the oil-rich Gulf States. The whole process came to an end in 1978 with Egypt suspended from membership after signing the Camp David Accords (q.v.). It was reformed in 1988, when Egypt was readmitted to Arab organizations, but has shown little ability to reduce dependence on outside sources for military equipment. However, following the Gulf Crisis of 1990-1991 the Gulf States planned to invest significant funds in the organization in an endeavor to achieve its original objectives.

ARAB MONETARY FUND (AMF). The AMF was founded in April 1976 following the meeting of the Economic Council of the Arab States at Rabat and came into force on 2 February 1977 with its headquarters in Abu Dhabi (q.v.). The AMF is run by a Board of Governors, composed of a Governor and Deputy Governor appointed by each of the member states for a five-year term. The Governors are the highest authority and formulate policy; however, some of their powers are delegated to the Board of Executive Directors, which consists of a president and eight directors, elected by the Board of Governors for a period of three years, with eligibility for reelection. The president of the fund is appointed for a renewable five-year period and supervises a Committee on Loans and a Committee on Investments, which make recommendations on policies to the Directors.

The fund was established to further the goal of Arab economic integration, and assists member states with balance of payments problems. The articles of agreement set out the following objectives for the fund:

- correction of disequilibria in the balance of payments of member states
- promotion of stability of exchange rates, realization of mutual convertibility, and removal of restrictions on current payments between member states
- establishment of policies for monetary cooperation to speed up Arab economic integration and economic development within member states
- provision of advice on investment policies, when requested;
- promotion of Arab financial markets
- promotion of the use of the Arabic dinar as a unit of account and of a unified Arab currency
- coordination of the position of member states in dealing with international economic and financial problems
- provision of a mechanism for settlement of payments between member states in order to foster inter-member state trade

The fund also acts as a bank and as such is empowered to:

- provide short- and medium-term loans to finance balance of payments deficits of member states
- provide guarantees to assist member states to enhance borrowing capabilities
- act as an intermediary in Arab and international markets for member states
- coordinate monetary policy of member states
- manage funds deposited by member states
- consult regularly with member states on their economic conditions
- provide technical assistance to monetary institutions in member states.

The bank provides loans at concessionary rates, or a uniform rate, which are designed to assist with balance of payments deficits. Loans are available to the level of 75 percent of a member state's paid-up subscription.

ARAB NATIONAL MOVEMENT (ANM). The ANM was founded in 1952 following a merger between two groups of staff and students at the American University of Beirut, with the objectives of promoting the unity of the Arab world, the liberation of Palestine (q.v.), and revenge against the Zionist State of Israel (q.v.). The ANM was extremely supportive of the Egyptian military coup of 1952 and of the United Arab Republic formed in 1958 between Egypt and Syria (qq.v.), and bitterly disappointed at its breakup in 1961. Failures of Egypt, Syria, and Iraq (q.v.) to unify left the ANM completely disillusioned with both Nasserism and Ba'athism (qq.v.) as unifying political forces.

The ANM found some expression in Kuwait (q.v.), through Dr. Ahmed al-Khatib, a member of the National Assembly, and through the National Cultural Club (Kuwait). The latter did well in the 1954 local elections, was active in pressing for a legislative assembly, and also did well in the 1961 general elections, emerging as the chief political force in the country. By then the ANM had achieved a measure of respectability such that the National Cultural Club was no longer necessary as a front. The ANM was also present in Bahrain (q.v.) but had little impact.

In terms of support for the Palestinians, the ANM set up a special section in 1964, with an armed section designed to pursue guerrilla activity against Israel (q.v.). However, the Arab defeats in the 1967 conflict with Israel destroyed the ANM's confidence in both Egypt and Syria and led to the movement ceasing to be pan-Arab and being divided into individual sections in different countries.

The ANM had considerably more support in South Yemen (q.v.), where it spearheaded the movement against British proposals to set up the Federation of South Arabia comprising Aden Colony and the Eastern and Western Protectorate states. In 1963, the ANM was instrumental in uniting the various nationalist groups active in South Yemen which brought into being the National Front for the Liberation of South Yemen (NLSY). The NLSY pursued a course of armed struggle that secured independence for South Yemen in 1967.

The ANM was also active in allying with supporters in the Dhofar Province of Oman (q.v.) to form a link with the Dhofari Liberation Front, which had started a guerrilla campaign in 1963 to obtain independence. The conflict lasted some 10 years but was ultimately a failure. By the mid-1990s the ANM was largely a spent force, particularly in terms of Pan-Arabism (q.v.).

ARAB NATIONALISM. The ideology of Arab Nationalism was defined in opposition to foreign rule, first by the Ottoman Empire (q.v.) and then by Great Britain and France, and it dominated the Arab world in the nineteenth century. In the nineteenth century, Egypt (q.v.) had been in the forefront in rebelling against the Ottoman Empire, which resulted in the Sultan recognizing Muhammad Ali as Viceroy of Egypt in 1805 and signifying that the Ottomans were prepared to assign Egypt a special place within the Empire. Due to the nature of the regime in Egypt, Cairo became a refuge for opponents of the Ottoman regime, and this helped to engender Arab Nationalism and Pan-Islamism (q.v.).

Following the opening of the Suez Canal in 1869, Britain supplanted the Ottomans in Egypt, and Arab Nationalism grew in opposition to the British presence. The opposition reached a peak in 1882, when Ahmad Pasha attempted militarily to end British interference in Egypt. But the attempt failed, leading to a British occupation of Egypt, thus providing a further force for nationalism.

In the Levant, Arab Nationalism found fertile ground in the educational institutions established by American and French missionaries during the 1860s, leading to the growth of secret societies such as Al-Ahd (The Covenant) and Al-Fatat (The Young Woman). The Ottomans suppressed these secret societies, and after 1882, many of the activists fled to Egypt.

The core premise of Arab Nationalism was that the Arabs are, and have been, a nation unified by a common language and a shared sense of history, but divided and dominated by outside powers. The ideology drew on elements of both Arab and Islamic heritages and incorporated a new Arab history with a pride in the past that was disseminated through the press and in novels, poetry, and popular histories aimed at all Arabs.

Little development was experienced during World War I, though the aspirations of the Arabs were fueled by Britain, which resulted in the Arab Revolt (q.v.) of 1916. Sherif Hussein (q.v.) of the Hedjaz, who had postwar pan-Arab aspirations, led the revolt. However, at the time of the outbreak Britain and France had agreed on a postwar settlement, assigning spheres of influence through the Sykes-Picot Agreement. The postwar settlement and the mandate system (q.v.) of the League of Nations largely followed this secret agreement, resulting in the Arabs feeling betrayed by the victorious allies.

In Egypt, Arab Nationalism developed through the evolution and activities of the Wafd, which had been founded in 1919, and elsewhere was centered upon the Hashemites in Iraq (q.v.) and Transjordan. At this stage it also became intermingled with the ideology of Pan-Arabism (q.v.), though this was severely damaged by the use of British troops by King Faisal II of Iraq in 1941 to crush the successful nationalist coup. It also received a further blow as a result of King Abdullah of Transjordan's secret discussions with Zionists over annexation of parts of Palestine (q.v.) in 1948/49.

The formation of the Arab League (q.v.) gave the ideology of Arab Nationalism a regional perspective and, from its base in Cairo, the organization set the scene for the integration of Egyptian nationalism into the larger Arab Nationalism. This followed the Free Officers coup of 1952 by nationalist republican army officers, among whom was Gamal Abdul Nasser (q.v.). It was the success of Nasser's nationalization of the Suez Canal, despite initial military setbacks, and the subsequent withdrawal of British troops which gave Nasser the mantle of leader of the Arab Nationalist movement.

However, Nasserism (q.v.) was distinct from Arab Nationalism and did not survive for very long after Nasser's death. It also faced competition as an ideology from Ba'athism (q.v.) which had emerged in Damascus, Syria, in 1954 and was a well-defined ideology, not linked to one individual, which spread in varying degrees to other Arab states.

However, Arab nationalism as an ideology received a severe blow when Iraq invaded and annexed Kuwait (q.v.) in August 1990, splitting the Arab League membership. Arab Nationalism has also been replaced by nation-state nationalist tendencies and this, together with Islamic radicalism, has largely filled the void.

ARAB ORGANIZATION FOR AGRICULTURAL DEVELOPMENT (AOAD). This is a specialized agency of the Arab League (q.v.) formed on 11 March 1970, based in Khartoum, Sudan, with membership drawn from all 21 members of the Arab League. Its objectives are to develop natural and human resources in the agricultural sector; to increase productive efficiency and achieve agricultural integration between the member states; to increase agricultural productivity to achieve self-sufficiency and to facilitate the exchange of agricultural products between member countries; to enhance agricultural venture industries; and to achieve an improvement in the standards of living of the labor force engaged in the agricultural sector.

The AOAD has a General Assembly, consisting of Ministers of Agriculture from the 21 member states; an Executive Council consisting of seven ministers; a Secretariat General; and seven technical departments dealing with food security, human resources development, water resources, studies and research, projects execution, and a technical scientific cooperation and financial administrative department. The AOAD has a number of specialist institutes: Arab Institute for Forestry and Research, which provides a two-year diploma course of training for member states; Arab Center for Information and Early Warning, which acts as a link between Arab sources of agricultural information and coordinates cooperation through use of new technologies to disseminate information; Arab Center for Agricultural Documentation and Information (ACADI), which assembles, updates, and disseminates information on Arab agriculture and participates in information coordination activities sponsored by the United Nations Food and Agriculture Organization; and Arab Center for Consultancy and Agricultural Projects, aimed at strengthening operational technical links between international and regional institutions through the provision of its expertise in areas that involve technical studies, training, and other developmental aspects of agriculture. It publishes *Arab Agricultural Statistics Yearbook, Annual Report of Agricultural Development in the Arab Countries, Arab Food Security Situation* (annual), *Annual Report of the Arab Organization for Agricultural Development, Agriculture, and Fisheries Sector in the Arab Countries* (annual), *Agriculture and Development in the Arab World* (quarterly), *AOAD Bulletin Newsletter* (monthly in Arabic, quarterly in English). *Arab Agricultural Research Journal* (biannual), regional country studies and symposia, seminars, and training programs (irregular).

ARAB ORGANIZATION FOR HUMAN RIGHTS (AOHR). The

AOHR was founded in 1983 and is based in Heliopolis, Cairo, Egypt (q.v.), with a membership from 16 regional and 14 other countries. Its objectives are to defend the fundamental freedoms of citizens of the Arab states and to assist political prisoners and their families in accordance with the Universal Declaration of Human Rights, the International Covenant on Economic, Social, and Cultural Rights, and the International Covenant on Civil and Political Rights. The AOHR is a nongovernmental organization that has consultative status with the United Nations Economic and Social Council. Every three years, the AOHR holds a General Assembly, which elects a 15-member Board of Trustees that meets annually. It publishes a *Newsletter* (monthly), *Annual Report*, the *State of Human Rights in the Arab World*, and other specialist publications in a series entitled *Nadwat Fikria*.

ARAB ORGANIZATION FOR INDUSTRIALIZATION (AOI). The AOI was formed in 1975 under the auspices of the Arab League (q.v.) with the objective of establishing a group to manufacture weapons for Arab countries. The main members were Egypt, Saudi Arabia (qq.v.), Qatar, and the United Arab Emirates (q.v.), which collectively contributed $1 billion of capital to manufacture advanced weaponry for all Arab countries. However, in 1979, Saudi Arabia proclaimed the dissolution of the organization following Egypt's signing of the Camp David Accords (q.v.). Egypt refused to accept the dissolution and sought agreements with Western countries, including agreements with American Motors to manufacture jeeps and with British Aerospace to manufacture anti-tank weaponry. *See also* **Arab Fund for Economic and Social Development**

ARAB ORGANIZATION FOR MINERAL RESOURCES. The Arab Organization for Mineral Resources was founded in 1979 and based in Rabat, Morocco. Although not affiliated with the Arab League (q.v.), it works in association with that organization. It merged with the Arab Industrial Development and Mining Organization in 1990 (q.v.).

ARAB ORGANIZATION FOR SOCIAL DEFENSE AGAINST CRIME. This organization was established by the Arab League (q.v.) in 1960 and is based in Rabat, Morocco. The aims of the organization are to study causes and remedies for crime, treatment of criminals, and the reinforcement of cooperation in legal, judicial, and correctional fields. The organization also has three specialist bureaus: Arab Bureau for Narcotics, Arab Bureau for Prevention of Crime, and Arab Bureau of Criminal Police.

ARAB ORGANIZATION FOR STANDARDS AND MEASURES. This specialized Arab League (q.v.) agency began activities in 1968 with the aim of unifying technical terms and standard specifications through the work of 31 Technical Committees. The organization cooperates with international standards activities, assists member states with the setting up of national bodies, and runs an Arab Center for Information and Documentation. The publication program consists of an *Annual Report* (French and English), *Standardisation* (10 per annum in Arabic, English, and French), and information pamphlets. It merged in 1990 with the Arab Industrial Development and Mining Organization (q.v.)

ARAB ORGANIZATION OF ADMINISTRATIVE SCIENCES. This organization was set up by the Council of the Arab League (q.v.) in 1961 but did not become operational until 1969. The aim of the organization is to foster cooperation in the promotion of administrative science and to improve the standards of administration in member states.

ARAB PERMANENT POSTAL COMMISSION. This agency of the Arab League (q.v.) was founded in 1954 as the Arab Postal Union with the aim of establishing postal regulations between member states and encouraging the development and modernization of services in member states. The commission publishes a *Bulletin* (monthly), a *Review* (quarterly), and annual *News*, together with occasional studies.

ARAB PETROLEUM INVESTMENTS CORPORATION. A joint undertaking through the Organization of Arab Petroleum Exporting Countries (q.v.), which was formed in 1975 and based in Dhahran, Saudi Arabia (q.v.). The objective of the corporation is the financing of petroleum investments in the Arab world and in developing countries and the creation of a regionally integrated petroleum sector. Among projects financed were gas liquefaction plants, petrochemicals, oil refineries, fertilizer plants, and shipping in member states and developing countries, with priority given to Arab joint ventures. The shareholders are Algeria, Bahrain, Egypt, Iraq, Kuwait, Libya, Oman (qq.v.), Qatar, Saudi Arabia, Syria, and the United Arab Emirates (qq.v.). It has an authorized capital of $460 million.

ARAB PETROLEUM SERVICES COMPANY. A joint undertaking

through the Organization of Arab Petroleum Exporting Countries (q.v.), which was founded in 1977 and based in Libya (q.v.). The prime function of the company is to provide petroleum services through a series of companies set up to provide specialist services to oil producers. Additionally, it provides training facilities and programs for specialist areas. It has a capital of 100 million Libyan dinars.

ARAB PETROLEUM TRAINING INSTITUTE. It was founded in 1979 and is based in Baghdad, Iraq (q.v.), with the objective of training high-level personnel in all aspects of the oil industry. The institute can be used by all member countries of the Organization of Arab Petroleum Exporting Countries (OAPEC) (q.v.).

ARAB PLANNING INSTITUTE (API). In September 1972, the government of Kuwait (q.v.) renamed the Kuwait Institute of Economic and Social Planning the Arab Planning Institute and gave it a regional role. The API has 15 participating members and is governed by a Board of Trustees, which has three members representing Kuwait and a member from each of the other participating countries. The Board is responsible for defining the general policy of the API and for following up the realization of its objectives. The director-general of the API is ex-officio a member of the board, but has no vote; he is responsible for the administration of the institute and supervises training and research programs.

The API has a major training program designed to address current developmental and economic decision-making in Arab countries, and provides certificated programs dealing with economic management and development in the region. It also provides a diploma course addressing issues relating to development policies, economic management and reform, the management of resources, and workshops aimed at high-ranking officials from member states. The institute also arranges conferences, symposia, and seminars for discussion of relevant current issues in Arab countries.

The research program of the API focuses on problems related to financial sector reform and foreign investment, social policy reform, public finance and tax systems, competitiveness and shifting comparative advantage, World Trade Organization and New Trade Agenda, information technology, and human resources development. Advisory services are provided to Arab governments and institutions on request on issues of economic and social development and planning. An advisory committee, comprising the director-general, the deputy director-general, the advisors of the institute, and three experts from member states, reviews the work program of the institute for consideration by the Board of Trustees. The publication program includes the *Journal of Development and Economic Policies* (bi-annual) and a series of working papers.

ARAB REVOLT (1916-1919). The Arab Revolt was an uprising of Arab nationalists against the Ottoman Empire (q.v.) during World War I. The revolt led by Sherif Hussein (q.v.) of the Hedjaz, a descendant of the Prophet Muhammad, and his four sons, Ali, Abdullah, Faisal, and Zaid. During the period of the Ottoman Empire, many Arabs had achieved high positions in the Ottoman administration, but opposition to the Ottomans had been growing in the Arab provinces. A separatist nationalist movement had attracted followers in Damascus, Cairo, Baghdad, and Jerusalem by the beginning of the twentieth century. Members of the movement formed secret societies as cultural or political organizations, which included groups of Arab officers in the Ottoman military. The Young Turk revolution of 1908 led to a policy of Turkification and attempts to repress Arab Nationalism (q.v.), which led to an intensification of opposition to the government, and increased demands for separation from the empire.

The Ottoman authorities had long suspected Sherif Hussein of disloyalty toward the Empire and the family had been in exile in Constantinople from 1893-1908. After his return to Mecca (q.v.), Sherif Hussein sought support from other tribes in the area to oppose conscription into the Turkish army, and the Turkish Governor-General of Mecca was forced to back down on the conscription order. The Ottoman policies led to Hussein seeking support from outside in order to combat further attempts to undermine his authority in the Hedjaz.

In February 1914, Hussein attempted to open negotiations with Great Britain by sending one of his sons to Cairo to negotiate with the British agent and consul general, Lord Kitchener, but Britain was not ready to support an Arab uprising against the Turks. However, Britain's view changed when Turkey entered the war on Germany's side in October 1914. The Ottoman attempts to raise support for a jihad (q.v.) among Muslims throughout Asia failed to win much support among the Arabs, as most notables were sympathetic to demands for independence, looking to Sherif Hussein for leadership. Relationships continued to deteriorate, with mass arrests of suspected Arab nationalists, resentment of conscription, and poor economic conditions.

In 1915, Sherif Hussein reopened negotiations with Britain through

Lord Kitchener's successor in Cairo, Sir Henry McMahon. An exchange of ten letters took place, which became known as the *McMahon–Hussein Correspondence* (q.v.), in which Sherif Hussein offered assistance against the Turks in return for a British promise to recognize the independence of the Arab provinces which were to become Iraq, Lebanon, Palestine, and Syria (qq.v.), and most of the Arabian Peninsula, and to endorse the proclamation of an Islamic Arab Caliphate. Britain refused to accept such a precise definition and granted recognition except where it deemed areas were not purely Arab. This difference in viewpoint was to have significant postwar implications with regard to the future of Palestine.

At the same time as the negotiations were drawing to a conclusion, the Ottoman authorities began a major crackdown on Arab nationalists and, in May 1916, 21 leading citizens of Damascus and Beirut were arrested and publicly hanged. Any vestiges of Arab loyalty were destroyed by these executions and they sparked widespread support for a revolt against the Turks. Opposition was further heightened in 1916 by famine; crops had been destroyed by a plague of locusts and, as a punishment for nationalist activities, the Turks refused to allow relief supplies into the area, with the result that some 300,000 people died of starvation.

In May 1916, Sherif Hussein gave orders for the tribes in the Hedjaz to strike against the Turkish garrisons and, at the same time, he proclaimed Arab independence. After three weeks, the Turkish garrison in Mecca fell, followed shortly by others in the main towns of the province. The Arab forces were supplied and financed by Britain, and military advisors, including Colonel T. E. Lawrence, served with the Sherif's army. Much of the activity was of a guerrilla nature, attacking Turkish garrisons and harassing military shipments on the Hedjaz railway, but the Arab forces did take Aqaba in the south. Also, as part of General Edmund Allenby's advance from Jerusalem, they also took Damascus in October 1919, under command of Faisal who established an Arab regime with himself as king. At the conclusion of the war Sherif Hussein alienated most of his Arab neighbors by proclaiming himself king of the Arab Countries, though Britain would only recognize him as king of the Hedjaz.

The Arab Revolt had a significant and controversial role to play in the postwar settlement, as the McMahon-Hussein Correspondence was in conflict with the secret agreements between Britain and France, the Sykes-Picot Agreement of 1916, over the fate of the Middle East on the defeat of the Ottoman Empire. The question of the future of Palestine was also to cause major problems in the immediate aftermath of the war.

ARAB SECURITY FORCE. *See* **SYMBOLIC ARAB SECURITY FORCE**

ARAB SATELLITE COMMUNICATION ORGANIZATION. This agency of the Arab League (q.v.) is responsible for the ARABSAT project that put up its first two satellites in 1965 to improve telephone, telex, data transmission, and radio and television in member states. A further satellite was launched in February 1992, with a 10-year operational life, and further launches were planned to further develop services.

ARAB SHIPBUILDING AND REPAIR YARD COMPANY. A joint undertaking through the Organization of Arab Petroleum Exporting Countries (q.v.) which was founded in 1974 and based in Bahrain (q.v.). The company operates two dry docks and two floating docks in Bahrain and engages in repair, servicing, and overhaul of tanker transport engaged in the shipment of hydrocarbons. It was hoped to eventually engage in construction, but developments in this sector have been affected by a world downturn in the shipbuilding industry. It has also been successful in the transfer of industrial technology and in the technical and managerial training for Gulf Arabs. Its operating capital is $340 million.

ARAB SOCIALISM. Arab Socialism originated as Egyptian socialism, with its leading proponent being President Gamal Abdul Nasser (q.v.), but was transformed into Arab Socialism following the establishment of the United Arab Republic (q.v.) in 1958. The doctrine was primarily of Nasser's creation, though it had been influenced by contacts with Yugoslavia's Tito and India's Nehru at conferences of non-aligned nations.

The breakup of the United Arab Republic in 1961 led to Arab socialism being pursued solely in Egypt (q.v.) and based on the abolition of feudalism and exploitation, redistribution of private property for the higher interests of society, and the incorporation of workers into management. Nasser intensified the pursuit of this policy after 1961, with measures targeted against the urban rich through the introduction of a progressive income tax and a program of nationalization.

Change in Egypt was to be implemented through the Arab Socialist Union, which was designed to be an alliance of peasants, workers, intellectuals, soldiers, and national capitalists. The union was charged with implementing the Charter of National Action, which was designed to facilitate the struggle against exploitation, to pursue equal opportunities, and to achieve the unity of all of the working forces of the population. However, it did not promote conflict between classes, as Nasser decreed that such conflict had to be peaceful, which differentiated Arab Socialism from Marxism. The Arab Socialist Union only survived Nasser's death in 1970 by six years, when it lost its political role after the parliamentary poll of October-November 1976. It formally ended in 1978 when its leader, Mustafa Khalil, became the head of President Anwar Sadat's (q.v.) National Democratic Party. President Abdul Gamal Nasser had been the only Arab politician to promote Arab Socialism, but he was not the only politician with a socialist ideology, as it was part of the ideology of the Ba'ath (q.v.). Arab socialism was also part of Muammar al-Qaddafi's (q.v.) Green Revolution, as he sought to radicalize Libyan politics. In his Green Book, Qaddafi proposed a political system based on direct popular consensual democracy set within an austere collective social structure but with due adherence to Islamic principles. *See also* **Nasserism**

ARAB SOCIETY OF CERTIFIED ACCOUNTANTS (ASCA). The ASCA was founded in 1987 and is based in Amman, Jordan (q.v.). It is a professional body whose prime function is to supervise qualifications for Arab accountants and to maintain standards. The ASCA also organizes the Arab International Accounting Conference and has a membership drawn from 21 countries. ASCA is a member of a number of international associations and committees, has been elected to the Board of the Economic and Social Council of the United Nations (q.v.), and has concluded professional cooperation agreements with a number of universities and institutions in Arab countries. It publishes *Arab Certified Accountant* (monthly), *ASCA Information Guide*, *International Accountancy Standards*, *International Audit Standards*, and the *Abu-Ghazaleh Dictionary of Accountancy*.

ARAB SPORTS FEDERATION. It was founded in 1976 and is based in Riyadh, Saudi Arabia (q.v.). It was designed to encourage regional cooperation in sport through the linking of national Olympic Committees. Its membership consists of 20 national Olympic Committees and 39 Arab Sports Federations.

ARAB STATES BROADCASTING UNION (ASBU). This is an agency of the Arab League (q.v.) founded in 1969 with membership from the radio and television stations of the member states and some associated foreign companies. The objectives of the ASBU are to promote Arab fraternity, to study and coordinate the study of broadcasting subjects, and to exchange expertise and technical cooperation in broadcasting. It also conducts training courses and undertakes audience research. It published the *ASBU Review* every two months.

ARAB TELECOMMUNICATIONS UNION (ATU). It was founded as an agency of the Arab League (q.v.) in 1953 with the aim of coordinating and developing telecommunications between member states, exchange of technical aid, and promotion of research. It also promotes the establishment of new cable communications networks in the region. The publication program includes economic and technical studies and the *Arab Telecommunications Union Journal* (quarterly).

ARAB TOURISM UNION (ATU). The Arab Tourism Union was founded in 1956 and is based in Amman, Jordan (q.v.). Its objectives are the promotion of tourism and a regional policy for the tourist industry. The union has members from the national tourist organizations of 21 Arab states and affiliates from the private sector. It publishes *Arab Tourism Magazine* (fortnightly in Arabic) and *Press Bulletin* (monthly in Arabic and English).

ARAB TOWNS ORGANIZATION (ATO). The Arab Towns Organization was founded in 1967 to assist Arab towns with the solving of problems and to ensure that planning preserves the natural environment and cultural heritage. The organization provides soft loans for needy members and has an affiliated Arab Urban Development Institute (q.v.) based in Riyadh, Saudi Arabia (q.v.), which provides its technical and scientific support. It publishes *Al-Medinah Al-Arabiah* (quarterly).

ARAB TRADE FINANCING PROGRAM (ATFP). The Arab Trade Financing Program is a specialized financial institution established by the Arab Monetary Fund (AMF) (q.v.) on 16 March 1989 with the objective of developing and promoting trade among Arab countries and enhancing the competitive ability of Arab exporters. As of December 1998 the ATFP was operating with paid-in capital of $488 million and reserves of $189 million. The ATFP is controlled by a General Assembly, which authorizes deposits from financial and banking institutions as well as borrowing from financial markets and any other sources.

The ATFP provides refinancing in the form of lines of credit to

Arab importers and exporters through national agencies designated by the monetary authorities of Arab countries. Refinancing includes pre-export, export and import, and buyer credits of goods with value added of at least 40 percent originating from primary sources and/or other domestic production factors of an Arab country. However, crude oil, used goods and re-exported goods are ineligible for refinancing.

The ATFP provides additional services through an Intra-Arab Trade Information Network (IATIN) which provides information on intra-Arab trade and Arab trade opportunities. It also organizes meetings of buyers and sellers of Arab goods and training programs on trade-related issues.

Three groups are allowed to participate in the capital of the organization: Arab Monetary Fund (q.v.), multilateral Arab financing institutions, and Arab public financial and banking institutions; private Arab financial and banking institutions; and international and joint Arab-foreign financial institutions. The General Assembly is the highest authority, with the management of the fund in the hands of a Board of Directors which comprises eight members elected by the General Assembly for a three-year renewable term under the chairmanship of the director-general and the chairman of the AMF. The Board of Directors formulates policy, passes internal by-laws and supervises its operations, while the director-general is responsible for the ATFP's management and day-to-day activities.

It publishes an *Annual Report* (Arabic and English), *Lines of Credit Rules and Procedures* (Arabic), *ATFP General Features-Objectives and Activities* (Arabic and English), and *IATIN Quarterly Bulletin* (Arabic).

ARAB UNION OF RAILWAYS. It was founded in 1979 and based in Aleppo, Syria (q.v.). The union aims to stimulate and coordinate the development of railways in the Arab world and, in particular, regional and international links. Its membership is drawn from the rail authorities of Algeria, Iraq, Jordan, Lebanon, Libya (qq.v.), Morocco, Syria (q.v.), Tunisia, and the Palestine Liberation Organization (q.v.). It publishes *Arab Railways* (quarterly in Arabic), *Annual Statistics of Arab Railways,* and a glossary of railway terms in Arabic, French, English, and German.

ARAB URBAN DEVELOPMENT INSTITUTE (AUDI). The Arab Urban Development Institute was founded in 1980 and has its headquarters in Riyadh, Saudi Arabia (q.v.). The AUDI is a regional, nongovernmental, not-for-profit urban research, technical, and consulting organization. The institute is affiliated to the Arab Towns Organization (q.v.), serves as its technical and scientific arm, and has a membership drawn from some 400 Arab towns and cities from 22 countries.

The AUDI is directed by a Board of Trustees and Officers with 11 members representing nine member towns and cities and managed by the chairman of the Board and a director-general. Members of the Board are elected for four-year terms. The main objective of the Institute is the enhancement of the quality of municipal services in member cities through the provision of professional and technical support. It is also dedicated to the improvement and preservation of the Islamic and Arab character and heritage of Arab towns and cities.

The institute organizes training programs, undertakes research, and organizes symposia and conferences such as one on "Urban Development Strategies for Arab Cities," which was held in Riyadh in April 2000.

ARAB WOMEN'S SOLIDARITY ASSOCIATION (AWSA). It was founded in Cairo, Egypt (q.v.), in 1982 by 120 women who agreed that the liberation of Arab women could not be separated from the struggle to liberate the Arab people. The AWSA is a nonprofit organization which has in excess of 3,000 members internationally, has consultative status with the Economic and Social Council of the United Nations (ECOSOC) (q.v.), and promotes Arab women's active participation in social, economic, cultural, and political life.

The primary aims of the AWSA have been to:

- establish an international network of Arab women
- hold general meetings and conferences
- develop income-generating projects for Arab women
- provide Arab women with social services and increase their visibility in social, political, and cultural spheres

The AWSA organizes international conferences, publishes literary magazines and books, and produces films about Arab women's lives.

ARABIAN GULF STATES FOLK HERITAGE CENTER. This center was established in 1981 and is located in Doha, Qatar. The center was founded because of concern that aspects of traditional folklore were disappearing because of development, modernization, and rapid social change. Its collection consists of objects representing folk crafts, poetry, music, stories, and oral histories. The center houses a library of 5,000 volumes, 110 journals, material on video-audio cassette, and photographic material.

ARAFAT, YASSER (1929-). Yassar Arafat is Chairman of the Palestine Liberation Organization (PLO) and of the Palestinian Authority and is the man most closely identified with the Palestinian cause. Arafat attended university at Cairo, majoring in Civil Engineering and was reportedly a member of the Muslim Brotherhood (q.v.) becoming active as a Palestinian student organizer and becoming leader of the General Union of Palestinian Students from 1952 to 1957. Arafat was in Prague in 1957 when some of his colleagues were arrested in Egypt (q.v.) due to activities within the Muslim Brotherhood. He remained in Europe studying in Stuttgart before going to Kuwait (q.v.), where he founded a successful contracting company, which brought him considerable wealth.

Arafat was one of the founding members of al-Fath (q.v.) in the late 1950s as one of the exiled Palestinians in the Gulf States who advocated an armed struggle to free Palestine. The group received training in Algeria and Syria (qq.v.) and achieved prominence after the 1967 Arab-Israeli War. The various guerrilla groups soon overshadowed the PLO, and in 1969 al-Fath and its allies won enough seats on the Palestinian National Council to elect Arafat as the chair of the PLO's executive committee. After being expelled from Jordan (q.v.) in 1970, the Palestinians set up their operational base in Beirut and began operations against Israel from southern Lebanon (qq.v.). Following the 1973 Arab-Israeli War, some Palestinians began to consider a settlement. On 13 November 1974, Arafat addressed the United Nations (q.v.) in a speech in which he offered both an olive branch and a freedom fighter's gun.

However, Arafat's career took a downward turn in 1975 with the outbreak of the Lebanese civil war. The Palestinians found themselves fighting both Maronite forces and Syrians, but still managed to maintain a foothold in Lebanon. In 1982, Israel invaded Lebanon; Arafat and some 10,000 Palestinian fighters were evacuated to Tunis. In 1984, Arafat held discussions with King Hussein of Jordan (q.v.) to seek a joint Jordanian-Palestinian negotiating position but these failed and Arafat was blamed for the failure. In 1987, the *intifada*, or Palestinian uprising, began in the occupied territories and although al-Fath was involved it was at a local level and not through the leadership in Tunis. This led many observers to write Arafat off together with the central PLO leadership, but these political obituaries were wrong as Arafat's leadership role survived. His survival was largely due to his ability to forge coalitions of vastly different factions from the left and right, and from communist and capitalist persuasions.

In 1988, Arafat and the old al-Fath elite took a major step toward recognizing Israel's right to exist, involving the principles of negotiation with Israel on peace in exchange for territory, and renunciation of terrorism. This allowed the United States to open up a dialogue with the PLO but negotiations were suspended when Arafat refused to condemn an attack on Israel by a Palestinian faction. In 1991, the Middle East Peace Conference (q.v.) was opened in Madrid, but the Israeli Likud government refused to recognize the PLO and the Palestinian delegation had to operate as part of a joint Jordanian-Palestinian delegation. Again some analysts wrote off Arafat and the PLO leadership as essential to a peace settlement.

In 1992, Arafat was injured in a plane crash in Libya (q.v.) and was convinced that he had been spared by providence for some reason. He also got married in 1991 or 1992 to Suha Tawil, daughter of a PLO activist, who had served as his secretary and who had converted from Christianity to Islam (q.v.). The couple had a daughter in 1994, and Suha Tawil has given a number of interviews to the media presenting a more intimate view of her husband. Following Likud's replacement by the Labor government of Yitzhak Rabin, a series of secret negotiations took place in Oslo using Norwegian intermediaries. The result of the Oslo accords was the Declaration of Principles on Interim Self-Government Arrangements, which was signed at the White House on 13 September 1993. Arafat was greeted by the U.S. President and, significantly, shook hands with Rabin, which confirmed that Arafat had survived his enemies within the PLO in Israel and in the United States.

Arafat was declared chairman of the Palestinian Authority which, under the agreement, was to take over self-government in Jericho and Gaza and eventually more of the West Bank. Arafat delayed his return to Palestine (q.v.), but on his return to Gaza, he was greeted with adulation by the population. This marked a personal vindication of Arafat's policy with regard to the peace process. Arafat is a Sunni (q.v.) Muslim but is staunchly opposed to the Islamic elements within the Palestinian movement, and is opposed by Hamas (q.v.), who view the Palestinian Authority as ineffective and corrupt.

The continuing peace process with Israel has been fraught with difficulty following the assassination of Yitzhak Rabin and the election of an intransigent Likud coalition which was reluctant to make progress and still pursued a policy of settlements in disputed areas. However, the following general election led to the return of a Labor government and under Prime Minister Ehud Barak progress was made in the peace process, with the return of a further area of the West Bank to Palestinian control. Agreement was also reached in January 2000 for a further 5 percent of the West Bank to be turned over to Palestinian control.

ARIF, ABDUL SALAM (1920-1966). Arif was born into a middle-class family in Baghdad, Iraq (q.v.), and trained as an officer at the Military Academy, serving with the Iraqi army in the 1948 Arab-Israeli conflict. However, the poor performance of the Iraqi troops in the war turned him against the pro-Western regime of King Faisal II. Arif played a leading part in the organization of the Free Officers coup that overthrew the monarchy in July 1958, and led the force that seized the capital.

In the new republic Arif served as Deputy Chief of Staff, Deputy Premier, and Minister of the Interior in the regime of Abdul Karim Qasim (q.v.). However, a clash with Qasim soon followed, as Arif planned to lead Iraq into the United Arab Republic (q.v.), a move opposed by Qasim. Arif lost all of his posts in September 1958 and was imprisoned on charges of attempting to assassinate Qasim and staging a coup. Arif was found guilty and sentenced to death but the sentence was commuted and he was released from prison in 1961. Once out of prison, he formed an alliance with Ba'athist officers, which led to a coup in February 1963 and the ending of Qasim's regime. Arif became president but lacked power. However, the Ba'athists were not united and he disposed of them, assuming full power in November 1963.

Arif was a firm admirer of President Gamal Abdul Nasser (q.v.) and he followed his policy of expanding the public sector through a program of nationalization. He also planned to unite Egypt (q.v.) and Iraq beginning with economic and military coordination and a joint presidential council. He also attempted to resolve the Kurdish problem and was on the verge of signing an accord with the Kurds (q.v.) when he was killed in an air crash in April 1966.

ARSUZI, ZAKI (1908-1968). Arsuzi was born into a lower middle-class household in Antioch (later Antakya) in the Syrian Province of Alexandretta and went to Sorbonne University, Paris, obtaining a degree in philosophy in 1931. In 1932, he became a teacher in Antakya and formed a club to help raise the appreciation of the arts, but the French mandatory authorities closed it. This action caused Arsuzi to turn his attention toward nationalist politics, but he became a refugee in Damascus when his province of Alexandretta was annexed to Turkey (q.v.) in

1939.

Arsuzi soon gathered together a group of acolytes and began to pursue his nationalist ideas, urging the group to bring about a renaissance in the Arab world. He was forced out of his job by the mandatory authorities but he did not give up his nationalist activities. On the departure of the French in 1946 attempts were made to unite the pan-Arab groups led by Arsuzi and Michel Aflaq (q.v.), and these came to fruition in April 1947 with the founding of the Arab Ba'ath Party (q.v.). One of the first recruits to the new party was Hafiz Assad (q.v.) and, following the Ba'athist coup of March 1963, Assad was assigned to the task of creating a military imbued with the Ba'athist ideology, turning toward Arsuzi for guidance. He became Assad's constant companion on tours of military barracks, where he lectured on Ba'athist ideology.

However, by 1965 the civilian and military factions of the party had split and a power struggle was developing, with Assad supporting the military faction. Arsuzi wrote editorials in party and military publications, and was the ideological thinker for the military faction, as the civilian faction owed allegiance to Michel Aflaq.

ASSAD, HAFIZ (1930-2000). Hafiz Assad was born into the family of a notable of the Alawi tribe in a village near Latakia, Syria (q.v.). He enrolled at the military academy in Homs in 1951, graduating four years later as an air force pilot. He underwent additional training in Egypt (q.v.). After the formation of the United Arab Republic (UAR) (q.v.) in 1958, he undertook further training in Russia. Assad was a member of the Ba'ath Party (q.v.) but it was suppressed by Gamal Abdul Nasser (q.v.) on the formation of the UAR. This left Assad disgruntled and, while in Egypt, he became a founder of the clandestine Military Committee. Once Syria ceded from the UAR in September 1961, the Military Committee became active and was the prime force behind the Ba'athist coup in March 1963.

In September 1963, Assad was elected to the regional high command of the Ba'ath Party, and he became commander of the Syrian air force in December 1964. In May 1965, he was elected to the national (i.e., all Arab) high command of the party and, in the growing rift between the moderate civilian and radical military arms of the party, he became firmly allied with the latter. In February 1966, the military faction launched a successful coup and Assad became Defense Minister, immediately adopting an Arab nationalist stance with the main objective the defeat of Israel (q.v.). His rival within the Ba'ath party, Salah Jadid, wanted Syria to pursue a socialist path and to revolutionize Syrian society, and the party was unable to resolve this split.

The conflict was partially resolved in February 1969 when Assad used his military support to take control of the Ba'ath high command and the government. However, he refrained from monopolizing power and retained Nur al Din Attasi, a Jadid ally, as president, with Jadid still powerful within the party. The climax came during the national congress of the Ba'ath at Damascus in November 1970, when Assad gained full control resulting in purges and the arrest of his adversaries. He then assumed the additional office of Prime Minister, leaving the presidency to his nominee, Ahmad Khatib. The new party high command under Assad then proceeded to draft a new constitution for approval by the People's Assembly.

In February 1971, the People's Assembly ratified Assad's nomination as president, which was confirmed by an affirmative 99.2 percent in a referendum in March 1971. The draft constitution adopted in January 1973 described Syria as a democratic, popular, socialist state. This was attacked by Muslim clerics as secular and atheistic; they demanded that Islam (q.v.) be designated as the state religion. Assad's attempt to defuse the situation was limited to amending the constitution to specify that the president must be Muslim, but this did not satisfy the clerics. Assad declared the 1973 war against Israel to be a jihad (q.v.), and in 1974 he went on a pilgrimage to Mecca (q.v.), which established him as a true believer. He was reelected president in 1978, 1985, and 1992.

Assad succeeded in putting Syria onto a firm institutional path with elections being held for the People's Assembly every four years. The Assembly is dominated by the Ba'ath-led National Progressive Front which was formed in 1972 and includes pan-Arabists, socialists, and communists. However, real power lies with the Ba'ath high command that is led by Assad backed by an intelligence network, which permeates all levels of the government and society. The only real opposition comes from the Muslim Brotherhood (q.v.), which is banned.

The affairs of Lebanon (q.v.) have also seen heavy involvement from Assad, based on the premise that Syria and Lebanon have a special relationship. He first intervened in the Lebanese Civil War in 1976 to bolster the Christians, which revived the Islamists within Syria resulting in a campaign of assassination and terrorism. In March 1980, this escalated to near insurrection in Aleppo and Hama, with an attempt being made to assassinate Assad in June 1980. He responded with a campaign to crush the Islamists, who went underground and consolidated before launching an insurrection in Hama in February 1982. Assad responded by using the forces at his command and regained control of the situation. In the following year he had a heart attack, and in November 1983 his younger brother, Rifat, failed in an attempt to seize power.

Assad finally gained complete control of the situation in March 1984, which coincided with his success in persuading Lebanon to abort the Lebanese-Israeli peace treaty. This treaty had been initialled by the Lebanese, under U.S. pressure, after the 1982 Israeli invasion of Lebanon. Assad was concerned that the defection of Lebanon to the U.S.-Israeli alliance would pose a serious security threat to Syria. Because of this Assad persevered with a presence in Lebanon and, in October 1990, the pro-Syrian side was victorious.

Relations with Egypt (q.v.) during Assad's time in power have also fluctuated, with ties strengthened during the 1973 Arab-Israeli War and the agreement to a coordinated military command. Assad became disillusioned with President Anwar Sadat (q.v.) when Egypt began to pursue policies, which resulted in the 1979 peace treaty with Israel. Assad firmly allied himself with the Palestine Liberation Organization (PLO) (q.v.) and opposed the readmission of Egypt to the Arab League (q.v.), from which it had been expelled in 1979.

The Ba'ath Party's national command (i.e., all-Arab) was dominated by Assad in Syria and by Michel Aflaq (q.v.) in Baghdad, and divisions emerged between the two. Assad remained cool toward Iraq (q.v.) both under Ahmad Hassan Bakr and then Saddam Hussein (q.v.); though there was a brief rapprochement in 1978, it was of short duration. Relations soured further when Syria sided with Iran in the Iraq-Iran War (1980-88) (q.v.), and Assad also joined the anti-Iraq coalition following Hussein's invasion of Kuwait (q.v.) in 1990, after failing to persuade Iraq to withdraw.

The one consistent policy throughout Assad's period as president has been the commitment to divest Israel of all territorial gains made in the 1967 war; however, he failed to retake the Golan Heights in the October 1973 war. Syria did reach a disengagement agreement with Israel and stopped guerrilla attacks on Israel from Syrian territory. Following Egypt's signing of the peace treaty with Israel in 1979, Assad embarked on an extremely costly policy of attempting to keep pace with Israel's military capability while, at the same time, trying to prevent other Arab states from reaching bilateral deals with Israel.

Assad considered the Palestinians an important part of any alliance dealing with Israel and wanted to maintain a close relationship with the Chairman of the Palestine Liberation Organization (PLO) (q.v.), Yasser Arafat, but the latter's desire to maintain the PLO's independence led to strained relations between the two men. The incitement by Assad of a revolt against Arafat within al-Fath (q.v.) in 1983 also weakened Assad's position in relation to the PLO.

The decline of the Soviet Union as a superpower led to Assad having to be more pragmatic in dealings with Israel, and in 1991 he agreed to participate in the Middle East Peace Conference (q.v.), held in Madrid. However, Assad did succeed in ensuring that the conference was based on United Nations Security Council Resolutions 242 and 338 (qq.v.), which had called for Israeli withdrawal from territory occupied in the 1967 war. In the talks with Israel, Assad maintained that Israel had to withdraw from the Golan Heights before any peace treaty could be concluded but these talks were inconclusive, as were those held in 1994, mediated by the U.S. Assad died on 10 June 2000 and the Ba'ath immediately nominated his son Basher as President.

ASSOCIATION OF ARAB UNIVERSITIES. It was founded in 1964 and is based in Amman, Jordan (q.v.), with a membership of 140 universities in 20 countries. The association aims to consolidate cooperation between member Arab universities and institutes, holds a scientific conference every three years, and promotes seminars and conferences. The Association publishes a *Bulletin* (twice per annum), *Directory of Arab Universities*, *Directory of Teaching Staff of Arab Universities,* and seminar proceedings.

ASSOCIATION OF ISLAMIC CHARITABLE PROJECTS (AICP). The Association of Islamic Charitable Projects was founded in 1930 in Beirut, Lebanon (q.v.), by Sheikh Ahmed al-Ajuz as a nonprofit international organization with the objective of propagating Islam (q.v.) and assisting the poor of Lebanon with social welfare, education, and economic projects. It was not until 1983 that the AICP assumed an international role. By 1995, it had representation in 40 countries worldwide, though still operating extensively in war-torn Lebanon with a program of social rectification and religious education. Membership of AICP is diverse and from across the social strata, and it is largely from these individual members that the organization obtains its funding.

The association is primarily concerned with sponsoring secular and religious education, with the provision of preschools, elementary schools, secondary schools, and weekend programs designed to act as a springboard to full-time education. It also has various broadcasting stations that transmit the teachings of Islam and information on forthcoming AICP events. The organization sponsors scouting programs for boys and girls, as well as social and craft programs for women. AICP also has an extensive publications program of magazines, books, and pamphlets through its Islamic Studies and Research Division.

ASSOCIATION OF MUSLIM RESEARCHERS (AMR). The Association was founded in 1989 and is based at the Islamic Cultural Centre in London. It is a nonsectarian, independent, voluntary body that provides a framework for Muslim intellectuals to exchange and pool knowledge and ideas. The aims of AMR are to:

- identify gaps in knowledge and promote relevant research programs to address these needs
- develop solutions to problems faced by Muslims in Great Britain
- develop models for successful individuals and societies in the modern world

The AMR operates according to a Vision Statement that was adopted in 1990, organizing courses and lecture programs and publishing materials arising from these activities. It structures its program through special-interest groups formed from the interests of its membership.

ASSOCIATION OF MUSLIM SCIENTISTS AND ENGINEERS (AMSE). The Association is a non-profit scientific, educational, and cultural organization of Muslim scientists and engineers who are citizens or reside in North America, founded on 6 September 1969 with its headquarters in Herndon, Virginia. The objectives of the AMSE are to:

- channel the talents of Muslim scientists and engineers by providing assistance and guidance to individuals and communities
- provide encouragement, guidance, and assistance to Muslim scientists and engineers in their education and careers
- improve the gathering, distribution, and dissemination of technical information and Islamic knowledge through journal publications, meetings, and similar media

The AMSE is run by an Executive Committee and draws its membership from Muslims who are graduates or postgraduates in the relevant academic disciplines. The AMSE holds an annual conference and publishes the proceedings.

ASSOCIATION OF MUSLIM SOCIAL SCIENTISTS (AMSS). The Association was founded in 1972 to fulfill the perceived need for an organization to promote Islamic positions in the various academic disciplines. The AMSS is controlled by an Executive Board, elected by the members at the annual convention; it serves for a period of two years. In terms of organization, the AMSS primarily exists to serve the interests of members operating through e-mail and regional representatives based at universities across the United States. A branch of AMSS also exists in the United Kingdom with a postal base in Richmond, Surrey. The objectives of the AMSS are to:

- generate Islamic thought and Islamic epistemology through crucial and scientific enquiry to improve the condition of Muslim communities and institutions
- assist members to develop and apply Islamic positions on contemporary issues in their research
- facilitate research and professional development opportunities for U.S.-based members
- encourage institutional development within Muslim communities in the U.S. and abroad through research and application
- create venues for civilized dialogue
- develop relationships with other academic institutions and professional organizations

The association holds an annual convention in October of each year which is designed to attract scholars from all over the world to establish critical dialogue in important issues. The U.K. branch is organized on a similar basis and also holds an annual conference. The AMSS publishes the *American Journal of Islamic Social Sciences* (quarterly) and a newsletter. A newsletter is also published by the U.K. branch.

B

BA'ATH SOCIALIST PARTY (BSP). The BSP is a pan-Arab political party whose official title is the Arab Ba'ath Socialist Party. The Ba'ath Party began in Damascus, Syria (q.v.), in March 1954 from a merger between the Arab Ba'ath Party, founded by Michel Aflaq (q.v.) and Salah al-Din Bitar, and the Arab Socialist Party, founded by Akram Hourani. The BSP was based on the principles of the unity and freedom of the Arab nation within its homeland, the overthrow of colonialism, and the promotion of humanitarianism. The party leaders believed that, in order to achieve these objectives, the BSP had to be nationalist, populist, socialist, and revolutionary. The Ba'ath did not believe in class conflict but favored land reform; public ownership of natural resources, transport, large-scale industry, and financial institutions; trade unions of workers and peasants; the cooption of workers into management; and the acceptance of nonexploitative private ownership and inheritance. In addition, the BSP stood for representative and constitutional forms of government, freedom of speech, and freedom of association within the bounds of Arab Nationalism (q.v.).

The Ba'ath believes that the Arabs form a single nation that has been divided into various regions (i.e., countries) and the structure of the party reflects this belief. The party is headed by a National Command which is the central executive authority, under which are Regional Commands in states where the party has enough of a presence to establish one. Within the Regional Command are branches made up of divisions of three-member cells. Until 1966, the National Command was based in Damascus but a split in that year led to a breakaway group establishing itself in Beirut, transferring to Baghdad following the Ba'athist coup in 1968. The BSP has a presence in Iraq, Jordan, Lebanon, Syria, and Yemen (qq.v.).

BAGHDAD PACT. This was an attempt to form an anti-Soviet security pact to create a regional northern-tier security organization on the lines of the North Atlantic Treaty Organization (NATO). In April 1954, Turkey (q.v.) signed a mutual assistance pact with Pakistan, which was then signed by Iraq (q.v.) on 24 February 1955, thus forming the core of the Baghdad Pact. The most avid supporter of the pact was the Iraqi Prime Minister Nuri al-Said (q.v.) who saw it as a lever against the influence of President Gamal Abdul Nasser (q.v.). Lebanon and Syria (qq.v.) refused to sign the pact under pressure from Egypt (q.v.). During the course of 1955, Great Britain and Iran (q.v.) signed the pact and a Middle East Treaty Organization was formed with headquarters in Baghdad.

The United States did not join the pact because it did not want to alienate Egypt and force Nasser into the Soviet orbit of influence. However, the arrangement met U.S. security requirements for the region and Washington was heavily involved in the various security guarantees. The 1958 revolution in Iraq led to the deaths of King Faisal and Nuri al-Said and Iraq's withdrawal from the Baghdad Pact, denounced as a vestige of Western imperialism. The group was then renamed the Central Treaty Organization (CENTO) (q.v.) and had no Arab states in membership.

BAGHDAD SUMMIT (1978). This Arab summit was held between 2-5 November 1978 to consider the Arab world's response to the Camp David Accords (q.v.). Iraq (q.v.) was the prime motivator behind the summit, which was attended by 20 Arab states and the Palestine Liberation Organization (PLO) (q.v.). The summit rejected the Camp David Accords and put forward a peace proposal based on United Nations Security Council Resolution 242 (q.v.), calling for Israeli withdrawal from the Occupied Territories, the establishment of a Palestinian state, and a recognition of the right to exist for all states in the region. The summit also threatened Egypt (q.v.) with severe penalties if it signed a peace treaty with Israel (q.v.), which would effectively mean the isolation of Egypt from the rest of the Arab world. Among specific measures to be adopted were expulsion from the Arab League (AL) (q.v.), removal of the AL headquarters from Cairo, and the halting of all economic and military aid. The summit also adopted measures to aid the remaining frontline states to prevent further defections, and a fund of $9 billion was set up to provide aid to Jordan, Syria, and the PLO (qq.v.). This action was crucial in discouraging Jordan from going against the Arab consensus.

A delegation was sent from the summit to see President Anwar Sadat (q.v.) on 4 November but he refused to meet with them. On 27 March 1979, the day after Egypt signed a peace treaty with Israel, the AL met to follow through the sanctions agreed at the summit, though representatives from Oman, the PLO, and Sudan were not present. The sanctions were imposed on 31 March and diplomatic relations broken off by all AL states except Oman. Egypt was expelled from the AL and AL headquarters were moved to Tunis.

BAHRAIN. The State of Bahrain in the Arabian Gulf consists of 33 low-lying islands some 15 miles off the eastern coast of Saudi Arabia (q.v.) to which it is linked by a causeway. The region became Muslim within two years of the Prophet Muhammad's death and, given its closeness to Iran (q.v.), it has been open to Iranian influence, coming under Iranian control from 1603 to 1783. The country was then taken over in 1783 by the al-Khalifa family of the 'Utab tribe who were based in the Nejd, belonging to the Anaza federation which also includes the al-Saud (q.v.). The family have remained in power ever since, but the majority of the population are Shi'i (q.v.) Muslims while the ruling family are Sunni (q.v.), which has become a continuing source of political weakness.

Bahrain came under British influence in 1816 and a succession of treaties in the nineteenth century led to it becoming a British protectorate in all but name. Despite periods of internal unrest this influence and control of foreign policy lasted until British withdrawal from the Gulf in 1971. The Bahrain economy had relied heavily on the traditional pearling industry for its prosperity, but in the 1930s the whole industry in the Gulf collapsed due to competition from the Japanese cultured pearl industry. However, Bahrain was protected from this slump by the advent of the oil era in 1932, which radically restructured the Bahrain economy into an industrial and oil industry-related economy with an emergent industrial working class and an improved educational infrastructure.

The period following World War II was also one of internal unrest, which was largely due to the growth of Arab nationalism (q.v.) in the Middle East, particularly following the 1952 Free Officers' coup in Egypt (q.v.), but also due to sectarian riots in 1953. This unrest resulted in the formation of a Council of National Unity designed to further Bahraini aspirations for independence, but this was suppressed in 1956 following British and French interventions in Suez. Despite attempts by the ruling family to win the support of powerful commercial families and the accession of Sheikh Isa ibn Salman in 1961 the country continued to experience industrial and political unrest. During this strike, the leftist Progressive Forces Front began to articulate political demands, including an end to the nine-year old state of emergency, the granting of trade union rights, and a legislative assembly.

Saudi Arabia (q.v.) was alarmed at activities in Bahrain and applied pressure on the ruler to ensure that opposition was met with repressive measures and numerous arrests. However, Bahrain's reputation for unrest and the political agitation led to its being excluded from the proposed Gulf Federation (later the United Arab Emirates) (q.v.), resulting in the ruling family attempting to reach an accommodation with the opposition, initially through the appointment of a 12-member advisory Council of State in 1970.

In 1971, following British withdrawal, the council was transformed into a Council of Ministers, and plans were discussed for a new constitution that would allow for a degree of popular participation. However, the left in Bahrain had allied itself with the Popular Front for the Liberation of Oman and the Arab Gulf (PFLOAG) (q.v.) and the Bahrain

National Liberation Front (BNLF), and general strikes were called in March and September 1972. This accelerated the process of change and a draft constitution was approved by Sheikh Isa in March 1973, with elections being held in December 1973. The franchise was restricted with only 30,000 electors being eligible to vote for 30 seats in the 42-man assembly, with the BNLF and the Bahrain Nationalist Movement fighting the elections, which were boycotted by PFLOAG. The radical bloc won 70 percent of the vote and became the majority bloc in the new assembly.

Riyadh continued to exert pressure on Bahrain to combat the growing radicalism and a new law on state security was promulgated in October 1974. The Assembly, refusing to endorse the law, was dissolved in August 1975, and members of PFLOAG were arrested. Political opposition was driven underground until the Iranian Revolution in 1979, which gave rise to massive demonstrations among the Shi'i majority on 15 May 1979. The demonstrations were put down by troops and 900 protestors arrested. The Shi'i leaders demanded that Bahrain be declared an Islamic Republic, the security laws reviewed, reinstatement of the assembly, and alleviation of economic hardship. The government promised to reinstate the assembly, but instead reneged on this promise, repressed all opposition, and expelled the Shi'i leader Said Hadi al-Mudarrisi. Tension was heightened by a growing alliance between the secular left and the Shi'i militants and the emergence of continuing links with the U.S. military, with Bahrain being used as a staging post during the U.S. Embassy hostage crisis in Teheran.

As a result Bahrain has continued to experience Shi'i radicalism instead of radicalism from the secular left. There were rumors of a coup in 1981, and an arms cache discovered in 1984 was evidence of a further coup. Although Iran had formally abandoned its claim to Bahrain in 1970, there were hints of a renewed claim to sovereignty, leading to further insecurity. In 1981, Bahrain signed a defense treaty with Saudi Arabia, which had made it plain that it would not tolerate political change in Bahrain, and in the same year joined the Gulf Cooperation Council (q.v.). In 1982, a further 60 arrests were made in the wake of a suspected coup.

During the Iraq-Iran War of 1980-1988 (q.v.), Bahrain actively supported Iraq and during the Kuwait (q.v.) crisis of 1990-1991 the Emir followed a strongly pro-Kuwait policy. However, dissent refused to go away, and in an attempt to defuse the situation the Emir appointed a 30-man Advisory Council in 1973. This, too, failed to meet demands, and further demonstrations broke out in December 1994, followed by large-scale arrests and curfews.

At one point Bahrain had been one of the richest states in the Gulf, its wealth based largely on pearl fishing, boatbuilding, fishing, and a significant entrepot trade with Saudi Arabia and Iran. Now only the entrepot trade survives. Bahrain benefited from a well-developed oil sector but production has been in steady decline from 1970. It now relies on the export of oil-refined products to sustain the industry, but only 16 percent comes from Bahraini production, the balance coming from Saudi Arabia. Bahrain also has access to gas from the Khuff formation in the Gulf, and this is used for reinjection in the oilfields to aid secondary recovery, as an industrial fuel, and for petrochemical production. The country does have a major offshore financial sector that is vital to its economy.

BANKING AND FINANCE. *See* **ARAB BANK FOR ECONOMIC DEVELOPMENT IN AFRICA; ARAB MONETARY FUND; ARAB TRADE FINANCING PROGRAM; GULF INVESTMENT CORPORATION; INTER-ARAB INVESTMENT GUARANTEE CORPORATION; INTERNATIONAL ASSOCIATION OF ISLAMIC BANKS; INTERNATIONAL MONETARY FUND; ISLAMIC BANKING; ISLAMIC DEVELOPMENT BANK; UNION OF ARAB BANKS**

BANNA, HASSAN AL- (1906-1949). An Egyptian Islamic leader and founder of the Muslim Brotherhood (MB) (q.v.), al-Banna was born into a religious family in Muhammadiya in the Nile delta and, following graduation from the Cairo Teachers College, he became a primary teacher at Ismailiya in the Canal Zone, occupied by Great Britain. In 1928, he established the MB as a youth organization to further social and moral reform through communication, information, and propaganda. The movement then turned into a political-religious movement which argued that Islam (q.v.) was a total ideology, that it was an all-pervasive system for the regulation of the political, economic, social, and cultural life for all believers.

The MB opened a base in Cairo, Egypt (q.v.), in 1933 and by 1940 there were 500 branches with membership drawn from students, civil servants, artisans, petty traders, and middle-income peasants. The post-World War II anti-imperialist struggle against Great Britain boosted its popularity and by 1946 al-Banna was claiming a membership of 500,000. He had also travelled to other countries in the Middle East to open up other branches and sent out trained theology students to set up branches in their own countries.

The Egyptian establishment was held responsible by al-Banna for the Arab defeat in the 1948 Palestinian war and the MB began to engage in subversive and terrorist activities. As a consequence Prime Minister Mahmud Fahmi Nokrashi banned the MB in December 1948, only to be assassinated by an activist three weeks after the ban. Further repression of the MB followed and on 12 February 1949, al-Banna was killed by secret service agents in Cairo.

BANNA, SABRI AL- (1939-   ). Sabri al-Banna, also known as *Abu Nidal*, worked as an agent for a number of Arab intelligence agencies before forming his own group in 1974 called *al-Fath*: the Revolutionary Council, not to be confused with al-Fath (q.v.). The main policy of the group was total opposition to the two-state solution then being considered by the Palestine Liberation Organization (q.v.). The group has been responsible for a number of assassinations of Arab, Israeli, and Palestinian diplomats and attacks at Rome and Vienna airports in 1985, on worshippers at an Istanbul synagogue in 1986, and passengers on a Greek cruise ship in 1988. In 1982, the Israeli ambassador to Great Britain was assassinated by al-Fath and this became the trigger for Israel's (q.v.) invasion of Lebanon. From 1974 to 1983 Abu Nidal was based in Iraq (q.v.) and from 1983 to 1987 in Damascus, Syria (q.v.), before moving to Libya (q.v.). A series of internal conflicts since that date have severely weakened the organization and its activities. The whereabouts of Abu Nidal are a matter of speculation, as there were reports in 1999 that he had been betrayed by Libya and was being held by the Egyptian authorities, but reports have not been substantiated and speculation remains rife in the Middle East press.

BARZANI, MASUD AL- (1946-   ). Masud Barzani is the son of General Mustafa Barzani (q.v.) and was born in Mahabad in Iranian Kurdistan. He was closely associated with the struggles of the Iraqi Kurds (q.v.) from 1968, but fled to Iran (q.v.) in 1975 following the collapse of the Kurdish revolt. Following his father's death, he took over the leadership of the Kurdistan Democratic Party (KDP), and experienced the chemical warfare of Saddam Hussein (q.v.) in 1988 at Halabjah and the assaults on Kurdistan following the Gulf War (q.v.) in 1991.

Following the end of the Gulf War, the Kurds controlled their own region in northern Iraq, but there was serious conflict between the KDP and the Patriotic Union of Kurdistan (PUK) over joint control of the region, and in May 1994 clashes resulted in some 1,000 deaths. Unrest flared again in 1995 and an investigation by Amnesty International found evidence of widespread human rights abuses with arbitrary arrests, torture, and arbitrary killings.

In February 1996, the allies agreed to continue arrangements to enforce the air exclusion zone to protect the Kurdish enclave, and in April Barzani led a delegation to Syria (q.v.) to discuss the situation in the Kurdish enclave and in Iraq (q.v.) as a whole. Despite continued conflict between Barzani's KDP and the PUK, both parties agreed to the continued mandate for the Kurdish National Assembly in which they shared power, and Iraq became involved in mediation attempts to resolve the conflict between the two parties.

Further conflicts flared during the remainder of 1996 and 1997, with the result that the enclave was split between the two factions. In April 1997, the United States initiated talks between Barzani and the PUK leadership and the Kurdish leaders reaffirmed their commitment to the reconciliation process that had begun in November 1996. In 1997, the KDP was also involved in action against the Turkish Kurds. The latter were using bases in northern Iraq for cross-border raids into southeast Turkey and this had led to Turkish military incursions into northern Iraq.

In January 1998, the PUK proposed peace and reconciliation but the KDP under Barzani refused to respond, though a cease-fire was negotiated. Although fragile, the cease-fire enabled the leadership of the two parties to agree to an exchange of prisoners and to establish a joint committee to promote cooperation in public health, education, and energy. However, the real issues remain unresolved. The KDP under Barzani remains committed to a strengthening of the Kurdish Federal State, the National Assembly, and the coalition with other parties to secure the unity of the Kurdish people.

BARZANI, MUSTAFA (1904-1979). Mustafa Barzani was born in the small village of Barzan in Iraqi Kurdistan. He took part in a Kurdish revolt led by his brother in the 1930s and was exiled to southern Iraq (q.v.) and then to the city of Sulaymaniya. It was here that Barzani met the intellectuals who founded the first nationalist organizations for the Iraqi Kurds (q.v.) and gave him his first political lectures. He was forced to flee from Sulaymaniya in 1943, and joined a new revolt in 1945 before having to take refuge in Iranian Kurdistan. Barzani was welcomed by Qazi Mohammed, president of the Kurdish Republic of Mahabad, and from then on became known as General Barzani. After the collapse of the Kurdish Republic in 1946, Barzani sought asylum in the Soviet Union in June 1947 with several hundred partisans, remaining there until 1958.

The July 1958 revolution in Iraq allowed Barzani to make a triumphal return as the revolutionary leader who had fought against the British and then against the Iraqi and Iranian monarchies. However, good relations with the new leader of Iraq, Abd al-Karim Qasim (q.v.), did not last, and in March 1961 Barzani fled from Baghdad to his village. The new regime could not solve the Kurdish problem and in September 1961 the area around Barzan was attacked, beginning a 14-year war, punctuated by cease-fires, with Barzani waging war against the four regimes in Baghdad during this period.

Barzani consolidated power over the Kurdish Democratic Party (KDP) and the area of Kurdistan which stretched from Syria to Iran (qq.v.), and in 1970 he forced Saddam Hussein (q.v.), then Iraqi vice president, to agree to autonomy for the Kurds in Iraq. Barzani also reached an agreement with the Shah of Iran, who provided military and logistical aid. In March 1974, fighting erupted again following failure of negotiations over the future of Kirkuk, capital of the oil-rich province. However, Kurdish resistance collapsed when Iran withdrew support following the 1975 Algiers Accord with Iraq. Barzani went into exile in Iran before dying of cancer in the United States on 2 March 1979.

BIN LADEN, USAMA (1953-). Usama Bin Laden is one of the most internationally notorious fundamentalists and extremely wealthy as a result of a large construction business, the Bin Laden Group, established by his father. Bin Laden fought in Afghanistan (q.v.), recruited thousands of Arabs to the cause, and funded and organized training camps to fight the Soviets. He returned to Saudi Arabia (q.v.) in 1989, but his anti-government activities led to his being exiled to Sudan in 1991 and he was then stripped of his Saudi citizenship. The 1991 Gulf War (q.v.) led to Bin Laden becoming extremely critical of U.S. presence in the region and viewing the troops as an occupying army of infidels. The Sudanese government expelled him in 1996 following U.S. pressure and he returned to Afghanistan, from where he issued a *fatwa* (q.v.) declaring war against the U.S. presence in the Gulf. Bin Laden's wealth is mainly used to fund fundamentalist groups and he has been implicated in attempts to assassinate President Hosni Mubarak (q.v.), the bombing of the World Trade Center in New York in 1993, bombing of a center for training National Guards in Riyadh, Saudi Arabia, and the bombing of U.S. embassies in Kenya and Tanzania in 1998. Bin Laden had been linked to terrorist organizations and incidents in Algeria (q.v.), Egypt, Ethiopia, the Philippines, London, Saudi Arabia, and Yemen (q.v.).

BLACK SEPTEMBER. The organization was founded as a direct result of the defeat of the Palestinians in the 1970/71 civil wars in Jordan (q.v.) and led by Salah Khalaf, also known as Abu I'yed, who was intelligence chief of the al-Fath (q.v.) organization. The first targets of the group were Jordanians, including Prime Minister Wasfi al-Tal, who was assassinated in November 1971. The group was also responsible for the attack on Israeli athletes at the September 1972 Munich Olympic Games in which 11 hostages and five of the commandos were killed. Black September was involved in a clandestine war with Israel (q.v.) since fought throughout the Middle East and Europe.

BORDER DISPUTES. The Middle East and Islamic North Africa have been beset by conflicts and problems over boundaries, many of which predate the evolution of the modern states, though statehood has exacerbated the various disputes. In terms of the Arabian Gulf, there have been disputes between Qatar and Abu Dhabi (q.v.), Abu Dhabi and Dubai, Qatar and Bahrain (q.v.), Dubai and Sharjah, and Oman (q.v.) and the United Arab Emirates (q.v.) over the Musandam Peninsula border. However, many of these disputes were resolved by the founding of the federation of the United Arab Emirates in 1971. Other disputes have taken place between Iraq, Kuwait, and Saudi Arabia (qq.v.), which were resolved in 1922 by the creation of shared neutral zones between the three states. Another tripartite dispute was that between Abu Dhabi, Oman, and Saudi Arabia over the Buraimi Oasis, fueled by the presence of water and of oil. The Buraimi dispute was the subject of failed arbitration and almost resulted in conflict with Great Britain, which acted on behalf of Abu Dhabi, before it was resolved in 1960.

In North Africa, there were problems between Algeria (q.v.) and Morocco over their common frontier, a long-standing dispute that came to a head in 1963 with open conflict at Hassi-Baida and Tinjoub. This was resolved as a result of the mediation efforts of the Organization of African Unity (OAU) (q.v.) *See Also* **Algerian-Moroccan Border Dispute; Irredentism**

BOUTROS-GHALI, BOUTROS (1922-). Boutros-Ghali was born into a prominent Coptic family that played an active part in nationalist politics in Cairo, Egypt (q.v.) He received his higher education at Cairo University before transferring to Paris University, where he obtained diplomas in political science and economics before being awarded his doctorate in international law in 1949. Boutros-Ghali then taught international law and international affairs at Cairo University. In 1960, he founded and edited *Al-Ahram Iqtisadi* (Economic Al-Ahram), a position which he occupied until 1975, and he also wrote extensively on international politics.

Boutros-Ghali's career took a different direction in 1977 when President Anwar Sadat (q.v.) made him Minister of State for Foreign Affairs and, in this capacity, he was involved in the negotiations that led to the Camp David Accords (q.v.) between Egypt and Israel (q.v.) in 1978. Boutros-Ghali retained office under President Hosni Mubarak (q.v.) and was elected to parliament as a member of the ruling National Democratic Party, becoming Deputy Minister for Foreign Affairs in 1991. In 1992, he became United Nations (q.v.) Secretary-General for five years, standing down in 1997 when his term of office expired and it became clear that the United States would oppose any attempt at re-election.

C

CAIRO SUMMIT CONFERENCE. A conference was held at Cairo, Egypt (q.v.), between 25-26 October 1976 to resolve questions of funding for the Arab Deterrent Force (q.v.) which was to be deployed in Lebanon (q.v.) as replacement for the Symbolic Arab Security Force (SASF) (q.v.) The conference resolved to set up a special fund into which each member of the Arab League (q.v.) would pay an unspecified sum to be administered by the President of Lebanon in consultation with the Secretary-General of the Arab League and states contributing at least 10 percent of the total. Initially, Saudi Arabia and Kuwait (qq.v.) agreed to contribute 20 percent each, the United Arab Emirates (q.v.) 15 percent, and Qatar 10 percent but as no other members of the League were prepared to provide funds Saudi Arabia and Kuwait had to fund the balance. The summit also endorsed all of the resolutions and statements issued by the Riyadh Summit Conference (q.v.) of 18 October 1976.

CAMP DAVID ACCORDS (1978). The Camp David Accords were negotiated at the presidential retreat of Camp David, Maryland, in September 1978, between Egyptian President Anwar Sadat (q.v.) and Israeli Premier Menachem Begin, with mediation by President Jimmy Carter. The accords were signed in Washington on 18 September 1978 and set out the framework for a peace treaty between Egypt and Israel (qq.v.) and a resolution of the Palestinian problem.

In respect of Egypt and Israel the accords provided for:

- Egypt would recover the Sinai in exchange for the signing of a peace treaty with Israel and normalization of relations
- security zones would be established in the Sinai and limits on forces set
- following the signing of a peace treaty a phased pullout of Israeli troops would take place within three to six months of the treaty and the last withdrawal two to three years later

In respect of the solution to the Palestinian problem, the following were the main agreements:

- West Bank and Gaza would gain autonomy and there would be an end to Israeli military rule over a five-year period
- Israel would maintain military camps on the West Bank
- Jordan (q.v.) would be invited to join negotiations and to have a security role, if it wished
- during the five-year transitional period, there would be talks on the final status of the West Bank and Gaza between Egypt, Israel, Jordan (if it wished), and elected representatives of Palestinians from these areas
- during negotiations, there would be a freeze on new Israeli settlements in the West Bank and Gaza Strip

The peace treaty between Egypt and Israel was signed on 26 March 1979 in Washington and ratified by the parliaments of both countries. Israel withdrew from two-thirds of the Sinai Peninsula on 23 January 1980 giving Egypt control of the area from El Arish on the Mediterranean coast to Ras Muhammad on the Red Sea. Ambassadors were exchanged on 26 February 1980 and the final Israeli withdrawal took place on 26 April 1982. The cost of the accords to the United States in terms of military and economic aid to Egypt and Israel was $10 billion, of which Israel was to receive two-thirds.

The Camp David Accords and the subsequent peace treaty split the Arab world and resulted in Egypt being ostracized by its neighbors. Egypt's membership in the Arab League (q.v.) and its associated agencies was suspended, and a number of years went by before it was accepted back into the family of Arab states. *See also* **Palestine**

CENTER FOR ENVIRONMENT AND DEVELOPMENT FOR THE ARAB REGION AND EUROPE (CEDARE). The Center for Environment and Development for the Arab Region and Europe was established as a result of an initiative by Egypt, the Arab Fund for Economic and Social Development (AFESD) (qq.v), and the United Nations Development Program (q.v.). CEDARE is based in Cairo and began operations in 1993. The objective of CEDARE is to become a center of excellence for the Arab region and Mediterranean Europe in order to assist with the pursuance of global environmental trends and in support of national environmental programs.

CEDARE is governed by a Board of Trustees that oversees the budget and the program, and evaluates the performance of the organization. An Executive Committee is drawn from the Board of Trustees consisting of the Chairman and Vice-Chairman, the Executive Director and three other trustees. Day-to-day operations are controlled by the Executive Director who manages CEDARE's activities and finances and appoints the leaders of the various programs. The Executive Director is advised by a Technical Advisory Committee which is comprised of specialists who advise on programs, budget needs of programs, and potential sources of finance for each program.

CENTER FOR RESEARCH IN ISLAMIC ECONOMICS. The center is based at King Abdulaziz University, Jeddah, Saudi Arabia (q.v.), and was founded in 1977 on the recommendation of the First Islamic Conference of Islamic Economics held in 1976. The objectives of the center are to conduct, coordinate, and support international research into Islamic economics.

CENTER FOR SOCIAL SCIENCE RESEARCH AND DOCUMENTATION FOR THE ARAB REGION. The center was formed in 1978 and is based in Cairo, Egypt (q.v.). Its prime objective is to foster cooperation between regional research bodies, with membership drawn from Egypt, Iraq, Kuwait, Saudi Arabia (qq.v.), and Tunisia. It publishes *Arab Comnet* (three times a year) and a *Newsletter* (three times a year).

CENTRAL TREATY ORGANIZATION (CENTO). The Central Treaty Organization was the successor to the Baghdad Pact (q.v.) following

Iraq's (q.v.) withdrawal after the 1958 revolution. The members of CENTO included Iran, Turkey (qq.v.), Pakistan, and Great Britain, with the United States as an associate member. The organization was conceived as a defense organization with the northern tier of Middle East countries that bordered the Soviet Union due to their strategic significance to the Cold War. Although not a full member the United States was an active supporter of the organization and obtained military bases and intelligence outposts in each of the northern-tier member states. However, by the end of the 1960s the organization was more important as an economic bloc and it became defunct after the 1979 Iranian Revolution.

CONFEDERATION OF ARAB REPUBLICS. The confederation was a union of Egypt, Libya, and Syria (qq.v.), which was planned but never implemented. In April of 1971, the three states signed an agreement establishing the Confederation of Arab Republics, which was to form the basis of a federal union of the three countries. In August 1971, a constitution was signed and approved by referendum in the three states. The capital of the new federation was to be Cairo and the Egyptian President Anwar Sadat (q.v.) was selected as the first President. The plan was destined never to be implemented. In 1973, a feud between Sadat and the Libyan leader Muammar al-Qaddafi (q.v.) led to the suspension of the project.

COOPERATION COUNCIL FOR THE ARAB STATES OF THE GULF. *See* **GULF COOPERATION COUNCIL**

COUNCIL OF ARAB ECONOMIC UNITY (CAEU). The Council consists of representatives from member states who meet twice a year and usually comprises Ministers of Economy, Finance, and Trade. Meetings are chaired on a rotating basis for one year. Members of the CAEU are Egypt, Iraq, Jordan, Kuwait, Libya (qq.v.), Mauritania, Palestine (q.v.), Somalia, Sudan, Syria, United Arab Emirates, and Yemen (qq.v). The operational activities of the council are carried out by the general Secretariat, which is entrusted with implementing the council's policies, and with proposing working projects. The Secretariat encourages participation by Arab states in the Arab Economic Unity Agreement and publishes studies on Arab economic problems and the implications of world economic trends on Arab economies.

The Secretariat coordinates the development plans of the individual member states, and seeks to formulate new joint Arab companies and federations, programs for coordination in agriculture, industry, and transport, and unified methods of statistical analysis and data collection. The CAEU has standing committees covering Arab common market development; permanent delegates; budget; customs and trade; planning and coordination; and statistics. Several ad hoc committees meet to consider tariffs, trade promotion, and trade legislation.

A number of joint ventures have been established in the agricultural and industrial sectors and, in order to further cooperation, existing industries are coordinated through the establishment of Arab Specialized Unions, which deal with problems of production and marketing and assist companies to trade as a group in international markets. The CAEU has also negotiated a number of multilateral agreements among members covering: basic levels of social insurance; reciprocity in social insurance systems; labor mobility; organization on transit trade; avoidance of double taxation and elimination of tax evasion; cooperation in the collection of taxes; capital investment and mobility; and settlement of investment disputes between host Arab countries and citizens of other countries.

Among the Joint Venture Companies are: Arab Company for Drug Industries and Medical Appliances, Amman, Jordan; Arab Company for Industrial Investment, Alwiyah, Baghdad, Iraq; Arab Company for Livestock Development, Damascus, Syria; and Arab Mining Company, Amman, Jordan.

The Specialized Arab Unions and Federations include: Arab Cooperative Federation, Baghdad, Iraq; Arab Federation of Chemical Fertilizers Producers, Kuwait City, Kuwait; Arab Federation of Engineering Industries, Baghdad, Iraq; Arab Federation of Leather Industries, Damascus, Syria; Arab Federation of Paper Industries, Baghdad, Iraq; Arab Federation of Shipping, Baghdad, Iraq; Arab Federation of Textile Industries, Damascus, Syria; Arab Federation of Travel Agents, Amman, Jordan; Arab Seaports Federation, Basra, Iraq; Arab Sugar Federation, Khartoum, Sudan; Arab Union for Cement and Building Materials, Damascus, Syria; Arab Union of Fish Producers, Baghdad, Iraq; Arab Union of Food Industries, Baghdad, Iraq; Arab Union of Land Transport, Amman, Jordan; Arab Union of the Manufacturers of Pharmaceuticals and Medical Appliances, Amman, Jordan; Arab Union of Railways, Aleppo, Syria; General Arab Insurance Federation, Cairo, Egypt.

The CAEU publishes: *Annual Bulletin for Arab Countries' Foreign Trade Statistics; Annual Bulletin for Official Exchange Rates of Arab Currencies; Arab Economic Unity Bulletin* (twice a year), *Demo-*

graphic Yearbook for Arab Countries; Economic Report of the General Secretary (twice a year); *Guide to Statistics Prepared by Secretariat; Statistical Yearbook for Arab Countries; Yearbook for Intra-Arab Trade Statistics; Yearbook of National Accounts for Arab Countries.* *See also* **Arab Common Market**

COUNCIL OF ARAB MINISTERS OF HEALTH. The Council of Arab Ministers of Health was formed in 1975 and is based in Tunis. Its main activity is the holding of meetings of regional Health Ministers to discuss matters of mutual interest.

COUNCIL ON ISLAMIC EDUCATION (CIE). The council was founded in 1990 in the United States with its headquarters at Fountain Valley, California. The CIE is a nonprofit resource organization comprised of scholars from a variety of academic disciplines. The objectives of the CIE are to contribute to the American K-12 education system, providing resources and research-based tools to textbook publishers, state education officials and policymakers, curriculum developers, and teachers.

Services provided by the CIE include in-service workshops, conferences, the Muslim Speakers Bureau, and a host program for international visitors. However, the main activity of the CIE is its publication of teaching units and other texts covering, among other topics, world history using Islam (q.v.) and Islamic history as case studies, the role of Muslim women in history, the Crusades, and perceptions of the Muslim world by European travellers. The CIE also organizes conferences designed to explore specific issues and to share expertise on a variety of topics, with the most recent being the 1998 Conference on World History Standards.

D

DEVELOPING EIGHT. This organization is based in Istanbul, Turkey (q.v.), and was founded in June 1997 at a meeting of the heads of state of Bangladesh, Egypt (q.v.), Indonesia, Iran (q.v.), Malaysia, Nigeria, Pakistan, and Turkey. Its objectives are to foster economic cooperation between member states in the world economy. Among the projects being examined by the Developing Eight are trade and industry, agriculture, human resources, telecommunications, rural development, privatization, banking, and Islamic insurance. A second summit meeting of the group was held in Dhaka, Bangladesh, in December 1997.

DEVELOPMENT AGENCIES. *See* ABU DHABI FUND FOR ARAB ECONOMIC DEVELOPMENT; AFRICAN DEVELOPMENT FUND; AFRO-ASIAN ORGANIZATION FOR ECONOMIC CO-OPERATION; ARAB AUTHORITY FOR AGRICULTURAL IN-VESTMENT AND DEVELOPMENT; ARAB FUND FOR ECO-NOMIC AND SOCIAL DEVELOPMENT; ARAB FUND FOR TECHNICAL ASSISTANCE TO AFRICAN COUNTRIES; ARAB GULF PROGRAM FOR THE UNITED NATIONS DEVELOP-MENT ORGANIZATIONS; ARAB INDUSTRIAL DEVELOP-MENT AND MINING ORGANIZATION; ARAB ORGANIZA-TION FOR AGRICULTURAL DEVELOPMENT; ARAB ORGANIZATION FOR INDUSTRIALIZATION; ARAB PLAN-NING INSTITUTE; ECONOMIC COOPERATION ORGANIZA-TION; ECONOMIC RESEARCH FORUM FOR THE ARAB COUNTRIES, IRAN, AND TURKEY; ISLAMIC CENTER FOR THE DEVELOPMENT OF TRADE; KUWAIT FUND FOR ARAB ECONOMIC DEVELOPMENT; OPEC FUND FOR IN-TERNATIONAL DEVELOPMENT; SAUDI FUND FOR DE-VELOPMENT; UNITED NATIONS ECONOMIC AND SOCIAL COMMISSION FOR WESTERN ASIA; UNITED STATES AGENCY FOR INTERNATIONAL DEVELOPMENT: WEST BANK AND GAZA MISSION

E

ECONOMIC COOPERATION ORGANIZATION (ECO). The organization was founded in 1985 as the successor to Regional Coop-eration for Development (founded 1964) which was originally a tripar-tite agreement between Iran (q.v.), Pakistan, and Turkey (q.v.). ECO now has a membership of Afghanistan (q.v.), Azerbaijan, Iran, Ka-zakhstan, Kyrgystan, Pakistan, Tajikstan, Turkey, Turkmenistan, and Uzbekistan. The Turkish Republic of Cyprus has been granted guest status and ECO has been granted observer status at the United Nations and the Organization of the Islamic Conference (qq.v.). The aim of ECO is to promote regional economic cooperation between the member states. Among the areas of cooperation are transport, telecommunica-tions, trade and investment, energy, minerals and environmental issues, industry, and agriculture.

ECO held summit meetings in Istanbul, Turkey, and Islamabad, Pakistan, where it established a series of action plans to determine long-term priorities. A joint Chamber of Commerce and Industry was established in 1980 and the Islamabad summit of 1995 approved the establishment of a Trade and Development Bank in Istanbul, a joint shipping company and airline in Iran, and a reinsurance company in Pakistan. The same meeting also approved the establishment of an ECO Cultural Institute in Iran and a Science Foundation in Pakistan and called for a strengthening of cooperation in the areas of transport and communications, trade and investment, energy and ecology, and protection of the environment.

An extraordinary meeting of ECO was held in Izmir, Turkey, in September 1996 at which a revised Treaty of Izmir was signed amending the original founding charter. A further extraordinary meeting was held in Ashgabat, Turkmenistan, in May 1997 at which the importance of the development of the transport and communications infrastructure and the objective of transnational pipelines in the ECO region was stressed. The fifth summit meeting held in May 1998 at Almaty, Kazakhstan, concluded a Transit Transport Framework Agreement and a memorandum of understanding to counter cross-border trafficking of illegal goods. The meeting also agreed to establish an ECO Educational Institute in Ankara, Turkey.

ECONOMIC RESEARCH FORUM FOR THE ARAB COUNTRIES, IRAN AND TURKEY. The forum was formed in 1993 and is based in Cairo, Egypt (q.v.), with the objectives of conducting in-depth economic research, compiling an economic database for the region, and carrying out a training program.

EGYPT. Egypt has been continuously inhabited for more than 8,000 years and Islam (q.v.) spread to Egypt in the seventh century so that most of the population are Muslim although there is a significant Coptic Christian minority, forming about 10 percent of the population of some 51 million. Following the defeat of the last of the Pharaohs by Alexander the Great, Egypt was ruled by foreigners for centuries. The country ended the nineteenth century under British control that began in 1882. In 1914, it was declared a British protectorate. In 1922, Egypt was recognized by Great Britain as a sovereign state under King Ahmad Fuad, who ruled until 1936, but the country remained under British military occupation.

During this period, an anti-imperialist movement began to grow, which was led by the Wafd party and culminated in the Anglo-Egyptian Treaty of 1936 granting Egypt a limited degree of independence under

King Farouk. However, Farouk's reign was largely ineffectual and unable to deal with the country's problems, with the poor performance of Egyptian troops in the 1948-1949 Palestine War being a further blow to the prestige of the regime. The situation encouraged nationalist army officers to plan a coup that was carried out in 1952 after fears that they were to be arrested by the King.

The coup was successful and King Farouk was overthrown with power passing to a new Revolutionary Command Council (RCC) under General Muhammad Nejuib, though the real inspiration behind the movement had been General Gamal Abdul Nasser (q.v.). A politician, Ali Mahir, agreed to act as Prime Minister but there was soon disagreement about the extent of the army's role in the new government. The situation was complicated by the fact that the officers had acted quickly and had no coherent set of policies to follow except for the elimination of corruption in the army and among the political elite, and to force the evacuation of the British military. Only one clear policy was evident and that was in the area of land reform, with a law being passed in September 1952 limiting the size of an individual landholding. The size was progressively reduced throughout the decade. The move was designed to better the lot of the peasants at the expense of the larger landowners, to increase agricultural production, and to release investment capital for industry.

Initially the RCC did not target foreign interests in Egypt as it was keen to encourage private investment, but the power of the landowners and merchants was seen as a hindrance to industrial development. In 1954, Nasser ousted General Nejuib and took control of the RCC, but opposition came from the Islamic fundamentalists (q.v.) who attempted to assassinate him on 26 October 1954. Nasser became more involved in international affairs, opposing the formation of the Baghdad Pact (q.v.) and becoming co-founder of the Non-Aligned Movement in April 1955 with President Nehru of India. In September 1955, Nasser signed an arms agreement with Czechoslovakia having failed to agree to terms with Britain, France, and the United States. Relations deteriorated further in July 1956 when the U.S. withdrew financial support and guarantees for the building of the Aswan Dam. Nasser was now president of Egypt and he retaliated by nationalizing the Suez Canal on 26 July 1956.

Britain and France responded by deciding to use force to recover control over the canal and they allied with Israel (q.v.) which was anxious to respond to the attacks mounted by Palestinian guerrillas from Egyptian territory. Israel invaded the Sinai on 29 October 1956 and reached the Suez Canal within two days followed by the landing of British and French troops ostensibly to separate the opposing forces. The action was condemned internationally and, under pressure from Washington, Britain and France agreed to a United Nations (q.v.) cease-fire on 6 November, followed by a withdrawal of troops. Egypt agreed to compensate the shareholders of the Suez Canal Company and the waterway was declared open to all ships, except those of Israel.

Although defeated militarily, Nasser had won a political victory in the eyes of the populace, and he was encouraged to pursue his dream of being the unifier of the Arab world. In 1958, Nasser set up the United Arab Republic with Syria (qq.v.), but the concept collapsed when Syria withdrew in 1961. Nasser also intervened in the civil war in North Yemen (q.v.) in 1962 in support of the army officers who were fighting against the Saudi-backed (q.v.) religious ruling dynasty. Despite remaining in Yemen until the end of the decade, the Egyptian action was totally unsuccessful.

Domestically Nasser consolidated his political power in the late 1950s and the early 1960s, pursuing a policy of nationalization of industries and greater state control over the economy. This policy of Arab socialism (q.v.) led to the creation of the Arab Socialist Union, which was an attempt to form one mass political party giving the regime legitimization, and to provide a forum for debate. The state began to play a greater role in the industrial sector, though the private sector was still important in manufacturing and totally dominant in domestic trade and the vital tourist industry. Egypt also received significant investment from the Soviet Union but relations between the two regimes were never smooth and harmonious.

Relations with Israel also continued to deteriorate, largely because of an upsurge in Palestinian guerrilla activity, and in May 1967 Nasser ordered the UN peacekeeping force out of the Sinai and closed the Tiran Straits to Israeli shipping. In retaliation on 5 June, Israel launched attacks on Egyptian and Syrian airforce bases, completely destroying their air capabilities. This was followed by the Israeli army, which swept through the Sinai and also occupied the Jordanian West Bank and the Golan Heights of Syria. The humiliating defeat of Egyptian forces undermined Nasser's position. On 9 June, he resigned, but agreed to return following public demonstrations in his support. Nasser purged the armed forces of officers accused of negligence or incompetence and accepted Russian aid to rebuild his forces. Over the period March 1969-August 1970 hostilities continued along the Suez Canal in a war of attrition.

Nasser died of a heart attack on 28 September 1970 and was succeeded by Anwar Sadat (q.v.), a fellow Free Officer, whom Nasser had made a vice president in December 1969. Sadat began to consolidate his position by arresting a number of members of the Arab Socialist Union and in May 1971 he signed a friendship treaty with the Soviet Union. However, this was short-lived and in July 1972 Sadat ordered all 15,000 Soviet military experts to leave the country.

Sadat had also promised the Egyptian people that Egypt would regain the Sinai, and on 6 October 1973, in partnership with Syria, attacks were launched on Israel through the Sinai and the Golan Heights. Initially, the Arab forces were successful but Israel counterattacked, and by 20 October the Egyptian Third Army had been surrounded. A UN-backed cease-fire was put in place on 22 October. Although not a military success the initial action had provided a morale boost for the Arab world and enhanced Sadat's role as a statesman in the region. After the war, Egypt attempted to regain the Sinai by negotiation and this meant a shift in alignment toward Washington due to American influence with Israel. With U.S. mediation Sadat reached two disengagement agreements with Israel in January 1974 and September 1975, with the latter seeing the return of the Sinai oilfields to Egypt. The U.S. also began to provide Egypt with economic aid which, by the middle of the 1980s, was running at $2.3 billion a year.

In 1974 Egypt also changed its economic policy by opening up the market to foreign investment, particularly through joint venture companies with the Egyptian partner holding at least 51 percent of the company. However, the change brought little in terms of productive investment, as the concentration was on the oil industry and banking, with the latter placing an emphasis on import finance. The economy continued to deteriorate despite external aid, and the foreign debt and government finance deficits increased. In January 1977, Sadat was forced to bring in austerity measures with a draft budget, which drastically cut food subsidies and increased prices on unsubsidized goods. The consequence was a series of demonstrations and riots among the urban poor who saw this as an attack on their already low standard of living.

The domestic economic crisis was soon overshadowed by Sadat's relations with Israel, as in 1978 he signed the Camp David Accords (q.v.), which covered the return of Sinai to Egypt and the problems of the West Bank. The agreements were formalized in a peace treaty signed in Washington on 26 March 1979. The Camp David Accords caused consternation throughout the Arab world and were immediately denounced by the Arab League (q.v.). Arab states cut diplomatic ties with Egypt, all Arab aid was stopped, and the Arab League headquarters was removed to Tunis.

Although Sadat had promised a more democratic system of government, the process of liberalization had only a modest impact. Political parties were allowed to operate, within constraints, and in July 1978 the Arab Socialist Union was abolished to be replaced by the National Democratic Party (NDP). The NDP regularly won elections under Sadat's leadership but opposition was gathering within Egypt, though outside of the normal political structures, and the Muslim Brotherhood and the Ikhwan (qq.v.) reemerged as potent forces.

The crisis deepened in 1981 with clashes in Cairo between Muslims and Copts. Sadat blamed these on agitators and he arrested some 1,500 protestors, including prominent journalists, writers and intellectuals. The crisis was heightened by the lack of progress on the Palestinian question and the lack of cooperation from the new administration in Washington under President Ronald Reagan. On 6 October 1981, Sadat was assassinated by a group of soldiers at a military parade to mark the anniversary of the 1973 war. The soldiers, led by Khalid al-Islambuli, belonged to the Jihad group who were Islamic activists who favored violence to achieve their objectives.

The transition of power was relatively smooth with the presidency passing to Hosni Mubarak (q.v.) who had been appointed vice president in 1975. In terms of foreign policy, Mubarak tried to pursue a more balanced policy by reestablishing diplomatic relations with the Soviet Union in 1984 and in improving relations with the Arab world, a process begun by the restoration of relations with Jordan (q.v.) in 1984. He also attempted to reduce corruption among the elite who had enriched themselves through Sadat's encouragement of private enterprise. However, the economy continued to deteriorate and Egypt had problems servicing its external debt, particularly when oil prices collapsed in 1986. Although Egypt was readmitted to the Arab League in 1989, opposition within Egypt began to increase, largely voiced by Islamic activists, who ranged from traditionalists calling for the application of *Sharia* (q.v.) law to those who rejected modernization and aimed at the overthrow of the state.

Mubarak declared an intention to make Egyptian politics more democratic and he authorized all political parties, with the exception of the Muslim Brotherhood and the communists, to take part in the May 1984 general election. The election only attracted a 20 percent turnout with the NDP taking 85 percent of the seats and the Wafd gaining 57 seats. However, Mubarak's government of technocrats was seen as indecisive and incapable of dealing with Egypt's grave financial problems. Mubarak was reelected to a second presidential term in October 1993 but opposition from militant Islamic groups continued to grow. The most extreme militant act to date has been the massacre of 60 foreign tourists at Luxor in November 1997 by Jama'a Islamiyya.

Egypt had been under a state of emergency with Islamic groups being subject to oppression although in April 1999 the authorities released some 1,000 suspected members of Muslim groups. However, the Jihad group has refused to renounce violence against the authorities and nine of its leaders were sentenced to death in absentia by a military court. It is evident that this struggle is far from over.

Egypt has historically been an agricultural country and remains the same today, but the increase in production is not sufficient to cope with the rise in population, expected to be 70 million at the millennium. A major industrialization program was put into effect in the 1960s, largely dependent upon aid and credits from the Soviet Union but the massive increase in capital expenditure had an adverse effect upon the balance of payments. The government also introduced a social welfare system and guaranteed employment to university graduates, resulting in a grossly inflated bureaucracy.

The Egyptian economy has suffered the reduction in oil prices and had to apply for funding from the International Monetary Fund (q.v.) but the conditions that had to be met with regard to subsidy reductions again caused protests and riots. The economy was also heavily reliant upon the remittances from foreign workers, which had become the largest single source of foreign exchange, and these were adversely affected by the Iraqi invasion of Kuwait (qq.v.) in 1990 and the return of workers to Egypt. Tourism and the Suez Canal revenues are also crucial to the regime, although oil still remains important. Egypt's population growth of 2.7 per cent will continue to present problems particularly in the provision of housing, social welfare, and employment, which have to be reconciled with the major financial problems faced by the regime. *See also* **Arab Socialism**

F

FATAT, AL-. The organization al-Fatat was founded in 1911 by a small group of Arabs from Syria, Lebanon, and Palestine (qq.v.) while studying in Paris. The original aim of the society was the administrative independence of the Arab lands from Ottoman rule. It was not an independence movement, as its members believed that both Arab and Turkish nationalities should remain united within the Ottoman Empire (q.v.), with equal rights and obligations but with each community controlling its own educational institutions. In 1913, al-Fatat moved from Paris to offices in Beirut and also established a branch in Damascus.

Following the outbreak of World War I and the execution by Turkey of Arab nationalists in 1915 and 1916, the society amended its political program to one of complete independence and unity of Arab lands. In 1915, al-Fatat enlisted the support of Emir Faisal, which led them into direct contact with his father Sherif Hussein (q.v.) of the Hedjaz and through him the British and the drawing up of the Damascus protocol. This protocol expressed the readiness of the Arab nationalists to join the British war effort, provided that Britain pledged to support complete Arab independence and unity. After the war, al-Fatat shifted its attention to the principle of pan-Syrian unity and reached the height of its political influence during Faisal's short-lived government in Damascus from 1918 to 1920. However, Faisal's dealings with the Zionists and the French created splits within the organization as did the different priorities of the Iraqi, Palestinian, and Syrian elements of the organization. After the collapse of Faisal's government in 1920, al-Fatat ceased to be a structured political organization, although many of its members continued to be active in the politics of Arab nationalism.

FATH, AL-. The Palestinian movement led by Yasser Arafat (q.v.), and also known as *Fatah*, has been identified with the leadership of the Palestine Liberation Organization (PLO) (q.v.) but predates that organization. The movement was founded by a group of Palestinian exiles living in the Gulf, including Arafat, and came into existence as an organization in 1962. The movement is led by a central committee and also has a military wing operating under the name *al-Asifa*, which began military activities against Israel (q.v.) at the end of 1964 and during 1965, though its actions had little impact. In 1964, the Arab League (q.v.), backed by Egypt (q.v.), created the PLO under the leadership of Ahmad Shuqayri. However, al-Fath and other guerrilla groups continued their training in camps in Jordan and Syria (qq.v.) and began to undermine Shuqayri's leadership of the PLO, such that he resigned in 1968.

As a result of the fourth and fifth Palestine National Council congresses in 1968 and 1969, the guerrilla groups won larger roles in the PLO and also succeeded in getting the Palestinian National Charter amended to support armed struggle. The 1969 congress also saw the election of Arafat to the chair of the Executive Committee of the PLO.

He became Commander-in-Chief in 1970, and with other leading al-Fath figures obtaining other key posts. As a consequence al-Fath has become closely intertwined with the PLO, and has developed as the main pro-negotiation faction as other rejectionist groups have withdrawn from the PLO.

During the *intifada* (q.v.) in Gaza and the West Bank in 1967, al-Fath leaders within the territories were the leaders of the uprisings, while the central leadership, led by Arafat, were pushing the PLO toward recognition of Israel's right to exist. Despite predictions that al-Fath would lose control of the PLO or that Arafat would be replaced, the organization remains in control and has backed the current peace process. As a consequence Hamas (q.v.) has become the main rejectionist group in Gaza and the West Bank and a severe critic of the Palestinian National Authority.

FATWA (Legal Opinion). This was historically used to resolve legal and social problems that were not known textually or had arisen in new contexts. In modern times, it has been used by Islamic fundamentalists (q.v.) as a way of fighting the government or evaluating people's behavior. The most notable recent case was the *fatwa* issued by Ayatollah Khomeini (q.v.) putting forward the view that Salman Rushdie should be killed for his scorn of Islam (q.v.) and the Prophet.

FEDERATION OF ARAB ENGINEERS. The federation is part of the World Federation of Engineering Organizations and was founded in 1963. It works in cooperation with the Arab League (q.v.) and other regional engineering federations. It holds a pan-Arab conference every three years on engineering subjects, and annual symposia and seminars in its member states. Its membership is drawn from engineering associations in 15 Arab countries.

FEDERATION OF ARAB SCIENTIFIC RESEARCH COUNCILS. The federation was formed in 1976 and comprises a membership of national science bodies in 15 countries. The objectives of the federation are to encourage cooperation in scientific research, to promote joint regional research projects, and to encourage the establishment of new institutions. It also holds conferences, seminars, and workshops and publishes the *Journal of Arab Scientific Research, Federation News,* and reports from programs.

FEDERATION OF ISLAMIC ORGANIZATIONS IN EUROPE

(FIOE). The federation was founded in 1989 as an independent Islamic organization to cater to the religious, social, and cultural interests of Muslims in Europe. The headquarters of the FIOE are in Leicester, England, and its membership is drawn from 19 European countries. The FIOE is run by an Executive Office which is divided into three departments: President's Office, General Secretariat, and Da'wah to Islam, the latter based in France.

The objectives of the FIOE are to:

- promote dissemination of the Islamic culture among Muslims in Europe
- assist the Muslims of Europe in performing their religious duties, preserving their cultural identity, and providing support for their social and religious needs
- reach out to the new generations of Muslims in Europe to enhance their sense of belonging to their religion and community
- coordinate and cooperate with all existing organizations in areas of mutual interest
- promote cultural dialogue between Muslims and groups belonging to other faiths in order to further the cause of a peaceful co-existence in European societies

The Da'wah (missionary) to Islam department is based at the Institut Européen des Sciences Humaines at St. Léger-de-Fougeret, France.

FIQH. *Fiqh* is Islamic jurisprudence and includes all aspects of religious, social, and political life. It covers ritual and religious observances, the law of inheritance, property and contracts, and criminal law. In terms of the Islamic state, *fiqh* also covers constitutional law, laws relating to the administration of the state, and the conduct of war. *See also* **Sharia**

G

GENERAL UNION OF CHAMBERS OF COMMERCE, INDUSTRY, AND AGRICULTURE FOR ARAB COUNTRIES. The union was formed in 1951 to foster Arab economic collaboration and productive capacity in the Arab world. It also facilitates the exchange of technical information between Arab states. Its membership is drawn from Chambers of Commerce, Industry, and Agriculture in 22 countries. It publishes *Arab Economic Report* (Arabic and English), an annual report, economic papers, and proceedings of conferences and seminars.

GLOBAL RELIEF FOUNDATION (GRF). The foundation is an organization based in Bridgeview, Illinois, with the objective of providing relief to the Muslim world through a range of activities. It relies on donations from individuals and contributions from *zakat*, or almsgiving, which is one of the Islamic obligations. Among the activities of the GRF are those covered by its emergency relief program with projects in Bangladesh, Kosovo, and Iraq (q.v.), the latter providing food for 100,000 Iraqi families. In May 2000, the GRF launched a major appeal to deal with famine in Ethiopia.

Health is another concern of the GRF, which runs a medical clinic in Kosovo, a surgical hospital in Kashmir, and a charitable clinic in Lebanon (q.v.). Education is supported through the Khadija school for girls in Bangladesh and a major project for combating illiteracy in Pakistan working with 42 schools in rural areas. The GRF also supports development projects in Afghanistan (q.v.) with a poultry breeding program to provide jobs for Afghan widows based in Kabul and with refugees in Peshawar, Pakistan. A vocational center has also been established at Jelalabad, Afghanistan, which provides basic training in carpentry, welding, plumbing, masonry, and steel bar bending. These are all income-generating trades, but these skills are also required to rebuild the shattered infrastructure of Afghanistan.

The final project sponsored by the GRF is the Imam Shafi'e school in Chechnya on the outskirts of Grozny. The school was opened in December 1997 and is designed to provide sponsorship and quality Islamic and academic education to hundreds of orphans. The school has the capacity to house 700 children and operates from buildings provided by the government.

GREATER SYRIA. Greater Syria comprises the territory enclosed by the Taurus Mountains in the north, the Mediterranean Sea to the west, the Arabian Desert to the south, and the Euphrates River to the east, an area of 110,000 square kilometers. Ottoman rule over this area was established in 1516. During the period 1831-1840, during a short break in Ottoman rule, Greater Syria was governed as a single entity under the Egyptian viceroy, Ibrahim Pasha. Once direct Ottoman rule was restored, Greater Syria was divided into several provinces. However, following the defeat of the Ottoman Empire (q.v.) in World War I, Great Britain and France split Greater Syria according to the Sykes-Picot Agreement of 1916 with the northern region, which later formed the republics of Lebanon and Syria (qq.v.), going to France, and the southern region, consisting of Palestine (q.v.) and Transjordan, going to Great Britain.

The mandates (q.v.) over these territories followed the lines of the Sykes-Picot Agreement and were confirmed by the League of Nations Supreme Council in 1920. The intention of the mandate was for the mandatory powers to lead the young nations toward independence, but France toppled the government of Faisal I ibn Hussein al-Hashemi and established a colonial regime administered from Damascus. France rearranged the borders of the mandated territory by allocating part of Syria to the area of Mount Lebanon, to create Greater Lebanon, and in 1921 surrendered sections of the province of Aleppo to Turkey (q.v.), thus reducing the size of Syria. As a result, when Syria gained independence in 1946, the territory occupied an area of 185,180 square kilometers. The question of Greater Syria did not end with the independence of the various Arab states and continued to be one of the long-term aims of the Syrian regime under President Hafiz Assad (q.v.). The objectives imply a relentless drive toward a Greater Syria which would include Lebanon, the Alexandretta area, Jordan, and Israel (qq.v.). This would also realize the dreams of Pan-Arabism (q.v.) and offset the influence of Egypt and Iraq (qq.v.).

GULF AIR. Gulf Air is a regional airline based in Bahrain (q.v.), which is jointly owned and operated by four Gulf States: Bahrain, Abu Dhabi, Oman, and Qatar.

GULF COOPERATION COUNCIL (GCC). The Gulf Cooperation Council is the more generally used title for the Cooperation Council for the Arab States and the Gulf, which was established on 25 May 1981 with six member states. As its name implies, it is an organization of states which border the Arabian Gulf, namely, Bahrain, Kuwait, Oman, Qatar, Saudi Arabia, and the United Arab Emirates (qq.v.).

The prime motivator for the establishment of the GCC was Saudi Arabia, the largest state in the region, and the major political and economic force. Regional insecurity and instability were the main reasons underlying the foundation of the GCC triggered by an armed uprising in Mecca (q.v.) in 1979, coupled with a fear of the possible consequences of the Iraq-Iran War (1980-1988) (q.v.) on the conservative Sunni (q.v.) Muslim-dominated oil-rich states of the Gulf, all of which are small countries, but strategically significant to the Western world because of their substantial oil and gas reserves.

All of the member states belong to the Arab League (q.v.), and were criticized by Iraq (q.v.) for setting up a separate regional organization, but the formation of the GCC was partly a result of member states feeling that the Arab League was not promoting Gulf unity and that the various bilateral agreements were not providing effective regional cooperation and integration.

The GCC is headed by a Supreme Council, comprising the heads of member states that meets annually, but can meet in an emergency if requested by two member states. The Supreme Council determines overall policy and discusses recommendations presented for consideration from the Ministerial Council and Secretariat General. The presidency of the council is undertaken by each state in turn in alphabetical order. The next layer of control is the Ministerial Council comprising the Foreign Ministers of member states, which meets quarterly and in emergency session if requested by two or more members. The Ministers are responsible for drawing up policies, recommendations, and projects aimed at developing cooperation and coordination among member states. The day-to-day affairs of the GCC are in the hands of the Secretariat General under a secretary-general who is appointed by the Supreme Council for a three-year renewable term. The member states all contribute equally to the budget of the Secretariat.

At its inception a number of spokesmen for the Supreme Council expressed the hope that the GCC would develop in the same way as the European Community. In its constitution, the GCC is described as providing "the means for realising coordination, integration and cooperation" in all economic, social, and cultural affairs, with no mention at all of regional security. However, the Iraq-Iran War (q.v.) ensured that the question of defense cooperation was on the agenda of the November 1981 meeting of the Supreme Council.

In the field of economic cooperation the GCC has had success with a range of agreements covering investment, petroleum, moves toward the abolition of customs duties, and uniform banking regulations. The formation of a common currency was among the stated objectives, but this has proved elusive. Progress has been made in these areas and the Supreme Council has also promulgated regulations allowing for free movement of workers among member states. The Supreme Council also approved the establishment of the Gulf Investment Corporation (q.v.) at its November 1982 meeting with the objective of promoting investment in the Gulf States, particularly in the fields of energy and transport.

Inevitably, energy policies and activities of the member states were to form a significant part of the cooperative policies of the GCC. A ministerial committee was set up in February 1982 to coordinate hydrocarbon policies and prices, and agreements were reached on the safeguarding of individual members against a cessation of oil production, the creation of a stockpile of petroleum products, and cooperation in downstream activities to avoid the expense and inefficient duplication experienced in the 1970s. Unified water and electricity charges were introduced in 1986 and studies have resulted in the formation of a project to establish a regional power grid.

Progress has also been made in other areas of economic activity, particularly industry and agriculture, and regional plans for transport policies have been developed, including highways between member states. A feasibility study has been undertaken into the construction of a rail link between Muscat and Iran (q.v.) that would then link into the European network, but no implementation plans have been finalized.

Despite the GCC's original focus on economic matters, the Iraq-Iran War, the Iraqi invasion of Kuwait (q.v.) in 1990, and the Gulf War (q.v.) in 1991 have led to the GCC having to consider the defense implications in an unstable region. The GCC provided financial support to Iraq in its war against Iran and tried without success to mediate in the war. Agreement in this sector has been minimal, but in October 1984, the GCC conducted joint military exercises in the United Arab Emirates, and the Supreme Council set up a rapid deployment force, under a Saudi general, at its November 1984 meeting. The main difficulties in the military sector are the special relationship between the United States and Saudi Arabia and the granting by Oman of military facilities to the United States. These policies are contrary to the wishes of the other member states, which want to have no foreign forces on GCC soil or military links with any external power. The GCC did participate in the Gulf War against Iraq by despatching the rapid deployment force to the Saudi-Kuwait border and troops and aircraft participated in the war.

In terms of regional politics the GCC is likely to be dominated, in the immediate future, by the consequences of the Iraq-Iran War, the Iranian Revolution, the Arab-Israeli conflict, and the Gulf War. The organization has endured a long period of instability and economic adversity caused by a large drop in oil prices and reduced world demand. Despite these constraints, the economic momentum of social cooperation has been maintained largely as a means of ensuring political stability within the member states. Success is also a result of the GCC's program, which is based on practical and pragmatic considerations and not influenced by ideological considerations. The complex mutual interests of its member states and the nature of their political infrastructures also strengthen the GCC.

GULF INVESTMENT CORPORATION (GIC). The GIC was established in November 1982 as the first joint venture of the Gulf Cooperation Council (GCC) (q.v.). The corporation initially had a capital of $2.1 billion, which was later raised to $3 billion and shared equally by investment from each of the states. The corporation began operations in 1984 with the objective of promoting the economic development and integration of the GCC states through the identification and support of new ventures in partnership with either public or private initiatives. The corporation has also been developing a capital market within the GCC states. It has largely been a successful venture, showing a healthy return on investments, and has assisted a significant number of projects either through loans or equity investment. It publishes the *GIC Gazetteer* (annually).

GULF NATIONAL FORUM. The forum was established in May 1992 following a meeting in Kuwait (q.v.) of professionals and businessmen from Bahrain, Kuwait, Qatar, Saudi Arabia, and the United Arab Emirates (qq.v.). Its goals are the promotion and protection of democracy, human rights, and basic freedoms in the member states of the Gulf Cooperation Council (q.v.).

GULF NEWS AGENCY. This was founded in 1976 as part of a Gulf-wide cooperative media program in order to serve the needs of the press in Bahrain, Iraq, Kuwait, Saudi Arabia, and the United Arab Emirates (qq.v.).

GULF ORGANIZATION FOR INDUSTRIAL CONSULTANCY (GOIC). The GOIC was established in 1976 by Iraq, Kuwait, Qatar, Saudi Arabia, and the United Arab Emirates (qq.v.) (each with a 17% share), and Bahrain and Oman (qq.v.) (each with 7.5%). The consultancy is based in Doha, Qatar, and its objectives are:

- collection and publication of data on industrial projects and industrial development policies
- preparation of proposals for establishment of joint industrial projects in member states
- recommending ways and means of coordination among industrial development projects
- development and coordination of technical and economic coopera-

tion among existing and planned industrial companies and estab-
lishments

- provision of technical assistance in preparing and evaluating industrial projects
- conducting studies on industry in general

In order to achieve these objectives, the GOIC undertakes a range
of activities, including the preparation of economic and industrial studies and reports, the preparation and promotion of manufacturing investment opportunity profiles for private sector implementation, a consultancy service to private sector companies, and an information service
to public and private sectors. The GOIC also maintains an industrial
data bank, with databases on industrial economy, trade, finance, and
technology, to provide an information service and to aid the preparation
of statistical data on Gulf Cooperation Council (q.v.) states. The GOIC
also organizes conferences and symposia, coordinates meetings of Gulf
industrialists, and provides short-term training courses relating to industrial projects. It publishes *GOIC Monthly Bulletin* (Arabic and English), *Al Tu'Awan al-Sinaie* (quarterly in Arabic and English), *Annual
Report,* and a series of specialized studies and reports.

GULF WAR (1991). The 1991 Gulf War, also known as the *Second Gulf
War*, was between Iraq and a coalition led by the United States. The
war has to be seen against the backcloth of the aftermath of the Iraq-
Iran War (q.v.) and the perceived need of the Iraqi government to divert
the attention of the population from internal economic problems. In
July 1991, Iraq (q.v.) complained to the Arab League (q.v.) about the
effect of the oil glut triggered by the actions of Kuwait and the United
Arab Emirates (qq.v.). Oil prices had plummeted to between $11 and
$13 a barrel as a result of the glut, whereas the Organization of Petro-
leum Exporting Countries (q.v.) reference price had been set at $18 per
barrel. Saddam Hussein (q.v.) also accused Kuwait of extracting oil
from Iraq's share of the cross-border oilfield at Rumallah, and resur-
rected Iraq's historical claim to Kuwait and its offshore islands.

On 31 July 1991, Iraqi and Kuwaiti officials met in Riyadh to try to
resolve the crisis, but the talks had failed by the following day and
100,000 Iraqi troops were already massed along the Kuwaiti border.
The Iraqi version of the outcome was that Kuwait had expressed no
willingness to compensate Iraq for the economic damage inflicted on
the Iraqi economy by the fall in oil prices; a $1 drop per barrel was
costing Iraq $1 billion per annum. According to the Kuwaitis, the talks

had collapsed because they had failed to agree to write off the $14 billion that Iraq had been lent during the Iraq-Iran War, refused to cede some territory on the border with Iraq, and rejected a demand to lease its Bubiyan and Warba Islands to Iraq.

On 2 August 1990, at 2:00 A.M. local time, Iraq invaded Kuwait and occupied the whole of the emirate. The Emir, Sheikh Jaber III al-Sabah (q.v.), and other members of the royal family fled to Bahrain (q.v.) and then to Saudi Arabia (q.v.) as the resistance to overwhelming Iraqi forces was ineffective. The United Nations (q.v.) Security Council met in emergency session and Resolution 660 (q.v.) was passed condemning Iraqi aggression, against Kuwait and demanding immediate withdrawal. Ancillary action saw the freezing of Iraqi and Kuwaiti assets by the United States, Great Britain, and France, while the Soviet Union halted arms deliveries to Iraq.

In regional terms, the Iraqi action caused splits within the Arab world, as indicated by the Arab League vote on 3 August 1990 condemning the action; five members abstained from voting on the motion. On 6 August, the United Nations imposed mandatory sanctions on Iraq and an embargo on Iraq and occupied Kuwait, which was followed by the Iraqi annexation of Kuwait on 8 August. Saddam Hussein made an offer of peace on 12 August based upon the withdrawal of Israel (q.v.) from the Occupied Territories in Palestine, Lebanon, and Syria (qq.v.), together with resolution of the Kuwait problem in accordance with UN resolutions, but this was rejected. Again on 15 November, following a massive build-up of U.S. troops the Gulf, Hussein proposed talks with Saudi Arabia over regional problems and with the U.S. over wider issues, but neither country responded to these overtures.

At the UN, the Security Council adopted Resolution 687 (q.v.) authorizing "all necessary means" to implement the earlier resolutions in order to restore peace in the region unless Iraq fully complied with the resolutions before 15 January 1991. Despite a series of meetings between American and Iraqi officials, no progress was made. On 12 January 1991, U.S. President George H. W. Bush was authorized to use military force by the U.S. Senate and House of Representatives. The Iraqi parliament met on 14 January 1991 and unanimously decided to go to war rather than withdraw from Kuwait.

The Gulf War commenced on 16 January 1991 with the allied forces consisting of a U.S.-led coalition of 28 other UN members, including nine Arab states. The Arab states were Bahrain, Egypt, Kuwait, Morocco, Oman, Qatar, Saudi Arabia, Syria, and the United Arab Emirates (qq.v), together supplying some 22,000 troops and a token force of aircraft and warships. Support for Iraq, though not in military terms, came from Jordan and the Palestinians (qq.v.). Jordanian support for Iraq cost the country dearly in terms of economic aid from the West and Palestinians in Kuwait were held responsible for demonstrations in support of Iraq in the Occupied Territories, suffering greatly as a result.

After a massive show of air power, missile attacks, and a ground campaign, Iraqi forces began to evacuate Kuwait City on 26 February and the remainder of the country on the following day. A truce was declared on 28 February after 42 days of warfare, with Iraqi losses estimated at 100,000 and coalition losses in the low hundreds. Damage to Iraq's infrastructure was put at $200 billion, with no figures available for the military operation, while coalition costs amounted to $82 billion.

After the truce was declared UN Security Council Resolution 687 required Iraq to implement a UN-monitored program of disarming itself of weapons of mass destruction, and intermediate and long-range missiles before UN sanctions could be lifted. The whole operation was to be supervised by a special UN Commission reporting to the Security Council through the UN secretary-general.

On 16 December 1998, after a number of crises during the truce, Iraq was subject to a four-day air campaign for refusal to cooperate fully with the UN weapons inspectors. These raids were carried out by U.S. and British forces only, against strenuous opposition from Russia and China, which considered them to be in breach of UN resolutions. Further raids have also taken place where Iraq has been accused of threatening British or U.S. planes policing the northern and southern no-fly zones designed to protect the Iraqi Kurds in the north and the Marsh Arabs in the south. There has been incessant conflict with Iraq over its failure to implement the program of disarmament and much dismay at the plight of the ordinary Iraqis suffering from the sanctions.

H

HADITH. The *Hadith*, Arabic for narrative, is the sayings and doings of the Prophet Muhammad. Following the death of the Prophet in A.D. 632, many of his companions settled in conquered territories where the population had been converted to Islam (q.v.). The Quran has 6,616 verses, but only 80 covered legal issues, mainly about women, marriage, family, and inheritance. However, there was an oral record of what the Prophet Muhammad had said or done as a judge and administrator, and many of his companions had kept a record of these for their own guidance. This later enabled the Prophet's *Sunna* (q.v.) to be codified when Muhammad ibn Idris al-Shafii ruled that all legal traditions not stemming from the Quran must be based on tradition going back to the Prophet Muhammad himself.

The outcome of this was the *Hadith* books of tradition with each tradition backed by text and the chains of authority going back to the source of origin. The six canonical works, called originally *Al-Hadith*, consisted of 2,700 acts and sayings of the Prophet Muhammad, and these were accepted by Sunni (q.v.) Muslims as being a secondary source of guidance after the Quran. Shi'i (q.v.) Muslims accepted only three traditions that could be traced through Imam Ali ibn Abu Talib and came up with their own collection. In the event of a dispute, a tradition from the *Hadith* can only be abrogated by another tradition.

HAJJ. The *hajj*, or Arabic for setting out, is the fifth pillar of Islam (q.v.) and is decreed by the Quran: "And pilgrimage to the House (of Allah) is incumbent upon people for the sake of Allah, (upon) everyone who is able to undertake it." The House of is ventered at a small building in Mecca (q.v.) called the *Kaaba*, which is believed to have been rebuilt several times since its original construction by Adam and which contains the sacred black stone. The *hajj* is of real significance to Muslims throughout the world as it is a pilgrimage that all believers should make at least once during their lifetime. It can also be regarded as another form of unity within the Arab world and creates a sense of belonging for all Muslims. The *hajj* attracts millions of pilgrims each year, represents a major source of income for Saudi Arabia (q.v.), and presents the authorities with major logistical problems in terms of transportation and accommodation. The number of pilgrims performing the rituals can be two million at a time and some have been trampled to death due to the sheer weight of numbers.

HAMAS. This is an acronym of Harakay al-Muqawama al-Islami, the Movement of Islamic Resistance, which is based in the West Bank, Gaza, and East Jerusalem. The organization was established by Sheikh Ahmed Yasin and six other leaders of the Muslim Brotherhood (q.v.) in the Occupied Territories soon after the outbreak of the *intifada* in December 1987. The charter of Hamas has as its short-term aim the reversal of Israel's (q.v.) occupation of the West Bank, Gaza, and East Jerusalem, and the founding of an Islamic state approved by a referendum. In the longer term, Hamas has the objective of establishing an Islamic state in the area of Palestine (q.v.) covered by the original mandate.

Hamas is financed by worldwide support from contributions made as part of supporters' Islamic tax, with funds largely spent on the construction and running of clinics and mosques. It also participates in the trade union movement and chambers of commerce.

Hamas was extremely active in the *intifada* and set up an armed wing called Izz al-Din Qassim, named after the leader of the 1936-1939 Arab Revolt (q.v.), and it opposed the Palestine Liberation Organization's (PLO) (q.v.) participation in the Middle East peace process. It also rejected the Israeli-PLO accord signed in Oslo in 1993. Hamas became the foremost opponent of Israel. Following the establishment of the Palestinian Authority in the Gaza Strip in May 1994, Hamas still regarded the Israeli settlements in the area as an occupying force to be resisted.

HANAFI CODE. The Hanafi Code is a Sunni (q.v.) Islamic legal code and is the school of the *Sharia* (q.v.) founded by Abu Hanifa al-Numan (A.D. 699-767), an Iranian merchant scholar based in Iraq (q.v.). Abu Hanifa did not codify established practices but applied logic and consistency to legal doctrines. This provided a method for dealing with future problems and expanding the jurisdiction of law in Muslim society. The Hanafi Code is liberal and oriented toward urban society and was adopted by the Abbasid Caliphs (A.D. 751-1258) before spreading to Afghanistan (q.v.), the Indian subcontinent, central Asia, and western China. It also became the school used by the Ottoman Turks and was incorporated into the Ottoman Empire (q.v.) (1517-1918) and became the official code of the empire. It has continued to have official status even in parts of the former Ottoman Empire, where a different school is followed by the local population.

HANBALI CODE. The Hanbali Code is the school of the *Sharia* (q.v.) founded by Ahmad ibn Hanbal (A.D. 780-855). The founder was opposed to a legal infrastructure built upon the Quran and the *Sunna* (q.v.), arguing that a legal decision could only be reached by referring directly to the Quran and the *Sunna* as they constituted the law and were not merely a source for the law. This interpretation stood the Hanbali Code apart from the Hanafi, Maliki, and Shafii (qq.v.) schools that had codified the Quran and *Sunna* into a system of jurisprudence.

The fundamentalist approach of the Hanbali Code lost support in the more sophisticated countries of the Fertile Crescent but retained its hold on the interior tribes of the Nejd. The code was revived in the Ottoman Empire (q.v.) when it was adopted by Muhammad Ibn Abd al-Wahhab (1703-1787), a Nejd cleric, who subsequently formed an alliance with its ruler, Muhammad ibn Saud, who adopted the Wahhabi (q.v.) doctrine.

HASHEM, HUSSEIN IBN ALI, AL- (c1853-1931). Hussein Ibn Ali al-Hashem was Sherif of Mecca (q.v.) and leader of the 1916 Arab Revolt (q.v.) against the Ottoman Empire (q.v.). Hussein and his family had been kept in Constantinople from 1898-1908 because of Sultan Abdul Hamid II's doubts about their loyalty. The Young Turk revolution of 1908 and the deposing of the Sultan allowed the family the opportunity to return to the Hedjaz, from where Hussein supported Ottoman action against the Al-Saud (q.v.) in 1910, and the Idrisi of Asir Province in 1911. However, these actions were as much about Hussein preventing these leaders from encroaching into areas where the tribes owed allegiance to him.

The Turkification policy of the Young Turks led Hussein to become more cautious in his dealings with the Ottomans, and he was particularly concerned with plans to extend the Hedjaz railway from Mecca to Medina and attempts by the Ottoman Governor to extend control over the province. In 1914, negotiations were opened by Hussein with Lord Kitchener in Cairo in an endeavor to obtain British support should the Ottomans attempt to remove him. At this stage Great Britain was not interested in concluding any deal with Hussein, but in October 1914 Turkey entered World War I on Germany's side, which led to negotiations being reopened.

The Turkish regime was also increasing the rates of conscription from the Arab provinces to the Turkish army and this was a cause of great resentment. The British representative in Cairo was now Sir Henry McMahon. A series of 10 letters were exchanged between the two men, which led to the declaration of the Arab Revolt in June 1916. The correspondence was, however, ambiguous, as Hussein felt that Britain had supported his claim to the Arab Caliphate and to Arab control over Syria, Iraq, and Palestine (qq.v.) after the war. The British interpretation of the correspondence was different, as it had been conditional on French interests in the region, and Palestine was excluded from consideration.

Hussein always maintained that the revolt was Islamic, more than Arab, but that the Arabs were the people to lead it. The revolt was backed by British military personnel and finance, which sustained the effort until the end of the war. The revolt tied down Turkish garrisons in the province, disrupted supplies on the Hedjaz railway, and did succeed in capturing Aqaba on the Red Sea, in what is now Jordan (q.v.). In 1919, the Arab army took Damascus, under Hussein's son, Faisal, and an Arab regime was established but proved to be short-lived because of Britain's wartime agreements with France.

Despite the military successes, Hussein never received credit in the Arab world because he was regarded as an agent of British and French imperialism. Other non-Arab Muslim countries did not forgive him for revolting against the Caliphate and for his treatment of pilgrims on the *hajj* (q.v.). Hussein's rule in the Hedjaz after the war was beset by problems and its economy suffered as Britain reduced, and eventually withdrew, its subsidy, largely because of his accusations of perfidy by Britain in the postwar settlement.

The downfall of Hussein had more to do with his inability to form a tribal confederation to withstand Ibn Saud and the Ikhwan (qq.v.), his harsh method of government, and the alienation of the influential and powerful merchant class. In March 1924, Hussein declared himself Caliph, but this was not recognized outside of the Hedjaz, and Ibn Saud eventually conquered the province, with Britain refusing to aid Hussein. Neither of his sons who ruled in Iraq and Transjordan would provide shelter and Hussein was exiled to Cyprus, returning eventually to Amman where he died in 1931. *See also* **McMahon-Hussein Correspondence**

HIZBULLAH. This is a Shi'i political party in Lebanon (q.v.), also known as the *Party of God*, which was established in 1982 and, by 1987, was the second most important Shi'i (q.v.) organization in Lebanon after Amal. The party has consistently followed the political and theological line of the Iranian government and has coordinated its activities with the government of Iran (q.v.). Hizbullah's policy rejected any accommodation with the Christian community in Lebanon, Israel (q.v.), or the United States. As a result of this policy, it attracted many members from Amal, particularly from the young, radical poor. The party is headed by a Consultative Council, which includes a number of clerics, and is organized on a geographical basis with branches in the Biqa valley, southern Lebanon and the suburbs of Beirut.

In 1983, Hizbullah gained international recognition when it was linked to attacks against United States, French, and Israeli targets in Lebanon and the abduction of Western hostages. The organization had been allowed by the Syrian (q.v.) army to retain its arms, as they considered the movement to be waging a legitimate struggle against the Israeli occupation of Lebanon. Hizbullah has waged a war against the Israeli troops occupying southern Lebanon and organized guerrilla attacks against Israel and Israeli settlements, including missile attacks.

Since the 1992 general election, Hizbullah has participated in the political process, won representation in the Lebanese parliament, and opened up a dialogue with its Christian and leftist opponents. It is also worthy of note that Hizbullah had been instrumental in setting up essential infrastructures in health, education, and social affairs in the area in which it is predominant and providing services that should have been provided by the central government.

HUSSEIN, SADDAM (1937-). Saddam Hussein was born in Auja, a village near Tikrit in Iraq (q.v.) in 1937, the son of a landless peasant who died before his birth, leaving him to be raised by a maternal uncle. Hussein went to Baghdad in 1955 to further his education and he became a member of the Ba'ath Socialist Party (q.v.). After the 1958 coup, he engaged in fights between the Ba'athists and the supporters of Premier Abdul Qasim (q.v.) and was a member of the team that tried to assassinate Qasim in October 1959. Hussein was injured in this attempt, after which he fled to Syria and then to Egypt (qq.v.), where he studied law at Cairo University.

The Ba'athists seized power in Iraq in 1963 and Hussein returned to Baghdad just before Abdul Salam Arif (q.v.) seized power from the Ba'athists. Hussein was involved in a failed attempt to overthrow Arif and was imprisoned, but he escaped in July 1966. He was elected secretary-general of the Ba'ath Party and spent two years reorganizing the party and building a power base ready for the return to power of the Ba'ath in 1968.

Initially, Hussein was not a member of the Revolutionary Command Council (RCC), but he still wielded influence due to his ties with the Chairman of the RCC, Ahmad Hassan Bakr, who was a cousin of his maternal uncle, and he secured a place on the RCC in 1969. The Hussein-Bakr alliance dominated the Ba'ath Party, mainly through the elimination of rivals on the RCC, and he continued to strengthen the party, while dealing with the Kurdish problem in northern Iraq. In the mid-1970s, Hussein had become the dominant partner, having exceeded Bakr in leadership, ruthlessness, and organizational ability.

In 1975, Hussein signed the Algiers Accord with the Shah of Iran (q.v.) to end a bitter feud between the two regimes and to settle a dispute over the Shatt al-Arab. By the end of the decade, Hussein felt powerful enough to overturn Bakr's strategy of conciliation with the Shi'i dissidents who had been inspired by the Iranian revolution. Hussein also discovered that Bakr had been in secret contact with President Hafiz Assad (q.v.) of Syria with a view to unifying the two regimes and, in mid-June 1979, he forced Bakr to resign. On the anniversary of the Ba'athist revolution in July 1979, Hussein assumed supreme power in Iraq. He consolidated his power base through the discovery of a major anti-state conspiracy in late July, which involved 69 top Ba'athist civilian and military leaders, all of whom were summarily tried and 21 executed. Following this action, a major purge followed of elements considered half-hearted in their support for Hussein within the militia, trade unions, student unions, and local and provincial governments. Although conciliatory toward senior Shi'i clergy and generous in funding the improvements to shrines and mosques, the regime suppressed militant religious bodies.

In September 1980, Iraq invaded Iran with the stated objective of retrieving the eastern half of the Shatt al-Arab waterway, which had been conceded to Iran in the Algiers Accord of 1975. However, the objective soon expanded into the incorporation of occupied areas of Iran into Iraq on the pretext that the majority of the inhabitants were ethnic Arabs. By mid-1982, Iraq had suffered military reverses such that all territorial gains had been lost and only two possible outcomes could be forthcoming, either a draw or an Iranian victory. The prospect of an Iranian victory was viewed with concern by outside forces, particularly the prospect of destabilization of the oil-producing Gulf States, and the United States, the Soviet Union, and France stepped up their military, economic, and intelligence aid to the Iraqi regime.

By 1984, Hussein had extended the war into the Arabian Gulf, Iranian oil facilities, and shipping, which, in 1987, drew the U.S. Navy into the Gulf to protect shipping against Iranian attacks. This included an operation to reflag the Kuwaiti oil-tanker fleet in order to protect Western oil supplies.

In the spring of 1988, Iraq staged a series of offensives to recover territory lost to Iran. This was effective due to the extensive use of chemical weapons. These actions forced Iran to accept unconditionally UN Security Council Resolution 598 (q.v.) of July 1987, which had called for a cease-fire, and a truce came into being on 20 August 1988. During the course of the war, Hussein had expanded his military forces from 250,000 to 1,250,000, built up his industrial-military capacity, and had succeeded in developing biological and chemical weapons. This power was now unleashed against the Kurdish dissidents in northern Iraq, who had largely sided with Iran in the Iraq-Iran War.

Hussein continued to use his intelligence service and his military power base to ensure complete control over the state. At the same time, he also reinforced his Islamic credentials through visits to, and funding of, Islamic shrines, and tried to restore Iraqi pride through a revival of Iraq's historical past, such as the Hanging Gardens of Babylon. At the same time, he began to adopt a pan-Arab (q.v.) stance by declaring that Iraq would be the leading nation in such a movement, which would succeed in retaking Arab lands lost in the Arab-Israeli wars.

In August 1990, Hussein invaded Kuwait (q.v.) on the pretext that Kuwait was extracting Iraqi oil from cross-border oilfields, despite that state's logistical and financial support for Iraq during the war with Iran. The U.S. reacted to this move by mobilizing international support and President George H.W. Bush put together a coalition of 29 Western and Arab nations to oppose Iraq. The support of the international community also extended to the UN (q.v.), which imposed a military and economic embargo on Iraq and ordered the withdrawal of Iraqi forces by 15 January 1991. The coalition then opened up an air campaign against Iraq and occupied Kuwait, setting in motion another Gulf War (q.v.).

The intense bombing campaign lasted 39 days and was followed by a four-day ground offensive, which resulted in the defeat of Iraqi forces, and Hussein was forced to withdraw from Kuwait. A temporary truce became effective on 28 February 1991. In April, Iraq was forced to accept UN Security Council Resolution 687 (q.v.) that detailed the cease-fire terms, war reparations, destruction of its medium-range missiles, nonconventional arms, and manufacturing facilities, all of which had to be met before economic sanctions would be lifted.

Despite the efforts of the Western powers, Israel, and Saudi Arabia (q.v.) to have Hussein assassinated or overthrown, he remained in power, largely because his military and intelligence mechanisms remained effective. However, although the imposition of a "no-fly" zone north of the 36th parallel effectively ended his control in the Kurdish region, and his position in the south was weakened by a "no-fly" zone to protect the Shi'i below the 36th parallel, neither move prevented ground forces, action in the two areas.

Economic sanctions against Iraq led to high inflation and a drop in living standards for the population, but did not result in popular dissent growing to a level that could destabilize the regime. Hussein had assumed that President Bush's failure in the November 1992 elections would ease matters, but he found that President Bill Clinton was prepared to continue the U.S. hard-line policy. This continuation of American policy was reinforced by an attack by the U.S. Navy on an Iraqi intelligence complex in Baghdad in June 1993, on the grounds that Hussein had planned to assassinate George Bush during a visit to Kuwait in April of that year.

Despite the defection of General Hussein Kamil Hussein, a son-in-law of Hussein, to Jordan (q.v.) in August 1995, Hussein overcame the crisis and won a referendum in October 1995, giving him 99.96 percent backing for a further seven-year presidential term. The situation in Iraq in 2000 was one where UN sanctions are still in force and Hussein is continuing to engineer crisis after crisis with the UN weapon inspectors and facing the possibility of further air strikes from the U.S. and Great Britain. *See also* **Kurds**

HUSSEIN IBN TALAL AL-HASHEM (1935-1999). King of Jordan (q.v.) since 1952 having succeeded his father, Talal ibn Abdullah al-Hashem, who was deposed due to mental illness in August of that year. Hussein did not fully exercise power until May of the following year as power was exercised by a regency council until his eighteenth birthday. A new constitution was promulgated in 1952, which provided for a multiparty two-chamber parliament with the King as the constitutional head of state. Elections were held in 1954, but the opposition demonstrated against electoral malpractice, rigging of the results by the King, and Hussein's proposal to join the Baghdad Pact (q.v.), which was to become effective in December 1955.

In response to pressure from the opposition Hussein dismissed General John Glubb as commander of the army and ordered fresh elections to be held in 1956. At the elections the nationalist-leftist alliance secured the largest bloc of seats and a government was formed under Suleiman Nabulsi. The new government immediately abrogated the 1948 Anglo-Jordanian Treaty, which had allowed Great Britain to maintain military bases in the kingdom, and Hussein did not challenge this decision. However, in April 1957, Hussein crushed a prospective coup of army officers, led by the new chief of staff General Ali Abu Nawar, and was immediately rewarded by U.S. aid under the Eisenhower Doctrine. This was followed by the dismissal of the Nabulsi government, dissolution of parliament, banning of political parties, and the imposition of martial law.

The emergence of the United Arab Republic (q.v.) led Hussein to foster a link with Iraq (q.v.) in early 1958 with himself as deputy head of the federation. The concept was short-lived and disintegrated in July 1958 following the military coup in Iraq. The regime has survived several attempts to overthrow it with a number having been backed by Egypt and Syria (qq.v.). Hussein survived because of his political acumen, the loyalty of the armed forces, and the subsidy that he has received from the U.S. in recognition of the freedom allowed to U.S. intelligence agencies.

Jordan was part of the Egypt-Syria defense pact during the build-up to the June 1967 Israeli War. As a result of the war Jordan lost control over the West Bank and had to cope with a massive influx of refugees from the area. These refugees swelled the numbers that had been in Jordan since 1948, but a new militancy began to develop within the Palestinian refugee community. This led to open conflict between the Jordanian army and Palestinian guerrillas, which climaxed in July 1971 when the last of the Palestinian commandos were expelled from Jordan.

During the 1973 Arab-Israeli War, Hussein refused to open up a third front against Israel, despite pressure from Egypt, Syria, and Saudi Arabia (q.v.), and accepted American advice to stay outside of the conflict. Subsequently, Hussein began to resume contact with Israeli leaders in order to secure a settlement that was to be based on an Israeli evacuation from the West Bank. However, a summit of the Arab League (AL) (q.v.) recognized the Palestine Liberation Organization (PLO) (q.v.) as the sole and legitimate representative of the Palestinians, and supported the right of the Palestinians to establish an independent national authority on any liberated Palestinian territory. Hussein reluctantly accepted this resolution and dismissed elected West Bank members of parliament, suspended the parliament, and advocated a comprehensive peace settlement through a United Nations (q.v.) sponsored conference.

In February 1977, Hussein received a PLO delegation to Amman which improved his standing in the Arab world, and he refused to participate in the peace process set in motion by the Camp David Accords (q.v.) of 1978 between Egypt and Israel (q.v.). He began to strengthen ties with the Soviet Union, concluding an arms deal in 1981, and backed Leonid Brezhnev's call for an international conference on the Middle East.

In the Iraq-Iran War (1980-1988) (q.v.) Hussein sided with Iraq, which accelerated the integration of the two economies, with Aqaba becoming the major source of imports for the Baghdad regime. In January 1984, the Jordanian parliament was revived and Jordan began to repair relations with Egypt in the face of AL opposition. In early 1985, Hussein concluded a deal with PLO Chairman Yasser Arafat (q.v.) on the forming of a future confederation of a Palestinian state and Jordan, and a joint approach to a Middle East peace settlement. This was subsequently rejected by the Palestinian National Council in April 1987. In the following year, Hussein severed all legal and administrative links with the West Bank.

Hussein was an active supporter of the Arab Cooperation Council (q.v.), which was formed in 1988 but disintegrated, with the Iraq invasion of Kuwait (q.v.) in 1990. Hussein worked strenuously to find an Arab solution to Iraq's invasion of Kuwait but failed. He blamed the U.S., Egypt, and Saudi Arabia for his failure and the fact that the crisis developed into a full-scale war. Public opinion in Jordan supported Iraq and the parliament, which was elected in November 1988 and had returned 32 Islamist deputies, was also supportive of Iraq. The critical stance against the U.S.-led coalition policy and the pro-Baghdad policy cost the regime dearly in Western capitals.

Following the Gulf War (q.v.) truce in 1991, Hussein tried to repair the damage by distancing himself from Saddam Hussein (q.v.) and he participated in the negotiations that preceded the 1991 Madrid Middle East Peace Conference (q.v.). However, he opposed the Israeli-PLO Accord when it became public in 1993 because it breached the joint strategy agreed between the Arab parties. This opposition was moderated following a meeting with Yasser Arafat.

However, Jordan continued to coordinate its peace talks with Israel and with Syria and Lebanon (q.v.). Fresh general elections were held, as scheduled, in November 1993, with a significant decline in the representation from the Islamist party. This, together with the apparent progress of the Israeli-PLO accord, led Hussein to open bilateral talks with Israel and, on 25 July 1994 in Washington, an agreement was signed with Israel ending the state of belligerency that had existed since 1948. On 26 October, a peace treaty was signed with Israel at a site in the Araba valley on the joint border, some 48 kilometers north of the Gulf of Aqaba.

During 1998, Hussein had been receiving cancer treatment in the U.S. and Crown Prince Hassan had been controlling the administration. However, Hussein went to Washington at the end of the year to try to assist in the brokering of a deal between the PLO and Israel to keep the peace process on track. Initially, this was successful, but was subsequently put on hold by the loss of support in the Israeli Knesset for Benjamin Netenyahu, and the calling of new elections.

On 25 January 1999, Hussein announced that his son Abdullah was to become crown prince and his successor. Hussein then returned to the United States for further treatment, which proved unsuccessful. He returned to Jordan where he died on 7 February 1999, being succeeded by his son, Abdullah.

I

IBADHIS. This is an Islamic sect named after Abdullah ibn Ibadh, a member of the Azd tribe of Oman, who started his life as a Khariji (q.v.). In A.D. 685, Ibadh split with Khariji (q.v.) extremists and Ibadhism developed as a pragmatist school within the Khariji movement. The aim of the sect was to restore Islam (q.v.) and the concept of the Islamic state to the condition that it was in before being supposedly corrupted by Caliph Othman ibn Affan (ruled A.D. 644-656). Ibadhis were to be found in Iraq (q.v.), the Hedjaz, Central Arabia, Oman, and Iran (qq.v.). In A.D. 850, the Omani tribes split from the Abbasid Caliphate and set up an independent state in the Jebal al-Akhdar. Today, two-thirds of Omani Muslims are Ibadhi, though adherents are also to be found in the Maghreb and Nigeria.

IBN KHALDUN CENTER FOR DEVELOPMENT (ICD). The center was founded in 1964 as a private sector organization based in Cairo, Egypt (q.v.). The overall policy direction of the ICD is controlled by a 32-member Board of Trustees, which meets four times a year to review and evaluate the ICD's work plan, funding, and proposals. Day-to-day operations are managed by a General Committee comprising the permanent staff of the center chaired by the Chairman of the Board of Trustees. All project proposals are considered by the committee and all project progress is reviewed on a monthly basis. The staff of the center is augmented by a large number of consultants, specialists, and researchers, either on a part-time or project-specific basis.

The ICD seeks to promote the use of available research in the social sciences in the policy-making process in Egypt and the Arab world, and aspires to be a model for vibrant civil society institutions. The conception of the ICD is that development encompasses social, political, and cultural dimensions with activities developed that comply with this goal. It publishes a newsletter *Civil Society* (monthly) and has embarked upon a major research project on civil society and democratization in the Arab world.

IJMA. *Ijma* is Arabic for consensus and is one of the four pillars of Islamic jurisprudence, which represents the consensus of the community. The function of the *ijma* is to settle the theory or practice concerning believers' behavior in matters specified through the Quran and the *Hadith* (q.v.). Until the Shafii Code (q.v.) founded the discipline of religious jurisprudence based on the four pillars of Islamic jurisprudence, *ijma* had been construed as consensus of the people, which embraced types of representatives of the community, including religious intellectuals, but this was enlarged by the Shafii to the whole community. In more modern times, *ijma* has been interpreted as standing for public opinion. *See also* **Sharia**

IKHWAN. As part of his alliance with the Wahhabi (q.v.) movement Abdul Aziz ibn Abdul Rahman Al-Saud (q.v.), the ruler of the Nejd, conceived the idea of settling nomadic tribes into colonies in order to teach the tenets of Islam (q.v.), and he called the settlers *al-Ikhwan*. The colonies were established from 1913 onward, and the settlers were fired with zeal to spread the Wahhabi version of Islam throughout the Arabian Peninsula and beyond. By 1920, the colonies were providing most of Ibn Saud's soldiers and, over the next few years, they helped him expand his territory to cover 80 percent of the Arabian Peninsula.

In 1927, Great Britain recognized Ibn Saud as King of the Hedjaz and Sultan of Nejd and its Dependent Territories, on the proviso that he recognized Britain as protector of Oman and the Gulf States, as well as the territorial integrity of Iraq and Transjordan (qq.v.) under the British mandate (q.v.). However, some Ikhwan commanders refused to recognize this agreement and continued to raid outside of their domain, leading to conflict with Ibn Saud. In March 1929, 8,000 Ikhwan faced 30,000 al-Saud troops and were defeated, but further unrest followed, and it was not until January 1930 that the last of the Ikhwan chiefs surrendered. The Ikhwan commanders who remained loyal to Ibn Saud received regular stipends and their units became transformed into the National Guard. *See also* **Saudi Arabia**

IMAM. This is the Arabic term to describe a person who can be seen as a model or one whose leadership is an example to be followed. In Islam (q.v.), the actual usage of the term varies between the Shi'i and the Sunni (qq.v.). Shi'i use Imams for their religious leaders at the highest level instead of Caliphs, as used by the Sunnis. The Sunnis use the term to describe the founders of their four legal schools, for example, Imam Muhammad ibn Idris al-Shafii. The term is also used to describe the leaders of prayers at any mosque.

IMAMIS. *See* **TWELVER SHI'IS**

INDIAN OCEAN RIM ASSOCIATION FOR REGIONAL COOPERATION (IOR-ARC). An intergovernmental meeting was held in Mauritius in March 1995 to promote an Indian Rim initiative and a charter establishing the IOR-ARC was signed at a ministerial meeting in March 1997. The aim of the association is the promotion of regional cooperation through trade, investment, infrastructure, tourism, and science and technology. The member states are Australia, India, Indonesia, Kenya, Madagascar, Malaysia, Mauritius, Mozambique, Oman (q.v.), Singapore, South Africa, Sri Lanka, Tanzania, and Yemen (q.v.).

INSTITUTE OF ARAB RESEARCH AND STUDIES. The Institute of Arab Research and Studies is a division of the Arab League Educational Cultural and Scientific Organization (q.v.) which was founded in 1953 and based in Cairo, Egypt (q.v.). The Institute provides specialist facilities for graduates of Arab universities to research into contemporary Arab affairs including national and international affairs, social studies, history, geography, law, and literature and linguistics. A special department of the Institute is devoted to the Palestinian question, the Arab cause, and the development of understanding of Arab nationalism (q.v.).

INTER-ARAB INVESTMENT GUARANTEE CORPORATION (IAIGC). The Inter-Arab Investment Guarantee Corporation was founded in 1970 by the Council of Arab Economic Unity and the Arab League (qq.v.), but did not come into effect until April 1974. The Corporation has 21 Arab states as members and is designed to provide insurance for Arab investors in the areas of inter-Arab investments and for export credits against noncommercial risks in the case of investments, and noncommercial and commercial risks in the case of exports. The noncommercial risks include nationalization, sequestration, or other measures that would deprive investors of their rights, or the risks to investors of being unable to transfer income from the host country. Commercial risks include insolvency of the debtor, abrogation or termination of the export contract, and bankruptcy. The corporation also undertakes the promotion of the flow of investments between Arab countries, including studies of the conditions governing the flow of investments and the identification of investment opportunities. The IAIGC has an authorized capital of $83.22 million and paid-up capital of $81.66 million as of December 1998.

The council is the highest authority of the corporation and comprises one representative from each member state. It determines the formulation of general policies, rules, and regulations, and takes decisions pertaining to guarantee, financial and administrative matters, appoints members of the Supervisory Committee, and elects the director-general and deputy director-general. The Supervisory Committee consists of six Arab experts, five of whom are of different nationalities, elected by the Council following recommendations from member states, and a sixth member appointed by the Council upon the recommendation of the General Union of Chambers of Commerce, Industry and Agriculture for Arab Countries (q.v.). The Supervisory Committee oversees the activities of the corporation and can advise, as appropriate, the director-general and the Council.

It publishes *Annual Report, Investment Climate in the Arab Countries* (annual), and *Investment Guarantee* (monthly). All publications are in Arabic except for the annual report, which is in Arabic and English.

INTER-ISLAMIC NETWORK ON WATER RESOURCES DEVELOPMENT AND MANAGEMENT (INWRDAM). The Organization of the Islamic Conference (OIC) (q.v.) established INWRDAM in 1987 as an intergovernmental, autonomous organization operating under the Oak's Standing Committee on Scientific and Technical Cooperation. It is based in Amman, Jordan (q.v.), and all of the OIC member states are members of the network. INWRDAM specializes in the identification of water resources management and development programs and its objectives are to:

- collaborate and cooperate in the areas of water resources development and management to assist member states to build up national capability, and in the development of the economic production sector relevant to the scientific field of the network
- exchange information, share experiences, and maintain a continuing dialogue on development in the fields of water resources development and management
- set up and maintain a data bank on developments in the subject area for the use of the member states
- initiate joint projects of research and development and to assist member states in the training of manpower

INWRDAM offers its member states consultancy and advisory services, maintains a table of water scarcity in OIC countries, publishes research papers, and provides technical support.

INTERNATIONAL ASSOCIATION OF ISLAMIC BANKS. The International Association of Islamic Banks was founded in 1977 and is

based in Jeddah, Saudi Arabia (q.v.), with branches in Cairo and Karachi. It is designed to link all banks that follow Islamic principles of
participation, and conducts research and provides training programs. It
has a membership of 192 Islamic banks and other financial institutions
from 34 countries. *See also* **Islamic Banking**

**INTERNATIONAL CENTER FOR AGRICULTURAL RESEARCH
IN THE DRY AREAS (ICARDA).** The ICARDA was founded in
1977 and based in Aleppo, Syria (q.v.), with members from 52 countries, and is part of a network of agricultural research centers supported
by the Consultative Group on International Agricultural Research. The
ICARDA aims to improve agricultural production in the countries of
West Asia and North Africa, working in the areas of water management, cereal and legume improvement, improvement to farming methods, and recovery of degraded rangelands. Publications include an *Annual Report, Faba Bean Information Services Newsletter* (twice a year),
Barley and Wheat Newsletter (twice year), *Lentil Experimental News
Service Newsletter* (twice a year), and *Caravan Newsletter.*

**INTERNATIONAL COMMISSION FOR THE PRESERVATION OF
ISLAMIC CULTURAL HERITAGE (ICPICH).** A subsidiary of the
Organization of the Islamic Conference (OIC) (q.v.), which was
founded in 1992 and based in Istanbul, Turkey (q.v.).

**INTERNATIONAL CONFEDERATION OF ARAB TRADE UNIONS
(ICATU).** It was founded in 1956 and based in Damascus, Syria (q.v.).
The ICATU has trade union membership from 18 countries, including
Morocco, Tunisia, Egypt, Bahrain, Jordan, Kuwait, Lebanon (qq.v.),
Mauritania, and Yemen (q.v.), and 12 affiliated international federations. However, member organizations that can be considered as free,
democratic, and representative are in a minority, with the majority being more representative of their governments than workers. It organizes
a congress every four years and publishes *Al-Amal al-Arab* (monthly).

**INTERNATIONAL INSTITUTE FOR ADULT EDUCATION
METHODS.** The institute was founded in 1968 by the United Nations
Educational, Scientific, and Cultural Organization (UNESCO) and Iran
(q.v.) and is based in Teheran. It collects, analyzes, and distributes information concerning the methods, media, and techniques used in adult
education programs. The institute maintains a documentation service
and library, organizes seminars, and publishes *Adult Education and*

Development (quarterly).

INTERNATIONAL INSTITUTE OF ISLAMIC MEDICINE (IIIM).
The institute was founded in 1993 by the Islamic Medical Association of North America and its secretariat is based in Brandon, Florida. The IIIM is dedicated to research and promotion of Islamic medicine, its history, impact on modern medicine, and its applications in contemporary times. One of the aims of the IIIM is to Islamize all existing knowledge of medicine, and to have all Muslim physicians become aware of their historical heritage and incorporate this heritage in their teaching of medicine to future generations.

The institute has organized four conferences on the history of Islamic medicine or on its applications to contemporary medicine. The conference held in 2000 at Hyderabad, India, was on "Islamic Medicine in the New Millennium."

The IIIM is funded by donations from founding members and fellows. It is using part of its funding to build up a library of materials relating to Islamic medicine and is engaged in developing a catalog of books on Islamic medicine and its history. It publishes a newsletter, *Al-Hikma,* which is designed to be quarterly, but, because of financial constraints, appears on an as-needed basis.

INTERNATIONAL INSTITUTE OF ISLAMIC THOUGHT (IIIT).
The institute was established in 1981 with its headquarters in Herndon, Virginia, and branches and offices worldwide. It is a private, nonprofit, academic and cultural institution concerned with general issues of Islamic thought. The IIIT is an intellectual forum working to promote and support research projects, organize intellectual and cultural meetings, and publish scholarly works.

The objectives of the IIIT are to:

- serve as a think tank in the field of Islamic culture and knowledge
- formulate a comprehensive Islamic view and methodology to assist Muslim scholars in their critical analysis of contemporary knowledge
- develop an appropriate methodology for dealing with Islamic legacy and contemporary knowledge
- develop an appropriate methodology for understanding and dealing with the present situation of both the *Umma* (religious groups) and the world in general, in view of contemporary challenges and opportunities

The IIIT's objectives are achieved through the direction of appropriate research and studies, the holding of seminars and conferences, support for researchers and scholars in academic institutions, joint research ventures with universities and research centers, and a program of publications.

The IIIT has organized a number of international conferences on Islamic thought and it applications and many of the proceedings have been published. Its publication program also includes *The American Journal of Islamic Social Sciences* (quarterly) and *Islamiyyat al-Ma'rifah* (quarterly in Arabic). The various worldwide branches of IIIT also publish their own local newsletters.

INTERNATIONAL ISLAMIC FEDERATION OF STUDENT ORGANIZATIONS (IIFSO). The IIFSO was established in 1969 as a federation of Muslim student organizations with the main objective of uniting Muslim students worldwide. It also seeks to strengthen Islamic fraternal bonds, to encourage the study of the Islamic faith and the Arabic language, and to spread the principles of Islam (q.v.). The IIFSO organizes seminars and youth camps and maintains an information center. The publication program includes a biweekly magazine *Al-Akhbar* (in Arabic and English), a monthly *Connection* (in English), and a monthly newsletter. The program also includes books on Islam in some 69 languages.

INTERNATIONAL ISLAMIC NEWS AGENCY (IINA). The agency was established in 1972 as a specialized agency of the Organization of the Islamic Conference (OIC) (q.v.) and is based in Jeddah, Saudi Arabia (q.v.). The budget of the IINA is dependent upon contributions from the member states of the OIC.

The IINA distributes news and reports projecting Islamic causes, the conditions of Islamic minorities, Islamic theological issues, and development projects. The daily news is disseminated through the Qatar News Agency, which then disseminates the news to 700 points in the Arab world, Europe, and America in Arabic, English, and Portuguese. Bulletins are also despatched electronically to the news agencies of Indonesia and Malaysia, the Associated Press of Pakistan, and to Central Asia and Russia. Africa is serviced via the Pan-African News Agency.

INTERNATIONAL ISLAMIC ORGANIZATION (IIO). The International Islamic Organization was founded in 1970 at Bandung, Indonesia, as a successor to the Afro-Asian Islamic Organization. The IIO's aim was to work toward the establishment of a new world order in accordance with the teachings of Islam (q.v.). The organization assists Muslim communities that are seeking independence, actively supports the study of the Arabic language, and promotes human rights in accordance with Islamic teaching. Based in Jakarta, Indonesia, the IIO draws membership from national groups in 23 countries: Afghanistan, Algeria (qq.v.), Australia, Cambodia, China, Cyprus, Egypt (q.v.), Germany, Hong Kong, India, Indonesia, Iraq (q.v.), Japan, Laos, Malaysia, Pakistan, the Philippines, Saudi Arabia (q.v.), Singapore, South Korea, Sri Lanka, Syria (q.v.), and Thailand.

INTERNATIONAL ISLAMIC RELIEF ORGANIZATION (IIRO). The International Islamic Relief Organization was founded in 1978 and has its headquarters in Jeddah, Saudi Arabia (q.v.), with over 100 offices worldwide. The IIRO is a humanitarian, nongovernmental organization, supporting humanitarian activities in more than 120 countries without any ethnic, linguistic, or religious considerations, though 80 percent of its work is with Muslims.

The funds of the IIRO are drawn from individual contributions from Saudi Arabian citizens, from the *zakat* (q.v.) paid by citizens and companies in Saudi Arabia, and bequests made in its favor. The IIRO has also created an endowment fund to generate a stable income to fund future activities.

The IIRO's activities are organized through various departments covering: urgent relief and refugees, health care, orphans and social welfare, education, agricultural projects, children's projects, and an architectural and engineering consultancy. A Department of External Affairs has also been established to coordinate the IIRO's activities with other nongovernmental organizations (NGOs), agencies, and international organizations.

The Department of Urgent Relief and Refugees was established in 1980 and is seen as a vital part of the IIRO with the objectives of responding to the most urgent victims of calamities, cooperating with other NGOs and international agencies to meet identified needs, and working with other organizations to facilitate repatriation of refugees and displaced persons. The department has established camps in Afghanistan (q.v.), Bangladesh, and Sri Lanka; assisted earthquake victims in Egypt (q.v.), Indonesia, Morocco, and Kyrghizstan; provided relief to the Balkan region; and assisted victims of armed conflict in

Burundi, Rwanda, and Somalia. This work has been undertaken in co-operation with the World Food Programme, the Islamic Development Bank (q.v.), and national and international agencies, with $85 million being spent between 1987 and 1995.

The Department of Health Care has established a health care network in Africa, Asia, and Europe with the aim of providing high quality health care, where needed. In Africa, 92 projects have been financed, 136 in Asia, and 51 in Europe and the Americas. One example has been the establishment of a medical network in Bosnia-Herzegovina with 48 medical projects. The department works closely with other agencies and spent $30 million between 1987 and 1995.

The Department of Orphans and Social Welfare is considered an important area of activity and works to sponsor 100,000 orphans throughout the world. The IIRO has established 25 centers and mother care facilities in 12 countries, provides support for 251 existing orphanages, and implemented 1,100 family projects to support orphans and needy families in Egypt (q.v.). The department has also established dress making projects for poor families in Bangladesh, India, Indonesia, Jordan, Lebanon (qq.v.), Sri Lanka, Philippines, and a number of African countries. The department spent $83 million between 1987 and 1995.

The Department of Education was established in 1985 and pursues a program of school building, sponsoring educational institutions and teachers, and providing scholarships for needy students to gain higher education. It also has a publication program of children's books that can be used as part of a planned curriculum. The department spendt $40 million between 1987 and 1995.

The Department of Agricultural Projects was established in 1993 to promote agricultural production through financial and technical packages, usually on a profit-sharing basis, and through creating a system of revolving credit with the objective of providing self-sufficiency. In this context, the department works to facilitate resettlement of displaced persons in order to reduce their reliance on relief. The department has been involved in vegetable growing, animal rearing, and seed production in Bosnia-Herzegovina, Iraqi Kurdistan, Azerbaijan, and other countries in Asia and Africa.

The Department of Architectural and Engineering Consultancy was established in 1987 as a technical unit to implement various IIRO construction projects using materials and skills locally available, at minimum cost, and within the shortest possible timescale. The IIRO also encourages entrepreneurs and sponsors viable economic projects and small businesses to help victims get back on their feet. The IIRO has a wide network of national and international contacts with various Islamic and non-Islamic relief organizations to achieve these aims.

INTERNATIONAL ISLAMIC UNIVERSITY ISLAMABAD (IIUI). The university was founded on 11 November 1980 at Islamabad, Pakistan, with the aim of producing scholars and practitioners capable of meeting the economic, social, political, technological, and technical needs of the Muslim community.

The objectives of the IIUI are to:

- provide an all round and harmonious development of the individual and society
- reconstruct human thought in all its forms on the foundations of Islam
- develop Islamic character and personality among the students, teachers, and support staff in the university
- encourage and promote education, training, and research in Islamic learning, social, natural, applied and communication sciences, and other branches of knowledge
- take practical steps for ideological, moral, intellectual, economic, and technological development in accordance with the norms, values, and principles of Islam

The IIUS has Faculties of Islamic Studies, *Shariah* and Law, Economics, and Arabic, and a Department of Computer Science. Aid is available for extremely deserving students from donations from Muslim countries and *zakat* (q.v.) donations.

INTERNATIONAL ISLAMIC UNIVERSITY MALAYSIA (IIUM). The university was founded in 1983 by the Government of Malaysia with support from the Organization of the Islamic Conference (OIC) (q.v.). The IIUM operates under the direction of a Board of Governors on which sponsoring governments and organizations are represented.

The university has Faculties of Economics, Engineering, Human Sciences, and *Shariah* Law. The international element of the IIUM is indicated by the fact that 92 countries are represented within the student community, being some 18 percent of the undergraduate and postgraduate student population.

INTERNATIONAL MONETARY FUND (IMF). The IMF was established in 1944 at the conference of Bretton Woods and provides financing for any of its 150 member states experiencing a balance of payments problem. Each member state is assigned a quota of funds that can be borrowed and repaid over 10 years, but the quota can be waived in times of serious crisis. The IMF often demands that borrowers make fundamental changes in their economies to try to avert future balance of payments problems. Among these changes are stabilization of exchange rates and government deficits, structural adjustment of economies through privatization of state enterprises, liberalization of trade, and reduction, or removal, of state subsidies. In January 1977, following an economic crisis, the Egyptian (q.v.) government was forced to reduce subsidies on basic consumer goods to secure IMF funding resulting in food riots in Cairo and Alexandria. Troops had to be used to restore order and in Cairo alone 77 people died. A similar situation was experienced by Morocco in 1984, with rioting following cutbacks in consumer subsidies due to IMF pressure. In Sudan, the Islamization policies of Muhammad Ja'far Numerie led to the IMF suspending aid payments to Sudan, leaving the country with a huge debt burden and state bankruptcy. In 1981, Saudi Arabia (q.v.) made a major commitment to the IMF, which made it the sixth largest contributor, and the Palestine Liberation Organization (q.v.) was granted observer status.

INTERNATIONAL MUSLIMAH ARTISTS NETWORK (IMAN).
The International Muslimah Artists Network was founded on 1st January 1997 by Norah Hammoude and Safiya Godlas as an international organization created by and for Muslim women artists. The main aim of IMAN is to promote the artistic achievements of Muslim women around the world, encouraging established artists and those aspiring to become established artists. IMAN is also developing a structure to mentor new artists and to support Muslim women artists through a variety of activities.

Among the objectives of IMAN are:

- to make visible the many skills, artistic achievements, and professional roles of Muslim women throughout the world in order to dispel the false images that are so widely spread
- to provide avenues, means, and resources for the development of the artistic potential and skills of all Muslim women
- to develop and present a coherent philosophy of art and art education from the viewpoint of Muslim women artists
- to articulate and present, through lectures, conferences, and other

educational activities, the important role of art in Islamic culture and social life and to establish beyond doubt its vital influence on this and future Islamic generations

- to establish once and for all the crucial function and importance of Islamic art as a religious "pointer," as a *dawa* tool, and as an ambassador for Islam in the Western world and other non-Islamic areas

INTERNATIONAL PLANNED PARENTHOOD FEDERATION (IPPF). The Arab regional office of the IPPF is based in Tunis, Tunisia and aims to advance education in family planning, to promote the use of family planning services through locally based voluntary associations, and to organize training for providers. Member associations in the Arab world can be found in Algeria, Bahrain, Egypt, Iraq, Jordan, Lebanon, Morocco, Palestine, Syria, Tunisia, and Yemen (qq.v.).

IRAN. Iran has an area of 1,648,000 square kilometers and an estimated population of 64 million. It is bounded on the north by the Caspian Sea and the republics of Armenia, Azerbaijan, and Turkmenistan; on the east by Afghanistan (q.v.) and Pakistan; on the south by the Persian Gulf and the Gulf of Oman; and to the west by Turkey and Iraq (qq.v.). Over half of the population live in urban areas, with Tehran accounting for some 6 million, Mashad some 1.5 million, and Tabriz and Isfahan about 1 million each. About 80 percent of Iran's population are of Iranian origin of whom the ethnic Persians are predominant, and mainly Shi'i (q.v.) Muslims. The Azerbaijanis form about 20 percent of the population with the Kurds (q.v.) making up 5 percent of the population, mainly in the provinces of Kurdistan, West Azerbaijan, and Kermanshahan, and most are Sunni (q.v.) Muslims. The Sunni Baluchis form 2 percent of Iran's population and reside in the Sistan/Baluchistan province. In addition to Islam (q.v.), there are three other officially recognized religions, with Christians numbering some 97,550, the Zoroastrians numbering some 33,000, and some 26,500 Jews.

Iran is extremely rich in mineral resources, with oil reserves representing about 10 percent of the world's total, and some 15 percent of the world's reserves of natural gas. During the decades of the 1960s and the early 1970s, the growth rate in the industrial sector was about 15 percent, the service sector grew by 14.3 percent, and agriculture by 4.6 percent. However, distribution of wealth was uneven, as the top 20 percent of the population saw their share of wealth increase from 52 to 56 percent, while the share of the bottom 40 percent from 14 to 11 percent. The end of 1980 saw a decline in the economy, as the period of revolutionary crisis led to the flight of skilled workers and entrepreneurs and the transfer of large sums of capital abroad.

The revolution of 1979 against the Shah was a populist uprising directed, initially from France, by Ayatollah Khomeini (q.v.). The situation was complex but the Shah's reforms had succeeded in alienating all sectors of the population and had eliminated the traditional foundation of the regime: the *ulama* (religious scholars), the bazaar merchants, and the landowning classes. The new Western-educated elites were unhappy with their lack of political power, the intelligentsia resented the abuses of human rights, and the *ulama* and the bazaar merchants resented Western lifestyles, which contravened Islamic traditions.

During this period of upheaval, the Shah was indecisive and the regime was weakened by a series of strikes and riots that the authorities were unable to control. On 16 January 1979, the Shah left for Egypt (q.v.), and Ayatollah Khomeini (q.v.) returned to Iran on 1 February 1979. On 11 February, the army commanders ordered troops back to barracks, and military installations were occupied by the people and pro-Shah commanders arrested. In April 1979, a referendum was held which approved the formation of an Islamic Republic, and in December 1979 a constitution was approved. The early 1980s were marked by intellectual conflict, armed struggle, secessionist movements, and repression of liberal and leftist movements in the revolutionary coalition, with the Islamic regime beginning to consolidate its position.

In 1980 the Iraq-Iran War (q.v.) broke out, arising from a long border dispute over the Shatt al-Arab from south of Basra to the Arabian Gulf. Iraq (q.v.) invaded Iran on 22 September 1980, occupying large areas of southwestern Iran and destroying the Abadan oil refinery. However, the war became bogged down in siege warfare. In May 1981, Iran recaptured the strategic town of Khorramshar and its forces entered Iraq. A war of the cities then ensued, with air and missile attacks. On 13 September 1986, it was reported that Iran had received United States missiles as part of an arms deal for hostages held by Hizbullah (q.v.), this becoming known as the *Iran-Contra Affair*. The war went into a period of stalemate until the war of the cities was resumed in 1988. In May 1988, the United States became directly involved through the reflagging of Kuwaiti oil tankers and, on 3 July 1988, the U.S. warship *Vincennes* shot down an Iranian civil airline, killing all 290 passengers. On 18 July 1988, Iran accepted United Nations (q.v.) (UN) Security Council Cease-fire Resolution 598 (q.v.). The eight-year war resulted several hundred billion dollars in damage and military expenditures and about one million casualties.

On 3 June 1989, Ayatollah Khomeini died and was replaced by President Sayyed Ali Khamene'I, but this election also marked a major shift of power from the radical left to the conservative right. The Islamic Republic of Iran is a theocratic republic, a hybrid of the absolute authority of the ruling Shi'i (q.v.) jurist combined with an elected president and parliament and an appointed chief of the judicial branch. The Islamic Republic has three central organizations to defend against foreign aggression, to perform police services, and to suppress opposition to the regime. Opposition to the regime largely comes from among some one million Iranian exiles supporting many different groups, each with its own, often conflicting, agenda.

The revolutionary regime also nationalized large sectors of industry and imposed severe controls on the banking and financial sectors. Meanwhile, Iran has experienced extreme economic hardship in the 1990s due to a decline in oil revenues and the lack of a coherent and consistent economic policy. Western attitudes toward the Iranian revolution and the Islamic Republic have been conditioned by Ayatollah Khomeini's avowed declaration to spread the Islamic revolution throughout the Arab world, thus threatening the conservative oil-producing Arab Gulf States, support for Hizbullah in Lebanon (q.v.), the United States Embassy hostage incident, and the issuing of a *fatwa* (q.v.) against Salman Rushdie. Sanctions imposed by the United States and other states, because Iran was regarded as a source of terrorism, further crippled the economy.

In recent years, however, there have been attempts by both sides to reach an accommodation and an acceptance by the West that the Islamic Republic is now established as the Iranian state. This has been reinforced by the elections in February 2000, which produced a less religiously dominated administration.

IRAQ. Iraq is relatively well-off in terms of natural resources, with an oil production capacity and reserves sufficient to fund both agricultural and industrial expansion. Given its size the population of 15 million is manageable in terms of its natural resources. The agricultural area is about one-sixth of the area of the country, but only two-thirds is under cultivation, and this is declining due to the rural-urban drift and inefficient irrigation methods. Iraq is completely landlocked except for a 40-kilometer-wide outlet at the top of the Arabian Gulf. About half of the country consists of mountains and deserts. The mountainous area is in the north, and the area south of Baghdad consists of the fertile plains of the Tigris and Euphrates and desert.

The population of Iraq is divided along both racial and religious lines with Arabs comprising 75 percent of the population, Kurds (q.v.) 18 percent, and the remainder smaller ethnic groups, such as Assyrians. About 90 percent of the population is Muslim, with the remaining 10 percent consisting of a variety of Christian sects and the Yazidi (q.v.) and Sabeean communities. The Muslim population consists of Sunni and Shi'i (qq.v.) communities, with the latter being in the majority, but with power resting with the Sunni minority of the cities who have ruled Iraq since the time of the mandate (q.v.).

At the end of World War I, the area that became Iraq had been part of the Ottoman Empire (q.v.), consisting of the provinces of Basra and Baghdad, and became a mandatory territory under Great Britain. Mosul was later added to the mandate, thus forming present-day Iraq. Faisal, the son of Sherif Hussein (q.v.), became king in 1921, heading a government with a democratic structure and a constitution and legislature but, in reality, every Iraqi minister was guided by a British advisor. Ultimate authority within the state in reality rested with the British High Commissioner, backed by the Royal Air Force, with political power resting in the hands of a powerful urban elite in uneasy alliance with tribal leaders.

In 1923, Iraq became formally independent, but real power still rested with the British authorities, the court, and professional politicians, though a succession of coups from 1936 onwards brought the military more directly into politics. A brief attempt to end British control was launched in 1941, but this was put down and the British reoccupied Iraq until 1945. At the end of World War II, a period of instability ensued, with 13 cabinets between 1945-1958 but with the same key personnel moving between portfolios. However, this group of professional politicians, led by the pro-Western Nuri Al-Said, was swept aside by the 1958 revolution.

At the time of the revolution, Iraq was a dependent and underdeveloped economy with land ownership in a few hands, little industry except for the oil industry, widespread poverty, and a population with no political power. This led to the growth of a clandestine, but disparate, opposition. Two factors united the opposition: hostility to the monarchy and court, and the continued British presence in Iraq, which was seen as providing support for a corrupt and aging elite.

In July 1958, a revolt began in the army, and soon developed into a nationwide insurrection that overthrew the old political order and the king and Nuri Al-Said were killed. The Free Officers movement, led by Brigadier Abd al-Karim al-Qasim (q.v.), headed the new cabinet. However, Qasim was unable to establish a base for his rule; the new government did not have a common vision, or even share a political ideology, and political differences soon developed. The main political clashes arose between the communists, who had been an active opposition since their formation in 1934, and those politicians who were essentially Arab nationalists.

One major area of disagreement was over the United Arab Republic (q.v.). The nationalists favored membership but it was opposed by the communists, who saw it as a threat to their position and the construction of a new social and political order. In this area, the communists were supported by Qasim who did not wish to be in a subservient position to Gamal Abdul Nasser (q.v.) although he did not share their political views and objectives and Iraq did not join the UAR. Over the next five years there were fierce battles between the two factions and in February 1963 an alliance of nationalists and Ba'athists seized power and waged a reign of terror against the left and the Communist Party, but the Ba'athists were pushed out of the alliance in November 1963. From 1963 to 1968, a further period of instability ensued, with a series of military governments preaching Arab unity and pursuing costly but unsuccessful actions against the Kurdish minority in northern Iraq.

On 17 July 1968, Ba'ath Party (q.v.) authority was reasserted through a military coup led by Ahmad Hasan al-Bakr and at the end of July became the government. The Arab defeat in the 1967 Arab-Israeli War and U.S. support for Israel (q.v.) meant that a regime which aimed to be regarded as revolutionary needed to be opposed to the U.S. and the West in general. Iraq therefore approached the Soviet Union for technical aid for the oil industry in June 1969, which greatly enhanced the regime's prestige at home. Soviet aid was aimed at developing the North Rumayla oilfield, which was a major deposit and crucial to an independent Iraqi oil policy.

At the same time, the Revolutionary Command Council (RCC) through its Vice-Chairman, Saddam Hussein (q.v.), opened talks with the Kurdish leader Mustafa Barzani (q.v.), which on 11 March 1970 led to an agreement on Kurdish autonomy. This was to prove a ruse by the government to buy time, but domestically it gave grounds for political optimism within Iraq. A National Action Charter was issued in 1971, putting forward a socialist social and economic program, and the Iraqi Petroleum Company was nationalized in June 1972. Iraq also signed a 15-year friendship treaty with the Soviet Union and oil began to flow from the North Rumayla oilfield. All of this did a great deal for the prestige and popularity of the Ba'ath, and nationalization of the oil industry was a major boost to the economy.

Iraqi relations with the Soviet Union were opposed by the West and by the conservative Arab states in the Arabian Peninsula. The autonomy agreement with the Kurds had not been implemented, and Iran (q.v.) began to take an interest in the affairs of the Kurds in Iraq in an attempt to destabilize the regime in Baghdad. Iran began to supply the Kurds with sophisticated weaponry and funds to enable them to sustain military actions against the Iraqi regime. This led to the communists supporting the Ba'ath regime to form a National Patriotic Front in July 1973, though the communists were very much the junior partner. The Kurds had been pushed further toward Iran and in the spring of 1974 a major insurrection broke out, which was supported by the bulk of the Kurdish population despite some suspicion as to the support being received from Iran.

In October 1974, King Hussein of Jordan (qq.v.) acted as a broker between Iraq and Iran, arranging a series of meetings to try to resolve the differences between the two regimes. The result was the Algiers Agreement between the two countries, signed in March 1975, with the most important provision being Iranian access to the Shatt al-Arab at the head of the Arabian Gulf. This was sufficient for Iran to withdraw its support for the Iraqi Kurds. Artillery support was withdrawn and the Iranian border closed to the Kurds; the supplies of weapons and funds were halted. As a result Kurdish resistance collapsed and Barzani went into exile.

The domestic impact was a further consolidation of the Ba'ath's status in Iraq, as the Kurdish question seemed to have been settled on Baghdad's terms, the frontier with Iran had been negotiated, and the solution was well received by Iraq's neighbors. It also meant that Iraq no longer needed to be so dependent on the Soviet Union, and the regime gradually moved into the orbit of the West and toward the moderate Arab states by the end of 1979. The period from 1975 to 1979 marked the diversion of power from the Ba'ath Party and the RCC into the hands of Saddam Hussein and a group of trusted subordinates.

The Ba'athists had also benefited from the rise in oil prices following the 1973 Arab-Israeli War. As the government was able to spend vast sums of money on welfare and infrastructural projects, this gave the Ba'athists confidence to move toward the creation of a political system under their total control and the party gradually became an instrument of the Iraqi leadership. The communist alliance with the

Ba'ath also collapsed when Iraqi communists were arrested and 12 of them executed for allegedly carrying out political activities in the army. In 1978 the RCC made non-Ba'athist political activity illegal; in the army, it was punishable by death.

Further action against the Kurds consisted of the clearing of the border areas with Turkey (q.v.) and Iran and forcible resettlement of the Kurdish population in southern Iraq or in specially constructed secure villages. However, by 1977 the Kurds had regathered their strength sufficiently to recommence guerrilla activity against the Iraqi military. Opposition had also begun to manifest itself within the Shi'i population, largely through an organization known as *al-Da'wa*, which was oppressed by the Iraqi authorities and some of its leaders executed. In terms of the leadership, Ahmad Hasan al-Bakr resigned on 16 July 1979 and announced that Saddam Hussein was to be his successor. An unsuccessful coup was discovered on 28 July, and five members of the RCC and 17 others of the elite were executed on Saddam's orders.

The revolution in Iran brought problems for Iraq, as the Algiers Agreement went into abeyance and there were fears that the Kurdish insurrection would also grow in strength. It was also feared that a defeat for the Shah would encourage Shi'i opposition within Iraq, but this proved to be unfounded, and Saddam calculated that action against a weakened Iranian army could preempt any such uprising. Saddam also saw action against Iran as a means to achieve his status as an Arab statesman and a defender of the Arab nation, and of making Iraq into a regional power, with the ability to control the Gulf. A war against Iran was irresistible due to the perceived weakness of the new regime and its inability to respond to any aggression.

The duration of the Iraq-Iran War (1980-1988) (q.v.) and the resultant stalemate left Iraq greatly weakened in terms of the economy and the political capacity of the regime. Both the Ba'ath Party and Saddam Hussein lost face because of the defeats suffered by the army, the devastation brought by the war, and the fact that an estimated 200,000, or one percent of the population, were dead or wounded. The regime only survived by a skilful propaganda exercise and the ruthlessness of the security forces in putting down any opposition. The situation also partially explains the Iraqi invasion of Kuwait (q.v.) in 1990, the war against the allied coalition, and the economic and political consequences of the Gulf War (q.v.)

The economy of Iraq is dependent upon oil and the United Nations (q.v.) embargo has placed great strains on the economy. The rural-urban drift in recent decades has also meant that the labor force in the agricultural sector has dramatically declined. Since 1960 Iraq has become a net importer of food and the economic sanctions and the reaction of the regime have exacerbated the distress caused by the situation. However, the regime of Saddam Hussein is still securely in power, though the plight of the people has been seriously affected by the recent wars and their aftermath.

Hussein has remained in power largely because his military and security mechanisms have remained effective, and despite the hard-line policy of the United States and Great Britain, the regime has overcome every crisis. In October 1995, Saddam Hussein easily won a referendum giving him a further seven-year term of office. However, the situation in Iraq in 2000 was one where UN sanctions are still in force and the disarmament resolutions of the UN Security Council have still not been fully met. Concerns are also mounting about the effects that the sanctions are having on the ordinary Iraqi people, particularly the lack of food and medicine and increasing death rates among children.

IRAQ-IRAN WAR (1980-1988). This war between Iraq and Iran (qq.v.), sometimes known as the First Gulf War, started as a week-long clash in a disputed border region in the central sector, with Baghdad claiming a victory on 10 September 1980. Immediately afterwards President Saddam Hussein (q.v.) abrogated the 1975 Iraq-Iran Treaty of International Boundaries and Neighborliness (Algiers Accord) and reclaimed the part of the Shatt al-Arab waterway ceded to Iran by the treaty. On 22 September, Iraq invaded Iran at eight points on the border and bombed military installations and economic targets. The end result was to be the largest conventional war of the twentieth century, with some 194,900 Iranian dead and Iraqi fatalities of 160,000-240,000.

The conflict can be divided into eight distinct phases from September 1980 to August 1988, with periods of stalemate, periods of attrition, missile attacks on cities by both sides, and conflict in the Arabian Gulf with attacks on oil tankers. At the beginning of the war Iraq had captured a significant amount of Iranian territory, but a wet winter resulted in a military stalemate, and despite strenuous efforts by the United Nations and the Organization of the Islamic Conference (qq.v.) no resolution was forthcoming.

In terms of impact on the region, the fifth phase of the war between April 1984 and January 1986 was significant, as all of the action took place in the air or in the Arabian Gulf. Iraq escalated attacks on Iranian oil tankers using French exocet missiles and increased its air raids on the Kharg oil terminal, which was a major outlet for Iran's exports. Iran retaliated by attacking Kuwaiti and Saudi ships in the Gulf on the grounds that both countries were providing financial and logistical aid to Iraq. In March 1985, Iran eventually managed to reach the Basra-Baghdad highway but was unable to hold the position in the face of Iraqi counterattacks. Iraq continued to intensify its attacks on Iranian shipping and on the Kharg oil terminal and, by the end of the year, had hit 33 ships in the Gulf, to Iran's 14.

The next phase of the war, from February 1986 to January 1988, was marked by United States intervention on the side of Iraq, with provision of covert U.S. expertise and intelligence data that allowed Iraq to make more effective use of its air force. In April 1986, Kuwait and Saudi Arabia (qq.v.) flooded the oil market, causing the price of oil to drop from $27 a barrel to $10 a barrel, and this had a severe impact on the income of the two combatants. Iraq, however, was cushioned by $10-$14 billion of aid from the Gulf States, the West, and the Soviet Union. In 1986, the shipping war in the Gulf intensified, with Iraq hitting 86 ships and Iran 47. On the ground, Iran came within 11 kilometers of Basra in January 1987, but could not take the city. In the north, in company with Kurdish allies, it succeeded in capturing part of Iraqi Kurdistan.

On 20 July 1987, the UN Security Council passed Resolution 598 (q.v.), which called for a cease-fire and a withdrawal of forces to international boundaries. The resolution also included a commitment to the setting up of an international commission to determine responsibility for the war, a major demand of Iran.

However, on 24 July a Kuwaiti supertanker in a U.S. Navy-escorted convoy hit a mine believed to have been laid by Iran, resulting in a major Western naval buildup in the Gulf with 60 American, British, and French warships being stationed in the region. Washington also took the decision to assist Kuwait with the reflagging of its tanker fleet through a U.S.-based company in order to safeguard Western oil supplies. In October 1987, the U.S. Navy sank three Iranian patrol boats near Farsi Island, after claiming that they had fired on a U.S. helicopter, and also destroyed two Iranian offshore oil installations in the Lower Gulf in retaliation for an Iranian attack on a reflagged Kuwaiti supertanker.

In February 1988, Iraq introduced long-range surface-to-surface missiles into the conflict and launched attacks on Teheran, demoralizing the civilian population. Iran retaliated by hitting Baghdad, which was much closer to the international border. Iraq also began to regain lost territories as it recaptured the Fao Peninsula between 16-18 April through the use of chemical weapons. Chemical weapons were also used by Iraq between 23 and 25 May in the central and northern sectors, primarily against the Kurdish insurgents, and then in the southern sector retaking Shalamche. Iraq also used poison gas between 19 and 25 June to recapture Mehran in the central sector, before retaking the Majnoon Islands in the south. The U.S. Navy was active in blowing up two Iranian oil rigs, sinking an Iranian frigate, severely damaging another, and sinking an Iranian missile boat.

Despite launching a major offensive, Iraq failed to take Iranian territory, as advances in the northern, central, and southern sectors showed limited success, except in the north, but reversed by Iran in the following week. In the Lower Gulf on 3 July 1988, a U.S. cruiser shot down an Iranian airbus with 200 passengers, having mistaken it for a combat aircraft. By 18 July, Iran had unconditionally accepted UN Security Council Resolution 598 as being in the interests of the Iranian revolution. However, it was not until 20 August that a UN-supervised truce came into effect.

In addition to the human costs, it is estimated that Iran spent $74 to 91 billion, plus military imports of $11.26 billion, while Iraq spent $91 to $112 billion, plus military imports of $41.94 billion. These figures were estimated by the Stockholm International Peace Research Institute, but in July 1990 Iraq's deputy premier, Tariq Aziz, put Iraq's military imports at $102 billion. Neither state lost much land and the regimes did not change in either nation. The war enabled Ayatollah Khomeini (q.v.) to consolidate his position and that of the Iranian Revolution, while Iraq, with over a million men under arms, emerged as the most powerful country in the region. Once the truce was in effect, Iraq agreed to abide by the 1975 Iran-Iraq Treaty of International Boundaries and Neighborliness, to withdraw its forces from occupied Iranian territory, and to exchange prisoners of war. However, relations between the Gulf Cooperation Council (GCC) states and Iran remained strained due to their support for Iraq and gifts and loans to Iraq by GCC states was also to cause problems in the immediate aftermath of the war. *See also* **Gulf War; Kurds**

IRREDENTISM. The Arab and Islamic states have been beset by various territorial disputes, which extend beyond mere border disputes (q.v.). Some of these are of long-standing origin and, in some cases, had remained dormant for years but have been reactivated due to the presence of valuable mineral resources.

In the Arabian Gulf, Iran (q.v.) has historically laid claim to

Bahrain (q.v.) and the Arabian Gulf islands of Abu Musa and Tunbs, largely because of the presence of offshore hydrocarbon reserves. The question of hydrocarbon reserves has also been a factor in disputes between all of the states on both sides of the Arabian Gulf with regard to continental shelf boundaries between the states. A further major territorial claim is that by Iraq over Kuwait (qq.v.), which dates back to the Ottoman Empire (q.v.) but was reactivated by Iraq in 1958, 1961, and in 1990 when Kuwait was invaded by Iraq and formally annexed.

Syria (q.v.) has also not totally abandoned her dream of establishing Greater Syria (q.v.), which also has its origins in the Ottoman Empire and has recently been rekindled by its interventions in Lebanon, particularly since the 1976 Lebanese Civil War. Egypt (q.v.) has also laid claim to territory in Sudan. This claim stems from the Anglo-Egyptian Agreement of 1899, and was reactivated by Egypt prior to Sudanese independence in 1955 through support of the Nationalist Party, which was thought to favor union with Egypt, in the Sudanese elections. However, on becoming prime minister, Ismail al-Azhari made it clear that he favored Sudanese independence. For Egypt the two main issues with regard to Sudan were access to the waters of the Nile and possible use of the underpopulated area of Sudan to absorb part of the growing Egyptian population.

In North Africa, the Libyan regime under Colonel Muammar al-Qaddafi (q.v.) revived territorial claims to part of Chad, having initially supported the Front de Libération Nationale du Tchad (FROLINAT) in its rebellion against the Chad government. In 1973, Libya occupied the mineral-rich Aozou strip in northern Chad to exploit its resources, basing its claim on a territorial agreement reached between Italy and the French Vichy government during World War II. Mediation was attempted by the Organization of African Unity (OAU) (q.v.), but this failed and Libya continued to be involved in the internal affairs of Chad. The OAU and France became instrumental in protecting Chad, and although agreement was reached in 1984 between Libya and France for the withdrawal of troops, it became clear that Libya had left some 5,000 troops in the Aozou strip.

Morocco has also been involved in various territorial disputes including one dispute over the Spanish enclave of Ceuta dating back to 1860. A dispute that has yet to be resolved is the Moroccan claim to the previous Spanish territory of Western Sahara (q.v.). Initially, the claim to the territory was a joint claim with Mauritania, but the latter withdrew its claim in 1979 after making peace with the Saharawi government in exile. At present, the whole area is under Moroccan control watched over by the United Nations Mission for the Referendum in Western Sahara (MINURSO) (q.v.) whose mandate is to determine whether the territory should unite with Morocco or become independent. However, the Saharawi government in exile has been recognized by a number of states and has been given a seat at the OAU.

ISLAM. Islam is one of the three important monotheistic religions, along with Judaism and Christianity, both of which influenced Islam. Islam was founded by the Prophet Muhammad (A.D. 570-632), who was born in Mecca (q.v.) and its followers are called *Muslims*. The scripture of Islam is the Quran, which is the Word of Allah as revealed to the Prophet Muhammad who was the last of the messengers from Allah to mankind, beginning with Adam and including Abraham, Moses, and Jesus. The next text important to Muslims is the *Sunna* (q.v.) (custom), which is the collected words and deeds of the Prophet. The Quran and the *Sunna* were later codified as the *Hadith* (q.v.), which came together to form the *Sharia* (q.v.) (Islamic Law) and covering all aspects of religious, social, and political life, including administration of the state and the conduct of war.

The term *Islam* means submission or peace and Muslims are those who surrender to God's law. All followers of Islam are part of a worldwide faith community, or *umma* (q.v.) and, as a result, believers have both a corporate religious identity and a duty to obey and implement God's will in personal and social life.

The spread of Islam was not instant, as the Prophet only had limited success and was subjected to a great deal of persecution from the beginning of his mission in A.D. 610 to A.D. 622. In A.D. 622, Muhammad and two hundred of his followers emigrated to Medina, in present-day Saudi Arabia (q.v.), and established an Islamic community, thus giving the Islamic movement a political form. Muhammad became prophet-head of a religio-political community and consolidated his leadership in Medina, subdued Mecca, and subsequently consolidated Muslim rule over the remainder of Arabia through diplomatic and military means and conversion.

The message of Islam was formulated in the formative centuries of classical Islam, providing a way of life whose duties were delineated by Islamic law and thus emphasizes practice more than belief. As a result, law, rather than theology, is the central religious discipline and locus for defining the path of Islam and preserving its way of life. The *Sharia* and its system of Islamic courts and judges is a comprehensive law which encompasses a Muslim's duties to God and society, including regulations governing prayer and fasting, family, and penal and international law. The sources of law are identified as the Quran, the *Sunna*, *ijma* (q.v.), or community consensus, and reason, based on rules derived from the Quran and *Sunna* by analogy.

The Muslim community is united in their common belief through God, the Quran, and the Prophet Muhammad, and the five pillars of Islam provide a unity of practice amidst the rich diversity of the various Islamic communities. The pillars are the five obligatory practices that all Muslims must follow: Profession of Faith which affirms Islam's monotheism and acceptance of Muhammad as the messenger of God; Worship or Prayer which involves the call to prayer five times a day, facing the holy city of Islam; Almsgiving or *zakat* (q.v.), which is a religious tithe based on accumulated wealth and assets; Fasting once a year for the month of Ramadan with abstention from food, drink, and sex from dawn to dusk by all healthy Muslims; Pilgrimage or *hajj* (q.v.), being the obligation of every adult Muslims who is healthy and financially able to make the pilgrimage to Mecca at least once in his or her lifetime.

Although it has no official status, jihad (q.v.) is often referred to as the sixth pillar of Islam and means to strive or struggle in the way of God, to lead a virtuous life and to spread the Islamic community through preaching, education, and example. However, it also includes the struggle for the defense of Islam, or holy war, which is not supposed to include aggressive warfare but this has occurred since the activities of the *khariji* (q.v.) in the early days of Islam through to contemporary groups such as Hamas (q.v.).

The early days of Islam and the period of the first four caliphs of Islam, the Four Rightly Guided Caliphs (632-661), is regarded by Sunni (q.v.) Muslims as the best of times and often used when the community needs guidance and inspiration. It was during this period that the spread of Islam and the conquest of Arabia was completed and Islamic rule extended throughout the greater part of the Middle East and North Africa. The Umayyad Caliphate in Damascus (661-750) and the Abbasid Caliphate in Baghdad (749-1258) saw the consolidation of Muslim power, the expansion of the Islamic Empire, and the development and flourishing of Islamic civilization. The Eastern Byzantine and Sassanian (Persian) Empires were overrun and the rule of Islam spread, with inhabitants of the conquered territories offered conversion to Islam, "protected" status if they were "People of the Book" (i.e., Jews or Christians), or combat or execution for those who rejected or resisted Muslim rule.

Islam was also spread by merchants, traders, and mystics who carried the message of Islam from Africa to Southeast Asia and from Central Asia to Spain, Portugal, and southern Italy. However, after the destruction of the Abbasid Empire by the Mongols in 1258, the Islamic world consisted of a number of local states or sultanates. The most powerful of these were the Ottoman Empire (q.v.) covering Turkey, most of the Arab world and Eastern Europe; the Safavid Empire in Persia; and the Mogul Empire in the Indian subcontinent. Although the Arab world is regarded as the heartland of Islam, the majority of Muslims are to be found in Africa and Asia, and Islam has grown significantly in many parts of Europe and the United States. Muslims constitute a majority in more than 48 countries and a significant minority in many others. There are an estimated 800 million Muslims around the world.

After the death of Muhammad the argument over the succession led to a split in the Muslim community resulting in two major divisions, the Sunni who represent about 85 percent of the world's Muslims and the Shi'i (q.v.) who constitute about 15 percent of the total, though there are some other minority sects such as the Ibadhi and the Alawis (qq.v.). The Sunni believed that Muhammad died without naming a successor. Thus, the political leader would be elected by the elders of the community. The Shi'i minority believed that the senior male of the Prophet's family, his son-in-law and cousin, Ali ibn Abi Talib, had been designated to lead the community. As a result the Shi'i believe that the Imam (q.v.) of the Muslim community must be a descendant of the family of the Prophet. The struggle for the succession resulted in the death of Hussein, the son of Ali, and he became a martyr to Shi'i Muslims whose death is ritually commemorated by the community.

The institutions of leadership represent the fundamental difference between Sunni and Shi'i Islam. In Shi'i Islam, the Imam is not just the political successor of the Prophet Muhammad but the religio-political leader of the community, and regarded by the community as religiously inspired, perfect, and sinless. Sunni Islam placed religious authority for interpreting Islam in the *ijma* of the *ulama* who represented the collective judgment of the community.

From the eighteenth to the twentieth centuries the Islamic world witnessed a protracted period of upheaval and renewal. Muslims struggled with the failure of their societies, the impact of European colonialism, superpower rivalry between the Soviet Union and the United States, and responding to the intellectual and moral challenges of a changing world. In the nineteenth century, a series of revivalist movements rose up, including the Wahhabi (q.v.) in Saudi Arabia, all of which were motivated by a conviction that the decline of Muslim fortunes could only be cured by a purification of their societies and way of life by a return to pristine Islam. In the late nineteenth and early twentieth centuries, modernist Islamic movements responded to the challenge of Western hegemony, wishing to bridge the gap between their Islamic heritage and modernity. Such intellectuals as Jamal al-Din al-Afghani (q.v.) sought to restore Islamic pride, emphasizing the compatibility of Islam with reason, science, and technology but arguing for the need to reinterpret Islam in the light of challenges and pressures brought about by modern life.

The modernism movements were primarily the reserve of an intellectual elite, as they failed to produce a systematic reinterpretation of Islam or organizations capable of propagating the message. This led to the emergence of Islamic organizations such as the Muslim Brotherhood in Egypt (qq.v.) which criticized the secular elites for emulating the West and modernists for trying to Westernize Islam. In their view, Islam was a totally comprehensive way of life and their objective was to establish effective organizations to implement an Islamic system of government and law through social and political action.

Following World War II, most of the Muslim world regained its independence, though many of the newly emerging states, including Iraq, Jordan, Lebanon, Syria (qq.v.), and Pakistan had been carved out by European colonial powers, which resulted in states with artificial or arbitrarily drawn boundaries and appointed rulers. Problems of nation-building were compounded by political legitimacy and national identity and unity. Turkey had become a secular state and Saudi Arabia became a self-declared Islamic state, but the majority combined Western ideas with a minimal recognition of the role of Islam because they were dominated by Western-oriented elites. As the West provided the models for development, the expectation was that modernization and development would lead to progressive Westernization and secularism. But this assumption was shattered by the Islamic revolution (1979-1980) in Iran raising the fear of the spread of a Khomeini (q.v.) style militant Islam.

The revival of Islam and the growth of Islamic fundamentalism (q.v.) were often the result of an appeal to religion for legitimacy and to mobilize popular support. Islamic organizations have constituted the leading opposition parties in Algeria (q.v.), Egypt, Morocco, Tunisia, the West Bank, Gaza Strip, Indonesia, and Malaysia. Islam has also been a significant factor in nationalist struggles and resistance movements in several states or regions, including Afghanistan (q.v.), Lebanon, Kashmir, and the Muslim republics of Soviet Central Asia. In some cases, movements have participated within the system such as the Muslim Brotherhood in Jordan, while others such as Hizbullah (q.v.) in Lebanon have used violence and terrorism in their attempts to destabilize and overthrow prevailing political systems. Radical movements operate on the assumptions that Islam and the West are locked in an ongoing battle and that Islam is a theological and political imperative with implementation an obligation incumbent on all true Muslims.

Islam has also generated organizations to cater for its specific needs in ordinary fields of human activity. In the political arena, this is represented by organizations such as the Arab League (AL) and the Organization of the Islamic Conference (OIC) (qq.v.), which are unifying factors at a political level, with each of these organizations generating others to deal with specific matters, such as the Arab League Educational, Scientific, and Cultural Organization (ALECSO) (q.v.) and OIC involvement in the Islamic Universities in Malaysia, Niger, and Uganda (qq.v.). In cultural fields, Islamic interests have led to the creation of organizations, such as ALECSO and the Islamic Educational, Scientific, and Cultural Organization (qq.v.), the latter being a specialized institution of the OIC.

In the banking, finance, and economic sectors, organizations have been set up at either the regional or international level to further the well-being of the Islamic community and, in some cases, to impose Islamic principles on areas of operation. In terms of economy and trade, this is illustrated by the Islamic Chamber of Commerce (ICC) and by the Organization of Arab Petroleum Exporting Countries (OAPEC) (qq.v.) which, in addition to its role in the world oil market, also has economic and political ramifications. The banking and financial sectors are of significance in terms of Islam due to the growth in importance of Islamic banking (q.v.) and the establishment of organizations such as the Islamic Development Bank (IDB) and the International Association of Islamic Banks (IAIB) which serve Muslim communities and operate on Islamic principles which forbid usury.

A further area of financial operations is the aid sector, designed to assist the developing world but with an emphasis on serving Muslim communities. In regional terms, this aspect is represented by the Arab Bank for Economic Development in Africa (q.v.) and by the aid organizations set up by Arab oil-producing states: Abu Dhabi Fund for Arab Economic Development (ADFAED), Arab Fund for Economic and Social Development (AFESD), Arab Monetary Fund (AMF), Kuwait Fund for Arab Economic Development (KFAED), and the Saudi Development Fund (SDF) (qq.v.), all of whom have broadened their operations to Muslim communities outside of the Arab world.

The concept of the Muslim world as a single community has also led to the creation of a number of organizations in a variety of fields to visibly demonstrate this vision of a single community. Identity links are illustrated by the Arab Women's Solidarity Association (AWSA), International Muslimah Artists Network (IMAN), Muslim World League (MWL), and the World Muslim Congress (WMC) (qq.v.). In a different area, this also finds expression through charitable and relief projects targeting the Muslim community through organizations such as the Aga Khan Foundation (AKF), the Association of Islamic Charitable Projects (AICP), International Islamic Relief Organization (IIRO), Islamic Committee for the International Red Crescent (ICIRC), and Islamic African Relief Agency (IARA) (qq.v.).

A large number of other organizations exist in the Muslim world to link together professions, trades, services, or common interests such as the Organization of Islamic Capitals and Cities (OICC) (q.v.) charged with preserving Islamic heritage and architecture. Groups of like-minded organizations are represented by the Federation of Islamic Organizations in Europe (FIOE), International Islamic Federation of Student Organizations, and the International Islamic Organization (IIO) (qq.v.). *See also* **Alawis; Banna, Hassan al-; Fatwa; Fiqh; Hamas; Hanafi Code; Hanbali Code; Ibadhis; Ikhwan; Islamic Call Society; Islamic Jihad; Islamic Thought Foundation; Jami'at –e Islami; Maliki Code; Muslim Women's League; Pan-Islamism; Popular Pan-Arab Islamic Conference; Shafii Code; Twelver Shias; Ulama; Zaidis**

ISLAMIC ACADEMY OF SCIENCES (IAS). The Islamic Academy of Sciences was founded in April 1987 and is based in Amman, Jordan (q.v.). The membership in June 1999 consisted of 71 Fellows from 25 different countries representing a variety of scientific disciplines.

The IAS is governed by a General Assembly, which meets annually to determine the future activities of the academy and to deal with administrative and financial issues. The program determined by the General Assembly is directed and managed by an 11-member Executive Council which is elected by the assembly for a four-year period and meets twice a year. The Secretariat of the IAS is based in Amman and is the executive arm of the academy responsible for the institutional infrastructure and implementation of the agreed action plans. The academy also has five standing committees, which were formed to generate programs and comprise: Science and Technology Policy Committee, Science and Technology Manpower Committee, National Resources Development Committee, High Technology Development Committee, and Environment and Development Committee.

The objectives of the IAS are to serve as a consultative organization of the member states of the Organization of the Islamic Conference (OIC) (q.v.) on matters related to science and technology. It is also designed to initiate scientific and technological programs and to encourage cooperation among research groups in the various Islamic countries on projects of common interest. The IAS is also charged with the promotion of research into major problems of importance for Islamic countries and to identify future technologies of relevance for possible utilization. The academy is also responsible for the formulation of standards of scientific performance and attainment and to encourage, through awards and prizes, centers of excellence in all science and technology disciplines.

The IAS also organizes a series of conferences on relevant issues, with the 1999 Teheran conference dealing with "Science Education and Technology Management for Development in the Islamic World." The academy also maintains close links with a number of institutions, among which are the Arab League Educational, Cultural, and Scientific Organization (ALECSO), the Islamic Development Bank (IDB) (qq.v.), and a number of national scientific organizations.

ISLAMIC AFRICAN RELIEF AGENCY (IARA). The agency was established in 1984 with its headquarters in Columbia, Missouri. It began purely as an emergency relief agency but developed into a sustainable development agency with the objective of guiding recipients to fulfill their own needs. Among projects supported by the IARA are flood relief in Bangladesh, displacement assistance in Kosovo and Sudan, rehabilitation programs in Bosnia, and war relief in Iraq (q.v.).

The IARA depends almost entirely on donations from individuals and targets aid to the provision of education and support for self-sustaining projects largely operated by local nongovernmental organizations (NGOs) and local development. The IIRA operates a Child Health and Education Program in several countries, including Afghanistan (q.v.) and Pakistan, and a Child Survival Project in Mali in partnership with the United States Agency for International Development.

ISLAMIC ASSEMBLY OF NORTH AMERICA (IANA). The assembly was formed in June 1993 by a group of like-minded individuals representing a number of Islamic centers within the United States and Canada. The headquarters of the IANA are at Ann Arbor, Michigan, with a regional office at Austin, Texas, and a Canadian office in Montreal. The objectives of the IANA are to:

- unify and coordinate the effects of different *dawah* (missionary) oriented organizations in North America
- spread the correct knowledge of Islam and assist in its dissemination among Muslim Americans and immigrants
- widen the horizons and understanding among Muslims concerning different Islamic contemporary issues
- observe and analyze current events in the Muslim world and assist Muslim Americans to understand the events and their implications
- assist oppressed and tyrannized scholars, Islamic workers, and Muslim masses in any locality
- produce a serious and effective media institute to serve the Islamic presence in North America
- create a program to serve Muslim youth and their needs and concerns in Western society and to protect the Islamic presence in North America
- create programs and institutions that will serve the needs of English-speaking Muslims in North America

The IANA seeks to achieve these goals through holding conventions, general meetings, the founding of like-minded institutions, and promotion of publications of an Islamic nature in both Arabic and English. It is also the intention of the IANA to mount a series of programs aimed at Muslim youth and investment projects to ensure ongoing development.

ISLAMIC ASSOCIATION FOR PALESTINE (IAP). The Islamic Association for Palestine was founded in 1981, has its headquarters in Dallas, Texas, and is a not-for-profit, public awareness and educational organization dedicated to advancing a just and comprehensive solution to the cause of Palestine (q.v.) and the Palestinians.

The IAP's main objectives are to:

- keep Palestine and its people free and justly ruled
- educate people about the Palestinian issue and promote a real peace based on freedom and democracy for all residents
- act as a coordinating force to rally efforts in the United States to

achieve a true solution to the Palestinian problem and to expose the dangers of the unconditional American aid to Israel (q.v.)

* sustain the Palestinian American community of refugees and immigrants

The IAP has grown into the largest Muslim, Arab, and Palestinian grassroots organization dedicated to the cause of Palestine and has regional and local offices throughout the United States. The organization has a national Board of Directors, an Executive Committee, and regional and local committees.

ISLAMIC BANKING. This form of banking has grown in Muslim countries, particularly those where the legal system is based on the *Sharia* (q.v.), and is related to the fact that the Quran forbids usury. There are three devices used by Islamic banks to circumvent this problem. *Muraabaha* is a device whereby a commodity is sold by contract with an agreement to buy it back at a later date at a premium, which is equal to the agreed interest. *Mudaaraba*, which means sleeping partner, involves a sleeping partner financing an active partner with any resulting profits being shared, the percentage split reflecting the financing provided by the sleeping partner. *Mushaaraka* involves a depositor being treated as a partner in the bank and sharing any profits or losses made by the bank. The system is used by a number of national banks in the Arab world and also by the Islamic Development Bank (q.v.).

ISLAMIC CALL SOCIETY (ICS). The ICS was founded in Libya (q.v.) in 1972 and is entrusted with the task of missionary activity. The Libyan Revolutionary Command Council (RCC) under Muammar al-Qaddafi (q.v.) had always defined the revolution as an Islamic revolution and founded the ICS as a means of achieving this aim within Libya and in other states. As part of the ICS statute concerned with the preparation of teachers and missionaries, the Faculty of the Islamic Call was established as a faculty within the ICS. The faculty began instruction in 1974/75 with a four-year period of study leading to the Islamic Mission License, with further study leading to a Ph.D. in Islamic Call. The majority of the ICS students come from Asia and Africa.

The ICS is directed by the Administrative Council, consisting of a minimum of five members, which plans and oversees all ICS activities, and elects a general secretary from within its membership. The general secretary is the external representative of the ICS. The final part of the infrastructure is the general assembly, which meets annually to evaluate the work of the Administrative Council. Funding for the ICS comes from the state, largely through the Jihad (q.v.) Fund which was set up in 1972, and the organization is exempt from all taxes and duties, has no restrictions on the transfers of capital, and can work with any organization if it assists the spread of Islam (q.v.). The ICS also has the right to fund branches in other countries, and one was established in Paola, Malta, with links to the Islamic World Studies Center and the journal *The Future of the Islamic World.*

In August 1982 the Second Conference for Islamic Mission held in Tripoli led to the formation of the World Council of Islamic Call (WCIC) with 36 members under the chairmanship of the general secretary of the ICS. It meets annually and members are elected every four years at the Conference for Islamic Mission. The WCIC is concerned with the international impact of the work of the ICS but also propagates Qaddafi's version of Islam as an arm of Libya's foreign policy. The ICS also oversees an organization of Muslims known as the World Islamic Call Society through a series of regional councils in the Caribbean, West Africa, Central and East Africa, and South Asia, in an attempt to tie Muslims to Libya and to counter the activities of the Saudi-funded Muslim World League (q.v.).

The ICS sends out missionaries and provides medical relief and financial aid to Muslim communities, but its success has been limited despite immense expenditure and there has been some concern expressed at the inefficiency of the organization. Part of its lack of success may be attributed to its adherence to the Qaddafi version of Islam, which is based solely on the Quran and rejects the *Hadith*, the *Sunna* (q.v.), and the four legal schools. The 1972 law establishing the ICS had the use of peaceful means as a basic tenet, but this was removed from the 1980 revision, largely due to confrontation with Saudi Arabia (q.v.), leading Qaddafi to call for a jihad to liberate the holy cities of Mecca (q.v.) and Medina. The ICS has limited activities within Libya, though it does organize Quranic recitation contests, produce new editions of the Quran, and undertake missionary work among non-Muslim workers in Libya.

The ICS has a publication program of missionary books and leaflets such as *How to Be a Muslim, How to Pray,* and three periodicals: *Al-dawah-al-Islamiyah* (weekly from 1980-1992 with English and French sections); *Risalat al-jihad* (monthly from 1982-1992 with occasional English and French editions); and *Majallat Rulliyat al-dawah al-Islamiyah* (annual since 1984/85 produced by the Faculty of the Islamic Call).

ISLAMIC CENTER FOR THE DEVELOPMENT OF TRADE (ICDT). The Organization of the Islamic Conference (OIC) (q.v.) determined at the Second Islamic Summit Conference held in Lahore, Pakistan, in February 1974 to develop economic and commercial cooperation among member states, and to create a number of subsidiary organs and institutions to achieve these objectives. The ICDT was founded in 1981 but the center did not begin operations until November 1982.

The ICDT was set up to:

- carry out research and studies concerning development of trade among member states
- contribute to the dissemination of commercial information and data between member states
- hold trade fairs and exhibitions to promote products of member states
- promote contacts between businessmen in member states involved in intra-community trade and organize meetings and seminars
- organize seminars, symposiums, and training courses for participants from member states
- help member states to set up organizations and associations for trade promotion, or strengthen existing bodies
- encourage exchange of ideas and experience for the promotion of intra-community trade
- offer advice to member states regarding commercial policies to be applied to promote intra-community trade
- pursue all other objectives that would permit the center to attain its objectives

The Islamic Commission for Economic, Social, and Cultural Affairs, which meets annually, acts as the General Assembly for the ICDT and is attended by all member states. It is responsible for preparing reports and recommendations for submission to the Council of Foreign Ministers, which meets under the auspices of the OIC.

The Board of Directors is responsible for the operation of the center and comprises nine members. Eight of the members are elected for three years and may be reelected once. The ninth member is a permanent member from the host country, Morocco. The OIC secretary-general and the director-general of the center are ex-officio members. The Board of Directors meets at least once a year and elects a chairman from among its members for a three-year period. The director-general is the chief executive of the center and responsible for the realization of its objectives.

The program of the ICDT is in five main areas:

- *information and documentation*—a documentary department has been established together with a Trade Information Network consisting of a number of relevant data banks fed by member states to ensure availability of up-to-date data
- *studies and research*—studies on inter-Islamic trade, foreign trade regulations analysis, and market and product studies
- *trade promotion* through the holding of Islamic Trade Fairs and liaison with trade promotion centers of member states
- *publication program*—designed to further trade information dissemination
- *training programs*—provision of training for commercial attachés of member states, training for trainers, economic advisors and experts from trade organizations, and private economic operators from member states.

Its publications include *Tijaris: International and Inter-Islamic Trade Magazine* (quarterly) and the annual *Inter-Islamic Trade Report.*

ISLAMIC CHAMBER OF COMMERCE (ICC). The ICC is an organ of the Organization of the Islamic Conference (OIC) (q.v.) and is composed of federations, unions, and national chambers of commerce in 46 countries, all of which are members of the OIC. The ICC is comprised of a General Assembly, an Executive Committee, a General Secretariat, a president, and six vice presidents representing the geographical distribution of the membership. The organization began operations in 1977 with its headquarters in Karachi, Pakistan, and is funded on a formula based on per capita income. The organization maintains offices in Pakistan, Morocco, Senegal, Syria (q.v.), Bangladesh, and Kuwait (q.v.). The ICC exists to promote: trade industry and agriculture throughout the Muslim world; preferential terms of trade for members; cooperation in finance, banking, insurance, and communications; arbitration of industrial and commercial disputes; fairs and joint showrooms, exhibits, seminars, lectures, and publicity campaigns; and the eventual establishment of an Islamic economic community.

ISLAMIC COMMITTEE FOR THE INTERNATIONAL RED CRESCENT (ICIRC). The ICIRC is affiliated to the Conference of the Islamic Organization (q.v.), founded in 1979, and based in Jeddah,

Saudi Arabia (q.v.). The objective of the ICIC is the alleviation of suffering caused by natural disasters and war. It is allied to the Red Crescent Society, which is a member of the International Red Cross and Red Crescent movement and is represented on the Standing Commission of the Federation, which promotes harmony in the work of the movement and examines matters of concern to the movement as a whole. The Standing Commission meets twice a year with representation from the international movement, the Red Cross and Red Crescent societies, and five members of national societies elected at the International Conference which meets every four or five years.

ISLAMIC CORPORATION FOR THE INSURANCE OF INVESTMENT AND EXPORT CREDIT. The corporation is based in Jeddah, Saudi Arabia (q.v.), and was established in 1994 by the Organization of the Islamic Conference (OIC) (q.v.). It aims to promote the flow of trade and investments among OIC member states through the provision of export credit and investment insurance services.

ISLAMIC DEVELOPMENT BANK (IDB). The IDB was established as an outcome of a meeting of finance ministers of members of the Organization of the Islamic Conference (q.v.) held in December 1973, with the bank formally opening in October 1975. The main objective of the IDB is to encourage economic development and social progress in member countries in accordance with the principles of Islamic *Sharia.*

The IDB is run by a Board of Governors, with a representative of each of the 44 member states, which meets annually as the Supreme Authority of the Bank. The general operations of the bank are controlled by the Board of Executive Directors, who are elected for three-year terms. The Board consists of 10 members, four of whom are appointed by the four largest subscribers to the capital of the bank, and the remainder elected by the Governors to represent the other member states.

In terms of its activities, the IDB adheres to Islamic law which forbids usury and does not grant loans or credit for interest. As an alternative the bank provided interest-free loans, with a service fee, mainly for infrastructure projects, which are targeted at long-term socio-economic development. Among the other activities are: provision of technical assistance through feasibility studies, equity participation in industrial and agro-industrial projects, leasing operations involving equipment such as ships, and profit-sharing operations.

Any funds not immediately needed for project finance are used to finance foreign trade, particularly for the importation of raw materials, with priority being given to trade between member states. The Bank also maintains a Special Assistance Account to provide emergency assistance, where appropriate, and to fund education in Islamic communities of non-member countries. The Bank also maintains an Islamic Research and Training Institute in Jeddah to research into the transformation of banking activity to conform with *Sharia* law, and to act as a training center for staff involved in development projects in the bank's member states. *See also* **Islamic Banking**

ISLAMIC EDUCATIONAL, SCIENTIFIC, AND CULTURAL ORGANIZATION (ISESCO). ISESCO was founded in 1982 as a specialized institution of the Organization of the Islamic Conference (q.v.) and works in association with the United Nations Educational, Scientific, and Cultural Organization (UNESCO). It publishes *ISESCO Newsletter* (quarterly), *Islam Today* (twice a year), and *ISESCO Triennial*.

ISLAMIC FOUNDATION FOR SCIENCE, TECHNOLOGY, AND DEVELOPMENT (IFSTAD). This is a subsidiary organization of the Organization of the Islamic Conference (OIC) (q.v.), which was founded in May 1979 and is based in Jeddah, Saudi Arabia (q.v.). Its aims are to: promote scientific and technological research and its applications in the Muslim world; encourage Islamic cooperation and coordination in the field; ensure integration of science and technology by Muslim states into their socio-economic plans and objectives; and provide advisory services and undertake scientific studies.

ISLAMIC FUNDAMENTALISM. Islamic fundamentalism is primarily the effort to define the fundamentals of Islam (q.v.), to adhere to them, and to protect the purity of Islamic precepts against non-Islamic influences. Behind the fundamentalist movements is a revival or renewed interest in Islam coupled with a drive to purify the religion in order to release its inner force. In the Middle Ages, the aim of purification was primarily to rid Islam of superstition and thus it was an internal process. However, modern fundamentalism is designed not only to remove historical scholastic additions but also to rid Islam of all ideas imbibed from the West. In terms of defining a state as fundamentalist the basic test is whether its legislation is derived solely from *Sharia* (q.v.), or Islamic law.

The modern form of Islamic fundamentalism which appeared at the beginning of the twentieth century was a reaction against modernist movements that were trying to Westernize the Muslim world, and a resistance movement to colonial influences, particularly those of Great Britain and France. However, Islamic fundamentalism was not a single force, as two differing approaches were followed. The reformist tendency, which was in a minority, advocated a return to the original model of Islamic society, with the *Sharia* being regarded as a system of universal reference but being interpreted and adapted to the realities of modern life. The conservative fundamentalist tendency advocates going back to the roots of Islam, with interpretation of the *Sharia* being rejected and with the belief that Islamic law should be applied literally to all fields of life.

All Islamic fundamentalist movements have the common objective of creating an Islamic state, but they differ in views on the strategies, structures, and socio-political organization of the resultant state. The moderate movements are opposed to violent action and are prepared to participate in a political dialogue to achieve their aims. Moderates consider that the Islamization of a society will lead to the creation of an Islamic state and education and teaching are highly valued as vehicles for achieving these aims. Among the moderate movements are the Muslim Brotherhood in Egypt (qq.v.) and other Arab states and the Front Islamique de Salut (FIS) in Algeria (qq.v.).

The radical Islamic fundamentalist movements believe that the Islamic state must be achieved through a top-down process and, if necessary, through violent action. These movements are not prepared to wait for the process of Islamization to evolve and reject compromise or political dialogue with existing regimes. Among the radical movements are the fundamentalists in Iran (q.v.), Islamic Jihad (q.v.), found in a number of Arab countries, and the Taleban in Afghanistan (q.v.).

In the Arab world Islamic fundamentalism has developed at different periods of time with the Wahhabi (q.v.) movement of the eighteenth century, the Muslim Brotherhood in the early twentieth century, and the Front Islamique de Salut (FIS), Hamas, and Hizbullah (qq.v.) in the 1970s and 1980s. However, the Iranian Revolution of 1979 and the war in Afghanistan have played an important role in spreading Islamic fundamentalism. The Iranian Revolution of Ayatollah Khomeini (q.v.) succeeded in transforming a secular state into a religious state and provided a model for other states to follow, as evidenced by Afghanistan.

Islamic fundamentalism has been perceived as a threat by some policy-makers in the West who see incompatibilities between the

West's secular, democratic tradition and that inherent in Islam and its political philosophies. This view was reinforced by the Iranian Revolution of 1979, the assassination of President Anwar Sadat (q.v.) in 1981, and the World Trade Center bombing in 1993. However, some scholars consider this to be a misconception based on a view of Islam in the Muslim world seen solely through violence and terrorism, without an understanding of the breadth and depth of contemporary Islam, whereas such developments are being more properly regarded as Islamic revivalism or Islamic activism as these have roots within the Islamic tradition.

ISLAMIC HUMAN RIGHTS COMMISSION (IHRC). The Commission was set up in 1997 as an umbrella organization for a variety of projects relating to Muslims and their rights both in the United Kingdom and abroad, and is based in London, England. The aims of the IHRC are to:

- champion the rights and duties revealed for human beings
- promote a new social and international order, based on truth, justice, righteousness, and generosity, rather than selfish interest
- demand virtue and oppose wrongdoing in the exercise of power from whatever base that power derives
- gather information about, and publicize, atrocities, oppression, discrimination, and other abuses of divinely granted rights
- campaign for redress and support the victims of such crimes
- campaign to bring the perpetrators and their accomplices to justice
- cooperate with other groups and individuals where such cooperation is likely to further the achievement of these aims

The work of the IHRC includes submitting reports to governments and international organizations, writing articles, monitoring the media, cataloging war crimes, producing research papers, and taking on cases of discrimination. Among the areas in which the IHRC is operating are Bosnia, Chechnya, China, Lebanon (q.v.), Turkey (q.v.), and the United Kingdom.

ISLAMIC INSTITUTE OF TECHNOLOGY (IIT). The IIT is a subsidiary organ of the Organization of the Islamic Conference (OIC) (q.v.), which was founded in 1981 and is based in Dhaka, Bangladesh. The IIT was established to develop human resources in OIC member states, with particular reference to engineering technology, technical and vocational education, and allied research. It offers four-year degree courses, a three-year higher diploma, a one-year master's degree, postgraduate courses, short courses, and seminars. The institute has a staff of 281, 11,000 students, and a library of 18,000 volumes. Publications include an annual *News Bulletin*, reports, and a human resources development series.

ISLAMIC JIHAD. The Islamic Jihad is a fundamentalist organization which can be found in a number of Muslim countries and is a militant movement, often having broken away from more moderate fundamentalist groups. However, the agenda of each group varies according to the socio-political conditions in the country in which it is based. In Lebanon (q.v.), the Islamic Jihad is a pro-Iranian group which was involved in hostage-taking, the bombing of the United States Embassy, the bombing of United States marines at Beirut airport, and the destruction of the Israeli military headquarters at Tyre. However, the rise of Hizbullah (q.v.) within Shi'i (q.v.) life led to a decreasing influence for Islamic Jihad. In Palestine (q.v.), Islamic Jihad grew out of dissatisfaction with the Muslim Brotherhood (q.v.) and became the militant wing of the struggle against Israel (q.v.). It was a major force behind the *intifada*. Islamic Jihad has followed a policy of violent attacks against Israeli targets in the West Bank and Gaza Strip, and has come into conflict with the Palestinian Authority in relation to the peace process. Other Jihad organizations are to be found in Egypt, Lebanon, and Palestine (qq.v.), and are growing in number in the Muslim world, but there is not necessarily coordination between the various groups.

ISLAMIC LAW. *See* **SHARIA**

ISLAMIC RELIEF. Islamic Relief is an international relief and development organization that was founded in 1984 in Birmingham, England, as an initial response to the famines in Ethiopia and Somalia. The objectives of the organization are: to reduce poverty and its causes by promoting greater community development in poor rural and urban areas, to encourage income-generating capabilities and community self-help for long-term sustainability in areas of health, education training, and skills; to provide emergency aid at times of crisis; and to give assistance to those in need.

Islamic Relief is controlled by a Board of Trustees who develop and authorize the strategic objectives and decisions that are implemented under the remit of the Executive Committee and the chief executive. Day-to-day management is in the hands of the Executive Committee, which is charged with ensuring that the directives are carried out in an effective and efficient manner. The organization works with other nongovernmental organizations (NGO), has consultative status with the Economic and Social Council of the United Nations (q.v.), and is a member of the International Islamic Committee for Relief. Islamic Relief also has offices throughout Western Europe and the United States of America, where most of its funds are raised.

Projects are being undertaken in 22 countries of the world in Africa, Asia, and Europe, either under the direct control of Islamic Relief or through partner organizations. Islamic Relief is heavily involved in water and sanitation projects, working in Afghanistan (q.v.), Bangladesh, Pakistan, and Sudan. In Afghanistan, the organization has dug wells in the north to provide water for Tajik refugees and supports Water Aid for Afghanistan, which specializes in the provision of clean water for the country.

Allied to the water and sanitation projects are those concerned with health care and nutrition, with projects targeted at malnutrition in Bosnia-Herzegovina and Sudan. Outpatient clinics providing general services, such as vaccinations, have been established in Albania, Bangladesh, and Sudan, with special projects being formed to deal with disabilities. Education is another crucial area for assistance with support being offered for schools in Albania, Azerbaijan, Bangladesh, Chechnya, and Sudan. Adult illiteracy is also targeted by the organization and it also supports existing facilities through the provision of school kits and books.

In order to equip individuals with the skills necessary to obtain employment Islamic Relief has a program of vocational education covering computer skills training, typing courses, sewing projects, food processing, and women's training centers. Vocational education projects are currently running in Sudan, Albania, and Bosnia-Herzegovina. An allied program is that designed to produce income generation so that the poor can be weaned away from reliance on relief. Two livestock projects are currently in operation in Sudan and Albania with a view to providing sustenance for families and products that can be sold to generate income. In Bangladesh, a Community Action Program has been established which aims to initiate income-generating activities through the founding of local savings and credit schemes, which, backed by Islamic Relief support, can be used to purchase tools, equipment, etc.

ISLAMIC RESEARCH AND TRAINING INSTITUTE. *See* **ISLAMIC DEVELOPMENT BANK**

ISLAMIC RESEARCH FOUNDATION (IRF). The foundation was established in February 1991 and is based at Mumbai, India. Its objectives are to promote the proper understanding and clarification of Islam and to remove misconceptions about Islam from among less aware Muslims and non-Muslims. The IRF utilizes modern technology to spread its message, using the Internet and telecasts on satellite and cable television, and public debates at its headquarters and other venues in the Muslim world.

ISLAMIC SOLIDARITY FUND (ISF). The ISF is a subsidiary organ of the Organization of the Islamic Conference (q.v.), founded in 1974 and based in Jeddah, Saudi Arabia (q.v.). The objectives of the ISF are to assist Islamic communities through the provision of emergency aid and finance to build mosques, Islamic centers, hospitals, schools, and universities.

ISLAMIC THOUGHT FOUNDATION. The foundation was established in 1984 and was initially known as the Foundation of Islamic Thought. The foundation is based in Tehran, Iran (q.v.), and has a membership of individuals dedicated to the spread of the knowledge of Islam (q.v.). Its main publications are *Altahira* (in Arabic), *Le Message de l'Islam* (in French), *Mahjuba* (in Farsi), *Message of the Revolution* (in English), *Nedai e Islamis* (in Urdu), *Sauti Ya Umma* (in Swahili), and *Sawtaluahda al Islamiyya* (in Arabic), all of which appear monthly.

ISLAMIC UNIVERSITY IN UGANDA (IUU). The IUU is a subsidiary organ of the Organization of the Islamic Conference (q.v.), which provides the bulk of its funding. It was founded in 1988 and based in Mbale, Uganda. The IUU was established to meet the educational needs of Muslims in English-speaking Africa and has faculties of Arts and Social Sciences, Education, Islamic Heritage, Management Studies, and Science. The IUU also aims to promote and enhance the civilization and scientific influence of Islam and to promote culture and science among African peoples. The university programs are designed to enable African countries to assimilate science and technology, to acquire scientific and technological know-how, and to use it in the best interests of African countries and their peoples. In addition to its degree programs, IIU has a Vocational Training Center open to all members of the public, with programs in carpentry, metal work, tailoring, and typing.

ISLAMIC UNIVERSITY OF NIGER (IUN). The IUN was founded in 1984 and is based in Niamey, Niger. The university provides courses in *Sharia* (q.v.) (Islamic law), Arabic language and literature, pedagogy, and teacher training. Funding is provided by the Islamic Solidarity Fund (q.v.) and contributions from the Organization of the Islamic Conference (q.v.) member states, of which the IUN is a subsidiary organ.

ISLAMIC WORLD STUDIES CENTER. *See* **ISLAMIC CALL SOCIETY**

ISMAILIS. The Ismailis are an Islamic sect that is part of Shi'i (q.v.) Islam, and are distinguished from other sects by the number of revered figures that they regard as Imams (q.v.). The first six are shared with the Twelver Shi'i (q.v.) but the seventh Imam revered by the Ismailis was Ismail, the older militant son of al Sadiq, who died in A.D. 762 before his father. This caused a rift between the Shi'i as not all accepted as Imam Ismail's younger brother, Abdullah Ibn Jaafar, who died without a son. Ismailis are also known as Seveners because of its symbolism as the total of spatial directions and, in the case of Imams, the ending of a cycle. An Ismaili group set up the Fatimid dynasty based in Cairo in A.D. 969, which rivalled the Abbasids based in Baghdad, ruling until A.D. 1171. In the present-day Middle East, Ismailis are to be found in Iran, Syria, and Yemen (qq.v.). The sect is one of the smallest of the Muslim sects and has been subject to persecution, particularly in Iran (q.v.).

ISRAEL. The State of Israel came into being on 14 May 1948 at the end of the British mandate (q.v.) and was immediately at war with its Arab neighbors. At the end of the war in January 1949, Israel had acquired 21 percent more land than that envisaged under the United Nations (q.v.) plans for a partitioned state. This initial period of hostilities has conditioned Israel's relationships with the front-line Arab states of Egypt, Jordan, Lebanon, and Syria (qq.v.) and the rest of the Arab world to the present day. For the Arab states, opposition to the existence of the State of Israel and Zionism has often been the main unifying factor in their relationships.

In terms of military conflict, each major confrontation has always resulted in victory for Israel for a variety of reasons associated with Israel's unity of purpose (with survival of the state at risk), its more efficient intelligence services, and the lack of cohesion and strategic planning among its enemies. However, in recent years some reverses have been experienced, especially following the June 1982 invasion of Lebanon (q.v.) and over the *intifada* in the Occupied Territories.

The relationship between Israel and its Arab neighbors has always been affected by superpower rivalry in the region, with United States support for Israel being countered by Soviet Union support, at various times, for Egypt, Syria, and Iraq (q.v.). At times support from the Soviet Union has been manipulated by the Arab recipients to match their own agenda, which was not always in sympathy with superpower objectives. U.S. support for Israel has been largely because of the efforts of the Jewish lobby in America, but also because Israel has been seen as a staunch democratic ally in a complex region with ever-changing alliances and (latterly) a perceived threat from Islamic fundamentalism (q.v.).

Instability in the region has also been engendered to by Israel's military successes beginning with the 1948-1949 Arab-Israeli War and the avowed intention of all Israeli governments to secure territorial security as the prime foreign policy objective. The first period of instability was caused by the mass exodus of Palestinian Arabs as a result of the fighting, with just under one million being forced into, or choosing, exile. This figure had increased by 335,000 after the 1967 Arab-Israeli War and the acquisition of the West Bank by Israel. The refugee problem placed great strains on the economy of the recipient states, particularly Jordan (q.v.), and by 1970 actually threatened the political stability of the kingdom.

Over the years Israel has attempted to deal with Arab states on an individual basis, but to no avail until 1978, due to the significance of the Palestinian question to the Arab world, which meant that no frontline state would deal separately with Israel. Despite strong support for Israel, which has never wavered despite some criticism on specific issues, the U.S. has also tried to push the peace process forward in order to pursue a wider regional agenda. The first real success of this policy was the 1978 signing of the Camp David Accords (q.v.) between Egypt and Israel, which was followed by the signing of a peace treaty in 1979. However, no further peace treaties were entered into until 1994 when peace was concluded with Jordan.

Negotiations between Israel and the Palestinians over a peaceful settlement of the Palestinian question have always foundered. However, following the failure of the Middle East Peace Conference (q.v.) held in 1991 at Madrid, Israel and the Palestinians entered into secret negotiations in Oslo, mediated by Norwegian government officials. An agreement was reached on 9 September 1993 with the signing of the Oslo

Accords. This was followed on 13 September 1993 by the signing of a Declaration of Principles by both sides in Washington, D.C.

This allowed for five-year Palestinian limited autonomy in the West Bank and Gaza, starting with Jericho and the Gaza Strip. This was to be followed by further withdrawals from the Israeli-occupied West Bank and a transfer of power to the Palestinian National Authority (PNA). A second agreement was signed on 28 September 1995, known as *Oslo II*, which provided for Israel's further withdrawal from less than 30 percent of the West Bank, but important aspects such as the status of Jerusalem and Jewish settlements were deferred under these agreements.

Negotiations were scheduled to take place between 1995 and 1999 but were beset by the assassination of Yitzhak Rabin, the election of a Likud government, and the establishment of further Israeli settlements. Negotiations were reopened following the general election and the new government of Prime Minister Ehud Barak, with a further 7 percent of the West Bank being handed over to the PNA in December 1999.

Relations with Syria have always been bitter and the seizure by Israel of the Golan Heights in the 1973 Arab-Israeli War has made negotiations between both sides difficult, as neither has been prepared to compromise on this issue. The relationship between Israel and Lebanon (q.v.), particularly the Christian community, has also strained relations due to Syria's military intervention in Lebanese affairs. Israel's invasion of Lebanon in June 1982 and the setting up of a security zone in southern Lebanon in alliance with the Christian Southern Lebanese Army had also prevented progress over peace negotiations with Syria. Israel's reputation was also marred by the attacks on the Sabra and Shatilla refugee camps in Beirut by Christian militia, attacks that many felt could have been prevented by the Israeli military. Israel's venture into Lebanon has not been without cost due to the activities of Hizbullah (q.v.), which has inflicted casualties within southern Lebanon and in Israel and is implacably opposed to any peace deal. Israel withdrew from the security zone in southern Lebanon, completing the move on 24 May 2000, and the southern Lebanese Army collapsed, allowing Hizbullah to move in to fill the vacuum.

The United Nations (q.v.) was heavily involved in the relationship between Israel and the Arab world before Israel's creation in 1948 through various proposals designed to replace the British mandate, and since the first Arab-Israeli War of 1948-1949 the organization has been used by both sides to try to resolve disputes or to assign blame for specific actions. This is evidenced by the number of resolutions relating to the subject, and, in terms of Palestine (q.v.), the UN even has an entire division of its Secretariat devoted exclusively to the promotion of the rights of Palestinians.

The main involvement of the UN on the ground has been the provision of various peacekeeping forces to police cease-fires on the borders between Israel and the front-line states and these have been in being since the creation of Israel, with varying mandates and for varying lengths of time. Among the various operations have been: United Nations Emergency Force I (q.v.) following the 1956 war; United Nations Emergency Force II (q.v.) following the 1973 war; United Nations Truce Supervision Organization (q.v.) following the 1948-1949 war; and various specific observer missions including the United Nations Disengagement Observer Force (q.v.).

In 2000, negotiations are still going on with the Palestinians over full implementation of the Oslo Accords, with problems over further Israeli withdrawals from the West Bank and failure over the drafting of a framework for a permanent peace. The crisis in negotiations has also been fuelled by the Palestinian National Authority (PNA) declaring 13 September 2000 as the deadline for a permanent peace with Israel as it planned to declare statehood by that date. Negotiations with Syria have also stalled over the question of the Golan Heights and on 7 March 2000 the Prime Minister of Israel, Ehud Barak, expressed doubt as to whether Israel could resolve its differences with Syria. This aspect of negotiations was further complicated by Israel's declared intention to withdraw from southern Lebanon in July, which was seen by Syria as a ploy to split Lebanon and Syria. The withdrawal was in fact accelerated by Israel and completed by May 2000.

J

JAMI'AT –E ISLAMI. The Jami'at –e Islami, or Islamic Society, began in Kabul in 1971 and was conceived as a group whose objective was to fight the increasing secular and leftist trends in Afghanistan (q.v.). In 1975, the party headquarters moved to Peshawar, Pakistan, and the organization became both a political movement and a guerrilla resistance organization dedicated to the overthrow of the Marxist Afghan government. In 1978, Burhanuddin Rabbani became its leader. The party advocated the establishment of an Islamic state and strict adherence to the *Sharia* (q.v.), and has links with other international movements, including the Muslim Brotherhood (q.v.). During the guerrilla war, the movement was part of the Islamic coalition and considered to be one of the most moderate. The following of the party is largely from northern Afghanistan.

Among its commanders are Ahmad Shah Mas'ud (q.v.) who commands the Panjshir valley north of Kabul and Ismail Khan who controls the Heart province. In 1992, the party returned to Kabul with other coalition members to take over the government; in 1993, Rabbani became President of Afghanistan in a rotating presidency, but he refused to leave office when his term expired in June 1994. This resulted in further internal disputes and conflicts with other groups, leading to bitter fighting largely centered on northwestern Afghanistan.

JERUSALEM. The city of Jerusalem is located on the West Bank of the Jordan (q.v.) and Arab East Jerusalem is currently annexed by Israel (q.v.); the city has also been declared the capital of Israel. The city is Islam's (q.v.) third most holy city after Mecca (q.v.) and Medina because of its association with pre-Islamic prophets and because Muhammad is reputed to have made the "Night Journey" there. Jerusalem houses the magnificent Islamic shrine, the Dome of the Rock (A.D. 688-91), built by the Caliph 'Abd al-Malik, and the famous al-Masjid al-Aqsa Mosque which was damaged in an arson attack in August 1969. Jerusalem is also sacred to Christians and Jews.

JIHAD. The term literally means effort, or struggle, which is waged in various forms with war being the most extreme. Historically Muslims have used the term to describe an armed struggle against unbelievers in order to advance Islam (q.v.), or in order to counter any danger to Islam. The concept of religious war against unbelievers is contained within the Quran but should only be launched after unbelievers have turned down the offer to embrace Islam, or to become non-believers (*dhimmis*) who live in a Muslim state and accept Muslim rule. In a country with a Muslim minority, a jihad is only permissible if the Muslims are being oppressed. The use of jihad to declare a holy war has been invoked at various times, particularly in World War I and in conflicts between the Arabs and Israelis.

JOINT DEFENSE AND ECONOMIC COOPERATION TREATY (JDECT). The treaty was concluded between the seven members of the Arab League (AL) (q.v.) in 1950, following the failure of the Arab armies in the 1948-49 Arab-Israeli War, and was aimed primarily at Israel (q.v.). An early decision under the treaty was to continue the wartime blockade against Israel on the premise that the January 1949 truce did not constitute peace. It is a basic requirement that any new member of the AL has to join the JDECT.

In the Arab-Israeli wars of 1967 and 1973, the combatant Arab states called for, and received, military aid from other members of the AL under the terms of the JDECT. Iraq (q.v.) tried to invoke the treaty in May 1982 during the Iraq-Iran War (q.v.), but this failed, partly because the enemy was not Israel, but also because some members of the AL, Libya and Syria (qq.v.), had sided with Iran (q.v.).

JORDAN. The area now known as the Hashemite Kingdom of Jordan became Muslim after A.D. 636, following the success of the Arab army against the Byzantine forces at the Battle of Yarmouk. The area was subsequently controlled by the Umayyad and Abbasid Caliphates followed by a short period of Seljuk rule, before becoming part of the Latin Kingdom of the Crusaders in 1099. The Crusaders were replaced by Saladin in 1187 before coming under the Ottoman Empire (q.v.), and Jordan remained under Ottoman rule for a period of four centuries.

The area known as *Transjordan*, which was to the east of the river Jordan, was part of the Vilayet of Damascus and under the Ottoman Empire was a relative backwater. Under the 1916 Sykes-Picot Agreement, Transjordan was included as part of the sphere of British influence. From the San Remo Conference of 1920 on, the area of Syria (q.v.) was mandated to France, while Palestine (q.v.) was mandated to Great Britain, under the League of Nations (q.v.). In December 1920, the two powers agreed to include Transjordan within the Palestine mandate and in April 1921, Abdullah, brother of Faisal, was recognized as de facto ruler of Transjordan.

In July 1922, the League of Nations allowed Britain latitude in its administration of the area east of the River Jordan and, on 15 May 1923, Britain formally recognized Transjordan as independent under Emir Abdullah. The new regime was totally under British control and reliant on British subsidies for its existence. The force of the Arab Legion formed by Peake Pasha and subsequently commanded by Glubb Pasha was used to bring order to the rural areas and to secure the allegiance of the Bedouins to the new state. A further degree of independence came with a new treaty in 1928, but Great Britain retained control over financial policy and foreign policy was subject to the advice of the British Resident based in Amman.

World War II delayed further moves toward independence, but it was finally accorded to Transjordan by the Treaty of London on 22 March 1946. Emir Abdullah was crowned king on 25 May 1946, and a new constitution was approved and the state renamed Jordan. Britain retained a special relationship with Jordan, part of which allowed a military presence to be maintained in the kingdom because of continuing close British ties, the treaty underwent cosmetic changes in 1948, as the United States and the Soviet Union had withheld recognition following the terms of the 1946 treaty.

In 1948, Jordan took part in the Arab-Israeli War and the army fought with distinction, especially in the defense of East Jerusalem. At the end of the war, the Jordanian army was left in control of most of east Palestine accorded to the Arabs by the United Nations (q.v.) partition agreement. The area was known as the *West Bank* and formally incorporated into Jordan in April 1950. However, the annexation of the West Bank and the overall Israeli success in the war led to an influx of some 400,000 Palestinian refugees into Jordan, resulting in severe economic problems for the new state. The situation led to the formation of the United Nations Relief and Works Agency for Palestinian Refugees (UNRWA) (q.v.) in 1949 to provide for their needs by mounting a large operation in Jordan and the Gaza Strip.

The 1948 war had political ramifications for Jordan because a patriarchal regime was no longer workable in the changed circumstances. New tensions within the kingdom led to the assassination of King Abdullah on the steps of the al-Aqsa Mosque in Jerusalem (q.v.) on 20 July 1951. His successor King Talal had a short reign as he stepped down due to mental illness, to be succeeded by King Hussein (q.v.) in 1952. A new constitution had been drafted which allowed for cabinet government to be accountable to parliament, which comprised a 40-man chamber elected by the people and a 20-man senate appointed by the king. Although more democratic, the king still retained a great deal of power as he could choose and dismiss the prime minister at will.

The population of Jordan was radically altered by the 1948 war, being formed of Transjordanians and Palestinians, with the former comprising those who resided in the east Jordan region prior to the war. It is estimated that Jordan absorbed 100,000 Palestinians in 1948 and a further 310,000 after the 1967 Arab-Israeli War. In addition, there are significant minority populations of Circassians and Chechens who came to Jordan in the nineteenth century.

The majority of the population, both Transjordanian and Palestinian, are Sunni (q.v.) Muslims, while the Chechens are Shi'i (q.v.) Muslims, and small groups of Druze live in the north of the country. About 6 percent of the population are Christian, with the largest group being Greek Orthodox, the second largest Greek Catholics, and small numbers of Roman Catholics, Protestants, and Syrian Orthodox.

The first four decades of King Hussein's rule were marked by periods of civil disorder, which threatened the future of the regime. A major source of discontent and a blow to Hussein's prestige was the failure of the regime to secure popular support for entry into the Baghdad Pact (q.v.) in 1955. The widespread demonstrations against this proposal led to Hussein having to back down from the decision to join the pact. Political unrest was fostered by the nationalist regimes in Egypt and Syria (qq.v.) and from the West Bank in response to Israeli raids on the territory.

In 1956 Hussein responded to these pressures by dismissing his Chief of Staff, General Glubb, and by allowing free elections which returned a radical parliament. The king also appointed a pan-Arab Nationalist Prime Minister, Suleiman Nabulsi, from the Nationalist Socialist Party. Nabulsi's main achievement was to negotiate the end of the Anglo-Jordanian Treaty of 1948. The problem was not resolved as a power struggle ensued between the monarch and his radical government. In 1957, Nabulsi was dismissed by Hussein, a clampdown was imposed on political activity, and the regime turned to the United States for support. The U.S. replaced Britain as the chief source of foreign aid. A further period of instability followed the assassination in 1958 of King Faisal II of Iraq (q.v.), Hussein's cousin, and, in 1963, evidence of a further coup was discovered and put down. The latter part of the decade was a period of stability for the regime and a more secure power base for the king.

Further damage to the regime resulted from the 1967 Arab-Israeli War, in which Jordan played an active role in concert with Egypt and Syria. The Arabs suffered a crushing defeat and Jordan lost the whole of the West Bank and Arab Jerusalem (q.v.); this dominated Jordanian foreign policy for the next two decades. It was not until July 1988 that the hopes to regain sovereignty over the West Bank were abandoned and Jordan formally severed its administrative and legal links with the West Bank. However, the 1967 defeat was to bring further instability to Jordan due to its swelling Palestinian population and the militancy against Israel (q.v.). The Palestine Liberation Organization (PLO) (q.v.) saw the 1967 defeat as evidence that it had to take charge of its own destiny, adopting radical policies and forming commando units to mount raids against Israel, many of them from Jordan. The Palestinian guerrillas became so powerful within Jordan that they began to challenge the authority of the state. King Hussein was forced to take action ordering the Jordanian army to move against the PLO, and most of the leadership fled to Lebanon after a brief, but bloody, struggle in September 1970.

Jordan did not participate in the 1973 Arab-Israeli War, as it was conscious of Israel's military prowess and because King Hussein had come to believe that a durable peace settlement could only be secured through negotiation. However, Jordan did send some troops and equipment to Syria as a gesture of Arab unity. As a result, the defeat of the Arabs did not have such a major impact on Jordan as had the 1967 war. At the Arab Summit in Rabat (q.v.) in 1974, Hussein recognized the PLO as the sole representative of the Palestinians but still maintained his claim to the West Bank as occupied Jordanian territory. However, Hussein prorogued the parliament with its West Bank representatives and only restored its legislative functions in 1984.

The Rabat decision in regard to the PLO resulted in a rise in Jordanian nationalism, maintaining that Jordan should be for the Jordanians. Nationalists on the East Bank began to demand a greater share of government appointments and the period to the mid-1980s saw Jordanians gaining a greater share of posts in the bureaucracy and government services. It was not until 1979 that there was a rapprochement between Yasser Arafat (q.v.) and Hussein with Arafat making several trips to Amman.

King Hussein's position in the 1980s became increasingly secure as he enjoyed support from the bulk of the Jordanian population regardless of their ethnic origin. The king still wielded considerable power within the kingdom and that rule is largely patriarchal but with a relatively careful observance of the constitution. Parliament had emerged as a significant debating chamber and a watchdog over government policy, being particularly concerned over issues of corruption and civil rights. The 1984 elections to replace members who had died since the last elections and the West Bank seats was a success for the Islamic fundamentalists (q.v.), and a failure for the leftists and pan-Arab parties (q.v.).

Jordanian foreign policy has been largely dominated by the question of Palestine (q.v.) and relations with the other front-line states. Relations with Egypt were severed in 1978 over the Camp David Accords (q.v.), and not restored until 1983. Relations with Syria had improved by 1985 but were still problematic and subject to sudden change. In the Iraq-Iran War (q.v.), Syria was a supporter of Iran (q.v.) while Jordan supported Iraq and allowed Aqaba to be used as a supply route for goods and war supplies in return for Iraqi loans. Another major regional ally has been Saudi Arabia (q.v.), which has supported Jordan through grant aid, discounted oil supplies, and loans from Saudi banks and government agencies. Also of significance are the remittances from Jordanian workers in the oil-producing states of the Arabian Gulf.

In the wider arena, Jordan is formally a nonaligned state but has always retained strong relations with the West and has extremely close ties with Britain and close political relations with the U.S. Links have also been forged with the European Union, which now maintains a liaison office in Amman. Britain and France have been major suppliers of military aid; although Jordan had also bought some arms from the Soviet Union, this was not significant and was more a gesture to indicate independence and nonalignment. However, Jordan had always maintained civil relations with the Eastern bloc in recent years because of its influences within Syria, until the demise of the Soviet Union, which has lessened this influence.

Following Saddam Hussein's (q.v.) invasion of Kuwait (q.v.) in August 1990, King Hussein struggled to find an Arab solution to the problem but failed. Jordan's stance during the ensuing Gulf War (q.v.) was pro-Iraqi and this was forcibly expressed by the population. However, after the war Jordan distanced itself from Iraq and tried to repair damaged relations with the West. At the Madrid Middle East Peace Conference (q.v.) in July 1991, King Hussein had agreed to a joint Jordanian-Palestinian delegation and on 26 October 1994 Jordan concluded a separate peace treaty with Israel.

In 1995, King Hussein had been receiving treatment for cancer in the United States and became involved in trying to keep the Palestinian-Israeli peace accords on track. Although initially successful, these accords were put on hold by the calling of a general election in Israel. On 25 January 1999, King Hussein announced that his son Abdullah was to become Crown Prince, and his successor. Hussein returned to the U.S. for further treatment, which was unsuccessful, and he returned to Jordan where he died on 7 February. He was succeeded by his son who became King Abdullah II. The new king's youngest brother, Prince Hamza, was named as crown prince.

K

KHALIFA, AL- DYNASTY. *See* **BAHRAIN**

KHARIJI. The term means *sector* in Arabic and is applied to an Islamic sect that emerged in A.D. 658. The sect arose out of a battle and subsequent arbitration over the succession to the Caliphate between Ali ibn Abu Talib and Muawiya ibn Suffian. The arbitration ruled against Ali, and several hundred dissenters and deserters from Ali's army left Siffin on the banks of the Euphrates and went to a nearby village. It was at this point that they became known as the Khawariji (plural of Khariji). In July 658, Ali attacked and defeated the Khawariji, but enough survived to continue the movement and to seek revenge, with Ali being assassinated by a Khariji in January of A.D. 661. A moderate school of the movement known as *Ibadhis* (q.v.) is the prominent sect in Oman today.

KHARTOUM ARAB SUMMIT. This was a meeting between leaders of 12 Arab states and the United Arab Republic (q.v.), held from 29 August to 3 September 1967, to agree on a response to Israel's (q.v.) occupation of Arab lands after the 1967 war. The summit agreed that Arab states would not recognize, negotiate with, or make peace with Israel. The summit also promised continued support to the Palestinians and Arab countries affected by Israel's occupation. This support was primarily financial with Saudi Arabia, Kuwait, and Libya (qq.v.) donating $400 million in aid to Jordan and the United Arab Republic (qq.v.). The Arab leaders also agreed to end the oil embargo on the United States and Great Britain for their support of Israel and agreed that oil production should be used solely to strengthen the Arab economies, especially those hit by the Arab-Israeli conflict. The summit also agreed to try to resolve inter-Arab strife, and Egypt and Saudi Arabia agreed to work toward an end to civil conflict in Yemen (q.v.). *See also* **Palestine**

KHOMEINI, AYATOLLAH RUHOLLAH AL-MUSAIWI (1902-1989). Khomeini was the leader of the Iranian Revolution in 1979. He came from an extremely religious family, studied jurisprudence, and was firmly opposed to the rule of the Shah. Khomeini's main criticism was directed against economic conditions and the influence of foreign powers in Iran, particularly the United States. In 1963, he was arrested by the authorities and imprisoned, but was released following protests from the people and the clerics. On his release, he ordered his supporters to boycott the 1963 elections. Again, he was arrested, being exiled to Turkey (q.v.) in 1964. Khomeini then moved to Iraq (q.v.) and later to Paris from where he continued to mobilize opposition to the Shah. His teachings against the regime were taped and smuggled into Iran for use at Friday prayers and for distribution among the people. Khomeini was supported by the masses, being viewed as an honest and moral leader who was dedicated to helping the farmers and the urban poor. This active opposition led to an Islamic revival which culminated in the 1978-1979 Iranian Revolution, the overthrow of the Shah, and the founding of an Islamic state led by Khomeini until his death in 1989.

KING FAISAL FOUNDATION (KFF). The KFF is a philanthropic organization established by the eight sons of King Faisal ibn Abdul Aziz al-Saud (q.v.), in recognition of the major role that he had played in the civic and cultural life of the kingdom. The KFF is intended to promote, both domestically and abroad, all the charitable endeavors that the late king had sought to accomplish: assisting fellow Muslims; expanding Islamic missionary activity; and fostering solidarity among Muslim states.

The foundation has three distinct entities: the King Faisal Center for Research and Islamic Studies; the King Faisal International Prize; and the King Faisal Foundation General Secretariat. The Center for Research has a library of some 70,000 books, 2,000 periodicals in 16 languages, and some 11,000 manuscripts. It also houses a children's library with some 15,000 books in Arabic, English, and French. The automated search services of the center provide students and researchers, free of charge, with full bibliographies on any topic related to the Arab world and Islam (q.v.).

The King Faisal International Prize is valued at $93,000 and is awarded annually to international figures, whose contributions are generally recognized, in five main areas: services to Islam, Islamic studies, Arabic literature, medicine, and science. The prize began in 1979 and an average of six scholars have won this award every year.

The KFF also finances philanthropic projects in Islamic states run by nongovernmental organizations, especially schools, hospitals, and orphanages. Any KFF finance is independent of any finance provided to the recipient nations by the Saudi government. The only requirements are that the recipient bodies must conform to the *Sunna* (q.v.), and that the fund be run on sound business principles. Students and scholars from anywhere in the Muslim world are also encouraged to pursue medical and engineering studies in advanced industrial countries, with most scholarships, open to men and women, going to non-Saudi nationals.

The KFF General Secretariat is divided into an investment section and a programs and research section with work coordinated by a steering committee. The foundation has some $350 million in assets, including: shopping malls in Riyadh, Abha, and Khanus Mushayrt; a five-star international hotel; a supermarket; a modern boarding school; a portfolio of bonds, stocks, and shares; and joint business ventures. Earnings from these investments are used to finance projects in the Muslim world accounting for about 50 percent of expenditure. Twenty-five percent is spent on administration, and 25 percent is placed in reserve to maintain existing facilities.

KURDS. The Kurds are members of an ethnic group who are descendants of Indo-European tribes which appear in the early histories of the early empires of Mesopotamia, tracing their history as mountain people to the seventh century B.C. The Kurds inhabit the Zagros and Taurus Mountains of southeastern Turkey, northwestern Iran, northern Iraq, and adjacent areas in Syria (qq.v.). In the seventh century A.D., the Kurds embraced Islam (q.v.), but retained their distinctive culture, and adopted the Sunni (q.v.) form of Islam.

Over the centuries, there were periodic Kurdish uprisings against the central powers of the Persian and Ottoman Empires (q.v.), but modern Kurdish nationalism emerged at the end of the nineteenth century. The Treaty of Sévres in 1920, resolving the future of the Ottoman Empire in the Middle East, specified that there should be an autonomous Kurdistan but this was not ratified. The Treaty of Lausanne in 1923 made no mention of the proposal, so Kurdish aspirations remained unfulfilled.

The position of the Kurdish communities has always been dependent upon the countries in which they are resident and there has often been dissent and conflict within the Kurdish communities themselves.
Kurds in Iran:
The Kurds account for about 9 percent of the population; they are predominant in Iranian Kurdistan, and are a substantial community in the provinces of West Azerbaijan, Kerman, and Ilam. The Kurds are represented politically by the Kurdish Democratic Party (KDP) which was established in 1945 when the Kurdish region of Iran was under Soviet occupation. The KDP demanded autonomy for the Kurds within Iran and founded the State of the Republic of Kurdistan, with Qazi Muhammad as president, but it only lasted a year, being overthrown by Reza Shah Pahlavi following the withdrawal of Soviet forces in May 1946. The KDP was then forced to become an underground movement.

In the early 1970s there was a revival of some armed resistance to the Shah and the KDP, now renamed the Kurdish Democratic Party of Iran (KDPI), began to flex its muscles. However, the situation was complicated by the fact that the Shah had been arming Kurds in Iraq in their conflict with Saddam Hussein (q.v.) but the Algiers Accord of 1975 with Iraq ended this aid. The KDPI took part in the revolutionary movement of 1977-1978 when the local Revolutionary Komitech (composed of followers of Sheikh Izz al-Din Husseini, a Sunni religious leader, and KDPI members) seized power in the northern region.

After the revolution in Iran the central government of Ayatollah Khomeini (q.v.) tried to establish control in the Kurdish areas and came into conflict with the KDPI. The Congress of the KDPI in April 1980 demanded the use of Kurdish in schools, offices, and courts, and the redrawing of provincial borders, so that the Kurds were resident in one province. However, negotiations with Tehran broke down and fighting broke out between the two sides. The situation changed again with the Iraqi invasion in September 1980, which led to an upsurge of national sentiment and the temporary suppression of ethnic differences. The KDPI backed President Abol Hassan Bani-Sadr in his confrontation with Khomeini in July 1981, and lost, later joining the Komala in the Natural Resistance Council headed by Bani Sadr and Masud Rajavi.

As the Iraq-Iran War (q.v.) progressed the KDPI began to side with Iraq. Its leader, Abdul Rahman Qasimlou, tried to reconcile Iraq and the Iraqi Kurds, managing to get Baghdad and the Patriotic Union of Kurdistan to begin negotiations, but the talks collapsed in 1985. After the end of the Iraq-Iran War, Jabal Talabani brokered a meeting between Qasimlov and Iranian officials in Vienna, but Qasimlov was assassinated, allegedly by Iranian agents. However, the KDPI with its 10,000 militia withstood the event.

Kurds in Iraq:

The Kurds in Iraq account for 19 percent of the total population and are mainly resident in the northern part of the country. The Kurdish problem for Iraq was largely created by the amalgamation by Great Britain in 1925 of the predominantly Kurdish province of Mosul with Baghdad and Basra to create the modern state. The Mosul province became even more significant in 1927 when the British-dominated Iraqi Petroleum Company discovered oil.

During World War II, the Kurdish leader Mustafa Barzani (q.v.), led a failed revolution against the Baghdad government, which was put down with British support. Following the failure, Barzani fled to Iran and later to the Soviet Union. He returned to Iraq in 1958 following the coup and the establishment of the republic. In return for Barzani's support, the Baghdad government legalized the Kurdish Democratic Party (KDP) and promulgated a constitution that recognized the Kurds as an integral part of the nation. In response, Barzani put forward a plan for Kurdish autonomy, but Baghdad rejected this, and fighting broke out in September 1961.

Fighting concluded in June 1966 when an agreement with Baghdad granted official recognition of the Kurdish language and proportional representation for the Kurds in the civil service. However, the agreement failed to end the mutual distrust between the two sides and fighting broke out again in March 1969, though by this time the Baghdad regime was in the hands of the Ba'ath Party (q.v.). This spell of fighting lasted a year and a further accord was reached between the two sides, which was to be implemented over a four-year period. The July 1970 constitution recognized the Kurds as one of two nationalities in Iraq, and the Kurdish language as one of the two languages in the region, but again the agreement failed to hold.

In March 1974, the Baghdad government imposed the Kurdish autonomy law, including the appointment of a Kurd, Taha Muhyi al Din Maruf, a diplomat, as vice president of the republic, the formation of the Kurdish Autonomous Region (KAR) consisting of the provinces of Dohak, Irbil, and Sulemaniya, and the establishment of a largely nominated Kurdish Legislative Council. All of this was undertaken without the support of the KDP and fighting erupted yet again. On this occasion, the KDP had the backing of the Shah of Iran, as he wanted to weaken the pro-Moscow regime in Baghdad. At one stage the KDP controlled a third of the KAR and 45,000 guerrillas were holding down 80,000 Iraqi troops and 650 tanks. The human consequences of the fighting were high with 60,000 civilian and military casualties, 300,000 refugees, and the destruction of 40,000 Kurdish homes in some 700 villages. However, the danger of an Iraq-Iran war was averted by the signing of the Algiers Accord in 1975 between the two states, which led to Iran cutting off aid to the KDP. Barzani again had to flee to Iran.

Five years later, Iraq invaded Iran and the Kurdish guerrillas, allied again with Tehran, forced the Baghdad regime to deploy troops in the northern area of Iraq which hampered its war effort elsewhere. The KDP, now led by Masud Barzani (q.v.), and the Patriotic Union of Kurdistan (PUK), led by Jalal Talabani, set up Kurdish liberated zones along the borders with Iran and Turkey. In 1988, however, Saddam Hussein (q.v.) unleashed an assault on Kurdistan, which began in February, lasted seven months, and included the use of chemical weapons against Kurdish villages. In all, some 3,800 villages were affected by the campaign and Baghdad regained all of the lost territory. The Kurdish leaders escaped to Iran and Syria.

In August 1990, Iraq invaded Kuwait (q.v.) and this diverted troops from the KAR, giving the Kurdish leaders the opportunity to return. Following Iraq's defeat in the 1991 Gulf War (q.v.), the Kurdish nationalists persuaded the 100,000 strong militia, comprised mainly of Kurds, to change sides and, within a week, the rebels controlled the KAR, large parts of the oil province Tamim, including the capital Kirkuk. International support was not forthcoming and in March 1991 Baghdad launched a counterattack which reversed all the Kurdish gains, and caused an influx of 1.5 million Kurds into Iran and Turkey. Having regained the region Baghdad signed a truce in mid-April and opened talks with Barzani, who was acting as leader of the Iraqi Kurdistan Front. A draft agreement, reached in June, allowed for predominant Kurdish military and political control within the KAR, but with joint control over the army and police. The Kurds were required to surrender all heavy weapons and to sever links with all outside powers, but the majority of Iraqi Kurdistan Front leaders failed to accept the agreement.

The United States-led coalition deployed 16,000 troops in a 5,760 square kilometer security zone in the Iraqi-Kurdish border region in response to mounting Western concern over the plight of the refugees. Iraq was forced to withdraw its troops in October 1991 and, when allied troops vacated the region at the end of 1991, a no-fly zone was imposed north of the 36th parallel to prevent Iraqi air attacks on the Kurds. Under this limited protection the Kurds conducted parliamentary elections in May 1992 and began to set up a rudimentary administrative infrastructure and embryonic social services, thus creating a de facto state.

Kurds in Syria:

The Kurds in Syria account for 6 percent of the population and are largely centered in the Jazira region in southeast Syria, and in the mountainous area north of Aleppo, with a small community in Damascus. The majority of the Kurds in Syria arrived following a failed revolt in Turkey in 1925 against Kemal Atatürk. As in Iraq, the Kurds formed a Kurdish Democratic Party (KDP) in 1957 demanding that the Kurds be recognized as an ethnic group entitled to its own cultural identity.

Following the creation of the United Arab Republic (q.v.) in 1958 the new regime, with its pan-Arab (q.v.) policies, suppressed the KDP and this policy continued after the republic collapsed in 1961. The Syrian government conducted a special census in the Jazira region in 1962 and deprived 120,000 Kurds of their Syrian nationality. The seizure of power by the Ba'ath Party in 1963 led to the expulsion of the majority of the Kurds along the frontier with Turkey, and many thousands lost their Syrian nationality.

The Ba'ath Party joined Iraq's actions against the Kurds and adopted a policy of settling Arabs into the Jazira region and scattering the Kurds into the interior. This action was intensified when oil was found in the region and by 1971 some 30,000 Kurds had left the region in a haphazard policy of resettlement.

The Syrian government then adopted a conciliatory position, with the Ba'ath Congress of 1971 recognizing that Kurds and Arabs had equal rights and that the Kurds had a right to their own nationality, but not to an autonomous regime or separate state. In late 1971, the government distributed land reform land to Kurdish peasants in Jazira and, in 1976, President Hafiz Assad (q.v.) renounced the population transfers from Jazira region.

Kurds in Turkey:

The Kurdish population in Turkey is mainly found in the southeast of the country and numbers anything up to 10 million but they are not recognized as a separate ethnic group and their language is illegal. In the 1980s, the potential threat of separatism among the Kurds became a major problem for the Turkish government.

The political movement among the Kurds in Turkey is the Kurdish Workers Party (Partiya Karkaren Kurdistan) (PKK) led by Abdullah Ocalan and outlawed by the Turkish government. The PKK have pursued the objective of a Kurdish homeland in Turkey and launched a violent guerrilla action against the Turkish authorities, mainly in the southeast province. The Turkish government responded by arresting Kurdish leaders, increasing the military presence in the region, establishing local militia groups, and imposing martial law on nine provinces in the region. However, by July 1987 martial law had been replaced by a state of emergency in all of the provinces under a district governor.

However, the PKK continued with its guerrilla campaign, concentrating its attacks on the local militia groups and civilians. In June 1988, Ocalan offered to call a cease-fire and exchange prisoners in return for the legalization of the PKK, but the offer was rejected by the Turkish government. As a result the PKK threatened to broaden its campaign to spread the conflict to Turkish cities and to attack Turkish diplomats and politicians if the government pursued a military solution. The government responded in April 1990 with severe measures to combat ethnic unrest, with restrictions on the media and an increase in the power of local officials to outlaw strikes and to impose internal banishment. Violence continued to escalate, and conflict in April and May 1990 between the Kurds and Turkish security forces resulted in 140 deaths.

Early 1991 saw some moves by the government to reduce tension by reviewing the Kurdish language ban and allowing the Kurds to celebrate the Kurdish New Year for the first time. However, by mid-1991 the violence had erupted again between the security forces and guerrillas, with three dead and 100 injured in July from clashes at the funeral of a Kurdish rights activist. Cross-border attacks from bases in Iraq led to the Turkish military launching attacks across the border to raid suspected PKK bases during 1991 and 1992, resulting in the deaths of hundreds of Kurdish civilians and Iraqi Kurdish refugees. In late 1992, Turkish planes attacked suspected PKK bases and 20,000 troops were sent into Iraq to attack the PKK, which was also being attacked by Iraqi Kurds, which aimed at forcing the PKK from Iraq. In December, most of the ground forces were withdrawn and the Turkish military directed its activity against PKK strongholds in southeastern Turkey.

In March 1993, the PKK declared a unilateral cease-fire, but this was broken in May with a declaration of war against all Turkish targets, with attacks on tourist resorts and the abduction of foreign nationals. Attacks were made on Turkish diplomatic missions and business interests in Europe, which led the government to postpone plans to allow the use of the Kurdish language in schools and the media. The government also withdrew plans for a degree of autonomy in the southeast provinces. The armed forces in the region, numbering some 200,000, were also allowed a free hand in dealing with the Kurdish problem. In March 1995, Turkish troops were again sent into northern Iraq to pursue PKK guerrillas, with a further action in July. By the end of 1995, the death total from the Kurdish conflict had reached 19,000.

On 15 March 1999, Abdullah Ocalan was kidnapped by Turkish agents while in Nairobi, Kenya, and was returned to Turkey for trial, where he was found guilty of treason and separatism in June 1999. Ocalan was sentenced to death, but carrying out the sentence was postponed pending an appeal before the European Court of Human Rights. In August 1999, Ocalan had declared a cease-fire and a withdrawal from Turkey in the hope of an amnesty for all PKK guerrillas. However, the Turkish government insisted that the estimated 4,500 guerrillas must surrender without preconditions. By this time the death toll, mainly Kurdish, had risen to some 37,000.

On 9 February 2000, the PKK announced an end to guerrilla activity against Turkey and the pursuance of a political struggle for Kurdish rights. This was part of a move to transform the PKK into a political organization following major military defeats and the Ocalan death sentence. The PKK pointed out that the phasing out of the PKK's armed wing would be dependent upon the democratic transformation of

Turkey and resolution of the Kurdish question, but that real peace hinged on the fate of Abdullah Ocalan.

KUWAIT. The state of Kuwait is located at the head of the Arabian Gulf near the Shatt al-Arab estuary, which marks the boundary between Iraq and Iran (qq.v.). The area occupied by the state includes 2,590 square kilometers from the former neutral zone shared with Saudi Arabia (q.v.), and nine offshore islands, the most important of which are Warba, Bubiyan, and Faylaka. The border with Iraq had been a matter of historical dispute but was finally demarcated by the United Nations (q.v.) after the Iraqi expulsion from Kuwait in 1991. Kuwait has only 150 mm of rainfall annually, is almost devoid of surface water, and most sources are saline.

Kuwait's status as an independent state dates from the arrival of the 'Utab tribes in 1710 from the Nejd, being part of the Anaza tribal confederation, from which the al-Saud also come. The country was nominally part of the Ottoman Empire (q.v.), but prior to 1710 had been a small fishing village of no significance, as the main pattern of trade was from Basra and the lower Arabian Gulf to the East. However, the 'Utub were able to develop trade with Syria (q.v.) and the Levant, which brought commercial significance to the port of Kuwait. In 1760, the 'Utub in Kuwait split into two factions, with the Khalifa migrating to Bahrain (q.v.) while the al-Sabah created the Emirate of Kuwait, which has continued until today.

British interest in Kuwait dates from 1776 through the setting up of an East India Company base in the Gulf, both as a commercial venture and as part of the control of access to the Indian Empire. In the early days, British interest in Kuwait was minimal, as was that of the Ottomans, who were content to allow the al-Sabah to rule as long as sovereignty was recognized and levies paid. However, the situation changed at the end of the nineteenth century when Great Britain feared that Kuwait was to be integrated into the Berlin-Baghdad railway project and Ottoman desire to reassert authority over the al-Hasa region. These fears led Britain to respond to approaches from the Emir of Kuwait for a degree of independence from Ottoman sovereignty and, in return for a subsidy, the Emir agreed not to cede any sovereignty to a foreign power.

The Emir attempted to further this status, but Britain did not respond, although it was happy to enter into a series of economic agreements. In 1914, the situation changed and Britain agreed that Kuwait should be an independent state under British protection, which followed the pattern of an agreement reached with the Ottomans in 1913 that had not been ratified by the outbreak of World War I. Kuwait tried to use its new status to consolidate its hold over territories in the northwest of the Gulf, but this was opposed by the al-Sauds. In 1920, Saudi forces advanced on Kuwait City and only withdrew in the face of a British threat to intervene. Britain subsequently negotiated on Kuwait's behalf the 1922 Treaty of Ugair, which cost Kuwait territory previously guaranteed under the 1913 Ottoman agreement. As part of the treaty, the border with Iraq was also guaranteed.

Apart from its border links with Syria and the Levant, Kuwait's economic prosperity rested on traditional pearl fishing, but the industry collapsed in the 1930s. However, oil prospecting had begun in the 1930s with a joint British-United States venture through the Kuwait Oil Company. The first commercial discovery was made in 1938 at the Burgan field, which at that time was the largest in the world, but exploitation was halted because of World War II, and production did not begin until 1946.

Oil wealth began to flow into Kuwait and the country benefited enormously from the interruption to Iranian supplies during the Musaddiq crisis between 1951-1953. This led to a large influx of Palestinians and Egyptians to service the needs of the oil industry and the developing infrastructure but it also changed the attitudes of Kuwaiti society toward the state's status. This rising tide of nationalism was accentuated by the impact of the Egyptian revolution of 1952, which began to lead to demands for change.

The nationalist sentiment drew strength from the 1956 Suez crisis and resultant war, followed by the collapse of the pro-British Iraqi monarchy in 1958. This was manifested through the activities of the National Cultural Club led by Ahmad Khatib. At this time the Emir, the conservative elements in the state, and the merchant class also recognized that changes were necessary if the nationalist element was to be controlled and negotiations with Britain were opened to secure independence. At the same time the Emir also announced plans to hold elections to a Constituent Assembly charged with the drafting of a constitution.

Kuwait became independent in June 1961, but was immediately threatened by the Iraqi regime under Abd al-Karim Qasim (q.v.), who claimed the territory on the grounds that it was once part of the Ottoman Province of Basra. Britain was forced to send troops to counter this threat but they were quickly replaced by Arab League (q.v.) troops, though the Iraqi threat turned out to be empty. The new constitution was promulgated in November 1962 and it provided for a 50-seat Assembly to be elected from a franchise, which was restricted to about 10 percent of the population as women and non-Kuwaitis had no electoral rights. Formal political parties were not permitted, all ministers were appointed by the Emir, and the Assembly had no executive power although it was given a role in the selection of the Emir.

The Assembly was elected in January 1963 to serve for a period of four years. Although the Kuwaiti government endeavored to ensure that the Assembly comprised members favorable to the regime, it did begin to develop a voice and reflected the views of the major power brokers in Kuwait: the tribal elders, the merchant class, business; and professional groups. It was clear that to dominate the Assembly the Emir needed support from the politically important merchant community, in particular the 15 leading families, and the major tribes in the state.

Opposition within the Assembly was limited and led by Dr. Khatib, but his impact was aided by the growth of the press in Kuwait, which was dominated by immigrant journalists. Radical criticism of conservative Gulf politics began to manifest itself in the 1970s, particularly with regard to the Palestinian problem, the Lebanese Civil War, and the 1973 Arab-Israeli War, with the latter leading to demands for a reduction in oil production, nationalization of the oil industry, and liberalization of press controls. The growth of radicalism alarmed the Emir but also caused concerns within Saudi Arabia and in August 1976 Emir Jabir suspended the Assembly and parts of the constitution. In 1977, the Assembly was dissolved and replaced by autocratic rule.

Further pressures on the traditional Kuwaiti regime arose from the 1979 Iranian Revolution, as the Khomeini (q.v.) regime was hostile toward the Gulf States and Kuwait had a sizeable Shi'i (q.v.) population. Tension increased with the outbreak of the Iraq-Iran War (q.v.) in 1980, as Kuwait's border was only 20 kilometers away from the Shatt al-Arab and the Iranian border and Iraq had also begun to pressure Kuwait for the use of Warba and Bubiyan islands as naval sites. Kuwait was one of the states that supplied financial aid to Iraq either in money or oil sales and, despite tensions, the border between the two states was agreed upon in 1984.

Greater pressure was being applied by Iran, which was furious at the level of Gulf aid to Iraq and began to instigate attacks on Kuwaiti ships in the northern part of the Gulf, leading to the reflagging of Kuwaiti vessels by the United States. Kuwait was also the scene of suicide bombings against French and American property in 1983, the hijacking of a Kuwaiti airliner to Tehran in December 1984, the bombing of cafes in Kuwait City in 1985, and an assassination attempt on the Emir. In regional terms, Kuwait has attempted to counter its insecurity by membership in the Gulf Cooperation Council (q.v.), which was founded in 1980 as a result of the perceived threat to regional security from the Iraq-Iran war. Kuwait was also not slow to criticize the U.S. for its pro-Israeli stance and tried to maintain good relations with the Soviet Union to achieve a balance between the superpowers.

At home, the Emir responded to the Iranian Revolution with a firm hand because of the Shi'i response to the event and the welcome accorded to the revolution by the immigrant Palestinian population. Further controls were imposed upon the press and all public meetings were banned, as was public discussion of political issues. The government also addressed the problem of the large immigrant Shi'i population with the expulsion of some 20,000 in 1980, with further expulsions following the disturbances of 1983 and 1985.

In 1981, the Emir agreed to demands to reconstitute the Assembly and elections were held in 1985, with the threat from the Islamic fundamentalists (q.v.) having been replaced by the growing strength of Arab nationalist groups. Although without executive power, the new Assembly did provide a release for public criticism of the government. Examples of this crucial role were opposition to reductions in aid to the frontline states of Jordan, Syria, and the Palestine Liberation Organization (q.v.) in 1984 and 1985, and attempts to reduce the costs and coverage of Kuwait's welfare system. The assembly also opposed government attempts to cover up some of the effects of the unofficial stock market collapse in 1982. The Assembly was again dissolved by the Emir, Sheikh Jaber III, in July 1986.

Following the end of the Iraq-Iran War, agitation again arose for the Assembly to be reconstituted and the Emir eventually granted a 75-member National Council with elections to be held in June 1990. However, one third of the council was to be nominated by the government, resulting in the opposition boycotting the poll. This demonstrated a weakness within the political elite in Kuwait and the insecurity of the regime. At the same time, the Kuwaiti government had depressed the oil market by exceeding oil quotas set by the Organization of Petroleum Exporting Countries (OPEC) (q.v.), as had Abu Dhabi (q.v.), which had a major impact on the Iraqi economy and which was struggling to recover from the devastation wrought by an eight-year war with Iran.

This was seized upon by Saddam Hussein (q.v.) of Iraq, who demanded that Kuwait compensate Iraq for its losses and cancel loans made by Kuwait during the Iraq-Iran War (q.v.). On 2 August 1990,

Saddam Hussein sent his troops into Kuwait and occupied the whole state. This resulted in the short but extremely damaging Gulf War. During the Gulf War (q.v.), the Iraqi occupation devastated the economy and the whole fabric of the state. The country was subjected to brutality, rape, and summary executions, with other Kuwaitis, including the royal family, forced into exile. Resistance in Kuwait was significant and women played a large part in this movement, but there was some disquiet that the royal family and other leading families had fled to safety. The occupation also caused a backlash against Palestinian immigrant workers because of the PLO's support for Iraq, and many of them were subjected to rough justice once the Iraqis had been expelled, usually on the grounds of collaboration with the occupiers.

In February 1991, Sheikh Jaber III was restored to the throne, and action was taken to deal with the oil-well fires and to rebuild the fabric of the state and the economy. Elections to the National Assembly were held in October 1992 and 31 of the 50 seats went to the opposition, despite the restored economy. Kuwait has continued to rebuild its economy but the threat from Iraq remains, and U.S. and British troops have stayed in the region, with the allied air forces maintaining no-fly zones in southern and northern Iraq. However, a large area of the border area with Iraq is still marred by the wreckage of war and minefields and clearance is a slow process. In May 1999, the Emir announced that the franchise would be extended to include Kuwaiti women, which is a major advance in the political development of the state.

KUWAIT FUND FOR ARAB ECONOMIC DEVELOPMENT (KFAED). The Kuwait Fund for Arab Economic Development is the oldest of the Arab aid agencies, having been established in 1961 when Kuwait (q.v.) gained independence. In terms of political motivation, the fund was a demonstration by the Emir that the newly independent state was a responsible member of the international community and prepared to use its oil revenues to aid others.

The fund is administered by a board of eight Directors who are Kuwaiti nationals, appointed by the Prime Minister, who chairs the Board of Directors. The Directors meet quarterly to make decisions, which are by majority vote though in specific instances a two-thirds majority is necessary, e.g., where a loan exceeds 50 percent of the project cost. The day-to-day operations of the fund are in the hands of the Director-General, who attends the meetings of the Board and participates in discussions, but has no vote.

In the early years, the KFAED concentrated all its efforts on providing aid only to other Arab states, and this policy was interpreted by some observers as being a political decision to preserve Kuwait's independence in an insecure region. However, in 1974, following the oil price rises, the capital base of the fund was increased to $3.55 billion and its sphere of operations was extended to include the developing nations of Africa, Asia, and Latin America.

During the first 10 years of operation, the fund was extremely cautious in its lending policy and advice was taken from the World Bank on the formulation of policies and procedures for development funding. Increasingly, however, the personnel of the KFAED acquired an expertise at both regional and international levels to such an extent that it became a model for other institutions, e.g., the Abu Dhabi Fund for Arab Economic Development (q.v.).

Due to its close relationship to the Kuwaiti government, the KFAED has also developed expertise in other areas and has acted in an advisory capacity on aspects of development policies and services. One example was the use of the fund's expertise to provide technical advice on the establishment of an industrial development bank in Kuwait. The fund also provided technical assistance to the Kuwaiti and other Arab governments on establishing Arab and international investment institutions and portfolios, and on related legal and economic issues.

The expertise of the KFAED has also been used in Arab regional cooperation at the collective level and was involved in the establishment of the Arab Fund for Economic and Social Development (q.v.). However, the KFAED reflected the thinking of the Arab League (q.v.) and did not create the Arab Fund for Social and Economic Development as a mirror image of the KFAED, but the Inter-Arab Investment Guarantee Corporation (q.v.) did reflect the fund's thinking and was a major success.

The fund was also heavily involved in the establishment of the Arab Bank for Economic Development in Africa (q.v.) and the Organization of Petroleum Exporting Countries Special Fund (q.v.) through the provision of technical assistance in the preparatory stages, and in detailed negotiations leading to the establishment of the two organizations. The KFAED was primarily established to strengthen Kuwait's newly gained independence and was therefore political in nature, but these influences are subtle and this can be seen from the fact that loan and technical assistance decisions are not overtly political in nature.

The administrators of the fund enjoy a high degree of autonomy but the Board of Directors and chairman are responsible for the policies of the fund, which is an effective political oversight. The fund has achieved a high level of professional competence, with sound procedures for the consideration, monitoring, and evaluation of loan applications and approved projects. The result has been a recognition that the fund's money has been effectively spent in relation to the objectives of Kuwait and the recipient nations. The KFAED's operations are mainly in the area of infrastructure, with loans evenly divided between agriculture, transport and communications, electricity, and industry. It publishes an annual report and has a regular publications program covering the activities of the fund and policies relating to development problems in the Arab world, particularly in areas of regional cooperation.

L

LEAGUE OF NATIONS. *See* **MANDATE SYSTEM**

LEBANON. The present-day borders of Lebanon were drawn up in 1920, the state having been part of the Ottoman Empire (q.v.) prior to World War I. The population, excluding Palestinian refugees, is just under three million, with the main peoples in the central mountain range being Maronite Catholics. They are based primarily in the north, but also in many of the southern areas. The Druze population lives mainly in the southern part of the range, numbers about 200,000, and is marked by a strong sense of community and solidarity. Sunni (q.v.) Muslims are to be found in the coastal cities of Beirut, Tripoli, and Sidon, while the Shi'i (q.v.) Muslims are found in the south of the country and in the northern part of the Biqa region. Muslims comprise some 60 percent of the population and Christians the remaining 40 percent. Lebanon has also been host to a large number of Palestinian refugees estimated at 360,000, the majority of whom are Sunni Muslims.

Lebanon came under the Ottoman Empire in 1516 and enjoyed a measure of autonomy for three centuries under local princes who owed ultimate allegiance to the Ottomans. During this period, the Druze were the predominant force in Lebanon, largely as a result of their military forces and their core of dominant landowners, but the Maronite Christians began to dominate largely because of their ability to take advantage of increasing commercial links with Europe. The affairs of Lebanon in the nineteenth century were marked by external influences and interests as well as internal struggles between the Druze and Maronites, but the economy prospered as Lebanese ports become major centers of trade and provided important links between Europe and the Arab world. The outbreak of World War I ended this prosperity and the economy rapidly collapsed, with the country being badly affected by famine. The peace settlement supervised by the League of Nations saw Lebanon and Syria come under the French mandate (q.v.) with the borders of the state as it is today.

In 1926, a new constitution was drafted under French auspices, which allowed for the division of power on the basis of religious confession, and a Lebanese president was elected to exercise office, but under French supervision. In 1937, the Maronite president, Emile Edde, appointed a Sunni Muslim to the post of prime minister and this created a precedent for the future. During World War II, Lebanon was occupied by Vichy French forces; these were ousted in 1943 by British troops, and the country gained full independence. A National Pact was negotiated, which formalized the practice of the president being a Maronite and the prime minister a Sunni Muslim, but it also added that the Speaker of the Chamber of Deputies should be a Shi'i Muslim, the commander of the army a Maronite, and the chief of staff a Druze. In addition, the legislature, executive, civil service, and army were to be staffed according to a ratio of six Christians to five Muslims.

The remainder of the 1940s were dominated by the activities of the Parti Populaire Syrien (PPS), which was still campaigning for the creation of a Greater Syria (q.v.), the Druze political party, the Progressive Socialist Party (PSP), led by Kemal Jumblat, and the Phalanges Libanaises dominated by the Maronites and led by Pierre al-Gemayel. In 1951, the prime minister was assassinated by the PPS leading to the resignation of President Bishara al-Khuri in 1952. On 18 September 1952, Camille Chamoun was elected president, aligning Lebanon closely with the West including acceptance of the Eisenhower Doctrine in 1957, which allowed American troops to be called in to help allies faced by outside threats. This caused problems with Jumblat and the Sunni Muslims and increased tensions with Syria and Egypt (qq.v.). The creation of the United Arab Republic (q.v.) in 1958 also heightened tension, as Lebanese Nasserists agitated for Lebanon to join the new union, while Jumblat stepped up opposition to Chamoun.

In the summer of 1958, civil war broke out in Lebanon and regional tension was heightened by the overthrow of the Iraqi monarchy in July 1958. Chamoun invited U.S. troops into Lebanon and on 15 July marines landed in Beirut, while British troops were sent to Jordan (q.v.) to protect the integrity of the pro-Western monarchy. This intervention calmed the unrest and Chamoun did not stand for reelection, being replaced by Fuad Shihab. After his election, Shihab set about increasing the powers of the state against the entrenched positions of the traditional leaders and reducing the reliance of the Lebanese economy on the service sector. In 1964, Shihab was replaced as president by Charles Helou, who attempted to follow the policies of his predecessor. However, attempts to strengthen the state were not really successful and it did not prove possible to develop industry as an alternative to the service economy.

Failures were, however, also due to external circumstances because the 1967 Arab-Israeli War proved to have disastrous consequences for Lebanon due to the Palestinian guerrillas who began to operate openly in Jordan and Lebanon. In 1969, Palestinians in refugee camps clashed with Lebanese security forces over demands to have responsibility for their own security within the camps and to be able to mount attacks on Israel from Lebanon. In October 1969, the Lebanese government signed the Cairo Agreement with the Palestine Liberation Organization (PLO) (q.v.), which accepted most of the Palestinian demands. Palestinian numbers were swollen in September 1970 by the arrival of guerrillas expelled by Jordan. Maronites opposed the Cairo agreement. In the 1970 election, the Shihabist candidate was defeated by Sulayman Frangieh, thus marking a return to the power of the traditional and factional leaders.

The attempts to diversify from the service sector were not really successful and development schemes were largely ineffectual, resulting in rural-urban drift, particularly to the poorer areas of Beirut. This drift was exacerbated by Israeli retaliation for Palestinian guerrilla activity, as large numbers of Shi'i from the southern region fled to Beirut for safety. Confrontations continued between the security forces and the Palestinians, with a major clash with the army taking place in 1973.

The political framework of Lebanon was fragile and by 1975 it began to disintegrate in the face of all the pressures. The growing strength of the PLO led the Maronite community to strengthen its own military resources to meet the perceived threat posed by links between the PLO and left-wing and Muslim groups, which were to form the Lebanese National Movement (LNM). The LNM was led by Jumblat and its prime objective was to reform the political system, end Maronite dominance, and abolish confessionalism. The alliance of leftists and Muslims also argued that their economic position could not improve while the Christians dominated, and they also unreservedly supported the Palestinians.

Maronites regarded political reform as a threat to Christian security and they resented the power and policies of the PLO. Tension between the Maronite militiamen and the Palestinian guerrillas grew, with frequent clashes taking place near the refugee camps and in Christian areas. The militias' objective was to reduce the power of the Palestinians before they could be combined with the numerically superior Muslims to threaten the security and privileges of the Christian community. As the main target of the Maronites was the Palestinians, the former gambled on receiving backing for their actions from Israel (q.v.), the West, and some Arab states.

In February 1975, a major round of fighting resulted from the assassination of a Sunni Muslim politician, involving the army and Muslim militias backed by Palestinian guerrillas. On 13 April, an attempt was made to assassinate the Phalanges Libanaises leader Pierre Gemayel and, in retaliation, Maronite militiamen killed 27 Palestinians in the Christian quarter of Beirut. A brief respite came in June 1975 with the formation of a new cabinet under Rashid Kamari and the signing of a cease-fire between the Lebanese army and PLO Chairman Yasser Arafat (q.v.). However, in September heavy fighting again broke out, throwing Lebanon into an all-out civil war that was to last until 1990.

The first phase of the war, from April 1975 to May 1976, was marked by the ascendancy of the LNM and the PLO, which controlled two-thirds of the country by April 1976. The Lebanese Front turned to Syria, which provided assistance through fear of Israeli intervention. Syrian intervention marked the second phase of the war until February 1978, with the prevention of the collapse of the Lebanese Front, a cease-fire brokered by Libya, and the holding of a presidential election in September 1976, won by the Syrian nominee Elias Sarkis. Fighting still continued in southern Lebanon, where guerrilla activity against Israel was being countered by Israeli-backed Christian militia, and in March 1978 Israel invaded the region. In May 1978, the Christian militia leaders visited Israel to obtain arms.

This period between November 1978 and May 1982 saw the consolidation of a mini-Christian state with the defeat of the National Liberal Party (NLP) by Phalange forces. In July 1981, a U.S.-brokered cease-fire was negotiated between Israel, Syria, and the PLO, covering the southern region. However, the Lebanese Front continued to receive arms shipments in preparation for an Israeli invasion planned by Defense Minister Ariel Sharon. The attempted assassination of the Israeli ambassador to Great Britain gave Israel a pretext for invading Lebanon on 3 June 1982. On 13 September, Bashir Gemayel was assassinated and the Phalange headquarters destroyed in an explosion. Israeli troops then occupied Beirut to maintain order, but failed to prevent the massacre of 2,000 Palestinian refugees by Phalange militia in the Shabra and Shatilla refugee camps in Beirut between 16 and 18 September. On 20 September, a Western multinational force from the U.S., Britain, France, and Italy was deployed and on 21 September Amin Gemayel was elected president. Israeli forces left Beirut on 29 September but fighting continued in Lebanon. On 23 October 1983, the U.S. and French military headquarters in Beirut were attacked by suicide bombers, with the deaths of 214 American and 59 French troops. Fierce fighting broke out in the Shi'i suburbs of Beirut in February 1984 resulting in the expulsion of the Lebanese army from West Beirut. On 7 February, the Western powers withdrew their troops from Lebanon. This led to the Syrians returning to Lebanon to restore order, and the U.S and Syria agreed to cooperate to secure political reform in Lebanon. In September 1988, parliament failed to agree on a successor to Gemayel. The latter instructed his chief of staff, General Michel Anoun, to form an interim military government, but the three Muslim officers selected by Anoun refused to join the cabinet.

In February 1989, Anoun attacked and suppressed the Lebanese Front, declaring a war of liberation against Syria, while Syria imposed a land and sea blockade. The Arab League (q.v.) formed a committee to resolve the Lebanese crisis, and in August 1989, 14 different Lebanese groups allied against Anoun. From 30 September to 22 October 1989, the National Reconciliation Charter was debated at Taif, Saudi Arabia, by the 58 surviving Lebanese parliamentarians. The charter was accepted by the Maronite Lebanese Front but rejected by Anoun; on 5 November 1989, the Lebanese Parliament elected René Muwaad as president. Muwaad was assassinated on 22 November, being succeeded by Elias Hrawi. Fierce fighting ensued from January-March 1990 between Anoun's forces and the Lebanese Front resulting in Anoun being left in control of only one-third of the Christian enclave. Elsewhere Syria had joined the U.S.-led coalition against Iraq (q.v.) and in Lebanon it joined government troops in defeating Anoun's forces and bringing the civil war to a close.

The war was a disaster for Lebanon due to the collapse in economic activity, the costs of the war, and the loss of some 150,000 lives. In political terms, the Lebanese Parliament passed a law on 9 May 1991 increasing its membership to 108 seats and giving parity to Muslims and Christians in the Chamber. On 22 May 1991, Presidents Elias Hrawi and Hafiz Assad (q.v.) signed the Lebanese-Syrian Treaty of Brotherhood, Cooperation, and Coordination, which required the two states to coordinate their affairs in foreign, defense, and economic policies. Elections to the new parliament held in October 1992 were boycotted by the Maronites, resulting in a strongly pro-Syrian government. Despite participation in the 1991 Middle East Peace Conference (q.v.) in Madrid, bilateral talks with Israel ended in impasse. The government called on Israel to withdraw from Lebanon and permitted Hizbullah (q.v.) to operate against the Israeli-backed Southern Lebanon Army. It was not until Israel decided to withdraw unilaterally from southern Lebanon in May 2000 that this infringement on Lebanese sovereignty was ended. Rebuilding efforts have made considerable progress and fresh elections were held in 1996. As part of the reforms, some of the powers enjoyed by the Christian president were transferred to a half-Christian, half-Muslim cabinet with all presidential decrees having to be countersigned by the Muslim prime minister.

In October 1995, the National Assembly approved a three-year extension to Hrawi's term of office. However, political and religious leaders still wield considerable power in the regions, making it extremely difficult for the central government to enforce its legislation and the law. On 15 November 1998, Emile Lahoud was elected president having been commander of the armed forces from November 1989 until his election. *See also* **Palestine**

LIBYA. *See* **ARAB-AFRICAN UNION; ARAB ISLAMIC REPUBLIC; CONFEDERATION OF ARAB REPUBLICS; MUAMMAR AL- QADDAFI; UNION OF THE ARAB MAGHREB**

M

MALIKI CODE. The Maliki Code is the canonical school of Sunni Islam (qq.v.) and was founded by Malik ibn Anas (A.D. 714-796), a jurist who resided in Medina. In common with other schools, it is based on the Quran, the *Sunna* (q.v.), and *ijma* (q.v.). However, in terms of the *Sunna*, or the tradition of the Prophet Muhammad, Malik ibn Abas excludes Caliph Ali ibn Abu Talib, who was a cousin and son-in-law of the Prophet, and regarded by Sunni (q.v.) as the last of the Four Rightly Guided Caliphs. In terms of the *ijma*, or consensus of the community, Malik ibn Abas stated that if it failed to produce a solution a jurist should use reasoning by analogy to find a solution.

Initially, the Maliki Code dominated the Arabian heartland of Islam but gave way to the Shafii Code (q.v.). In essence, the doctrine was conservative and has survived in pastoral communities, being the leading code in North Africa, West Africa, and Sudan.

MANDATE SYSTEM. The mandate system was established after World War I under the auspices of the League of Nations to administer former territories of the defeated German and Ottoman empires (q.v.). Under this system the victors were given responsibility for governing former territories of the defeated power as mandates granted by the League. The goal of mandates was to develop each mandatory territory toward full independence. The mandates were either: Class-A territories, provisionally recognized as independent until able to stand on their own; Class-B, territories requiring additional development before qualifying for independence, and for which mandatory powers took full responsibility for administration and promotion of the social and material welfare of the inhabitants; Class-C, territories best integrated into the territories of the mandatory powers. All of the previous Ottoman territories in the Middle East became Class A mandates.

The granting of the mandates was, however, tempered by public and secret agreements made during the war, including the Sykes-Picot Agreement of 1916 and the Balfour Declaration of 1917. Great Britain was given the mandate for Iraq and Palestine (later Palestine and Transjordan) and France got Syria (later Syria and Lebanon) (qq.v.). The mandates were to be supervised by the Permanent Mandates Commission, which never followed an aggressive policy against the interests of the mandatory powers. This was demonstrated by the fact that by 1924 Britain had split the Palestine mandate into Palestine and Transjordan, making Sherif Hussein's son Abdullah Emir of the territory, and France had split the Syrian mandate into Syria and Lebanon, to provide protection for the Lebanese Christians. The mandate for Iraq remained intact.

The Class-A mandated territories did achieve independence as required by the mandate system. Iraq secured independence in 1932 (although Britain retained significant diplomatic and military concessions), Syria and Lebanon in 1941, and Transjordan in 1946 as the Kingdom of Jordan. Palestine remained within the mandate system and was transferred by the League of Nations to the United Nations (UN) (q.v.), as part of its trusteeship program. In 1947, Britain transferred the problem of Palestine to the UN for resolution. The result was approval of a plan to partition the area into two states, one Arab, one Jewish, with Jerusalem as an international city. The plan was never implemented, as the 1948 Arab-Israeli War broke out, leading to the creation of the State of Israel, which joined the UN in 1949.

MCMAHON-HUSSEIN CORRESPONDENCE. This was an exchange of 10 letters between Sherif Hussein (q.v.) of the Hedjaz and Sir Henry McMahon, the British High Commissioner in Egypt (q.v.), written between 14 July 1915 and 30 March 1916. The correspondence set out the terms under which the Sherif would ally with Great Britain against the Turks, in return for British support for Arab independence. Hussein asked Britain to support independence of the Arab countries in the Arabian Peninsula, except Aden, all of Iraq, Palestine, Syria up to Turkey (qq.v.) in the north and Persia in the east, and Transjordan (q.v.). In response, McMahon accepted the principles but excluded certain areas in the proposed boundaries: coastal regions along the Gulf area of Arabia; the province of Baghdad, which would be placed under British supervision; and in areas where Britain was free to act without detriment to the interests of France. The Arabs assumed that Arabia, northern Iraq, central Syria, and Palestine were part of the area that was to be independent.

The Arabs revolted against the Turks in May 1916 which assisted Britain in defeating the Turks in the region, largely through guerrilla warfare, tying up of Turkish garrisons, and attacks on the Hedjaz railway. The Arab forces did, however, take Aqaba and Damascus from the Turks and established an Arab regime in the Syrian capital in 1919.

After the war, the Arabs felt betrayed because Britain had entered into a secret agreement with France in 1916, known as *the Sykes-Picot Agreement,* which conceded Syria to France, and had also entered into a promise to help in the establishment of a Jewish homeland in Palestine, through the Balfour Declaration of 1917. The British always maintained that Palestine was not to be included in the McMahon pledges. The interpretation of these letters has been disputed, and is not helped by the deliberate vagueness of the British position. The letters were not made public until 1939, following the publication of George Antonious's *Arab Awakening,* which forced Britain to publish an official version. *See also* **Arab Revolt**

MECCA. The city of Mecca is in the Hedjaz Province of Saudi Arabia (q.v.) and has as its center the Kaaba, which is the most sacred building in Islam (q.v.). Traditionally, the Kaaba was built by Adam and rebuilt by Abraham, who is also venerated as a prophet by Muslims. The Kaaba, located in the center of the courtyard of the Great Mosque is a cube-shaped building, made out of local grey stone and draped with a black curtain embroidered with verses of the Quran. In the eastern corner is set the Black Stone. The Kaaba and the Great Mosque have both been renovated, especially since 1952. Mecca is the center of the annual pilgrimage, or *hajj* (q.v.), from all Muslim countries and is of great significance to Saudi Arabia in terms of prestige and status within the Muslim world. The *hajj* attracts millions of pilgrims, which presents Saudi Arabia with major logistical problems during the pilgrimage, but is a major source of income to the city and the region. Mecca can also be a center of political intrigue due to its status. One major disturbance was experienced during King Khalid's reign when, in 1979, there was an uprising led by a religious zealot, Juheima ibn Saif al-Utaiba (q.v.) who occupied the Grand Mosque on the eve of the Muslim New Year. Although the uprising was put down it took a long time to clear all the cellars and passages and it was thought that the uprising might be a forerunner of other violent outbreaks inspired by Islamic fundamentalists (q.v.). Another view was that this was an aberration which appeared in Islamic society from time to time, and the peace that has prevailed since would seem to support this view.

MIDDLE EAST DESALINATION RESEARCH CENTER (MEDRC). The MEDRC is located in Muscat, Oman (q.v.), and was founded in December 1996, an outcome of the Middle East multilateral peace process, as an international organization dedicated to research in the area of desalination technology. The center seeks to bring together scientists and engineers from the Middle East and North Africa to work in areas of basic, applied, and sponsored research designed to reduce the costs of desalination in recognition of the fact that the economy of the region is inextricably linked to the desalination of sea water and brackish groundwater.

The objectives of the center are to conduct, facilitate, promote, coordinate, and support the following activities:

- basic and applied research in the field of water desalination and related technical areas with the aim of discovering, developing, and improving methods of water desalination which are financially and technically feasible
- training programs which develop technical expertise and scientific skills through the Middle East in the field of water desalination
- information exchange, including electronic networking technology, to ensure dissemination throughout the Middle East and internationally of technical information concerning water desalination methods and research
- relations with other states maintaining organizations, as will foster

progress in the development, improvement and use of water desalination in the Middle East and elsewhere

The MEDRC is being supported and funded by the European Union, Israel, Japan, Korea, the United States, and the Sultanate of Oman and interest has been expressed by other countries in the objectives of the center.

MIDDLE EAST NEUROSURGICAL SOCIETY (MNS). The MNS was formed in 1958 and is based in the Neurosurgical Department of the American University Medical Center in Beirut. Its objectives are to promote clinical advances and scientific research, and to spread knowledge among its members and the medical profession in the Middle East. Membership is drawn from 17 Arab states.

MIDDLE EAST NEWS AGENCY (MENA). The agency was founded in 1956 to provide an alternative to Western news agencies and is based in Cairo, Egypt (q.v.), being nationalized by the government in 1962. MENA is run under the jurisdiction of the Ministry of Information and is the main provider and controller of news in Arabic, English, and French in Egypt. MENA also supplies its reports free to other news agencies in the Arab world, and the news agencies of Qatar, Oman, and Saudi Arabia (qq.v.) channel their foreign reports through the Agency. MENA runs training programs for journalists, radio and television personnel, engineers, media administrators, and accountants. The bulk of MENA's budget comes from contracts with Reuters and Agence France-Presse, photo exchange services, and television services. It publishes *Cairo Press Relations* (daily in English) and *Party Press Review* (with English translations of opposition press material).

MIDDLE EAST PEACE CONFERENCE (1973). Following the October 1973 Arab-Israeli War, a peace conference was convened at Geneva on 21 December under the co-chairmanship of the United States and the Soviet Union. The conference was attended by Egypt, Israel, and Jordan (qq.v.) but boycotted by President Hafiz Assad of Syria (qq.v.), and instructed Egypt and Israel (qq.v.) to disengage their forces. The conference was suspended due to the imminent general election in Israel but, following the Labor Party's victory on 31 December, Israel did not return to Geneva as planned on 7 January. The Israelis approached the U.S. Secretary of State, Henry Kissinger, to use personal diplomacy to bring about an agreement with Egypt and this approach was agreed to by President Anwar Sadat (q.v.).

During the administration of President Jimmy Carter (1977-1980), attempts were made by the joint chairmen to reconvene the full conference, but these failed. The bilateral talks between Egypt and Israel did culminate in the Camp David Accords (q.v.) of 1978, followed by the signing of a peace treaty in 1979.

MIDDLE EAST PEACE CONFERENCE (1991). Following the Gulf War (q.v.), the United States began to lobby actively for a Middle East peace conference. The concept came to fruition when President Hafiz Assad of Syria (qq.v.) made concessions in order to attend and the Palestine National Council also agreed to participate. The conference began on 30 October 1991 in Madrid under the co-chairmanship of the U.S. and the Soviet Union (later Russia) and was attended by Israel, Syria, Lebanon, and Jordan (qq.v.), the delegation of the latter including Palestinians from the Occupied Territories. All participants agreed to abide by United Nations (q.v.) Security Council Resolution 242 of November 1967 which called for the withdrawal of Israel from the Occupied Arab Territories in exchange for the peaceful coexistence of all the states in the region.

The Madrid Conference was followed by bilateral talks outside of the Middle East between Israel and the three Arab delegations. The talks between Israel and the Jordanian delegation evolved into separate talks between Israel and Jordan and Israel and the Palestinian delegates, directed by the Palestine Liberation Organization (q.v.). Negotiations between Israel and the Palestinians were held in secret and an accord reached in Oslo in September 1993, with agreement on the stages and measures necessary to secure a peace between the two parties. The talks with Jordan also proved positive, with a peace treaty being signed on 26 October 1994 with the agreed borders being largely based on the lines demarcated by the British mandate in 1922. Israel conceded Jordanian sovereignty over 381 square kilometers of occupied territory. Jordan, in return, leased 300 square kilometers back to Israel.

Negotiations between Israel and Syria began in 1994, mediated by the U.S., but little progress was made largely due to the intransigence of both sides over the question of the Golan Heights. Talks between Israel and Lebanon were placed on hold pending progress in the Israeli-Syrian talks, which was in accord with the 1991 Lebanese-Syrian Treaty of Brotherhood, Cooperation, and Coordination.

MIDDLE EASTERN REGIONAL RADIOISOTOPE CENTER FOR THE ARAB COUNTRIES. The Center was founded in 1963 and is based in Cairo, Egypt (q.v.). It provides training for specialists in the application of radioisotopes, particularly in the fields of medicine, agriculture, and industry. Research is also promoted in the fields of hydrology, tropical and subtropical diseases, fertilizers, and entomology. The center also promotes the use of isotopes in the Arab world. It publishes a *Bulletin* (twice a year) and an *Annual Report*.

MOROCCO. *See* **ALGERIAN-MOROCCAN BORDER DISPUTE; ARAB-AFRICAN UNION; UNION OF THE ARAB MAGHREB; WESTERN SAHARA**

MUBARAK, MUHAMMAD HOSNI (1928-). Hosni Mubarak was born in the Nile Delta village of Kafral Musaliha, the son of a court functionary. He graduated from the air force academy in 1950 and served as a fighter pilot until 1954, before taking a teaching post at the air force academy, of which he became director-general. Mubarak was appointed commander of the West Cairo airbase in 1961. He undertook courses at the Soviet General Staff Academy and, in 1964, he spent a year at the Frunze Military Academy in the Soviet Union.

Following the defeat in the 1967 Arab-Israeli War, Mubarak was returned to his earlier post of Director-General at the air force academy and promoted to Air Vice-Marshal. In the 1973 Arab-Israeli War, the Egyptian air force performed well in the opening stages and Mubarak was promoted in 1974 to Air Marshal. In 1975, President Anwar Sadat (q.v.) appointed him vice president, largely because he did not have the potential to develop a competing center of power. Mubarak became chairman of the ruling National Democratic Party (NDP) in 1976 and followed Sadat's line in domestic and foreign affairs.

After Sadat's assassination in October 1981 Mubarak took over as president and leader of the NDP. Initially, he moderated Sadat's policy with regard to the Islamic fundamentalists (q.v.) but this soon changed and the hardline policy was reinstated. Although maintaining a close alliance with the United States, Mubarak also fostered relations with the Soviet Union. Following Israel's (q.v.) invasion of Lebanon (q.v.) in 1982, he withdrew his ambassador from Tel Aviv, but refused to break off diplomatic relations. Mubarak continued Sadat's policy of aiding Iraq in the Iraq-Iran War (qq.v.), hoping to make progress toward ending Egypt's (q.v.) isolation by other members of the Arab League (AL) (q.v.). The policy was successful in 1984 when Jordan reopened diplomatic ties with Egypt.

In 1987, Mubarak was reelected president, being the sole candidate. In early 1989, he took Egypt into the Arab Cooperation Council (q.v.), and was allowed to rejoin the AL. Following Saddam Hussein's (q.v.) invasion of Kuwait (q.v.) in August 1990, he led the majority in the AL opposing Iraq's action and demanding an immediate and unconditional surrender. Mubarak sent Egyptian troops to Saudi Arabia (q.v.) to bolster its defenses against Iraq and joined the coalition against the Iraqi regime, though Egyptian troops did not enter Iraqi territory.

Mubarak's policies proved unpopular with certain segments of Egyptian society and almost all of the opposition groups boycotted the 1990 elections; the militant Islamic groups also intensified their campaign against the regime. Despite this Mubarak was reelected president in 1993 and was to play a significant part in the accord between Israel and the Palestinians reached in Oslo (q.v.) in 1993.

MULTINATIONAL FORCE AND OBSERVERS (MFO). The Multinational Force and Observers was designed as a peacekeeping operation to oversee the peace process set out in the Camp David Accords (q.v.) of March 1978. The MFO was not mandated by an international organization, but drew its legitimacy from the Camp David Accords and was organized by the United States. The United Nations Emergency Force (q.v.) had been withdrawn following the completion of the peace treaty between Egypt and Israel (qq.v.) in 1979, but the MFO benefited from the experience of the United Nations (q.v.) force. The composition of the MFO was some 2,000 troops from Colombia, Fiji, and the United States, covering the neutral zone between Egypt and Israel (qq.v.), with Italy providing naval forces and Australia and New Zealand contributing air support.

The command structure of the MFO followed that of the United Nations and the headquarters in Rome coordinates operations through a Director-General. The MFO liases with the United Nations Truce Supervision Organization, the United Nations Interim Force in Lebanon, and the United Nations Disengagement Observer Force (qq.v.).

MULTINATIONAL FORCES I (MNFI). Israel invaded Lebanon (qq.v.) in June 1982 in retaliation for attacks on Israel by the Palestine Liberation Organization (PLO) (q.v.) and the PLO forces were pushed northward until they were cornered in Beirut. At this point the United States intervened in an attempt to prevent large-scale conflict between Israel and the PLO fighters, with the proposal for a multinational peacekeeping force. The suggestion received the approval of the Arab League (q.v.), which had supported the Arab Deterrent Force (q.v.) in eastern

Lebanon. The MNFI was not mandated by any international organization but based on a series of bilateral agreements between the participants and the Lebanese government. The deployed force consisted of a United States contingent of 800 marines, an equal number of French troops, and 400 Italian troops.

The MNFI provided assistance in the evacuation of the PLO from Beirut to Tunis and guaranteed the safety of PLO families remaining in Beirut. The force was also instrumental in protecting the civilian refugee camps from the Israeli and Christian Phalange forces, and withdrawn once the PLO evacuation was complete. At this time, the force was one of three peacekeeping forces in Lebanon: the Arab Deterrent Force, the United Nations Interim Force in Lebanon, and the United Nations Truce Supervision Organization (qq.v.).

MULTINATIONAL FORCES II (MNFII). Following the withdrawal of the Multinational Forces I (q.v.) from Lebanon (q.v.) in September 1982, two massacres took place at the Sabra and Shatilla refugee camps by Christian Phalange forces that were not prevented by Israeli Defense Forces. This second operation mirrored the first in that there was no international mandate but a series of bilateral agreements between the participants and the Lebanese government. MNFII consisted of 1,400 United States marines, 1,500 French troops, 1,400 Italian troops, and 80 British troops with armored cars.

The initial objective of MNFII was to provide a buffer zone between the Israelis, their opponents, and the refugee camps. A longer-term objective was to assist the Lebanese government to extend its control over the country. The force had no centralized control and coordination between contingents was lacking, with each responding directly to directions from their home government. This affected the credibility of MFNII as it was not seen to be neutral in its aims and objectives. In terms of Lebanese reactions, only the Italians, because of their humanitarian program, were seen as neutral, while the U.S. and French forces were regarded as being in the pockets of the Lebanese government. As a result, U.S. and French forces became the targets for various factions in the civil war and the U.S. forces in particular suffered heavy losses. The U.S. changed its rules of engagement to allow naval bombardments and air attacks to support its ground forces. Both U.S. and French forces suffered from car bomb attacks on 23 October 1983, and during February and March 1985 MNFII forces were withdrawn.

MUSLIM BROTHERHOOD (MB). The MB was first established in Egypt by Hassan al-Banna (qq.v.) in 1928 as a youth club committed to pursuing moral and social reform through propaganda and an information program. However, in 1939, in response to the popular movement against the 1936 Anglo-Egyptian Treaty and the Palestinian uprising against the mandate (q.v.), the movement transformed itself into a political entity. According to al-Banna the MB was a political organization, an athletic group, a scientific and cultural union, an economic enterprise, and a social idea. The growth of the movement was such that by 1940 it had established 500 branches each with its own centers, mosques, schools, and clubs.

During World War II, the MB's membership was swollen by students, civil servants, artisans, petty traders, and middle-income peasants. After the war, it participated in the anti-British struggle and volunteers fought in the 1948 Palestine war, having received military training from Egyptian officers who had adopted the ideology of the MB. The creation of the State of Israel (q.v.) led the MB to blame the political establishment for the defeat and it resorted to terrorist and subversive activities against the Egyptian government. The government declared martial law and banned the party in December 1948, with further repression following the assassination of Prime Minister Mahmud Fahmi Nokrashi by a member of the MB. On 12 February 1949, al-Banna was himself killed by secret service agents in Cairo.

The ban on the MB was lifted in 1950 and it was allowed to function as a religious body, being permitted to participate in politics in 1951 following the election of a moderate leader, Hassan Islam al-Hudaibi. The MB allied itself with the government, supporting the abrogation of the Anglo-Egyptian Treaty, and participating in the January 1952 riots in Cairo. Following the Free Officers coup in July 1952, political parties were banned but the MB was allowed to continue as it was regarded as a religious body and members of the new Revolutionary Command Council (RCC) had been close to the movement. However, the MB turned against the government when it realized that its main aims were to spread secular education, grant rights to women, and support land reform. As a result the MB was banned again in February 1954.

In October 1954, an activist of the MB tried to assassinate President Gamal Abdul Nasser (q.v.) and six Brethren were executed, more than 4,000 activists arrested, and several thousand fled the country. In 1964, Nasser declared a general amnesty and the Brethren were released, but reconciliation did not last. Three more assassination attempts were made on Nasser's life, 365 MB activists were put on trial, and their leaders executed in August 1966.

Following the death of Nasser and the appointment of Anwar Sadat (q.v.) as president, the policies regarding the MB were reversed, prisoners released, and the *Sharia* (q.v.) was promised as the source of legislation. Exiles had also returned from other Arab states, thus strengthening the movement within Egypt. Sadat refused to allow the MB to participate in the 1976 general election as an entity but some activists were elected as independents or as members of the Arab Socialist Party. However, the economic policies of Sadat and the peace negotiations with Israel led to the MB opposing Sadat, and a large number of activists were arrested in September 1981. In October 1981, four soldiers who were members of the MB assassinated Sadat.

President Hosni Mubarak (q.v.) also pursued an intensive policy designed to crush the Islamic militants, and the MB was banned from participation in the 1984 and 1987 elections, though it succeeded in obtaining representation by candidates standing for other parties. The MB boycotted the 1990 election due to the government's refusal to lift the state of emergency and for the election to be overseen by a nongovernmental body.

During the Kuwait (q.v.) crisis and the ensuing Gulf War (q.v.), the MB allied itself with the Iraqi (q.v.) regime and fuelled pro-Islamic feelings, which led to an increase in terrorist acts by militant groups against tourists in an effort to destabilize the regime.

The MB is active in Jordan and Palestine (qq.v.) with branches being established by Hassan al-Banna between 1942-1945. The movement also became active in 1954 following the arrival of activists from Egypt when the MB was banned. The MB was established in Syria (q.v.) in the 1930s by students of theology who had been educated at Egyptian universities, and has undergone a similar stormy relationship with the Syrian government. All the various movements owe their origins to the MB in Egypt and share common principles, but they operate as separate entities within the various countries in which they have a presence.

MUSLIM WOMEN'S LEAGUE (MWL). The Muslim Women's League is a nonprofit American organization based at Los Angeles, California, which works to implement the values of Islam (q.v.) and to reclaim the status of Muslim women worldwide. The MWL operates through the establishment of study groups, spiritual retreats and conferences, and seminars. It also networks with other relevant organizations and has a publication program of position papers, articles, and texts that are allied to its objectives and the *MWL Newsletter* (monthly).

MUSLIM WORLD LEAGUE (MWL). The MWL was founded in 1962 and is based in Mecca, Saudi Arabia (qq.v.). It holds observer status at the Organization of the Islamic Conference (OIC), United Nations (qq.v.), and the United Nations Educational, Scientific, and Cultural Organization, and is dedicated to the advancement of Islamic unity and solidarity. It provides financial assistance for the promotion of Islamic education, medical care, relief work, and women's development, operating through 30 offices around the world, including offices in Indonesia, Great Britain, the Maldives, Bangladesh, Malaysia, Pakistan, France, the Philippines, and throughout Asia and Africa.

The MWL is organized through a Constituent Council, which is the policy-making body that determines the goals of the League and comprises 62 scholars and thinkers of the Muslim world. The executive wing of the League is that of the secretariat-general with a Secretary-General responsible for the implementation of the decisions and recommendations of the Constituent Council. The secretary-general is also responsible for the administrative and financial structure of the league and is the link with its offices throughout the world. Also part of the league are the World Supreme Council for Mosques, the Islamic Jurisprudence Council, and the Commission on Scientific Signs in the Holy Qur'an and Sunnah. The MWL publishes *Akhbar al-Alam al-Islami* (weekly), *Muslim World News* (weekly Arabic and English), *Majalla Rabitat al-Alam al-Islami* (monthly), *The Journal* (monthly in English), and a *Guide to Hajj and Accommodation* (several languages).

N

NAHAYYAN, ZAID IBN SULTAN AL- (1918?-). Sheikh Zaid was born in Abu Dhabi (q.v.) and raised in the desert in the tradition of the Bedouin, which remained as a major influence in his later life. In his early development, Zaid operated in the Al-Ain oasis region from 1946-1966 and he earned a reputation as a reformer through astute use of funds allocated to the region from oil revenues, which began to flow from 1962. In August 1966, the al-Nahayya family elected Zaid as ruler of Abu Dhabi; he began to develop a modern city with a modern infrastructure, and he also extended aid to neighboring emirates. In February 1968, following Great Britain's proposed withdrawal from the Gulf, Zaid formed a union with Dubai and invited other emirates to join them. The outcome was the federation of the United Arab Emirates (UAE) (q.v.) consisting of Abu Dhabi, Dubai, Sharjah, Ajman, Umm al-Qaiwain, and Fujairah. Zaid was elected president and Sheikh Rashid of Dubai vice president. Ras al-Khaimah joined the federation in 1972.

Zaid has been responsible for consolidating the federation and creating a federal infrastructure with a central security and defense oganization, while at the same time carefully reconciling modernization with tradition. The UAE was the first Arab state to announce an oil embargo on the countries that supported Israel (q.v.) in 1973 and was also involved in trying to end the Iraq-Iran War of 1980-1988 (q.v.). Zaid also gained respect in the Arab world for his attempts to reconcile inter-Arab differences and for his support for the Palestinians. He was also the prime motivator at the November 1987 summit in Amman for the return of Egypt (q.v.) to membership in the Arab League (q.v.), and was the first leader to visit Egypt in an effort to restore diplomatic relations.

During the 1991 Gulf War (q.v.), Zaid participated in the coalition against Saddam Hussein (q.v.), providing both ground troops and fighter planes as part of an overall contribution from the Gulf Cooperation Council (GCC) (q.v.) member states.

NAJIBULLAH (1947-   ). Najibullah was born in Kabul and his family was an Ahmadzai family of the Gilzar Pahktum. He studied medicine at Kabul University, graduating in 1975. Najibullah was active in politics in his youth and was a founding member of the People's Democratic Party of Afghanistan (PDPA) in 1965. The PDPA split in 1967 and Najibullah became leader of the Parcham faction in company with Babrak Karmal. He was exiled as ambassador to Iran (q.v.) in 1978 but returned to Kabul in 1980, when Babrak Karmal became president, and was appointed president of the Afghan Secret Police, a task which he pursued with enthusiasm and ruthlessness. In 1986, he became secretary-general of the PDPA and president of Afghanistan (q.v.).

Najibullah was a powerful and ruthless ruler who made a number of attempts to unite the country. He attempted to pacify the Islamic resistance by tempering the Marxist ideology of the PDPA, moving the country away from socialism, and restoring the role of religion in the state. However, he was unable to reach an accommodation with the mojahedin and his government collapsed in 1992.

NASSER, GAMAL ABDUL (1918-1970). Gamal Abdul Nasser was born in Bani Mor village in the Asyut province of Egypt (q.v.), the son of a postal clerk. He attended the Royal Military Academy in Cairo, and then served in Sudan for two years before returning to the Academy as an instructor in 1941. In the 1948-1949 Arab-Israeli War, Nasser served as a major in the Egyptian army, being promoted to colonel and appointed as lecturer at the Royal Military Academy.

Nasser became a member of the underground secret Free Officers Movement and was the leader of the move which ousted King Farouk on 22 July 1952. After the coup, Nasser set up the Revolutionary Command Council (RCC) with Brigadier General Muhammad Neguib at its head. Neguib favored a return to the parliamentary system, but this was successfully opposed by Nasser. In January 1953, the RCC banned political parties, but in turn sponsored its own Liberation Rally party. A power struggle continued between Neguib and Nasser, and this intensified following the declaration of a republic in June 1953 with Neguib as president.

The differences between the two men came to a critical point in February 1954 when the RCC banned the Muslim Brotherhood (q.v.) without consulting Neguib. He resigned in protest, thus creating a power vacuum and a crisis as different military units were mobilized by the two rivals. A compromise was reached in April 1954, with Neguib retaining his role as president but having to relinquish the post of prime minister, though this was a short-lived solution. In November, the RCC dismissed Neguib, placed him under house arrest, and chose Nasser as their chairman. A new constitution was promulgated in 1956 and Nasser was elected president for a six-year term, being reelected twice.

Initially, Nasser had been committed to ridding public life of corruption and not to any particular ideology. However, this changed, as he became ideological and radical in the face of attempts to smother his Arab nationalist (q.v.) regime by Egyptian conservatives and Western powers. Nasser was greatly influenced by the nonalignment philosophies of India's Nehru and Yugoslavia's Tito, and one success was his stopping the expansion of the Baghdad Pact (q.v.).

In 1956, the United States refused to sell military equipment to Egypt. Nasser accepted an offer from Czechoslovakia, acting as a proxy for the Soviet Union. The U.S. reacted by withdrawing financial support for the Aswan High Dam and, with Great Britain, refused to provide the guarantees required by the World Bank, which also withdrew support. In retaliation, Nasser nationalized the Suez Canal and accepted further aid from the Soviet Union, but then faced opposition from Britain, France, and Israel, who launched the Suez War in 1956. Due to U.S. pressure, the aggressors were forced to withdraw from Egypt in

March 1957 and, although defeated militarily, Nasser had won the political war, as the Suez Canal remained nationalized and his prestige rose in Egypt and in the region.

Various attempts were made to assassinate Nasser but all failed. In 1958, Egypt and Syria (q.v.) came together as the United Arab Republic (q.v.) and Nasser was elected president of the merged states. However, Nasser antagonized the Syrians by imposing Egyptian policies on them, and in 1961 they seceded from the union. This was a major setback to Nasser's pan-Arab dream of uniting the Arab east under his leadership. At home Nasser hastened the implementation of socioeconomic reforms in Egypt by consolidating the program of land reform and a further nationalization of industries and services.

In 1962 at a convention of intellectuals, workers, and peasants, Nasser inaugurated his form of Arab Socialism (q.v.) through the formation of the Arab Socialist Union. Also in 1962, he provided support for the republicans in North Yemen (q.v.) who were waging war against the royalists, supported by Saudi Arabia (q.v.). Nasser found himself upstaged by Syria in 1966, when the Ba'athist (q.v.) regime came to power and provided support for the escalation of Palestinian guerrilla attacks on Israel (q.v.). As a counter, Nasser signed a defense pact with Syria, which provided for a unified military command in the event of a war.

Tension rose in the region at the beginning of 1967, with Israel issuing warnings to Syria about guerrilla attacks mounted from its territory. The sense of crisis was increased when Nasser demanded that the United Nations Emergency Force (q.v.), posted in the Sinai, should be withdrawn. After the United Nations (UN) (q.v.) withdrawal, Nasser increased the regional tension by closing the Straits of Tiran, at the mouth of the Gulf of Aqaba, to Israeli shipping. In May 1967, King Hussein of Jordan (q.v.), who had been critical of Nasser, signed a peace pact with Egypt thus increasing his power and status in the Arab world.

On 5 June 1967, Israeli aircraft launched preemptive attacks on Egyptian, Jordanian, and Syrian air bases, having been convinced that international pressure would not force Egypt to reopen the Straits of Tiran. For the Arabs, the 1967 Arab-Israeli War was a rout and almost totally destroyed Nasser and Nasserism (q.v.), and although he tried to show the defeat as a victory he eventually resigned. However, popular demonstrations made Nasser retract his resignation and also rethink some of his policies. Nasser moderated his domestic socialist policies and, at the same time, accepted UN Security Council Resolution 242 which called for the peaceful coexistence of Israel and her neighbors in return for an Israeli withdrawal from occupied Arab territories.

Nasser used aid from the Soviet Union to fully reequip his military. In 1968, he instigated a war of attrition against Israel to prevent it from consolidating control over the Occupied Territories. Egypt resisted all diplomatic efforts to end the conflict with Israel, and responded to air attacks and raids into its territory by installing a Soviet-designed air defense system, which severely curtailed Israeli incursions.

Nasser reached a compromise with King Faisal ibn Abdul Aziz (q.v.) over the situation in North Yemen by withdrawing troops in December 1967. Despite these setbacks, Nasser remained as the elder statesman for the progressive Arab world and was used as a mediator, first by the Palestine Liberation Organization (PLO) (q.v.) and Lebanese in their conflict, resulting in the November 1969 Cairo Agreement, and second between Jordan and the PLO following their battles in September 1970. Nasser had a heart attack and died from strain and overwork shortly afterwards. *See also* **Lebanon; Palestine**

NASSERISM. The socio-political doctrine of Nasserism is based on the thoughts and actions of Gamal Abdul Nasser (q.v.), President of Egypt (q.v.) from 1954-1970. The doctrine began as pan-Arab Nationalism (q.v.) but soon evolved into Arab Socialism (q.v.) emerging as an ideology based on the practical responses to the domestic and foreign policy problems faced by the Revolutionary Command Council following the 1952 coup. The ideology was developed by Nasser and then a political organization was created to implement the ideology once the Free Officers had seized power. During Nasser's lifetime, Nasserite parties emerged in a number of Arab states, including Iraq, Jordan, Lebanon, Saudi Arabia, Syria, and North and South Yemen (qq.v.), but shortly after Nasser's death they ceased to exist or lost all significance. In Egypt, they were denied a license to operate as a political entity and most of the Nasserites joined the National Progressive Unionist Alliance.

NEUTRAL ZONE. The neutral zone is an area shared by Iraq, Kuwait, and Saudi Arabia (qq.v.) as the boundary between Kuwait and Saudi Arabia, demarcated by the Anglo-Turkish Convention of 1913, was not ratified due to the outbreak of World War I. Following the recognition of the sovereignty of Ibn Saud (q.v.) in 1915, a compromise was reached on the boundary by the creation of a 7,044-square-kilometer neutral zone. This was incorporated in the Uqayr Conference in 1922, which established a similar zone between Iraq and Saudi Arabia, abutting the Saudi-Kuwait neutral zone. The convention allowed the parties to explore on an equal basis for natural resources but did not address the question of sovereignty. In fact, each of the states administers the neutral zone as if it were part of its territory but oil and gas discoveries have pushed sovereignty to the forefront of regional politics. The state of the neutral zone was not altered as a result of the 1991 Gulf War (q.v.).

O

OBSERVER DETACHMENT DAMASCUS (ODD). The Observer Detachment Damascus consists of approximately 35 peacekeepers to provide support and logistics to the Observer Group Golan (q.v.), which is part of the United Nations Truce Supervision Organization (q.v.)

OBSERVER GROUP BEIRUT (OGB). The Observer Group Beirut was established by the United Nations (q.v.) in August 1982, following the Israeli invasion of Lebanon (q.v.) and attacks on Beirut. The group was set up to monitor the movements of both Palestinian and Israeli forces around Beirut, but the size of the group was reduced from 50 to eight personnel following the Israeli withdrawal to southern Lebanon in 1983. The observers were drawn from the United Nations Truce Supervision Organization (q.v.).

OBSERVER GROUP EGYPT (OGE). The Observer Group Egypt was set up by the United Nations Truce Supervision Organization (q.v.) following the ending of the United Nations Emergency Force (q.v.) mandate which had been rendered obsolete by the peace treaty between Egypt and Israel (qq.v.). The objective of OGE is to maintain a neutral presence along the Israeli-Egyptian frontier. The groups consist of 50 personnel operating from six static outposts and mobile patrols in the Sinai and at Ismailia, with headquarters in Cairo.

OBSERVER GROUP GOLAN (OGG). The Observer Group Golan was set up to ensure that Israel and Syria observe the disengagement agreement which followed the 1973 Arab-Israeli War. The group consists of some 138 observers and operates in support of the United Nations Truce Supervision Organization (q.v.).

OBSERVER GROUP LEBANON (OGL). After the United Nations

Interim Force in Lebanon (q.v.) was established in March 1978, the United Nations Truce Supervision Organization (UNTSO) (q.v.) ceased to monitor the Israeli-Lebanese cease-fire line. However, the 1948 armistice line between the two states continues to be monitored and the 65 UNTSO peacekeepers were organized as OGL, operating five static observation posts and mobile patrols.

OIL EMBARGOES (1967 and 1973-1974). Oil embargoes were imposed by the Arab petroleum-exporting countries in 1967 and 1973-1974 against Western states that provided aid to Israel (q.v.) in its war with Arab adversaries. The speed and success of Israeli attacks on the Egyptian, Jordanian, and Syrian air bases in June 1967 led the Egyptians and Jordanians to conclude that both London and Washington must have participated in the planning. The Arab exporting countries met in Baghdad at an emergency meeting and decided to cut off oil supplies to Great Britain, West Germany, and the United States, but not to France, which had condemned the Israeli action. The boycott lasted until the end of August 1967 and was followed by the establishment of the Organization of Arab Petroleum Exporting Countries (OAPEC) (q.v.) in January 1968.

War with Israel broke out again in October 1973 and the OAPEC ministers met on 16 October in Kuwait (q.v.) to determine their response to President Richard Nixon's airlift of weapons to Israel. On 17 October, OAPEC ministers decided to cut production by 5 percent and to maintain the cuts on a month-to-month basis until Israel withdrew from the Occupied Territories and recognized the rights of the Palestinians. The OAPEC ministers divided the oil-importing nations as friendly, neutral, or hostile to the Arab cause, with friendly nations to be supplied at the September 1973 level, neutrals at a reduced level, and hostile nations to receive no supplies at all. This was determined in addition to the steep price rises already put into effect by the Organization of Petroleum Exporting Countries (OPEC) (q.v.). Iraq (q.v.) ignored the OAPEC decisions.

The impact of the 1973 embargo was greater than that of 1967 because it took effect in the autumn and winter and because the U.S. had become a significant importer of Arab oil. However, OAPEC resolve began to weaken as the embargo progressed, and Saudi Arabia (q.v.) was particularly concerned at the possible weakening of the West in relation to the communist bloc. President Anwar Sadat (q.v.) and Henry Kissinger persuaded King Faisal of Saudi Arabia to end his embargo and to persuade the other OAPEC members to follow suit. The embargo was eventually lifted on 18 March 1974 as a sign of "a token of Arab goodwill" to the West, but it had not achieved its objective as there had been no Israeli withdrawal and no restoration of the rights of the Palestinians. The embargo did have an impact on the Western economies, which suffered from slower growth. *See also* **Palestine**

OMAN. *See* **SAID BIN TAIMUR AL-BU SAID; QABOOS BIN SAID BIN TAIMUR; POPULAR FRONT FOR THE LIBERATION OF THE OCCUPIED ARAB GULF; POPULAR FRONT FOR THE LIBERATION OF OMAN AND THE ARAB GULF**

OPEC FUND FOR INTERNATIONAL DEVELOPMENT. The OPEC Fund for International Development was established by the member states of the Organization of Petroleum Exporting Countries (OPEC) (q.v.) on 28 January 1976 as an addition to the existing bilateral and multilateral agencies used by member countries to extend assistance to other developing countries. The agreement was reviewed in 1980, changing the fund from a joint international account into a multilateral agency for financial cooperation and assistance, endowed with an international legal identity. The fund was initially resourced with funds of $800 million, which were replenished three times and, at the end of January 1999, stood at $3.4 million.

The fund is controlled by a Ministerial Council with each of the 12 member states being represented by its Minister of Finance, or other authorized representative. The general operations of the fund are controlled by a Governing Board composed of one representative and one alternate from each member state. The business of the fund is controlled by the director-general, appointed by the Ministerial Council, under the direction of the Governing Board.

Beneficiaries of the fund's assistance program are the governments of developing countries that are not members of OPEC and international development agencies whose beneficiaries are developing countries. Special attention is paid to the least developed of the eligible countries and, as of 31 January 1999, its cumulative commitments stood at $5.2 million and disbursements at $3.6 million. Since its inception the fund has approved 778 loans totalling $4.0 billion to 105 developing countries in Africa, Asia, Europe, Latin America, and the Caribbean. As of 31 January 1999 the fund had provided 478 grants totalling $420.9 million in support of technical assistance, food aid, research activities, and emergency assistance.

The objective of the fund is to reinforce financial cooperation between member states and other developing countries. In particular, the fund is empowered to:

- provide concessional loans for balance of payments support and for the implementation of development projects and programs
- make contributions and/or provide loans to eligible international agencies
- finance technical assistance activities
- participate in the financing of private sector activities

The 12 member states include the eight Arab States of Algeria, Iran, Iraq, Kuwait, Libya (qq.v), Qatar, Saudi Arabia, and the United Arab Emirates (qq.v.).

The fund has a major publication program that includes: *Annual Report, OPEC Aid and OPEC Aid Institutions—A Profile, The Unique Experience of the OPEC Fund, The OPEC Special Fund—A New Approach to International Financial Assistance, The OPEC Fund in Africa, The OPEC Fund in Asia, The OPEC Fund in Latin America and the Caribbean,* and *OPEC Fund Newsletter* (quarterly). The fund also publishes a series of occasional papers on OPEC aid, oil and energy conservation issues, and world trade issues.

ORGANIZATION OF AFRICAN UNITY (OAU). The Organization of African Unity was established on 25 May 1963 at Addis Ababa, Ethiopia, on signature of the heads of state of 32 independent African states. The OAU aims to:

- promote the unity and solidarity of the African states
- defend the sovereignty of members
- eradicate all forms of colonialism
- promote international cooperation having due regard to the Charter of the United Nations and the Universal Declaration of Human Rights
- coordinate and harmonize members' economic, diplomatic, educational, health, welfare, scientific, and defense policies

Among the member states are the Arab and Islamic states of Algeria, Egypt (qq.v.), Eritrea, Libya (q.v.), Mauritania, Morocco, Tunisia, and Sudan.

The supreme organ of the OAU is the Assembly of Heads of State and Government which meets annually to coordinate policies of member states, with provision for extraordinary meetings. The Council of Ministers consists of Foreign Ministers, or other designated ministers, from member states and meets twice a year to approve budgets and to prepare for the Assembly of Heads of State. Day-to-day management of the OAU is handled by a secretary-general, who is appointed by the Assembly of Heads of State, with the assistance of five elected assistant secretaries-general.

The OAU has been instrumental in setting up an African Economic Community, with the Lagos Assembly in July 1979 agreeing on a comprehensive economic development program covering actions needed at national, regional, and subregional levels, and the role of the OAU Secretariat in implementing the programs. The objective was to launch the economic community by 2000. Other Assembly meetings have dealt with the economic problems facing Africa and the debt crisis burdening some member states.

The March 1995 Council of Ministers, held in Cairo, ratified an agenda to relaunch Africa's socio-economic development. The Cairo Agenda was significant in that it was an indication of what African governments were committed to carrying out themselves and the areas which required international support and assistance. The agenda gives priority to the establishment of peace, stability, security, and good governance in Africa, food security, and the building of critical capacities as a basis for embarking on programs of socio-economic development.

ORGANIZATION OF ARAB PETROLEUM EXPORTING COUNTRIES (OAPEC). OAPEC was formed in Kuwait in January 1968 following the Arab defeat in the 1967 Arab-Israeli War. Initially, membership was restricted to Algeria, Iraq, Kuwait, Libya, and Saudi Arabia (qq.v.), as oil had to be the main source of national income in order to secure membership. Qatar then joined OAPEC and in 1971, when the condition about oil in relation to income was dropped, Bahrain, Egypt, Syria, and the United Arab Emirates (qq.v.) joined the organization. The main objective of OAPEC was to safeguard the interests of its members and to foster economic cooperation in the petroleum and allied industries.

OAPEC is controlled by a Council of Ministers with the supreme authority for the organization, and the participants are usually the Ministers of Petroleum. The council is responsible for drawing up general policy, directing its activities, and determining its governing rules. The council meets twice a year as a minimum requirement with the chair rotating on an annual basis.

The council is assisted by an Executive Bureau, which draws up the agenda for council meetings, reviews the budget for council endorsement, approves staff regulations, and considers matters of interest to OAPEC. The bureau meets twice a year prior to the council meetings, but may meet on two other occasions. Membership of the bureau comprises senior officials from member states and the chair is rotated on an annual basis.

The Secretariat implements the resolutions of the council and consists of five departments: Financial and Administrative Affairs; Legal; Information and International Relations; Petroleum Projects; Library and Documentation. The Secretariat also runs an Arab Center for Energy Studies, which was established in 1983, and a training unit. In addition, there is a Judicial Tribunal comprising nine judges from Arab states that is charged with: settlement of differences in interpretation and application of the OAPEC charter, arising between member states or between OAPEC and its affiliates; disputes among member states in oil activities; and disputes submitted by the Council of Ministers.

OAPEC organizes or participates in conferences and seminars, many of which are held in cooperation with other Arab and non-Arab organizations, covering such topics as industrial development for Arab States, use of solar energy, and the integration of the Arab petrochemical industry. Training programs are also organized for Arab states, primarily for middle management and above.

OAPEC has largely stayed out of involvement in pricing or production decisions, leaving these for the Organization of Petroleum Exporting Countries (OPEC) (q.v.). OAPEC was mistakenly held responsible for the oil price rises of 1973, which was actually a decision taken by OPEC, though the boycott of nations deemed hostile to the Arab and Palestinian cause was prompted by the Arab producers led by Saudi Arabia. OAPEC members met on 16 October 1973 and agreed to cut production by 5 percent on a month-by-month basis until Israel withdrew from the Occupied Territories and recognized the rights of the Palestinians. In addition, the OAPEC ministers divided the oil-importing nations as friendly, neutral, or hostile to the Arab cause, with friendly nations to be supplied at September 1973 levels, neutral at a reduced level, and hostile nations to receive no supplies at all.

OAPEC was involved in the 1970s in setting up a number of joint ventures in projects related to oil and gas production, as well as downstream activities. The organization provided a forum for cooperation that led to a reduction in the excessive duplication of projects that had been taking place. However, these developments failed to continue into the 1980s because of the divisions among the Arab states caused by the Camp David Accords (q.v.), reached in 1978 between Egypt and Israel (qq.v.), and the decline in oil revenues, which cut investment dramatically resulting in a loss of impetus within the organization. These joint ventures include, among others, the Arab Engineering Company, Arab Maritime Petroleum Transport Company, Arab Petroleum Investments Company, and Arab Shipbuilding and Repair Yard Company (qq.v.). OAPEC publishes *The Annual Report of the Secretary-General, Annual Statistical Report, Energy Resources Monitor* (quarterly), and *Oil and Arab Cooperation* (quarterly), *Oil and Arab Development* (fortnightly), and the *OAPEC Bulletin* (monthly).

ORGANIZATION OF ISLAMIC CAPITALS AND CITIES (OICC). The OICC is an affiliated institution of the Organization of the Islamic Conference (OIC) (q.v.), founded in 1980 and based in Jeddah, Saudi Arabia (q.v.). The OICC seeks to promote and develop cooperation among OIC members, to preserve their heritage, to implement planning guidelines for the growth of Islamic cities, and to upgrade standards of public services and utilities in Islamic cities.

ORGANIZATION OF ISLAMIC SHIPOWNERS ASSOCIATION (OISA). The OISA is an affiliated institution of the Organization of the Islamic Conference (q.v.), founded in 1981, and based in Jeddah, Saudi Arabia (q.v.). The objective of the OISA is to promote cooperation among marine companies in Islamic countries. In 1998, OISA established the Bakkah Shipping Company in order to enhance sea transport in the region.

ORGANIZATION OF PETROLEUM EXPORTING COUNTRIES (OPEC). The Organization of Petroleum Exporting Countries was established in 1960 to coordinate and unify members' petroleum policies and to safeguard their interests individually and collectively. The organization has 11 member states, seven of which are Arab states, namely, Algeria, Iraq, Kuwait, Libya, Qatar, Saudi Arabia, and the United Arab Emirates (qq.v.).

The Conference of OPEC is the supreme authority with responsibility for the formulation of its general policy and decision-making based on reports and recommendations submitted by the Board of Governors. The Conference has representatives from each country, usually at ministerial level, meets at least twice a year, and confirms the appointments of Governors from each country, elects the chairman of the

Board of Governors, appoints the secretary-general, and determines the budget as submitted by the Board of Governors. The Board of Governors directs the management of the organization, implements resolutions of the Conference, and draws up an annual budget. Each member state has one Governor appointed for a two-year period and the Board meets at least twice a year. Day-to-day functions are carried out by the secretary-general under the direction of the Board of Governors.

The Economic Commission of OPEC is a specialized body operating within the framework of the Secretariat, which is designed to assist the organization in promoting stability in international petroleum markets at equitable price levels. The Commission consists of a Commission Board, National Representatives appointed by the member states, and a Commission staff.

The member states of OPEC have attempted to set aside political differences in order to protect their economic interests. In the early part of OPEC's history, a leapfrogging technique was developed in negotiations with oil companies in order to gain incremental improvements in oil revenues. These gains increased OPEC's international stature and attracted new members to the organization, but each member state still had its own agenda. The main disagreements were over pricing strategies, with states such as Algeria (q.v.), with small reserves and large populations, seeking higher prices to finance development, while Saudi Arabia (q.v.), with large reserves and a small population, appealed for moderation so that consumers would not switch to alternative fuels.

The 1970s saw a boom period in terms of oil revenues, largely due to the 1973 Arab-Israeli War and the subsequent oil embargo imposed by the Arab states to try to force the West to resolve the question of the aspirations of the Palestinian peoples. However, the reduced production levels and higher prices resulted in a drop in demand for oil due to conservation measures and increased production by non-OPEC producers. The oil market at the start of the 1980s was extremely weak and OPEC attempted to reach a voluntary consensus on production levels in order to regulate prices. A voluntary production-sharing plan came into effect in 1982, but it was largely ignored by member states, and in 1983 it was replaced by a mandatory system. OPEC also tried to stimulate demand by reducing prices, and an external accounting firm was hired to monitor production in order to prevent cheating.

However, the quota system was flawed in that Saudi Arabia refused to agree to a formal quota arguing that it presented an unacceptable limit on its sovereignty. Saudi Arabia became marginalized within OPEC and the state of the market led to a decline in the demand for

OPEC-produced oil. This depressed market led to Saudi Arabia enduring more than a proportional share of demand reduction, and by mid-1985 oil production in Saudi Arabia fell to below 3 million barrels a day. As a result, Saudi Arabia chose to set production levels to meet its own economic needs. Supplies burgeoned while prices dropped to below $10 a barrel in June 1986, and although prices have recovered, they have not recovered to pre-1985 levels. However, reduced production has led to record post-1986 prices and there is a growing concern that higher prices could stall economic growth worldwide and should be lowered.

OPEC as an organization has continued to be divided by political conflict and it has even been termed "the Organization of Political Enemy Countries." The organization was split by the Iraq-Iran War (1980-1988) (q.v.) and could not even agree on a new secretary-general when it was Iran's turn to nominate one of its nationals. An Iraqi Assistant Secretary-General had to serve in an acting capacity from 1983 to 1988. Meetings of OPEC were held in a climate of hostility and the organization's usefulness as a strategy forum was rendered ineffective. The end of the Iraq-Iran War provided an opportunity to mend OPEC fences but the invasion of Kuwait by Iraq (qq.v.) and the resultant Gulf War of 1991 (q.v.) brought fresh problems.

One of Iraq's justifications for the invasion was Kuwait's overproduction of oil and the further depressing of oil prices, but this charge could be levelled against every member state. Increased production levels were used to counter low crude oil prices, and to maintain oil revenues in order to counter domestic difficulties. United Nations (q.v.) sanctions against Iraq severely restricted Iraq's oil production, but this has been countered by increased production by other OPEC states, resulting in a continuance of conflicts over production ceilings and quota allocations. Ecuador left OPEC in 1993 to escape the organization's attempts to discipline the market and Mexico refused to join for similar reasons. Due to these political divergences and opposing interests, it is clear that oil prices will continue to fluctuate and will continue to be affected by OPEC policy. Moreover, this policy will alternate as some countries press for higher prices and thus higher oil revenues while others prefer lower, more stable prices, which do not harm worldwide economic growth and provide more regular long-term income.

Among OPEC's publications are: *Annual Report of OPEC; Facts and Figures; OPEC at a Glance; OPEC Bulletin* (monthly); *Selected Documents of the International Petroleum Industry; OPEC Monthly Oil Market Report*; and *OPEC Review* (quarterly). *See also* **OPEC Fund for International Development**

ORGANIZATION OF THE ISLAMIC CONFERENCE (OIC).

Following an arson attack on the al-Aqsa mosque in Jerusalem in August 1969, the Islamic world was in a state of shock, and a meeting was convened at Rabat, Morocco (q.v.), through the initiative of King Faisal of Saudi Arabia (q.v.). The summit was held in September 1969 and attended by representatives of 24 Muslim countries. The conference led to the establishment of the OIC in 1971 with its headquarters in Jeddah. This was the first official pan-Islamic institution of intergovernmental cooperation open to all states with a Muslim majority. It currently has 49 members, including the Palestine Liberation Organization (q.v.).

The OIC charter was adopted in 1972 and its aims were to:

- promote Islamic solidarity
- coordinate efforts to protect Islamic holy places
- support the Palestinian struggle for national rights
- increase social, cultural and economic cooperation among members

The organization is funded primarily by Saudi Arabia, which saw the OIC as a means of projecting the image of Saudi leadership of the Islamic world. It also had the objective of providing a counter to Soviet and radical Arab influences in the Middle East, but has developed into a forum for dealing with major political issues.

The OIC did fail as mediator in the Iraq-Iran War (q.v.) as it could not secure a cease-fire in 1981 and meetings were boycotted by Iran (q.v.) in 1984 (because of the OIC's refusal to inspect the effects of Iraqi [q.v.] bombing on civilian targets), and in 1987 (when the OIC meeting was scheduled for Kuwait [q.v.], which was deemed to be supporting Iraq). In Iran's absence, the 1987 meeting again called for a cease-fire in the war.

The OIC also has a number of subsidiary organizations, specialized and affiliated institutions, as follows: International Commission for the Preservation of Islamic Cultural Heritage, Islamic Center for the Development of Trade, Islamic Association of Islamic Banks, Islamic Committee for the International Red Crescent, Islamic Development Bank, Islamic Chamber of Commerce, Islamic Educational, Scientific and Cultural Organization, Islamic Institute of Technology, Islamic Solidarity Fund, Islamic University of Niger, Islamic University in Uganda, Organization of Islamic Capitals and Cities, and Organization of Islamic Shipowners Association (qq.v.).

ORGANIZATION OF THE ISLAMIC REVOLUTION IN THE ARABIAN PENINSULA (OIRAP). The existence of the OIRAP came to light in Saudi Arabia (q.v.) in November 1979 during the Ashura processions by Shi'i (q.v.) in Saudi Arabia to celebrate the martyrdom of Hussein, the oldest surviving son of Ali. This celebration had been banned in Saudi Arabia, but the rise to power of Ayatollah Khomeini in Iran (qq.v.) led to the Shi'i breaking the ban and turning the processions into pro-Khomeini demonstrations. The Saudi government deployed the National Guard to suppress the rioting and, for two months, sporadic riots and demonstrations took place resulting in the deaths of 57 guards, 99 Shi'i, and the arrests of about 600 people.

The authorities then proceeded with a campaign of repression against the OIRAP, and its leader Said Saffran was forced into exile in Iran. However, the movement continued to operate clandestinely. The OIRAP continued to make contact with Iranian pilgrims during the *hajj* (q.v.) and Saffran continued to broadcast commentaries from Iran against the Saudi ruling family.

OSLO ACCORDS. *See* **Israel; Middle East Peace Conference (1991); Palestine Liberation Organization**

OTTOMAN EMPIRE. The Ottoman Empire was founded in the late thirteenth century and survived until the end of World War I, when it was formally dissolved by the peace treaties. The Ottoman Turks took over some of the Byzantine Empire's territories and several Balkan states, part of Persia (now Iran), and the Arab lands. The empire was a multiethnic, multireligious, monarchical Muslim empire, which reached its peak in the sixteenth and seventeenth centuries. The empire comprised some 1.9 million square kilometers and had a population of some 16 million with its capital at Constantinople (now Istanbul). The empire had declined by the outbreak of World War I, but in the Middle East it still included all the Arab lands.

At this time, the empire's administration was based upon provinces (*vilayets*), divided into districts (*sanjaks*) and subdistricts (*kazas*), with each province having its own Governor. However, the bureaucracy was cumbersome, grossly inefficient, and corrupt. In the Arab lands, agriculture was the basic economic activity with landholdings being small, though large estates developed in the late eighteenth century as new land was cultivated, particularly in eastern Syria and Iraq (qq.v.). The Ottomans coped with the multireligious aspects of the empire by organizing the various ethnic and religious communities into religious nations called *millets*. Each *millet* was led by its own religious leader and was allowed to organize, fund, and administer its own religious and educational facilities.

In the Arab provinces, many of the leading Arab families were part of the Ottoman infrastructure in Constantinople and some served as officers in the Turkish army. All Arabs were treated as citizens of the Ottoman Empire with full rights and the links were strong because of their common religion and the position held by the Sultan as Caliph. Toward the end of the nineteenth century the empire was experiencing grave problems and was regarded by the Western nations as "the sick man of Europe." Although some Arab intellectuals were questioning their role and position within the Ottoman Empire, such political thinking had only considered autonomy for the Arab provinces within the Ottoman Empire.

Attitudes changed with the Young Turk revolution of 1908, which effectively turned the Sultan into a figurehead with real power resting with the Committee of Union and Progress. The change in power at the center was followed by a policy of Turkification, which began to alienate the Arab intellectuals, politicians, and army officers. As a result thinking developed into demands for total independence for the Arab lands, with the entry of Turkey into World War I on the side of Germany accelerating the process. The desire for independence led to the negotiations with Great Britain over support for the allied cause in return for postwar independence. The defeat of Turkey in World War I and the subsequent peace negotiations marked the end of the Ottoman Empire, which, for seven centuries, had been a unifying factor in the region.

The advent of the Turkish Republic and the reforms of Atatürk and subsequent regimes, many dependent on or related to the military, have led to the country becoming increasingly secular and playing down its Islamic credentials. It has also become increasingly oriented toward Europe, to the point of seeking membership in the European Union (EU) with a matching decline in interest in, and relations with, Arab and Islamic states. As a result Turkey has not been a member of many of their organizations and has only recently shown an interest in becoming a "bridge" between Europe and the Middle East and also increasing relations with the now independent Central Asian Republics.

P

PALESTINE. Palestine became a modern political entity with the collapse of the Ottoman Empire (q.v.) at the end of World War I. Prior to this, the area was part of a geographic region known as *southern Syria* (q.v.) with its boundaries defined by the Ottoman provincial administration. The Ottoman Empire revised its administrative structure in 1864 with the introduction of *vilayets*, or provinces. The largest part of Palestine and Transjordan became part of the *vilayet* of Damascus, the northern part of the country was part of the *vilayet* of Beirut with Jerusalem (q.v.), Gaza, Hebron, and Beersheba becoming a *sanjak*, or district, of Jerusalem because of its religious significance. The Jerusalem *sanjak* was also governed directly from Constantinople (now Istanbul).

At this time, the population of the Palestine region was some 500,000, more than 80 percent of whom were Muslim Arabs, 10 percent Christian, 4 percent Jews, and 1 percent Druze. The southern part of the region was largely desert and was only sparsely occupied by Bedouin tribes. The Turkish government also introduced land reforms designed to aid the efficient collection of taxes, but most of the peasant farmers evaded registration, fearing higher taxes or conscription into the Turkish army. As a result, land was registered under the names of wealthy urban notables with the peasant farmers becoming hired workers, such that by the end of the nineteenth century, 250 Arab families owned half of the cultivated land.

The Arab population of the area considered themselves as distinctive but they did not regard the Ottoman presence with hostility. The Palestinian elite benefited from the Ottoman reforms and many of them held influential posts in the region and in the Constantinople establishment. The Jewish population of some 24,000 largely resided in the district of Jerusalem, were not linked to political Zionism, and lived in reasonable harmony with their Arab neighbors. The first really significant Jewish immigration was in 1882 and these newcomers were Zionists who settled in what had been exclusively Arab areas. The results were quarrels over grazing rights, crops, and land rights, and armed clashes resulted from the purchase of land by immigrants from absentee Arab landlords and the eviction of the peasant farmers.

These tensions increased after the Young Turk revolution of 1908 and the policy of Turkification, which led to intellectuals identifying with the newly emerging Arab nationalism and a growing resistance to the perceived Zionist threat. Opposition to the Ottomans increased during World War I because of severe economic problems caused by a locust plague, drought, and famine which the Ottoman administration failed to handle. Indeed, repressive measures were imposed by the Turkish rulers. Palestine was occupied by British forces under General Sir Edmund Allenby in 1917 and placed under a military administration for the Occupied Enemy Territory South that lasted until July 1920, when it was replaced by a British civil administration.

As a result of this military administration, Palestine acquired fixed boundaries, its own government, and a separate political identity from the adjacent parts of the Ottoman Empire carved out by Britain and France as part of the Sykes-Picot Agreement. Palestine was accorded international recognition as a separate identity when Great Britain was granted the mandate (q.v.) for Palestine and Transjordan by the League of Nations in July 1922. In the following year, Great Britain unilaterally split the mandated territory into Transjordan, east of the Jordan River, and western Palestine.

The terms of the mandate required Great Britain to be responsible to the League of Nations for the governance of the country, but in reality it was governed as a colony and controlled by a High Commissioner responsible to the Colonial Office in London. The High Commissioner had authority to make all government appointments, laws, rules, and regulations, and was backed by British military forces and police. The government had its own postal service, police force, customs, transportation network, and currency, with all of the inhabitants regarded as Palestinians and British subjects.

British policy over Jewish immigration was ambivalent because it was affected by the provisions of the 1917 Balfour Declaration, which called for the establishment in Palestine of a national home for Jewish people and had been incorporated into the mandate. Britain did attempt to introduce some measurement of self-government during the 1920s and 1930s but all attempts failed due to arguments over representation. The Jewish community objected to the use of proportional representation as it would have relegated them to a minority status and prevented their objective of establishing a Jewish national home. Arab leaders also feared underrepresentation and others refused to participate because it would have implied recognition of the mandate.

All attempts to bridge the gap between the two communities failed and they developed largely in isolation from each other. Various investigative committees and a Royal Commission failed to find a solution to the problems and by 1939 Great Britain was trying to retreat from its obligations under the mandate. Each community developed its own educational, health, welfare, cultural, political, and labor organizations.

The Jews had their own schools where the language was Hebrew and their own Hebrew University, while the Arab schools were conducted in Arabic with their own curriculum and run by the mandatory Education Department. The two communities also lived separately, with the Jews in the urban areas while the Arab sector was predominantly rural.

The period from 1918 to 1948 saw the Jewish population increase through immigration from 60,000 to 600,000, while at the same time the Arab population doubled to some 1.3 million, largely through natural increase. The population change was also reflected in an increase in the number of rural collectives, cooperatives, and private farms run by Jewish settlers, and Jewish-owned industry was the dominant feature of the economy. The Jewish sector was still mainly urban, with only 7 percent of the land being Jewish owned, but this represented about one-quarter of the cultivated area.

The Jewish population was much more effectively organized, developing its own political parties and self-governing institutions, with the elected Knesset running the day-to-day affairs of the Jewish community. There were a number of political parties, grouped into four categories: general Zionists, Orthodox religions, Sephardi or Oriental, and Ashkenazi. The Arabs were much more loosely organized, with the traditional elite forming the Muslim-Christian Association in 1918, which cooperated with the British authorities but was strongly opposed to the concept of the Jewish national home. The younger politicians founded the Literary Club and the Arab Club with the former dominated by the Nashashibi family and the latter, the Husayni family. Both clubs were ardently Arab nationalist and initially supported joining Faisal's Kingdom of Syria. They were less willing to accept British rule and demanded immediate independence.

After the demise of Faisal's government in Damascus, the Palestinian Arabs concentrated on affairs at home and sought to plead the case for an independent Arab state, but to no avail. The most influential of the Arab leaders was Al-Hajj Muhammad Amin al-Husayni, who had been appointed by the mandatory government as Mufti of Jerusalem and leader of the Supreme Muslim Council. The Mufti was extremely influential, and was supported by the Husaynis, but opposed by the less-militant Nashashabi family. The opposing groups also formed political parties in the 1930s, with the Palestine Arab Party organized by the Husayni and the National Defense Party headed by the Nashashibi.

In 1936, the Arab groups came together to organize a general strike against the British and the Jewish community which was led by the

Arab Higher Committee (AHC) chaired by the Mufti and representing all political organizations. In 1937, the Nashashibi left the AHC, leaving it in the hands of the Mufti and his supporters, but it was banned by the British and several of its members deported. The Mufti and some of his associates fled to Syria, Iraq, and Lebanon (qq.v.) from where they tried to keep the rebellion alive. The Arab cause was damaged even further by clashes between the two main groups in which many Arabs were killed, with many more killed in clashes with Zionist, British, and Transjordanian forces. The use of force by the British authorities and the conflict within the Arab community caused the rebellion to peter out by 1939.

During World War II, political activity in Palestine was dormant, and after the war attempts to revive the AHC failed due to continued conflict between the Husaynis and the Nashashibi and the absence of many exiled Arab leaders. A version of the AHC was set up by the Husaynis but opposed by other factions. It was replaced by a membership determined by the Arab League (q.v.) in 1946. In the immediate postwar period, the AHC rejected all the compromise proposals put forward by Great Britain and the partition proposals of the United Nations (q.v.). A civil war broke out in December 1947 between the Arab and Jewish communities that intensified after Israel's declaration of independence in May 1948. After that, Arab volunteers and units of Arab armies joined the conflict until their ultimate defeat in January 1949.

As a result of the first Arab-Israeli War about half of the Arab population had fled or been expelled from Palestine to neighboring states. The State of Israel was established in May 1948; the Gaza Strip was occupied by Egypt (q.v.) and the West Bank by Jordan (q.v.). As a result Palestine ceased to exist as a separate political entity but in 1964 the Palestine Liberation Organization (PLO) (q.v.) was formed and represented the Palestinians in their struggle to establish a Palestinian presence in those parts of the country that were outside of the borders of Israel.

The history of the Palestinian struggle has been dominated by a series of Arab-Israeli wars and by guerrilla activity mounted by the PLO and other radical Palestinian factions. It was not until the Camp David Accords (q.v.) of 1978 that successful efforts were made to achieve peace between Israel and its Arab neighbors. By 1999 peace had been negotiated between Israel and Egypt and Jordan, with a Palestinian National Authority established to run the Gaza Strip and part of the West Bank following agreement between the two sides in secret negotiations held in Oslo (q.v.). Much still remains to be done, but at the beginning of 2000 peace negotiations continued, with more of the West Bank being handed over to Palestinian control and peace negotiations reopened with Syria (q.v.).

PALESTINE LIBERATION ORGANIZATION (PLO). The Palestine Liberation Organization was formed at an Arab summit held in East Jerusalem (q.v.) in 1964. The PLO became the institutional structure of the Palestinian national movement and the political representative of six million Palestinians, many of whom were refugees. However, the Arab states which backed the formation of the PLO saw it as a means of containing Palestinian nationalism and preventing guerrilla groups from taking independent action to liberate Palestine and destabilize the region.

The Palestinian National Council (PNC) was convened in May 1966 with 422 members. It elected an Executive Committee which selected as chairman a lawyer, Ahmed Shuqayri. The PNC also adopted a national charter which called for the elimination of Israel (q.v.) and the restoration of Palestine (q.v.) to the Palestinians. It also established a Palestinian Liberation Army which was attached to the armies of Egypt, Jordan, and Syria (qq.v.).

The Arab-Israeli War of 1967 saw the defeat of the Arab states and the discrediting of the Arab and PLO leaders. The guerrilla groups, of which al-Fath (q.v.) was the most powerful, moved to fill this political vacuum with increased attacks on Israel. On 21 March 1968, Israel retaliated at Karma in Jordan, meeting stiff resistance from the Jordanian army and the Palestinian guerrillas. This incident became a symbol of the struggle against Israel and al-Fath gained thousands of new recruits and financial support from the Gulf states as a result.

In 1968, groups such as al-Fath gained control over the PLO, and its leader Yasser Arafat (q.v.) was elected leader of the PLO and Chairman of the Executive Committee. The PLO was transformed from an Arab-controlled organization to an umbrella of disparate military and political groups. Although their common goal was the liberation of Palestine, their tactics and ideology differed widely. The most powerful group was al-Fath with its biggest rival being the Popular Front for the Liberation of Palestine (PFLP) led by George Habash. It was the PFLP that challenged Jordan's sovereignty in 1970, beginning a civil war that led to the Marxist-dominated group and other guerrilla groups being defeated and forced to relocate to Lebanon (q.v.). A number of these splinter groups developed and did much to damage the Palestinian cause by working at cross-purposes or being responsible for costly blunders such as involvement in Lebanon's civil war and the 1990 Gulf crisis.

The fragmentation of the Palestinian cause was largely prevented by the dominance of al-Fath and the leadership of Arafat, which allowed the PLO to develop military, political, and socio-economic institutions in Lebanon until 1982, when they were forced to flee to Tunis following the Israeli invasion. The foremost institution of the PLO was the PNC, which was the Palestinian parliament representing all ideological tendencies and groups including the guerrilla organizations, the labor unions, and representatives of the Palestinian communities. The infrastructure in Lebanon operated as a state within a state, providing welfare services for themselves and poor Lebanese, running light industry and businesses, and supervising the operation of many clinics and hospitals.

These operations enhanced the PLO's prestige and legitimacy and in October 1974 at the Rabat Conference (q.v.) the PLO was recognized as the sole legitimate representative of the Palestinian people. In November 1974, Arafat addressed the United Nations (q.v.) and the PLO was accorded observer status. In 1976 pro-Jordanian mayors in the West Bank and Gaza were voted out by the Palestinians and replaced by supporters of the PLO. However, withdrawal from Lebanon was a major reverse in PLO fortunes.

The PLO also experienced setbacks in relation to the question of Israel and the peace process being sidetracked by President Anwar Sadat's (q.v.) signing of the Camp David Accords (q.v.) in 1978, and entering into a separate peace with Israel in March 1979. The peace plan proposed by U.S. President Ronald Reagan in 1982 was based upon the Camp David autonomy program and again excluded the PLO. In 1983, there was a split within al-Fath led by Abu Musa and supported by Syria, which wanted control over the PLO, and this prevented Arafat from reestablishing a presence in Lebanon. Israel also attempted to further undermine the PLO by bombing its Tunis headquarters in October 1985, but the leadership escaped.

The PLO shifted its priorities toward diplomatic activity to try to reach a compromise settlement. In 1974 and 1977, the PLO moderated its stance from the liberation of all of Palestine to one of establishing a state in the West Bank and Gaza. It supported the Saudi Arabian proposals from King Fahd in 1982 that also implied a two-state solution. In 1987, the *intifada* began in the Occupied Territories. The *intifada* was so successful in terms of the level of disruption that by November 1988

Arafat was able to endorse the concept of an independent Palestinian state. At the same time, the PNC endorsed the United Nations General Assembly Resolution 181 of 1947, recognized UN Security Council Resolution 242, renounced terrorism, and accepted Israel's right to exist. This led to the United States opening up a dialogue with the PLO, but Israel refused to acknowledge a change in the PLO's policy toward the peace process.

Israel's refusal to accept a change in the stance of the PLO was partly responsible for Arafat lending support to Saddam Hussein (q.v.) during the 1990-1991 Gulf War (q.v.), but this was a major blunder because it resulted in the loss of funds from the Arab Gulf States. The PLO had also lost the financial support of the Soviet Union due to the collapse of the Soviet regime in 1991, and feared that it would be sidelined once again in any peace process. This led Arafat to agree to participate in the U.S.-led peace initiative, which resulted in the 1991 Madrid Middle East Peace Conference (q.v.) between Israel and the Arab states, though the PLO had to participate as part of a joint Jordanian-Palestinian delegation.

Despite 10 rounds of negotiations over nearly two years, the talks proved fruitless and the PLO regarded the framework as unfair and the middle-level U.S. officials as pro-Israeli. However, the Norwegians established a secret channel of negotiations in Oslo between the PLO and Israel, which, on 9 September 1993, led to the signing of the Oslo Accords. This was followed on 13 September 1993 by the signing of a Declaration of Principles by both sides in Washington, D.C. This allowed for five-year Palestinian limited autonomy in the West Bank and Gaza, starting with Jericho and the Gaza Strip. This was to be followed by further withdrawals from the Israeli-occupied West Bank and a transfer of power to a Palestinian National Authority (PNA).

In May 1994, Israeli Defense Forces withdrew from Jericho and most of the Gaza Strip and the Palestinian police assumed the security role on behalf of the PNA. A further agreement was signed on 28 September 1995, known as Oslo II, which provided for Israel's further withdrawal from less than 30 percent of the West Bank. This process was a major triumph for the PLO and Arafat, but important aspects were deferred under these agreements, such as the status of Jerusalem, Jewish settlements, and the return of 1948 refugees. The remainder of the negotiations were scheduled to take place between 1995 and 1999 but were beset by the assassination of Yitzhak Rabin, the election of a Likud government, and the establishment of further Israeli settlements. Negotiations reopened following the general election and the new government of Prime Minister Ehud Barak, leading to a further 7 percent of the West Bank being handed over to the PNA in December 1999.

If the peace process is an overall success, then the PNA and the PNC should become the dominant factions in any Palestinian state. The PLO could cease to exist as an organization at that point as its objectives would have been fulfilled. However, the opposition of Hamas (q.v.) to the peace process and the PNA, together with that of other radical Palestinian groups, could result in further discord and the excluded elements are those least capable of resolution.

PAN-ARABISM. The doctrine of Pan-Arabism is one which maintains that all Arabs, wherever they live, are members of a single community. It first emerged in the Arab provinces of the Ottoman Empire (q.v.) between 1876-1878 when the constitution promulgated by Sultan Abdul Hamid II granted a small measure of free expression. Pan-Arabism reemerged in 1908 after the Young Turks came to power, but was forced underground again when the Turkish government adopted the policy of Turkish superiority.

The declaration of the Arab Revolt (q.v.) by Sherif Hussein (q.v.) of the Hedjaz in 1916 led to his adoption of the leadership of the pan-Arab movement, with a plan to see all the Arab territories become an independent state after the defeat of the Ottomans. This concept was based on agreements reached between the Sherif and Sir Henry McMahon of the Arab Bureau (*see* **McMahon-Hussein Correspondence**) and the support provided by Great Britain to the Arab army. However, all of this was at odds with the secret Sykes-Picot Agreement of 1916 made between Great Britain and France with regard to spheres of influence in the Middle East, assuming an allied victory.

The peace negotiations at the end of the war led to the Arabs' wishes largely being ignored, as the mandate system (q.v.) was based on the spheres of influence contained in the Sykes-Picot agreement. However, the Hashemites had been installed by Britain as rulers in Iraq and Transjordan (qq.v.) and these countries became the repositories of Pan-Arabism. This state of affairs changed in 1948 when King Abdullah of Transjordan tried to reach an agreement with the Zionists in order to annex parts of Palestine to Transjordan; he was regarded as a traitor by pan-Arab nationalists.

The 1948 Arab-Israeli War and the creation of the State of Israel (q.v.) led to Pan-Arabism being directed toward the struggle to regain Palestine (q.v.) from the Israelis. The leadership of the pan-Arab movement fell to Gamal Abdul Nasser (q.v.) following the Free Officers coup in Egypt in 1952. Up to that time, Egypt (q.v.) had contributed little to the movement, other than acting as host to the Arab League (q.v.). The first real manifestation of Pan-Arabism was the creation of the United Arab Republic (q.v.) between Egypt and Syria (q.v.) in 1958, but it failed three years later. Despite this failure, Nasser was still able to lead a joint military command of Egypt, Jordan (q.v.), and Syria into the 1967 Arab-Israeli War.

The crushing defeat of the Arab armies led to Pan-Arabism again centering on the regaining of all the territories lost to Israel. The next test for Pan-Arabism came with the 1973 Arab-Israeli War and the alliance between Egypt and Syria supported by the rest of the Arab world, the oil power of the Gulf States being used as a lever against supporters of Israel through the use of production quotas and oil embargoes (q.v.). This unsuccessful war against Israel proved to be a great setback to the movement, as the signing of the peace treaty between Egypt and Israel in 1979 destroyed the consensus that had existed against the making of unilateral peace with Israel. As a result Egypt lost its leadership of Pan-Arabism, leaving the banner to President Hafiz Assad (q.v.) of Syria, who was still committed to retrieving all of the Occupied Territories.

As part of the propaganda war with Iran, Saddam Hussein (q.v.) tried to utilize the concept of Pan-Arabism to secure support for his struggle against perceived Iranian expansionism. The attempt was only partially successful as some Arab states of significance–Algeria, Libya (qq.v.), and Syria–sided with Iran (q.v.) during the Iraq-Iran War of 1980-1988 (q.v.). Also, Hussein's invasion and annexation of Kuwait (q.v.) in August 1990 split the Arab League and fatally weakened the concept of Pan-Arabism. The last remaining expression of Pan-Arabism is the Arab League itself, but even this has been weakened by the creation of the Gulf Cooperation Council and the Arab Maghreb Union (qq.v.).

PAN-ISLAMISM. Pan-Islamism is a doctrine that maintains that no matter where Muslims live they belong to a single community, or *umma* (q.v.). The doctrine transcends linguistic, cultural, and other ethnic differences among Muslims.

Pan-Islamism was used in the nineteenth century by the Ottomans during the reign of Sultan Abdul Hamid II (1876-1909) when he tried to regenerate cohesion in the Ottoman Empire (q.v.) by mobilizing the masses around the Islamic banner and encouraging a Pan-Islamism movement. Hamid showed his commitment to Pan-Islamism by personal piety, appointing Arabs to important positions at the court, and the construction of a railway from Damascus to Mecca (q.v.) to promote the *hajj* (q.v.).

The Sultan was actively backed by a number of religious personalities, including Jamal al-Din Afghani (1838-1897) (q.v.) whose role in the religious-political life of all of the significant Islamic regions–Turkey, Egypt, Iran (qq.v.), India, and Central Asia–meant that the Sultan acquired a pan-Islamic perspective and a realization that the Islamic community, as a whole, was threatened by the European powers.

The Ottoman Empire was dissolved following World War I and the Caliphate was abolished in 1924 by the Republic of Turkey, which represented real blows to the Pan-Islamism movement. However, the movement was relaunched as a popular movement with the founding of the Muslim Brotherhood in Egypt (qq.v.) in 1928, which spread quickly to Syria, Transjordan, and Palestine (qq.v.). The Muslim Brotherhood reached its zenith in Egypt in 1949 when its leader Hassan al-Banna (q.v.) was killed by security forces in Cairo. It became a suppressed organization following the 1952 army officers' coup. In Egypt, the dominant forces became Pan-Arabism and Arab Socialism (qq.v.).

The Pan-Islamism center then moved to Saudi Arabia (q.v.) with King Faisal ibn Abdul Aziz attempting to promote the movement as a counter to Arab Socialism, but the attempt failed. However, an attempted arson attack in 1969 on the al-Aqsa Mosque in Jerusalem provided the motivation for King Faisal to sponsor the Organization of the Islamic Conference (q.v.), which is a multilateral body not restricted to the Arab world.

In terms of international impact the Iranian Revolution in 1979 brought Pan-Islamism to the fore, with the new regime basing Article 10 of its constitution on a requirement that the government's policies had to be geared to "the merging and union of all Muslim peoples," while Article 152 requires Iran's foreign policy to be founded on "the defense of the rights of all Muslims." The impact outside of Iran has been minimal in real terms, except in countries with significant Shi'i (q.v.) communities, such as Lebanon and Iraq (qq.v.), but it has led to a fear elsewhere of Pan-Islamism and Islamic fundamentalism (q.v.). One outward manifestation of this fear was the action of the Algerian military in 1991 to abort the election victory of the Front Islamique de Salut. The pan-Islamic movement remained a utopian ideology as its leadership was weak and the rivalry between Sunnism (q.v.) and Shi'ism could not be surmounted.

PEACEKEEPING. The Middle East and North Africa have hosted a number of peacekeeping forces under the auspices of the United Nations (q.v.) as a result of the various Arab-Israeli wars since 1948, the Western Sahara (q.v.) dispute, and the Yemen Civil War. The Arab states themselves have also been involved in peacekeeping operations through the Arab Deterrent Force, created under the auspices of the Arab League (q.v.), which was deployed to try to keep peace in Lebanon (q.v.) when the civil war broke out in 1976. Other peacekeeping operations have also been carried out by the Organization of African Unity (OAU) (q.v.), particularly in Chad.

The Arab League (q.v.) has also been involved in peacekeeping through mediation between member states which have not resulted in a military role as has the OAU in mediation between Libya (q.v.) and Chad and Algeria (q.v.) and Morocco. There have also been individual attempts at a peacekeeping role such as efforts by Jordan and Yemen (qq.v.) separately to try to produce a settlement to the Iraqi invasion of Kuwait (qq.v.) in order to prevent hostilities between Iraq and the Allied coalition. *See also* **Arab Deterrent Force; Arab League Force in Kuwait; Border Disputes; Multinational Forces: Observer Detachment Damascus; Observer Group Beirut; Observer Group Egypt; Observer Group Golan; Observer Group Lebanon; Riyadh Resolution; Symbolic Arab Security Force; United Nations; United Nations Disengagement Observer Force; United Nations Emergency Force I; United Nations Emergency Force II; United Nations Guard Contingent in Iraq; United Nations Interim Force in Lebanon; United Nations Iran-Iraq Military Observer Group; United Nations Iraq-Kuwait Military Observer Mission; United Nations Mission for the Referendum in Western Sahara; United Nations Observation Group in Lebanon; United Nations Special Commission in Iraq; United Nations Truce Supervision Organization; United Nations Yemen Observation Mission**

POPULAR FRONT FOR THE LIBERATION OF OMAN AND THE ARAB GULF (1971-1974) (PFLOAG). At its third congress held in 1971, the Popular Front for the Liberation of the Occupied Arab Gulf (q.v.) lowered its sights from achieving a socialist revolution to effecting a national democratic revolution. It also modified its name, but not its acronym. In its new guise, the movement succeeded in withstanding British-backed Omani attacks and aid had to be secured by the Sultanate from Egypt, Jordan, and Iran (qq.v.) which resulted in severe military reverses for the movement. The position of the PFLOAG had also weakened as a result of the social and political reforms introduced by

Sultan Qaboos and the major investment in the Dhofar Province through the Civil Aid Program. In July 1974 at its Congress, the PFLOAG decided to limit its activities to Oman and renamed itself the Popular Front for the Liberation of Oman.

However, the PFLOAG had established a base in Bahrain (q.v.) and, following British withdrawal in 1971 from the Gulf, it began to flex its muscles. The ruler Sheikh Isa al Khalifa had made some minimal moves toward power sharing with his ministers and the PFLOAG joined forces with the Bahrain National Front in calling for a general strike. Sheikh Isa agreed to hold elections to a constituent assembly but refused to release all political prisoners, or to grant votes to women, which led to a boycott of the polls by the PFLOAG, repeated at the general election in December 1973. The parliament was dissolved in August 1975 and, in the crackdown that followed, most of the leaders of the PFLOAG were imprisoned. *See also* **Popular Front for the Liberation of the Occupied Arab Gulf**

POPULAR FRONT FOR THE LIBERATION OF THE OCCUPIED ARAB GULF (1968-1971) (PFLOAG). The Popular Front for the Liberation of the Occupied Arab Gulf grew out of the Dhofar Liberation Front when, at its second congress in September 1968 in South Yemen (q.v.), it decided to extend its activity to the remainder of Oman and the other Arab Gulf States. The movement was based on opposition to neoimperialism, neocolonialism, and local oligarchies, and committed to achieving a socialist revolution. The PFLOAG saw Dhofar as a link between South Yemen and the remainder of the Arabian Gulf and was backed by the Marxist regime in South Yemen and by the People's Republic of China.

After two years of terrorist activity, the PFLOAG had succeeded in gaining control of about two-thirds of Dhofar Province and began to extend activities to the remainder of Oman. Great Britain had a special relationship with the Sultanate and was so alarmed at these developments that it assisted in a coup to replace Sultan Said bin Taimur (q.v.) with his son, Qaboos bin Said bin Taimur (q.v.), which was effected in July 1970. The new regime under Sultan Qaboos instituted a series of socio-political reforms and launched a major community development program in the troubled Dhofar Province.

The Sultan built up his armed forces with British assistance and also accepted military aid from Iran, Egypt, and Jordan (qq.v.), and the tide began to turn against the PFLOAG, especially in terms of support among the Dhofari population. In 1976, South Yemen withdrew its support as a response to pressure from Saudi Arabia and the PFLOAG agreed to a cease-fire in 1976. The following year saw the withdrawal of Iranian troops, and the PFLOAG took the opportunity to regroup, but its effectiveness had been destroyed and its activities were restricted to sporadic attacks and assassinations. In 1982, South Yemen and Oman signed a normalization agreement and the PFLOAG ceased to exist. *See also* **Popular Front for the Liberation of Oman and the Arabian Gulf**

POPULAR PAN-ARAB ISLAMIC CONGRESS. The leader of the Muslim Brotherhood (q.v.) in Sudan, Hasan al-Turabi, led the first major split with the International Organization of the Muslim Brotherhood (q.v.) setting up the Popular Pan-Arab Islamic Congress in order to loosely represent the major Islamic movements. The first conference of the Congress was held in Khartoum in 1991 and the second in 1993 when the word *Arab* was retained despite opposition from Iran (q.v.), which regarded the term as racist. The third Congress took place in 1995 and 80 states were represented, including representatives from the Muslim Brotherhood, the Front Islamique de Salut, and Iran. At this conference a decision was taken to set up branches throughout the Islamic world. The Congress does not believe in centralization and gives more autonomy to local movements, believing that they should cooperate as independent units functioning in differing environments. The Arab Islamic Congress accepts that what may be helpful in one movement may not be appropriate for another, whereas the Muslim Brotherhood tends to adhere to the decisions of central authorities.

Q

QABOOS BIN SAID BIN TAIMUR (1940-). Sultan Qaboos was born in Salalah, Dhofar Province, becoming ruler of Oman (q.v.) after a coup against his father, Sultan Said bin Taimur (q.v.), on 23 July 1970. Qaboos was educated privately in Salalah before attending a private college in Great Britain. He then attended the Royal Military Academy at Sandhurst and served briefly with British forces in West Germany before returning to Britain to study sociology and political administration. Qaboos was recalled to Oman in 1965 and placed under surveillance at the royal palace. Among his visitors were British expatriates, some of whom were used by London to plot the coup to overthrow his father, who had kept Oman underdeveloped, isolated, and under attack from leftist guerrilla groups based in Yemen (q.v.).

On accession, Qaboos had also become responsible for the offices of Prime Minister, Defense, and Foreign Affairs. He encouraged exiled, educated Omanis to return to assist with the rebuilding of the nation, including Omanis who had been living in Zanzibar for a number of years, and brought in expatriates to fill other crucial posts associated with development and modernization needs. Qaboos ended Oman's isolation by joining the Arab League and the United Nations (qq.v.) and expanding Oman's diplomatic representation throughout the world.

As part of a campaign against the Dhofari rebels and the Popular Front for the Liberation of Oman and the Arab Gulf (q.v.), Qaboos instigated a Civil Aid Program aimed at winning over the hearts and minds of the people. The objective was to bring education and health, agricultural and welfare services to the province to remove some of the underlying causes of unrest. On the military front, the army was expanded with a large intake of foreign mercenaries, especially from Pakistan; in 1973, Qaboos accepted an offer of troops from Iran (q.v.). Further aid came from Egypt, Jordan, Saudi Arabia (qq.v.), and Britain, enabling Oman to defeat the rebels in 1975. For the next two to three years, the threat was only from sporadic raids or assassination attempts, but did not present a serious threat to the regime.

Qaboos made great strides in developing the state through considerable investment in infrastructure projects. Initially, Oman had to rely on expatriate labor to provide the expertise necessary for development. As a result of this program, Oman now has a good education system, including a teacher-training college, a medical school, a university, and a program aimed at eradicating adult illiteracy. Qaboos has also brought Oman into the modern world through an investment program in the health services, social services, telecommunications, expansion of the economy, and social justice.

A great deal has been achieved since 1970, but Oman is not without problems, particularly in relation to the succession, future economic problems, and social stability. Prospects for the immediate future are good, with reserves of oil and gas providing revenue well into the twenty-first century. Oman also has the advantage of an agricultural and fishing base with development potential, and mineral resources not found elsewhere in the Gulf. However, the pace of economic diversification must be maintained if Qaboos is to satisfy the social and economic aspirations of the population.

Qaboos has always pursued an independent foreign policy and he was the only Arab leader who did not condemn Egypt for signing the Camp David Accords (q.v.). In 1980, he signed an accord with the

United States, allowing access to Oman's ports and harbors and permitting the U.S. to stockpile military supplies on its soil. Qaboos ended his regional isolation in September 1980 by supporting Iraq's position in the Iraq-Iran War (q.v.) and he was a cofounder of the Gulf Cooperation Council (q.v.) in 1981. However, he adopted a non-participatory stance in the Iraq-Iran conflict due to the proximity of Iran (q.v.) across the Strait of Hormuz. In the 1991 Gulf War (q.v.), Qaboos provided ground and air forces for the U.S.-led coalition. He also endorsed the 1993 Oslo Accord (q.v.) between the Israelis and the Palestinians (qq.v.) and hosted a multilateral conference in Muscat in 1993 as part of the peace process.

Although refusing to abandon any of his powers, Qaboos established a Consultative Council to advise on socio-economic matters, for which elections are held, and he makes regular consultative visits throughout the Sultanate.

QADDAFI, MUAMMAR AL- (1942-). Muammar al-Qaddafi was probably born in the spring of 1942 to a Bedouin family near Sirite in northern Libya (q.v.). Qaddafi did not begin school until he was 10 years old, when he attended a local mosque school before attending secondary school from 1956-1961. He was expelled from school in Sabha and completed his education in Misurta before joining the Libyan Military Academy, graduating in 1965. After completing a course in Great Britain, Qaddafi was posted to Benghazi, where he established a network of conspirators planning to overthrow the monarchy. This was achieved in a bloodless coup on 1 September 1969 while King Muhammad Idris al-Sanusi was in Turkey (q.v.).

The group called themselves the *Free Unionist Officers.* Following the coup, they established a Revolutionary Command Council, which, by December 1969, was given full authority to govern the country. At that time, Qaddafi was revealed as leader of the group and, although he still serves as head of state, he holds no formal position of authority. At this time, Qaddafi was an admirer of Gamal Abdul Nasser's (q.v.) brand of Arab Nationalism (q.v.) and also a devout Muslim, which is testified to by his reputation for personal integrity. Initial policies included the banning of alcohol and closure of churches and night clubs. This was followed by the closure of British and U.S. military bases, expulsion of the remaining Italian residents, and nationalization of all foreign-owned banks. Arabic was also made the only language recognized in all official and public communications.

During the mid-1970s, Qaddafi had become disenchanted with

Egyptian policies and particularly with Nasser's successor, President Anwar Sadat (q.v.). Also at this time, Qaddafi became a political visionary, publishing three volumes of the *Green Book* in which he developed his "Third International Theory," which was designed to replace competitive and single-party politics. Qaddafi instituted a system of popular congresses and committees, composed of elected members, to run the country, including national policy review and implementation, management of state enterprises, local administration, and control of the universities.

At the same time, Qaddafi had introduced a series of economic reforms which were based on a radically egalitarian vision of economic relations based on equal partnerships, and by nonprofit state-run distribution of goods and services. The outcome was that enterprises were taken over by workers, landlords lost their property to tenants, and retail trade disappeared. The outcomes were shortages of goods, hoarding of basic commodities, a halt to housing construction, and an increase in the already widespread economic inefficiency. The country only survived the chaos that these parallel reforms produced because of its significant oil revenues and the existence of a substantial expatriate workforce.

However, by the end of the 1970s, Qaddafi had become disenchanted with the ineffectiveness of the congresses and committees. He introduced a series of revolutionary committees to act as a watchdog, but they only succeeded in obscuring lines of authority because they were not equipped to resolve the problems brought about by inexperience and the unrealistic expectations that had been placed upon the congresses and committees. These domestic failures were attributed by Qaddafi to foreign and domestic subversion, and the revolutionary committees were charged with responsibility for "liquidating the enemies of the revolution" both at home and abroad.

Qaddafi was branded by Western nations as a sponsor of international terrorism due to his support for various radical, militant Palestinian factions, the Irish Liberation Army, and the assassination of Libyan opponents of his regime in exile. His condemnation of the 1978 Camp David Accords (q.v.), large arms purchases, and further acts of terrorism were instrumental in the United States bombing Tripoli and Benghazi in April 1986, targeting Qaddafi personally. His adopted daughter was killed and members of his family injured. Nonetheless, he continued working for Arab unity, only this time with neighboring nations. In 1981, he entered an Arab-African Union with Algeria and Morocco (qq.v.). In 1989 Libya joined a Union of the Arab Maghreb (q.v.)

with Algeria, Mauritania, Morocco, and Tunisia.

After these raids, Qaddafi adopted a lower international profile, which was also determined by severe economic problems and the 1991 demise of his superpower patron, the Soviet Union. In the 1980s, Libya suffered acutely from the collapse in oil prices and the imposition of sanctions by the U.S. and other Western nations. As a result, some of Qaddafi's domestic reforms had to be reversed, with a resumption of small-scale retail trade and the release of some political prisoners. The handing over of the Libyans suspected of involvement in the Pan Am bombing over Lockerbie, Scotland, for trial has also eased tensions and resulted in the lifting of economic sanctions. However, there is no evidence that Qaddafi has changed his utopian vision with regard to the future of Libya and support for the freedom of other Arab peoples in the Middle East.

QASIM, ABD AL-KARIM (1914-1968). Abd al-Karim Qasim was born into a poor Baghdad family. His father was a Sunni (q.v.) Muslim and his mother a Kurdish Shi'i (qq.v.). Qasim taught for a year in a primary school before going to military college in Iraq (q.v.), graduating in 1934. As an Iraqi officer, he fought in the 1948 war against Israel (q.v.) and was bitter at the Arab defeat, which he attributed to the corruptness of the Arab monarchies.

The Free Officers coup in Egypt (q.v.) in 1952 reverberated throughout Iraq, as there was dissatisfaction among the Iraqi military as a result of the failed anti-British coup of 1941 and the repression of the nationalists. The Iraqi officers formed themselves into underground cells and Qasim joined the organization in 1955, soon becoming Chairman of the Central Committee of Free Officers. On 14 July 1958, the officers staged a successful coup, which resulted in the killing of the royal family and Prime Minister Nuri al-Said (q.v.). Qasim became president and prime minister of the new republic, with his fellow officer, Abd al-Salam Arif (q.v.), becoming deputy prime minister. The first rift between the two officers came over Iraq's policy toward Egypt: Qasim wanted to keep his distance while Arif favored rapprochement and eventual membership in the United Arab Republic (q.v.).

Qasim was anti-Western in his policies, withdrawing Iraq from the Baghdad Pact (q.v.), restoring relations with the Soviet Union, and signing an arms agreement with the Soviets. Domestically, he introduced agrarian reform and passed legislation giving women additional rights in matters of divorce and inheritance. In 1961, Qasim stripped the foreign-owned Iraq Petroleum Company of 99.5 percent of its concessionary territory.

For a time, political parties had freedom to operate, but Qasim's lenience toward the activities of the communists led to dissatisfaction among the population and the army. The rift with Arif was exacerbated by this unrest and Qasim had him arrested and imprisoned. Qasim also had to cope with Kurdish separatists: a revolt started by Mustafa Barzin (q.v.) in 1960 lasted, with brief cease-fires, until 1963, which weakened the legitimacy of the regime. Qasim faced regional problems when he revived vague historical claims to Kuwait (q.v.), which had been given its independence by Great Britain in 1961. In response to a perceived threat, Great Britain sent troops for Kuwait's defense, later to be replaced by a force from the Arab League (q.v.), thus isolating Qasim from his Arab neighbors.

During this period, the Ba'athist Party (q.v.) and nationalists had been organizing themselves; they mounted a successful coup on 8 February 1963. Qasim was arrested and executed on 9 February with Arif succeeding as president, with a Ba'athist prime minister, and a civilian government.

R

RABAT ARAB SUMMIT. This summit was held on 25 October 1974 with the foreign ministers of the Arab League (q.v.) at Rabat, Morocco, to coordinate an Arab strategy with regard to Israel (q.v.). The main issue was representation of the Palestinians and the agenda relating to the formation of a Palestinian state. On 26 October, the heads of state met and approved the proposals from the foreign ministers that the Palestine Liberation Organization (PLO) (q.v.) should be the sole representative of the Palestinian people in negotiations with Israel. The summit also agreed to support the PLO's claim to any territory vacated by Israel to enable the establishment of an independent state.

Only Jordan (q.v.) voted against the proposals as it had previously represented the West Bank Palestinians in negotiations with Israel, and Muammar al-Qaddafi (q.v.) refused to attend the summit. Also approved at the summit was a multibillion-dollar package of aid to the front-line states of Egypt, Syria, Jordan (qq.v.), and the PLO. This summit is seen as having paved the way for a two-state solution to the regional crisis with Arab states approving creation of a Palestinian state, based on the West Bank and Gaza, while allowing the State of Israel to exist. *See also* **Palestine**

REGIONAL ARAB INFORMATION TECHNOLOGY NETWORK (RAITNET). The network was founded in 1996 by members and participating institutions of the Regional Information Technology and Software Engineering Center (RITSEC) (q.v.) with the support of the International Telecommunications Union (ITU) and the United Nations Educational, Scientific, and Cultural Organization (UNESCO), and is based in Cairo, Egypt (q.v.).

The main objectives of the RAITNET are to:

- encourage and promote exchange of information between the Arab members and the international community for the benefit of national and regional development
- promote and participate in the development of high-quality information and telecommunications infrastructure for the benefit of Arab states
- facilitate coordination of the activities between the RAITNET and the other international networks
- act as a consultative voice on information technology issues that have a national, regional, or international dimension
- organize meetings, training courses, and workshops for the development of human resources in the Arab region
- stimulate, design, coordinate, or participate in the implementation of training activities, projects, and studies at the national, regional, or international level in the fields of informatics, communication, and networking information systems

It is intended that these objectives should be met using open standards and the most advanced technology available.

REGIONAL INFORMATION TECHNOLOGY AND SOFTWARE ENGINEERING CENTER (RITSEC). The center was established in January 1982 as a joint project between the Arab Fund for Economic and Social Development (AFESD) (q.v.) and the United Nations Development Program (UNDP) (q.v.) with the government of Egypt (q.v.) acting as host to the RITSEC in Cairo. The RITSEC has been created as a regional, nonprofit organization to provide technical, professional, and developmental services to the agencies, institutions, and governmental organizations in the Arab region.

The objectives of the RITSEC are to:

- contribute to and empower the development and utilization of

knowledge through the provision of education and professional development using traditional and distance learning approaches
- help build software engineering capacities, use, and development of IT tools, products and services
- lead regional and global cultural heritage preservation using information technology tools and techniques
- contribute to the development of new initiatives in high-priority areas, such as e-commerce, distance education, and intellectual property rights

The RITSEC has launched a series of programs for regional development, as well as business development, in the area of information technology to promote the transfer of knowledge and experience in the region. Among the services offered by the center are: consultancy, project formulation, project management, project design and implementation, training, product and system development, and technical support. The programs supported by the center are: Culture Preservation Program, Human Resource Development Program, Regional Distance Learning Program, Environment Information Program, Communication and Networking Program, and the Arab Child of the Twenty-First Century-Little Horus.

The Little Horus project is a web site for children launched in June 1997 in Arabic and English, designed as an investment in the future to prepare Arab children for the new millennium. Among the activities of the project is the Cyber Café, aimed at the population under the age of 20. By the end of 1999, 40 centers had been established in the region and the Web site had attracted over 2.5 million visitors.

RESEARCH CENTER FOR ISLAMIC HISTORY, ART, AND CULTURE (IRCICA). The IRCICA was founded in 1979 and is based in Istanbul, Turkey (q.v.), as a subsidiary of the Organization of the Islamic Conference (q.v.). The center holds exhibitions, seminars, and lectures, conducts research programs, and maintains a research database. The objective of the IRCICA is to study the cultural legacy of Muslim countries, to foster understanding among Muslims, and to oppose foreign misconceptions and prejudices against Islam (q.v.). Additionally it seeks to correct distortions of Islam found in textbooks, and encourages the exchange of books on history, art, and culture among universities and research institutions. The center also acts as the Secretariat of the International Commission for the Preservation of Islamic Cultural Heritage (q.v.). Its main publication activities are the *Library*

Accession List (in English), a *Newsletter* (quarterly in Arabic and English), and an *International Directory of Islamic Cultural Institutions* (in English with irregular updates).

RIYADH ARAB SUMMIT CONFERENCE. The summit was convened by Prince Fahd of Saudi Arabia (q.v.) on 16 October 1976, following Syria's (q.v.) entry into the Lebanese Civil War, which had been in progress for some 18 months. The summit called for a cease-fire to be imposed by an Arab Deterrent Force (q.v.), which, in effect, legitimized the Syrian presence as they provided 25,000 of the 30,000 troops, under Syrian command. Although the summit succeeded in halting full-scale war, the fighting did not stop, and the withdrawal of armed men and weapons was not implemented. The summit also rejected Yasser Arafat's (q.v.) attempts to raise the issue of the Israeli (q.v.) presence in South Lebanon. The summit was restricted to representatives from Egypt, Kuwait, Lebanon, Syria, and the Palestine Liberation Organization (PLO) (qq.v.), and its resolutions were ratified on 25 October 1976 at an Arab League (q.v.) meeting in Cairo, Egypt.

RIYADH RESOLUTION. This resolution was adopted at the Riyadh Arab Summit Conference (q.v.) of the Arab League (q.v.) on 18 October 1976 and outlined the functions of the Arab Deterrent Force (q.v.) which evolved from the Symbolic Arab Security Force (q.v.) and was intended to keep peace in Lebanon (q.v.). According to the resolution the force was to ensure observance of the cease-fire, disengage the belligerents, deter any violation of the agreement, maintain internal security, supervise the withdrawal of armed forces to positions held on 13 April 1975, supervise the collection of heavy weapons, and assist the Lebanese authorities where necessary.

S

SABAH, AL-. *See* **KUWAIT**

SADAT, MUHAMMAD ANWAR (1918-1981). Anwar Sadat was born in Mit Abul Kom in the Nile Delta, the son of a minor civil servant, and raised in Cairo. He graduated from the Cairo Military Academy in 1938 and was jailed in the summer of 1942, having been found guilty of spying for Germany. Sadat escaped in 1944 and went underground until the detention order was lifted. He spent a further two years in jail from 1946-1948 as a suspect in the assassination of Ahmad Osman, a Cabinet Minister, but was acquitted.

Following release from prison, Sadat went into business, but this failed. In 1949, he rejoined the army with his former rank of Captain, being posted to Rafah in the Sinai Peninsula, where he met Gamal Abdul Nasser (q.v.). Sadat participated in the Free Officers coup of 1952 and secured a seat on the Revolutionary Command Council (RCC), acting as liaison with the Muslim Brotherhood (q.v.), with whom he had friendly relations. He also edited the regime's newspaper *Al-Gumhuriya* (The Republic), was Speaker of the parliament from 1959-1969, and from 1964-1966 was one of four vice presidents.

Sadat was chosen as secretary-general of the Islamic Congress in 1965, and represented Egypt (q.v.) at international gatherings, including the summit that founded the Organization of the Islamic Conference (q.v.) in 1969. At the end of 1969 Sadat was appointed a sole vice president by Nasser and, on Nasser's death in September 1970, became acting president. In October 1970, he was elected president in a referendum, being the only candidate. Sadat had been engaged in a power struggle with Ali Sabri, secretary-general of the Arab Socialist Union, but this ended in May 1971 when he arrested Sabri and his close aides. In September 1971, Sadat promulgated a new constitution, which was less socialist that its predecessor. In mid-1973, he purged the Arab Socialist Union of leftists.

Sadat signed a 15-year Egyptian-Soviet Friendship Treaty in May 1971, but in July 1972 he demanded that all Soviet advisors had to leave Egypt within 10 days. Some 15,000 Soviet personnel left, taking fighter aircraft, interceptors, and surface-to-air missiles, though some returned after October 1972 and others after February 1973. A rapprochement was reached with Moscow in March 1973, heralding the renewal of Soviet arms shipments.

In 1973, Sadat began to plan an invasion of the Israeli-occupied Arab territories, which took place in October and in which the Egyptian forces performed well, capturing land in the Sinai that they held against Israeli counterattacks. This incident enhanced Sadat's reputation at home and in the region but, instead of pursuing peace through the United Nations (q.v.), Sadat opted for U.S. mediation in talks with Israel (q.v.), thus breaking with Arab ranks. Two interim disengagement agreements were reached with Israel in 1974 and 1975 over the Sinai, but after these agreements, the peace process was stalled.

At home, Sadat pursued a policy of economic liberalization that involved the reduction or removal of government subsidies, which triggered violent bread riots in January 1977. The riots were only stemmed when the price rises were withdrawn. Sadat appealed for aid to the U.S., which responded positively, but the Soviet Union's refusal to reschedule Egypt's $12 billion debt caused Sadat to unilaterally abrogate the Egyptian-Soviet Friendship Treaty.

In November 1977, Sadat took the unprecedented step of addressing the Israeli Knesset, which raised his status in the Western world; the U.S. began to provide Egypt with military aid. On 18 September 1978, Sadat signed the Camp David Accords (q.v.) with Israel Premier Menachem Begin. In the following year, Sadat signed a bilateral peace treaty with Israel. At home, Sadat feared a military coup and he dismissed his chief of staff and defense minister, and charged Mustafa Khalil, leader of the National Democratic Party (NDP), with leading a peace government of academics and technocrats. However, the peace treaty had led to Egypt's isolation in the Arab world, with expulsion from the Arab League (q.v.) and the breaking off of diplomatic relations.

Sadat assumed greater power domestically by dissolving parliament and then rigging the first multiparty elections in June 1979, with his NDP securing 83 percent of the seats. The last of the experts from the Soviet Union were also expelled and Egypt became even more reliant on American aid. Sadat forced Khalil to resign in May 1980 and he became prime minister. Sadat immediately held a stage-managed referendum that abrogated that part of the constitution limiting the presidency to one six-year term. The peace treaty with Israel and rising corruption within the Egyptian elite alienated Sadat from the Islamic forces within Egypt and the dismantling of Nasser's economic policies fuelled inflation, bringing severe hardship to the working and lower middle classes.

Sadat became even more autocratic and contemptuous of the opposition, whether secular or religious, and he banned strikes and demonstrations. In September 1981, he instigated a crackdown on dissidents, resulting in some 2,000 arrests. On 6 October 1981, he was assassinated by Islamic militants during a parade to mark the anniversary of the 1973 Arab-Israeli War. Sadat's death did not cause popular unrest or lead to demonstrations of public grief, such as those seen after the death of Nasser.

SAID, NURI Al- (1888-1958). Nuri al-Said was born in Baghdad to a Sunni (q.v.) family of mixed Arab-Kurdish origin. Said graduated from the Istanbul Military Academy and became a commissioned officer in the Ottoman army. In 1914, he joined one of the Arab secret societies,

Al-Ahd (The Covenant), and he defected from the Ottoman army in 1916 to join the Arab Revolt (q.v.) led by Sherif Hussein (q.v.) of the Hedjaz. Said became chief of staff in the army of Faisal ibn Hussein and, after Faisal became King of Iraq (q.v.) in 1921, Said was appointed chief of army staff. He became minister of defense from 1922 to 1924 and 1926 to 1928, becoming prime minister in 1930.

Said founded a political party named after the Arab secret society, Al-Ahd, though he had abandoned Pan-Arabism (q.v.) and reached an accommodation with the British mandate, formalized in the Anglo-Iraqi treaty of 1930, which provided for the appearance of, if not the substance of, independence. In 1939, Said was appointed prime minister but, despite his pro-British leanings, dared not join the Allies in World War II because of the strong anti-British feeling in Iraq. In March 1940, he resigned as prime minister, but agreed to join the cabinet of Rashid Ali Gailani, which lasted until January 1941, remaining out of the next Gailani government which took office in April 1941. Great Britain overthrew the Gailani government in May 1941 and Said again became prime minister, declaring war against Germany in 1943. By the time he relinquished office in June 1944 he had been involved in the groundwork for the launching of the Arab League (q.v.).

Following the end of World War II, Said served as prime minister in 1946-1947, 1949, and 1950-1952, before Faisal II came of age in 1953. After the general election of June 1954, Said was again appointed prime minister in order to oversee renegotiation of the 1930 Anglo-Iraq treaty, which was due to expire in 1955. However, Said's joining of the Baghdad Pact (q.v.) and his failure to condemn the aggressors in the Suez War of 1956 caused Iraq's isolation from the rest of the Arab world.

Said had become increasingly dictatorial, had manipulated the electoral system, and had banned political parties, which made the regime increasingly unpopular. Following the Free Officer coup in 1958, Said and the royal family were assassinated.

SAID BIN TAIMUR AL-BU SAID (1910-1972). Said was Sultan of Oman from 1932 to 1970 having succeeded, aged 25, on the abdication of his father. His prime objective was to rescue the Sultanate from insolvency and to reduce the influence of Great Britain, which had propped up a number of rulers since 1800. In this aim, he was generally successful, though at the expense of development in the state, and his manner of rule was autocratic. On his accession, Said had inherited a split country, as the Imamate in the interior was run as a separate entity, having been developed from the 1920 Treaty of Sib. It was only in 1959 with British support that the Imam's forces were defeated and reunification achieved.

Oil revenues began to flow in the 1960s but Said found it impossible to alter his parsimonious policy and development, unless oil related, was almost nonexistent. Unrest began to manifest itself within the state and it was evident that Said had lost touch with the needs of the country fuelled by returning Omani workers from neighboring oil states. An uprising began in Dhofar Province, led by the Dhofar Liberation Front and backed by left-wing activists from Yemen (q.v.), which in turn became the Popular Front for the Liberation of the Occupied Arab Gulf (q.v.) and then the Popular Front for the Liberation of Oman and the Arab Gulf (q.v.). The unrest then spread into northern Oman, threatening the oilfields, and insurgents were now receiving backing from the Soviet Union and the People's Republic of China.

Modest programs of development initiated by Said were too late to dispel the level of social unrest and resentment. It was clear by 1970 that the position of Said was untenable and key Omanis and British expatriates helped to plan a coup, which placed his son, Qaboos bin Said, on the throne on 25 July 1970, while his father was in London having medical treatment.

SAUD, AL- DYNASTY. *See* **SAUDI ARABIA**

SAUDI ARABIA. The Kingdom of Saudi Arabia is the largest country in the Arabian Peninsula, occupying an area of 2,150,000 square kilometers (much of which is barren and lacking in water), and a population of some 18 million. The Nejd, the most populous part of the kingdom, receives some winter rainfall and has significant reserves of groundwater. It is also the home of the Saudi royal family and the center of Wahhabism (q.v.), which has determined the evolution of the kingdom. The Nejd is also an agricultural center making the kingdom self-sufficient in wheat and poultry.

The western area of the kingdom covers the Hedjaz, with the holy cities of Mecca (q.v.) and Medina, borders the Red Sea, and contains the commercial port of Jeddah and the industrial complexes at Jubail and Yanbu. The central mountainous area houses the city of Taif, which is the seat of government in the summer, and the southern part comprises Asir Province, which is a highly populated area. The eastern province is separated from the Nejd by the desert area, including the Rub'al-Khali, or Empty Quarter, which occupies about one quarter of the kingdom. This province borders the Arabian Gulf and in the south are the biggest oilfields around Dhahran, Abqayq, and Hufuf.

The Kingdom of Saudi Arabia is dominated politically and culturally by the inhabitants of the Nejd, the Nejdis, though the term is now used to describe the desert and small-village people throughout the kingdom. The Nejdis are of pure Arabian stock, independent, strong-willed, and aloof, largely as a result of their ability to have survived in a harsh environment prior to the discovery of oil. The major political influence was wielded through the tribal structure, which was weakened in the 1950s when the oil-based economy had developed, but tribal origins still have social importance.

Cultural dominance of the Nejdis is also based on their having been devotees of Wahhabism (q.v.), or more properly Unitariansim, founded by Muhammad ibn 'Abd al-Wahhab. The origins of the movement are traced back to 1745 when the chieftain of the village of Diriyya, north of Riyadh, Muhammad ibn Saud became a patron of al-Wahhab and his revivalist movement. The movement was based on the strict Hanbali (q.v.) school of Islamic jurisprudence and sought to cleanse society of the corrupt practices which had grown up since the death of the Prophet. The propagation of the creed was, and remains, the basis of the Saudi state, and the descendants of al-Wahhab are strong supporters of the Saudi royal family and occupy ministerial and judicial posts in the government.

Outside of the Nejdis the next most significant group are the Hedjazis who comprise the urban populations of Jeddah, Taif, Mecca, Medina, as well as Yanbu and other towns of the central part of the Tihama plain and the mountainous areas in the west of the kingdom. The occupants of this province are not all of pure Arabian stock, but are descended from a mixture of races, including settlers from the desert and descendants of pilgrims who came to Arabia from Africa, Egypt, Iran, Syria, Turkey, Yemen (qq.v.), India, and central and southeast Asia.

The Hedjazis are Sunni (q.v.) Muslims, which does not conflict with the Nejdis who follow the same sect of Islam (q.v.), but stripped to its bare essentials. Prior to the Saudi conquest of the Hedjaz province in 1925-1926 the region followed the Hanafi (q.v.) school of jurisprudence but since then has followed the Hanbali (q.v.) school. The province also houses the holy cities of Mecca and Medina, but this is not a factor in cultural differences within the kingdom, though it does give the state added international prestige. Rivalries between the Nejdis and the Hedjazis are still evident, though this is not detrimental to the stability of the kingdom.

The inhabitants of Asir Province are of similar stock to the Yemenis, but they are orthodox Sunni Muslims and their politics and religious beliefs are similar to those of the Hedjazis. The only other significant group is the Shi'i population, most of which resides in the Eastern Province at the oases of Qatif and in al-Hasa. A small number reside in Medina, which is of significance to the Shi'i sect as it contains the tombs of members of the Prophet's family and four of the Twelve Imams who originally led the sect. The Shi'i population in Saudi Arabia numbers some 400,000 out of a total Saudi national population of some 18 million.

The state in its modern form began as an alliance between Muhammad Ibn Saud and Muhammad ibn 'Abd al-Wahhab in 1745. The ambition of the Saud family and the religious zeal of al-Wahhab led to their establishing authority over the Arabian Peninsula and the creation of the first Saudi state. The followers of al-Wahhab, the *Ikhwan* (q.v.), or brethren, provided the military forces for the Sauds' expansionist policies and in 1806 they conquered Mecca and Medina from the Ottomans. In response, the Sultan asked his viceroy in Egypt (q.v.), Muhammad Ali, to invade the Nejd and after seven years his son, Ibrahim Pasha, succeeded in retaking the territory. The Sauds were forced to retreat back into the Nejd and Riyadh became the capital of the kingdom

The kingdom suffered further problems in dealings with the al-Rashids and the Ottoman Empire (q.v.), but under the leadership of Abd al-Aziz ibn Abd al-Rahman ibn Faisal, who later became known as *Ibn Saud*, the Rashids were defeated and the Sauds gained control of all of the territory, with the exception of the Hedjaz. During World War I, the Sauds remained neutral, largely through a British subsidy, but after the war the Hedjaz was occupied and incorporated into the Kingdom of Saudi Arabia.

Saudi Arabia is a monarchy headed by a king drawn from the royal al-Saud family and all rulers since 1953 have been directly related to Ibn Saud who ruled from 1902-1953. The ruler holds the reins of power but is not an absolute monarch, as he is required to rule according to Islamic principles and tribal tradition. As such all significant decisions are only taken after gaining the consensus approval of the inner circle of the royal family and, in matters relating to Islam, the religious leaders.

The 1930s also saw the discovery of oil in Saudi Arabia following a concession granted to Standard Oil of California in 1933. Commercial deposits were discovered at Damman in 1938 and further significant discoveries were made in the early 1940s. World War II delayed commercial exploitation, but production began in 1945. In 1948, the Arabian American Oil Company (ARAMCO) was created by Exxon and Mobil in partnership. This development was of great significance to the American oil companies and the U.S. government, as the country was about to become a net importer of oil. Oil brought considerable wealth to the kingdom and enabled major socio-economic development to take place.

Prior to the oil boom, Saudi Arabia was a poor state, almost totally dependent upon the *hajj* (q.v.) for its revenues, with no modern infrastructure and an illiterate, uneducated population. The massive oil incomes enabled the kingdom to be transformed such that by 1980 it had become a highly developed social welfare state. Great strides have been made in education, with literacy rates now around 70 percent and the state has a well-developed university sector, of which three institutions specialize in Islamic disciplines.

Despite its vast oil wealth, the lack of organization and structure within King Saud's administration brought the state to the verge of bankruptcy with the riyal having been devalued and loans having to be sought from the International Monetary Fund (q.v.). In 1958, Prince Faisal, heir to the throne, was appointed finance minister. He brought the balance of payments into order and balanced the budget, but the role was again assumed by King Saud resulting in financial chaos. The situation was critical as the Middle East was under the influence of Gamal Abdul Nasser (q.v.) and his republican and nationalist theories and policies. Saudi Arabia was subjected to daily propaganda broadcasts from Cairo, some Saudi air force officers defected to Egypt (q.v.), and a few of King Saud's younger relatives fled to Lebanon (q.v.) and then Egypt, having declared themselves as republicans. The situation was further complicated in 1963 with the outbreak of the civil war in Yemen (q.v.) with Egyptian troops supporting the republicans while Saudi Arabia provided financial assistance to the royalists.

The situation led to speculation as to the survival of the monarchy, but the precarious nature of the state was resolved by the appointment of Prince Faisal as prime minister following pressure from within the royal family. Immediately, Faisal appointed his brothers to key government positions and these appointments were to become key elements within the government, achieving a measure of consensus and stability.

However, relations between Faisal and the king continued to deteriorate with a series of disagreements about the government and its policies, and this caused the royal family deep concern. The outcome was that King Saud was persuaded to go into voluntary exile in 1964 and King Faisal acceded to the throne. Saud died in Athens in 1969.

Faisal had more experience of the modern world than his father and had proved his administrative abilities in his previous roles as finance minister and prime minister. King Faisal's philosophy was to pursue a careful process of modernization while still retaining traditional social and religious values, and this has been the policy adopted by successive Saudi governments. Faisal was an austere and strict ruler with an obsession with communist influence and regarded all opposition as subversive, incarcerating many of his opponents. External pressures lessened with the resolution of the Yemeni Civil War, the subsidies being paid to the front-line states, and a more conservative climate of Arab politics that emerged in the 1970s.

During King Faisal's reign, a modern infrastructure was developed and modern health and education systems introduced, including provision for women, which did promote some public unrest. Oil revenues greatly increased in 1974 as a result of the Arab oil embargo (q.v.), which was designed to alter U.S. policy with regard to Israel (q.v.) in the wake of the 1973 Arab-Israeli War. Further increases were brought about by the gradual nationalization of ARAMCO and huge increases in production levels. However, Faisal's reign ended on 25 March 1975 when he was assassinated by a deranged nephew in revenge for his brother's death in the 1965 riots, following the introduction of television.

The throne passed smoothly to King Khalid, who was an extremely capable and pious man, but not expected to play an active role in government. Crown Prince Fahd was moved from the Interior Ministry to the post of first deputy prime minister backed by a cabinet of technocrats. In fact, King Khalid took an active role in government and was the mastermind behind a major development push that began in 1975. The reign was a period of great prosperity with a number of major projects being completed and a significant number of advances in the infrastructure, particularly in the areas of telecommunications, transportation, post facilities, hotels, and a major gas system in the Eastern Province.

Throughout King Khalid's reign, the kingdom enjoyed an annual budget surplus, much of which was invested abroad by the Saudi Arabian Monetary Agency. The king was more liberal than his brother and, during his reign, a large number of political prisoners were released and the reputation of King Saud restored. One major disturbance during King Khalid's reign was the uprising inspired by Juheima ibn Saif al-Utaiba (q.v.), a religious zealot, who occupied the Grand Mosque at Mecca on the eve of the Muslim New Year. Although the uprising was put down, it took a long time to clear all the cellars and passages, and it was thought that the uprising might be the forerunner of other violent outbreaks inspired by Islamic fundamentalism (q.v.). King Khalid died of a heart attack in June 1982 and was succeeded by Crown Prince Fahd.

The start of King Fahd's reign was marked by the beginnings of a recession brought about by a rapid decline in the world demand for oil which dramatically affected Saudi Arabia as a major producer. In this respect, the king had the misfortune to begin his rule in difficult circumstances and following a period of rapid economic development. At that time the Third Five-Year Development Plan (1980-85) was still in operation and this largely completed the planned infrastructure with the opening of new airports at Riyadh and Jeddah, an expansion in hospital provision, and the establishment of significant industrial complexes at Jubail and Yanbu with refining and petrochemical facilities. A major expansion was realized in the agricultural sector, assisted by subsidies and interest-free loans such that by 1985, it was producing more wheat than the country could consume, self-sufficiency had been achieved in poultry and eggs, milk production was almost meeting need, and fruit and vegetable production was expanding.

Recession really began to bite at the end of 1985, with oil exports collapsing to one million barrels a day, followed by an almost 50 percent decline in oil prices in 1986. Government revenues from all sources had declined to about one-third of their 1981 peak levels. The new Fourth Five-Year Development Plan was never properly published and the recession had made its stated objectives rather irrelevant, although the underlying principles of human manpower development and encouragement of the private sector are still guiding economic policies.

In political terms, King Fahd tried to pursue a plan to bring peace between the Arab states and Israel, based on the withdrawal of Israel from all Arab territories occupied in 1967 and dismantling of all Jewish settlements in those areas in return for a recognition of, and peaceful coexistence with, Israel. This policy was adopted by the Arab League (q.v.) and remained official Arab policy until the Madrid Middle East Peace Conference (q.v.) of 1991. King Fahd also responded to the Iraqi invasion of Kuwait (qq.v.) in 1990 by eventually calling for the United

States and Arab states to come to the defense of Saudi Arabia and the expulsion of Iraq from Kuwait. The costs incurred by Saudi Arabia in meeting most of the costs of the Gulf War (q.v.) and on a program of rearmament, together with the revenue reductions, caused a balance of payments problem necessitating the raising of loans by the government.

However, rising corruption within the ruling elite and repressive measures toward the opposition led to the rise of an Islamic fundamentalist movement, which sought a return to the principles of true Wahhabism. In an attempt to counter this opposition, the king appointed a 60-member Consultative Council with an advisory role in 1993. Further corruption allegations emerged in 1994 and there were a series of arrests of opponents of the government. Unrest continued with the offices of the Saudi National Guard being bombed in 1995 and over 400 dying in a bombing attack on a military housing complex at al-Khobar near Dhahran. Further problems arose over borders with Yemen and Qatar, but there were improvements in relations with Iran, Jordan, and the Palestine Liberation Organization (PLO) (qq.v.).

On the economic front the Saudi economy was boosted in 1997 by an increase in oil prices, but expenditure was above forecast. In 1998, efforts were made to control capital and recurrent public expenditure and some projects were frozen or scaled down. Efforts were made from 1995 onwards to control the problem of illegal immigrants and between 1995 and 1997 600,000 were voluntarily repatriated or expelled. The 1995-2000 development plan was assessed by the International Monetary Fund which recommended a radical restructuring of established institutions and practices through privatization, deregulation, and modernization. Further oil price rises at the end of 1999 and the beginning of 2000 assisted the government's expenditure plans, but control of public expenditure, diversification of the economy, and further privatization were still crucial elements of government policy.

SAUDI FUND FOR DEVELOPMENT (SFD). The SFD was established in 1974 to participate in the financing of development projects in Third World countries through the granting of soft loans with an emphasis on projects that promote social and economic well-being in low-income countries. The fund is based in Riyadh, Saudi Arabia (q.v.), and has a legal entity with autonomous financial status. It is governed by a charter and administered by a Board of Directors chaired by the minister of finance and national economy. The Board of Directors is the supreme authority that administers the fund's affairs with the vice chairman assuming the executive authority of the fund and responsible for implementing the decisions of the Board of Directors.

The fund consists of eight departments: Technical, Capital, Loan, Research and Economic Studies, Legal, Computer, International and Public Relations, and General Administration and Financial Affairs. The capital of the SFD was $1,350 million but steadily increased between 1974-1982 to meet demands, with loans being granted to countries in Africa and Asia in about equal percentages. Aid to Africa grew steadily as a result of cultural and historical links between Saudi Arabia and Africa in the hopes of forging an Afro-Arab alliance.

Recipients of aid from the SFD are able to spend loans on technology, equipment, and technical assistance from any source, with no requirement for loans to be recycled through the Saudi Arabian economy. This is largely because Saudi Arabia does not have the technology, or produce the capital goods, to meet the needs of the recipient countries. The SFD does not operate on the same scale as the aid funds operated by Abu Dhabi or Kuwait (qq.v.).

It publishes *Annual Report, Charter of the Saudi Fund for Development, General Conditions Applicable to Loan Agreements, Procedures for Withdrawal of the Proceeds of SFD Loans,* and *Guidelines for the Borrower on Procedures for Withdrawal of the Proceeds of SFD Loans.*

SEVENERS. *See* **ISMAILIS**

SHAFII CODE. This code is part of the Sunni (q.v.) Islamic school and was named after Muhammad ibn Idris al-Shafii (A.D. 767-820), a student of Islamic law in Medina at the same time as Malik ibn Anas, founder of the Maliki school (q.v.). He also familiarized himself with the Hanafi school (q.v.) through visits to Baghdad. Shafii settled in Cairo, Egypt (q.v.), and had a great influence on the legal and administrative apparatus of the Abbasid Empire (A.D. 751-1258). He founded the science of religious jurisprudence based on four pillars: the Quran; the Prophet's *Sunna* (q.v.), recorded in the *Hadith* (q.v.); analogical reason; and the consensus of the community. Analogical reasoning allowed for the incorporation of new situations into the *Sharia* (q.v.) without affecting the primacy of the Quran and the *Sunna*. The Shafii Code also allowed individual opinions and preferences as sanctioned in the *Hadith* by the Prophet Muhammad who states that "The differences of opinion among the learned within my community are God's grace." This enabled the clergy to merge the teachings of the Prophet Muhammad with Arab and non-Arab traditions to create a canonical system applicable to the life of all Muslims whether Arab or non-Arab. The systematic code of *Sharia* provided a foundation on which to build a common identity for Muslims scattered around the world. The Shafii School was founded in Egypt and spread to southern Arabia, from where it was spread by Arab traders to East Africa and Southeast Asia. The code is still predominant in Yemen (q.v.).

SHARIA. The *Sharia*, Arabic for way or road, is the Islamic law consisting of divine revelation in the form of the Quran, and the traditions of the Prophet Muhammad, the *Sunna* (q.v.), as recorded in the *Hadith* (q.v.). The *Sharia* completely governs the individual and the social life of the believer, and is used as a basis for judging actions as good or evil. The Quran provides the principles and the *Hadith* the details of their application. The *Hadith* was a six-book canonical collection of religious jurisprudence covering all human actions and categorizing them as: obligatory, recommended, indifferent, undesirable, and prohibited. Differences existed between the Sunni and the Shi'i (qq.v.) with regard to the obligatory actions, with the former having five obligations and the latter 10.

Jurisprudence then advanced into describing how the obligatory and recommended acts were to be performed and minutely pondered all of the bodily functions. The ways in which these were to be performed or dealt with are described with the stress being laid on the purity of the body. In parallel, there was also an all-encompassing code dealing with social behavior, and the two together presented a difficult set of rules for the true believer to observe without failure. However, these codes have ensured that there is a common behavioral pattern among all Muslims regardless of where they reside. The major codes are the Hanafi, the Hanbali, the Malik, and the Shafii (qq.v.).

SHERIF HUSSEIN. *See* **HASHEM, HUSSEIN IBN ALI, AL-**

SHI'I. The Islamic sect of Shi'i derives its name from Shi'it Ali, Partisans of Ali; Ali was a cousin and son-in-law of the Prophet Muhammad. Ali advocated strict adherence to the Quran and the *Sunna* (q.v.) and came to represent idealism in Islam (q.v.). His support came largely from pious Muslims and non-Arab Muslims who felt discriminated against by Arab Muslims. The Shi'i were a significant part of the coalition that ended the Umayyad caliphate in A.D. 751 and brought its replacement by the Abbasid Caliphs, on the grounds that the former had deviated widely from the true Islamic path. However, the Abbasid Caliphs also began to deviate from the true Islamic path, which allowed the Shi'i to claim to be the sole repository of the vision of ideal Islam. The outcome was the subjugation of the Sunni Caliph in Baghdad in A.D. 932 by a Shi'i, Muizz al-Dawla al-Buyid, the emergence of an Ismaili (q.v.) Shi'i Caliphate, the Fatamids, in Cairo in A.D. 969. By this time, the Shi'i had crystallized into three branches—Zaidis, Ismailis, and Imamis (q.v.)—and two collections of Shi'i *Hadith* (q.v.) had been codified.

Shi'i domination lasted for several generations, only losing its power in 1055 in Baghdad and in Cairo in 1171. The Shi'i today are a minority, comprising only 12-15 percent of the world Muslim community of about 1 billion. In the Organization of the Islamic Conference (q.v.), which has 54 member states, only Bahrain, Iran, and Iraq (qq.v.) have a Shi'i majority population.

The Shi'i community differs from the Sunni (q.v.) in terms of doctrine, ritual, law, theology, and religious organization. The Shi'i belief consists of five basic principles and 10 duties. The principles, the first three of which are shared with the Sunni, are as follows:

- monotheism, i.e., there is only one God
- prophethood, which is a means of communication between God and humankind
- resurrection, i.e., the souls of human dead will be raised by God on their Day of Judgment and their deeds on earth judged
- imamat, i.e., that Prophet Muhammad designated Ali as his successor and that the Imam (q.v.) must be designated by Allah, through the Prophet Muhammad, or another Imam. The Imams, being divinely inspired, are infallible
- *aadth*, justice based on the just nature of Allah

In terms of duties the Shi'i have 10, which is five more than the Sunni sect. These include: daily prayers; fasting during Ramadan; *khums* (an Islamic tithe); *zakat* (q.v.) (alms tax); *hajj* (q.v.) (pilgrimage to Mecca); encouraging virtue; striving; discouraging evil; loving Shi'i Imams and their followers; and disassociating from enemies of the Imam.

The Shi'i believe that only those in the lineage of the Prophet Muhammad and his daughter Fatima and husband Ali can govern Muslims on Allah's behalf, and that the Imams are divinely inspired and infallible. Shi'i also insist that the ruler must be just and that the Quran bears a pledge of sovereignty of the earth to the oppressed, and that within this pledge are the return of the hidden Imam, or Mahdi, and the rehabilitation of society. The sect also believes that history is moving toward a predetermined goal that will see the defeat of injustice, and this acts as a spur toward radical activism.

In terms of ethos the two sects are also different, as the Shi'i find emotional outlets to mourn previous martyred Imams: Ali (assassinated), Hassan (poisoned), and Hussein (killed in battle); this finds expression through the Ashura, the annual passion plays about the martyrdom of Imam Hussein. In terms of physical manifestation, this is expressed by the self-flagellation of the faithful to expiate the guilt and pain felt by the original inhabitants of Kufa, who abandoned the Imam after having invited him into their city.

In terms of the organization of religion and religious activities, differences also exist between the two sects. Shi'i religious leaders maintain religious colleges and social welfare activities independent of the state, unlike Sunni states where religion is organized under the aegis of the state. The Shi'i also rank their clerics, with *ayatollah* (sign of Allah) being the highest ranking, whereas in the Sunni sect titles are not awarded, except to government-appointed officials.

Shi'i differ from Sunnis because of their radical activism,which is guided by the concept of the return of the hidden Imam and the defeat of the forces of injustice, as part of a predetermined historical goal. They also believe that asceticism and self-suffering removes the humiliation and persecution inflicted upon them and this can find expression through radical fundamentalist movements, such as Hizbullah (q.v.).

SPECIAL BUREAU FOR BOYCOTTING ISRAEL. This is a specialized institution of the Arab League (q.v.), formed in 1951 and based in Damascus, Syria (q.v.). The role of the bureau is to prevent trade between Arab countries and Israel, and to enforce a boycott of countries outside of the region that trade with Israel (q.v.). *See also* **Arab Boycott**

SUNNA. The Arabic meaning of *Sunna* is custom, or path, and in pre-Islamic times stood for social practices based on ancestral precedents. After the rise of Islam (q.v.), early followers took their customs from the behavior of the Prophet Muhammad or the residents of Medina, which was the capital of the Islamic realm. However, for converts living away from Medina the codes were based partly on the *Sunna* but also incorporated local traditions. The Shafii code (q.v.), however, stated that all legal decisions not stemming from the Quran must be based on tradition going back to the Prophet Muhammad himself; this led to a serious effort to compile the Prophet's sayings and actions, based on eyewitness accounts. The *Sunna* of the Prophet was therefore codified by *Hadith* (q.v.). The authority of the *Sunna* was reinforced by jurists testing the genuineness of individual traditions and the *Sunna* was then employed in the exposition of the Quran and in Islamic jurisprudence.

SUNNI. The Sunni are the leading Islamic sect, whose name stands for "People of the Path," and who regard the first four Caliphs to have been "Rightly Guided." Sunni also belong to one of the four schools of jurisprudence—Hanafi, Maliki, Shafii, and Hanbali (qq.v.)—and accept the six authentic books of the *Hadith* (q.v.).

The Sunni differ from the minority Shi'i (q.v.) sect in doctrine, ritual law, theology, and religious organization, and share only three of the five doctrines of Shiism:

- monotheism, i.e., there is only one God
- prophethood, which is a means of communication between God and humankind
- resurrection, i.e., the souls of dead humans are raised by God on their Day of Judgment and their deeds on earth judged

The five obligations imposed on Sunni Muslims—recitation of the central Islamic precept; daily prayers; fasting during Ramadan; the *zakat* (q.v.) or alms tax; and the *hajj* (q.v.), or pilgrimage to Mecca)—are fewer than those required of the Shi'i. Sunni also regard the Caliphs as fallible interpreters of the Quran, do not share the Shi'i concept of Mahdi, and view Islamic history as a drift away from the ideal community that existed under the first four Rightly Guided Caliphs.

Differences between the two communities are also apparent in the organization of religion and religious activities. The Sunni sect regard religious activities as the exclusive domain of the Muslim state and, when the *ulama* (q.v.) (scholars) act as preachers, judges, or educators, they do so within the confines of the state with little scope to organize religion outside of the state. In terms of ethos, Sunni and Shi'i are also different, as the Sunni have no emotional outlet for mourning the martyrdom of historical Islamic leaders, such as in the Ashura of the Shi'i. Also, Sunni clerics are not given the religious titles of their Shi'i counterparts, except for government-appointed religious officials, such as judges, mufti, or professional theological teachers.

SYMBOLIC ARAB SECURITY FORCE (SASF). The Symbolic Arab Security Force was mandated by the Arab League (q.v.) on 8 June 1976 at a special session held in Cairo. The action was in response to the Lebanese civil war but, in particular, to Syrian intervention on 1 June 1976, which had as its pretext the protection of the Maronite Christian population. The SASF mandate was to maintain security and stability in Lebanon (q.v.) and was seen as a replacement for the Syrian forces, although Syria (q.v.) would be a participant in the force.

The SASF was organized along the lines of United Nations (q.v.) peacekeeping forces, and a force of 2,500 men was in place by mid-1976, comprising Libyan, Syrian, Saudi Arabian, and Sudanese troops. The Libyan troops were not welcomed by the Lebanese government, but remained until November 1976 when they were withdrawn by Tripoli. The Syrian contingent included 600 men of the Palestine Liberation Army. The SASF established itself around the international airport but it was ineffective due to its size, Christian refusal to deployment in east Beirut, and opposition by Syria to plans for replacing its troops by SASF forces. In October and November 1976, the level of hostilities increased, and the SASF was unable to contain the violence, largely due to its size and limited mandate. As a result, Saudi Arabia (q.v.) called the Riyadh Summit Conference (q.v.) on 16 October 1976, which established the Arab Deterrent Force (q.v.).

SYRIA. Syria is topographically varied, with mountains in the west, a plateau to the east of the mountains, and a narrow coastal plain. The highest mountain ranges reach over 2,500 meters with the highest peak, Mount Hebron, being over 2,814 meters high. The population of Syria is estimated to be some 14 million and is growing at about 4 percent per annum with the majority being under 25 years of age. About 85 percent of the population are Muslims with about 70 percent of these being Sunni (q.v.) Muslims in the Arab, Kurdish, Turkoman, and Circassion communities. The remaining 15 percent belong to three splinter Shi'i (q.v.) sects: the Alawis (q.v.) from the mountainous interior of coastal Latakia and Tartus provinces, who comprise 12 percent of the population; the Druze from the Jabal Druze region in the south-west comprising some 3 percent of the population; and the Ismailis (q.v.) from central Syria. The remaining 15 percent of the population belong to a variety of Christian sects with the majority being Greek Orthodox. The Christians are mostly based in Aleppo and Damascus and tend to be involved in the professions or commerce.

In historical terms, Syria has been a land bridge between the

Mesopotamian and Nile Valley civilizations and provided a link between Europe, Asia, and Africa. It has been host to a variety of ideas and people, resulting in a cultural diversity that is probably the most varied in the region. Islam (q.v.) arrived in Syria in the seventh century, brought by armies from the Arabian Peninsula, and there was a gradual conversion to the new religion and the adoption of Arabic as the first language. Syria has a long history and had been part of the Assyrian kingdom, and the Persian, Hellenic, and Roman empires before becoming part of the Arab world.

The arrival of the Arab armies from the Hedjaz resulted in the Umayyads establishing their capital in Damascus, but the capital was moved to Baghdad following the Abbasid revolution of A.D. 749. A variety of dynasties then ruled Syria including Christian Crusaders, Saladin, the Safavids, and the Mamluks. In 1516, Syria was invaded by the Ottoman Empire (q.v.) and the country remained part of that empire until nearly the end of World War I. In October 1918, the Arab army under Sheikh Faisal entered Damascus and this marked the end of Ottoman rule in Syria. However, the peace settlement for the Middle East gave France a mandate (q.v.) over Syria, a move that was unpopular with the population, and Faisal's rule was overthrown by the French authorities. There was a major rebellion against French control in 1925, which began in Jabal Druze and took two years for the French to put down.

French mandatory rule was a period of friction. At the beginning of World War II, control over Syria passed to the Vichy government, but this was short-lived. Vichy forces were defeated by British and Free French forces in 1941, with Syria being granted independence, though, in reality, this was nominal. It was not until 1946 that the French left for good with Syria gaining full independence. The post-independence period was turbulent and there were three coups d'etat in 1949, largely resulting from the Arab defeat in the 1948-1949 Arab-Israeli War, which had discredited the ruling elite. In March 1949, an army coup took place, with the resultant military rule lasting for five years under a number of rulers. Instability within Syria was also due to the inability of Syrians to identify with the new state, as it did not match their concept of Greater Syria (q.v.) and, as a consequence, the borders of mandated Syria were regarded as an obstacle to Arab unity.

The concept of Arab unity ensured that Syria would become involved in a variety of regional disputes and rivalries, and throughout the 1950s it was courted by Egypt and Iraq (qq.v.) with these two powers backing different factions within Syria. In regional terms, Syria tried to maintain a position of neutrality: its purchase of arms from the Soviet bloc aroused apprehension in the United States and caused further external pressures. This instability resulted in a number of internal power struggles largely due to regional, sectarian, class, and ideological cleavages with the most significant of these being the struggle between the landowning and urban mercantile elite and those who perceived a need for reform and modernization.

One radical group was the Ba'ath Party (q.v.), a pan-Arab, secularist, socialist movement, which was well organized and an advocate of radical change, with a significant power base among the officer corps, peasant, and minority communities. The Ba'ath did not ally with the traditional parties, such as the Nationalist Bloc, but advocated and pursued the idea of union with Egypt, which was achieved in 1958 with the creation of the United Arab Republic (q.v.). The union failed due to resentment of Egyptian dominance and the process of social reform was bitterly opposed by the business class. Syria seceded from the union in 1961, following a coup that restored the political elite to power.

However, the Ba'ath Party continued to grow in power, particularly in the armed forces, and a secret committee of Ba'athist officers led a coup in March 1963. A radical wing of the party came to power in 1966 under Salah Jadid. The new government that was formed had Hafiz Assad (q.v.) as defense minister and pursued radical socioeconomic policies designed to achieve land reform, nationalization of key sectors of the economy, and a redistribution of wealth and power. The new regime was also opposed to conservative Arab governments elsewhere in the region.

The Ba'ath did not draw its power from the traditional elite, as its main leaders were recruited from the officer corps who had come from the rural areas or small towns in remote provinces, with minorities being heavily overrepresented, in particular the Alawi community. The Ba'ath government successfully weathered the effects of the defeat by Israel (q.v.) in the 1967 Arab-Israeli War, but divisions arose internally as to where the responsibility lay for the defeat, resulting in a struggle between the socialist wing of the party, led by Jadid, and the nationalist wing, led by Assad.

In 1970, Assad mounted a successful coup, moving the party back to the center and pursuing a policy aimed at broadening support for the party. Assad was a pragmatist, and he liberalized the economy and ended regional isolation by improving relations with Syria's conservative neighbors. In 1971, Assad confirmed his authority through a referendum and the following year saw the establishment of the Ba'athist-led National Progressive Party, which incorporated other sympathetic political parties. The base laid by Assad enabled Syria to take advantage of the 1973 oil price explosion, and the economy showed rapid growth with a significant rise in real incomes further consolidating Assad's position.

The Syrian army performed credibly in the 1973 Arab-Israeli War, but initial successes were reversed with the loss of much of the Golan Heights. Assad lost some of his political prestige by intervening in 1976 in the Lebanese Civil War on the side of the Christians to prevent the defeat of the Christians by the Muslim-Palestinian alliance. This caused unrest within Syria, as many felt that its Arab nationalist credentials were tarnished and that the Alawi Muslim credentials were also questionable. Intervention proved costly in financial terms due to the costs of the operation, but also because the oil-rich states cut back on aid to Syria, inflicting serious damage on the economy. The Lebanese intervention and a catalog of corruption, nepotism, and sectarianism within the elite led to internal discontent and an upsurge in support for the Muslim Brotherhood (q.v.). The Muslim Brotherhood began to organize a series of demonstrations against the regime, which developed into a wave of bombings and assassination attempts on prominent Alawis. Between 1976 and 1982, several hundred Alawis lost their lives, with the population polarized along sectarian lines, while the regime pursued policies designed to clamp down on the Islamic fundamentalist (q.v.) opposition. Insurrections were mounted at Aleppo and Homs in March 1980 and an attempt was made to assassinate Assad in June of that year.

In 1982, another insurrection broke out at Hama, and the regime extracted severe retribution by using 12,000 troops to seal off the city. Over a two-week period somewhere between 5,000-10,000 civilians were killed and large sections of the city destroyed, finally crushing the opposition. However, in November 1983, Assad suffered a heart attack, and his power base was unsuccessfully challenged by his brother Rifat. But Assad eventually recovered and in 1985 sent his brother into temporary exile while, at the same time, securing another seven-year term of office.

Syria's relations with the West were dealt a severe blow with the arrest in October 1986 of Nizar Hindawi, a Jordanian supposedly working in collusion with the Syrian embassy in London, for attempting to plant a bomb on an Israeli airliner in London. Great Britain broke off diplomatic relations and the United States withdrew its ambassador and placed Syria on the list of nations supporting international terrorism. Although the ambassador returned in 1987, Syria still remained on the list of terrorist nations. Despite this Syria has emerged as one of the region's leading powers with influence far beyond its borders, particularly in relation to the Israeli peace process and the affairs of Lebanon (q.v.).

Continued intervention in Lebanon was justified by Assad on the grounds that Syria could not allow that country to become part of the U.S.-Israeli camp, and in 1990 the pro-Syrian side finally triumphed in Lebanon. Assad attempted to achieve military parity with Israel (q.v.) with the aid of the Soviet Union but this was a considerable economic drain, taking 30 percent of total government expenditure. The decline of the Soviet Union from 1989 caused Assad to moderate his policy with regard to Israel. Syria took part in the 1991 Madrid Middle East Peace Conference (q.v.), but bilateral talks failed over the question of the Golan Heights.

Assad's pragmatic leadership recognized the emergence of the U.S. as the sole superpower and following his attempts to persuade Saddam Hussein (q.v.) to leave Kuwait (q.v.) Syria joined the U.S.-led coalition against Iraq (q.v.) in the Gulf War (q.v.). Syria also sent troops to Saudi Arabia (q.v.) to aid in the defense of that country, this being another example of Assad's ability to adapt to changing circumstances not only to ensure his own position in power but that of Syria within the region. In regional terms, relations with Turkey (q.v.) have been strained by the question of access to water from the Euphrates River, over which Turkey (q.v.) has refused to enter into a permanent accord. Syria and Iraq are also concerned about the effects on the river flows of the Birecik dam in Turkey, and they blame Turkey for an increase in pollution levels in the river. The question of water access is crucial to Syria's objective to increase the acreage under irrigation in order to increase agricultural production.

Relations with Turkey have also deteriorated over the question of the Turkish Kurds (q.v.), as the militant Kurdish Workers Party (PKK) has training bases in the Bekaa valley in Lebanon, which is controlled by Syria. In 1995, Kurds crossed the Turkish border from Syria in a series of attacks on Turkish military targets. The situation deteriorated even further in 1996 when it was disclosed that Israel and Turkey had signed a military accord allowing the Israeli air force to use Turkish bases for training purposes; this was denounced by the Syrian government and the press. Turkey retaliated by denouncing Syrian support for the PKK and accusing Syria of not abandoning its ambition to create a Greater Syria. Almost by coincidence, Turkey temporarily closed the flood gates of Euphrates dams for technical reasons in April 1996, causing water shortages in Damascus. In May 1996, a series of small bombs exploded in Syrian cities, and it was speculated that Turkey was responsible, with the actions being a retaliation for Syrian support for the PKK.

Syrian-Jordanian relations had also deteriorated following the Jordanian peace treaty with Israel in 1994. Syrian officials complained that Jordan (q.v.) was working with Turkey and Israel to undermine the Assad regime. Jordan countered that Syria was sponsoring terrorist activity in Jordan to destabilize their regime. Relations improved following a meeting between Assad and King Hussein (q.v.) and action by Syria against Palestinians and other Arabs alleged to have been involved in attacks in Jordan, or in Israel through Jordan. Fences were also mended between Assad and Yasser Arafat (q.v.), and in early 1997 Syrian authorities warned the Popular Front for the Liberation of Palestine and other groups based in Damascus that their offices would be shut down if military operations against Israel continued.

In 1995, rallies were held to mark Assad's 25 years in power and some political prisoners, including members of the Muslim Brotherhood, were released, though Assad's control was not lessened. A poster campaign was mounted in 1997 to prepare for Assad's only surviving son, Basher, to succeed as leader of the Ba'ath and president. On 10 June 2000, President Assad died and the Ba'ath nominated Basher as leader and president, though the constitution has to be amended to allow the succession to take place as he was not aged 40, as required by the previous constitution. At the time of writing this process had not been completed. *See also* **Palestine**

SYRIAN SOCIAL NATIONALIST PARTY (SSNP). The Syrian Social Nationalist Party was founded in 1932 by Antun Sa'ada, a Greek Orthodox Lebanese who had been inspired by fascist ideologies, and had as its main objective the uniting of the Syrian nation, including Lebanon (q.v.). The party was originally known as the *Parti Populaire Syrien* and operated in secret until 1935, when Sa'ada was arrested by the French authorities. Sa'ada fled to Brazil and remained there until 1947, when he returned to Lebanon.

The SSNP is headed by a president and a high council with a dean's council, executive units, and management units. The party's ideology, as defined by Sa'ada, was based on the unity of the Syrian nation and all its components. This concept of Syria (q.v.) covered natural boundaries extending from the Taurus mountain range in the northwest and the Zagros Mountains in the northeast, to the Suez Canal and the Red Sea in the south, and included the Sinai Peninsula and the Gulf of Aqaba. Also included was the Mediterranean coastline, including Cyprus, to the arch of the Arabian desert and the Persian Gulf in the east.

Lebanon was declared to be part of Syria and this led Sa'ada into conflict with the Lebanese authorities. In 1949, Sa'ada declared an armed revolt against the government and called on his supporters to attack police stations. However, the Lebanese authorities, aided by the Syrian leader, Husni al-Za'im, retaliated and Sa'ada was arrested. He was executed in 1949 and this led to the overthrow of Za'im in Syria and a rise in popularity of the SSNP in the 1950s.

However, the killing of a Ba'ath (q.v.) party official and conflict between the SSNP and Arab nationalist, lost the party support in Syria. In the Lebanese unrest of 1958, the SSNP allied itself with President Camille Chamoun against the pro-Arab nationalist forces. The membership of the party in Lebanon at that time was some 25,000. In 1961, the SSNP was involved in an unsuccessful coup against the government, and many of its leaders were arrested, with others fleeing the country or leaving the party. During the Lebanese Civil War from 1975 to 1976, the SSNP fielded 2,000 fighters in Beirut and other cities but the party was divided. One faction retained the original ideology while a splinter group, led by In'am Raad, believed it possible to introduce Marxism into the party and to adopt violence as a legitimate means of achieving political aims. Ra'ad and his supporters left the SSNP in 1977 to join the Lebanese National Movement, and the party, as such, became a spent force. *See also* **Greater Syria**

T

TABA DECLARATION. *See* **ARAB BOYCOTT**

TA'IF ACCORD. The Arab Tripartite Committee comprised of Algeria, Morocco and Saudi Arabia (qq.v.) met in July 1989 to make recommendations for the ending of the Lebanese Civil War. These included expanded Lebanese sovereignty, a pullback of Syrian forces, and formalization of Syria and Lebanon's relationship with Israel (q.v.). The recommendations were promptly rejected by Syria. In September 1989, at Ta'if, Saudi Arabia, representatives of the various Lebanese factions accepted a new Charter of National Unity. Under the agreement Syria was to restrain the Iran-backed Shi'i (qq.v.) groups in exchange for recognition of Syrian dominance in Lebanon and the isolation of the Christian faction led by Michel Anoun. Syria was also empowered to become involved in reconstituting the authority of the national government, and the redeployment of its forces confirmed its control over territory strategically significant to Beirut. Finally, the governments of Syria and Lebanon were empowered to enter into secret agreements.

TRADE UNIONISM. *See* **ARAB FEDERATION OF PETROLEUM, MINING, AND CHEMICALS WORKERS; ARAB FEDERATION OF TEXTILE WORKERS; ARAB LABOR ORGANIZATION; INTERNATIONAL CONFEDERATION OF ARAB TRADE UNIONS; UNION SYNDICALE DES TRAVAILLEURS DU MAGHREB ARABE**

TRANSJORDAN. *See* **JORDAN**

TREATY OF FRONTIER AND GOOD NEIGHBORLY RELATIONS (IRAN-IRAQ). On 6 March 1975, Iraq's (q.v.) vice president, Saddam Hussein (q.v.), and the Shah of Iran (q.v.), signed an accord in Algiers. The accord had two main provisions: the first was an agreement to delimit their fluvial boundaries along the Shatt al-Arab waterway, according to the median line of the deepest channel; the second an agreement to end all infiltration of a subversive nature which was largely directed against Iran's support for Iraqi Kurdish insurgents. The accord was transferred into the Treaty of Frontier and Good Neighborly Relations that was signed in Baghdad on 13 June and ratified by both countries on 17 September 1975.

A joint commission was appointed to demarcate the new land border in Iran's Qasr e-Shirin area to resolve Iraq's claim that Iran retained territory in contravention of the 1913 Protocol of Constantinople. The commission was also charged with demarcating the new border within the Shatt al-Arab, which had hitherto been Iraqi territory. The treaty was a victory for Iran, which had been trying for 60 years to obtain guaranteed rights in the waterway. Baghdad largely agreed to the treaty due to exhaustion in the struggle with the Kurds (q.v.) and the promised withdrawal of Iranian support.

On 17 September 1980, Iraq accused Iran of violating the treaty as it had renewed support for the Kurdish insurgents and refused to hand back land in the Qasr-e-Shirin area. Saddam Hussein, now president, abrogated the treaty and insisted that all shipping in the Shatt al-Arab must fly the Iraqi flag and use Iraqi pilots. Iran refused these demands.

On 22 September 1980, Iraq invaded Iran and started the Iraq-Iran War (q.v.), which lasted until 1988.

TURKEY. *See* **OTTOMAN EMPIRE**

TWELVER SHI'IS. The predominant category among Shi'i (q.v.) are the Twelvers or Twelver Shi'I, which derive their name from a belief in 12 Imams (q.v.). It is their belief that Muhammad al Qasim, the infant son of the eleventh Imam, went into a state of occulation, or hiding, in A.D. 873, leaving four special assistants. The last of the assistants failed to name a successor and the line of divinely inspired Imams was deemed to have become extinct in A.D. 940. The Twelver Shi'i believe that the last Imam will end his occulation at the end of time, and will bring justice and order to the world and punishment to the enemies of Allah.

U

ULAMA. This is the term used collectively for religious-legal scholars of Islam (q.v.), and they are the ultimate authority on the issues of law and theology. In Sunni (q.v.) countries, they have now become part of the government and only a minority pursue an independent line on theology and canon law.

UMMA. The term *umma* appears several times in the Quran and alludes to ethnic, linguistic, or religious groups who were part of Allah's plan of salvation. As Islam (q.v.) spread in the early days *umma* changed from being used to describe the community of all Arabs, irrespective of religion, to the community of all Muslims. In modern times, the term is used to describe the worldwide Islamic community as an entity.

UNION OF ARAB BANKS (UAB). The UAB was founded in 1972 and is based in Beirut, Lebanon (q.v.). Its aims are to foster cooperation between Arab banks, to improve efficiency within the sector, and to undertake project feasibility studies.

UNION OF ARAB HISTORIANS. It was founded in 1974 with membership from 22 countries in the region. It publishes *Arab Historian*.

UNION OF ARAB JURISTS (UAJ). The UAJ was founded in 1975 to facilitate contact between Arab lawyers, to protect and develop legislative and judicial language, and to enable all Arab lawyers to handle cases in any Arab country. It also promotes the study of Islamic law (q.v.) and has membership from the bar associations of 16 countries. It publishes *Al-Haak* (The Law), *Al-Hukuki al-Arabi* (Arab Jurist), and specialist studies.

UNION OF ARAB STOCK EXCHANGES AND SECURITIES COMMISSION. It was founded in 1982 and based in Safat, Kuwait (q.v.), with a remit to develop capital markets in the Arab world.

UNION OF THE ARAB MAGHREB (UAM). The UAM was founded in 1989 and is based in Rabat, Morocco (q.v.), with the objective of encouraging joint ventures and the creation of a single market. The UAM is headed by a Supreme Council of Heads of State, which meets annually, a Council of Ministers of Foreign Affairs, a Consultative Council of 30 delegates from each member state, a judicial court, and four specialized ministerial commissions. The Chairmanship of the Supreme Council rotates between the heads of state. The members of the UAM are Algeria, Libya (qq.v.), Mauritania, Morocco, and Tunisia.

By the end of 1994, the joint projects that have been approved, or were actively being considered, were as follows:

- establishment of a Maghreb Investment and Foreign Trade Bank to fund joint agricultural and industrial projects
- free movement for citizens within the UAM
- transportation improvements covering railways and a UAM highway
- creation of a customs union
- establishment of a North African common market through a free trade zone resolution adopted in April 1994
- protection of the environment through a Maghreb Charter adopted in November 1992

The UAM also represents the interests of its members in negotiations with the European Union (EU), Arab and African regional organizations, and international organizations.

The member states of the UAM, particularly in North Africa, have a long history of tense relations and the organization can be seen as an attempt to secure a regional balance of power through a political arrangement. However, the UAM should primarily be viewed in economic terms as a reaction to the Single European Act (1986) of the European Union and the enlargement of the EU to include Spain, Portugal, and Greece. This shift in emphasis to economic imperatives marked a new phase in the history of attempts at regional reconciliation, with tensions over issues such as the Western Sahara (q.v.) being temporarily shelved due to dire economic prospects for the future.

The economic emphasis is largely the result of the one-sided reliance that the Maghreb has on trade with Europe, which exposed UAM states to the repercussions of economic conditions and labor policies of the EU. The expansion of the EU, for example, threatened the market for UAM agricultural products, particularly for such products as fruit, wine, and olive oil. Economies were also threatened by the potential loss of labor remittances if UAM guest workers in the EU were replaced by labor from Spain, Portugal, and Greece.

Another factor was the possibility of coordination of industrial development among member states in order to prevent duplication of effort, and five committees were established to promote a cooperative development strategy and to minimize intraregional competition. This regional experiment in cooperation and unity was effectively a response by reluctant participants to external challenges, rather than a regionally inspired move.

UNION SYNDICALE DES TRAVAILLEURS DU MAGHREB ARABE (USTMA). The USTMA was established in 1989 and is based in Tunis, Tunisia, representing the trade union movements in the member states of the Union of the Arab Maghreb (UAM) (q.v.) comprising Algeria, Libya, Morocco (qq.v.), Mauritania, and Tunisia. It is also affiliated with the International Confederation of Arab Trade Unions (ICATU) (q.v.). The leadership has been fiercely critical of the Union of the Arab Maghreb and the lack of progress toward meeting the objectives that it set when founded in 1989 and, in particular, the absence of a policy on social progress within the member states. The USTMA has also been critical of the lack of rights accorded to workers by the member states and has continued to stress that policies should be based on social justice, democracy, and dialogue with all the political and civil forces of the region, including tripartite cooperation between government, employers, and trade unions.

UNITED ARAB EMIRATES (UAE). The United Arab Emirates is a federation of seven sheikhdoms at the southern end of the Arabian Gulf, and borders Qatar, Saudi Arabia, and Oman (qq.v.). The federation occupies an area of some 82,880 square kilometers, with Abu Dhabi (q.v.) the largest of the emirates, occupying 87 percent of the total. Dubai occupies 5 percent; Sharjah, 3 percent, and the remainder is occupied by Ajman, Ras al-Khaimah, Fujairah, and Umm al-Qaiwain. The federation comprises a flat coastal plain, an interior desert which is part of the Rub' al-Khali, or Empty Quarter, an elevated plateau, and the Hajar Mountains, which are shared with Oman. Rainfall is minimal and temperatures reach in excess of 46° C, with high levels of humidity on the coast.

In 1968, the population of the seven emirates was 180,000 but by the mid-1990s it had risen to two million, largely due to the growth of expatriate workers and their dependents, who comprise some 80 percent of the population. The population is mainly urban, with the cities of Abu Dhabi and Dubai having populations of some 500,000 each and the city of Sharjah some 250,000. All of the UAE nationals are Muslim with 85 percent Sunni (q.v.) Muslims, as are most of the expatriate workers with the exception of the Indians and Filipinos.

Traditional tribal affiliations are still important in all of the emirates with the rulers being drawn from the leading families of the dominant tribes. The ruling families were already in place when Great Britain entered into treaty negotiations with the emirates in 1820 to end piracy in the Gulf. These arrangements were made more permanent by a series of treaties with Great Britain resulting in the area becoming known as the Trucial States. A British presence continued in the area with the Political Resident wielding considerable power. The borders of the emirates were largely determined in the 1930s as a result of the exploration for oil but many disputes remained unresolved and islands such as Abu Musa and the Tunb Islands are disputed with Iran (q.v.) today, largely because of offshore oil and gas deposits.

The dominant power in the region was Great Britain until 1970 when it announced that it was to withdraw from the region due to financial cutbacks. Initially, Great Britain tried to encourage a federation of nine states, which would have included Bahrain (q.v.) and Qatar. This concept failed for a variety of reasons, but the same remaining emirates combined to form the United Arab Emirates, with Bahrain and Qatar becoming independent states. The prime movers behind the federation were Sheikh Zaid of Abu Dhabi and Sheikh Rashid of Dubai and they became president and vice president, respectively. Historical border disputes between the emirates and with Oman and Saudi Arabia (q.v.) threatened the long-term stability of the federation and it has largely been through the patience and commitment of Sheikh Zaid that the federation has survived and flourished.

The constitution of the UAE provides for federal legislative, executive, and judicial institutions with the political system a mix of presidential and parliamentary features with the greatest power resting in the Federal Supreme Council, which comprises the rulers of the seven member states. The legislature is the Federal National Council (FNC), also known as the *Federal National Assembly,* and it has responsibility for scrutinizing all federal legislation. It has a membership of 40 drawn from the seven emirates, with Abu Dhabi and Dubai each having eight seats, Sharjah and Ras Al-Khaimah each having six seats, and Ajman, Fujairah, and Umm al-Qaiwain each having four. Selection of members is left to each emirate but all are selected by the rulers and tend to represent the merchant class. The FNC sessions, each of six months, begin in November and members serve for two-year terms, indefinitely renewable. All federal legislation is referred to the FNC, but it is only advisory as its recommendations can be overridden by the Federal Supreme Council. Despite this the FNC takes its responsibilities seriously and the rulers always give its advice serious consideration.

The individual emirates still have considerable powers and are still governed in a traditional manner by their rulers and often act independently in areas, which should be covered by the federal constitution. This has been manifested in the pursuit of individual oil policies and in foreign policy with Dubai and Sharjah maintaining relations with Iran during the Iraq-Iran War (q.v.) while the federal government supported Iraq (q.v.). President Zaid has always favored a centralized federation while the others, especially Dubai, have continued to favor the existing loose confederation.

In terms of foreign relations, the UAE generally has good relations with its neighbors and most of the internal and external border disputes have been resolved. The UAE has also played an important role in the Gulf Cooperation Council (GCC) (q.v.), which promotes economic and security ties with the other member states of Bahrain, Kuwait (q.v.), Oman, Qatar, and Saudi Arabia. During the 1990-1991 Gulf War (q.v.), the UAE joined the anti-Iraq coalition and provided troops for the coalition forces. Sheikh Zaid has also assumed a major role in the Arab world with support for Egypt's (q.v.) reintegration in the Arab League and the Oslo Accords (qq.v.) between Israel and Palestine (qq.v.).

In terms of the economy, oil and oil-related industries are the only real source of revenue. Abu Dhabi is the largest producer and has one tenth of the world's reserves while Dubai, Ras al-Khaimah, and Sharjah have smaller deposits. Dubai is still important as the major trading center in the Gulf and has continued to develop through the free trade zone of Jebal Ali. The economy is dominated by Abu Dhabi and Dubai with the former providing the bulk of the federal budget.

Despite some gloomy predictions at its founding and during the early years of its existence as to the uncertain and perhaps short life of the federation, it has survived for nearly 30 years. The long-term survival of the UAE has been largely due to the leadership of Sheikh Zaid and, latterly, to its membership of the GCC, which is a tangible example of regional cooperation in the Arab World.

UNITED ARAB REPUBLIC (UAR). On 1 February 1958, Egypt and Syria (qq.v.) agreed to merge to form the United Arab Republic. Syria shared Egypt's anti-Western stance and many Syrian politicians respected President Gamal Abdul Nasser's (q.v.) advocacy of pan-Arab (q.v.) unity, but Syria was in a weak position due to internal political instability and external threats. As a result the Syrian Assembly in November 1957 called for union with Egypt, which was agreed, by Nasser, but only on his terms, namely, full union rather than a federation. The formation of the UAR was announced by Nasser and Syrian President Shakri al-Quwatli on 1 February and a referendum was held on 21 February to approve the union, with Nasser as president.

In March 1958, new governmental institutions were formed with four vice presidents, two Egyptian and two Syrian, and with one of the Egyptian vice presidents being commander of the UAR military. A regional Council of Ministers was appointed for each province, together with a unified cabinet with members appointed in October 1958. A new National Assembly was established in March 1960 with all of the delegates appointed by Nasser, the majority of whom were Egyptian. The one-party system as operating in Egypt was also imposed by Nasser and only the National Union established in Egypt in May 1957 was allowed to operate.

The UAR was the first significant step toward Arab union and was seen as a threat by the Western powers, particularly when the UAR began to talk to other states about union. Yemen (q.v.) was also drawn into the United Arab States, which lasted until 1961, and talks were held with the 1958 post-revolutionary Iraqi (q.v.) government but they did not come to fruition. In response to the formation of the UAR and its expansionist plans, the U.S. and Lebanon (q.v.), respectively, and British troops were sent to Jordan (q.v.) to bolster the anti-UAR governments.

However, Syria soon became disenchanted with the UAR as Nasser introduced into the Syrian part of the republic his policies of nationalization of banking, insurance, and major industries, which alienated a significant social class within Syria. He had also succeeded in alienating all politicians in Syria through a ban on political parties, and by creating a unified military command in which Syrian officers were placed in secondary positions, thus alienating the Syrian officer corps. All of these factors combined to cause much unrest within Syria and eventually led to its withdrawal from the UAR in September 1961, following a coup and some fighting, but Nasser decided against enforcing unity by force of arms and there was much bitterness between the two partners. The dissolving of the UAR was a blow to Nasser's prestige and the dream of pan-Arab unity, though it was not until 1971 that Egypt dropped the title of UAR, becoming the Arab Republic of Egypt.

UNITED NATIONS (UN). The involvement of the United Nations in the Middle East has been primarily concerned with the Arab-Israeli dispute, providing peacekeeping forces to monitor the various cease-fires from the first Arab-Israeli War (1948-1949) to date and similar operations in Lebanon, Yemen and the Western Sahara (qq.v.). Further involvement came with the securing and monitoring of the cease-fire to end the Iraq-Iran War (1980-1988) (q.v.) and in the Gulf War (1990-1991) (q.v.) following the Iraqi invasion of Kuwait (q.v.).

In terms of the Gulf War, the UN was involved in two main areas. The UN Security Council was responsible for passing resolutions against the Iraqi actions in Kuwait and authorizing the use of all possible means to enforce its resolutions, which paved the way for the allied coalition to take military action. However, once the war was underway leadership passed to the United States, which directed the operation, often at variance with the wishes of some of the members of the UN. The other main area of involvement was in the enforcement of sanctions against Iraq (q.v.) after the invasion of Kuwait and continued enforcement after Iraq's defeat. The only exception to the sanctions was the limited sale of oil to enable Iraq to purchase food and medicine.

The UN was also instrumental in providing protection for the Iraqi Kurds (q.v.) in northern Iraq and the Marsh Arabs in the Basra area through the imposition of no-fly zones for Iraqi aircraft. The UN was also involved in a program, imposed as part of the cease-fire agreement, to eliminate Iraq's weapons of mass destruction and ballistic missiles with a range of more than 150 kilometers. This program was to be implemented and supervised by a United Nations Special Commission on Iraq (UNSCOM) (q.v.) and the commission was also to work in partnership with the International Atomic Energy Authority over the nuclear areas of the resolution. The mission was partly successful but was pulled out following disputes with Iraq over the methods and reports of the weapons inspectors.

The UN is also represented in the area through the activities of its specialist agencies, including the Economic and Social Commission for Western Asia (ESCWA), the United Nations Development Program (UNDP) (qq.v.), and the Food and Agriculture Organization (FAO). The United Nations High Commission for Refugees (UNHCR) is also active throughout the region, dealing with, among others, Somali refugees in Yemen (q.v.), Sahrawi refugees in Algeria (q.v.), Afghan and Iraqi Kurdish refugees in Iran (q.v.), and Palestinian refugees in Lebanon (q.v.). The vast majority of Palestinian refugees are cared for by the United Nations Relief and Works Agency (UNRWA) (q.v.). The United Nations Educational, Scientific, and Cultural Organization (UNESCO) is also active in the regions and among its projects are work in the Nile Valley and in the Roman city of Jerash in Jordan.

In the UN, the Arab states tend not to operate as a bloc because of differences and rivalries between the various regimes, particularly the socialist republics and the monarchical conservative regimes. However, members tend to act together when faced with issues involving the Palestinians and the question of Jerusalem (qq.v.), or in regional groupings such as the Arab League or Gulf Cooperation Council (qq.v.), in which they present a unified position. At times the Arab states also act in concert with member states of the nonaligned movement. Usually the Arab states have one nonpermanent seat on the Security Council, which means that they have relatively little power there as opposed to the five permanent members (China, France, Great Britain, Russia, and the United States). But, due to their number, the Arab states, often with backing from Islamic states, have considerable influence in the General Assembly and other bodies.

UNITED NATIONS DEVELOPMENT FUND FOR WOMEN (UNIFEM). The United Nations Development Fund for Women mandate for Western Asia includes all of the countries of the Arabian Peninsula, Egypt (q.v.), and the Occupied Territories. The UNIFEM Western Asia regional office was established in Amman, Jordan (q.v.), in 1994, and works through national counterparts, both governmental and nongovernmental, and local women's organizations and networks. UNIFEM recognizes that the lives of Arab women and the roles that they play vary widely according to their socio-economic class, religious and ethnic group, the economy, and the judicial and political systems under which they live. UNIFEM also recognizes that in the main the participation of women in public life and in decision-making remains intangible and invisible, but that where national governments see a role for women, major structural and institutional changes are being made to ensure gender equity and to bridge gender gaps.

In the Arab states, UNIFEM focuses on three main areas. The first is an Economic Empowerment Program, which attempts to strengthen women's economic capacity as entrepreneurs and producers, particularly in relation to new trade opportunities and new technology. The second area is that of Governance, where UNIFEM is directing its attention to the strengthening of the institutional capacities of women's organizations and the promotion of women's participation in the decision-making process. The last area of involvement is in the area of Women's Human Rights, where the prime objective is to eliminate all forms of violence against women and to transform development into a more peaceful, equitable, and sustainable process.

UNIFEM has five Economic Empowerment projects running in the region, eight Governance projects, and a regional project aimed at the elimination of violence against women. At present, UNIFEM has a mandate for, but no presence in, Iraq and the member states of the Gulf Cooperation Council (qq.v.)

Among its publications are an annual report (English/Arabic) and irregular newsletters.

UNITED NATIONS DEVELOPMENT PROGRAM: PROGRAM OF ASSISTANCE TO THE PALESTINIAN PEOPLE (PAPP). The United Nations Development Program (UNDP) was asked, in December 1978, by the UN General Assembly to undertake development activities on behalf of the Palestinian people. This resulted in the establishment of a Program of Assistance to the Palestinian People, which has now developed into a leading development organization working with the Palestinians through periods of occupation, the *intifada*, and the establishment of the Palestinian Authority. At the end of 1999 PAPP had over $145 million invested in projects active in the West Bank and Gaza Strip and a staff of 130, principally Palestinians.

PAPP's activities are firmly rooted in the official Palestinian Development plan, contributing directly to the priorities identified by Palestinian Authority ministries. Among the units set up by PAPP are the Agriculture, Rural, and Economic Development Unit; Governance and Public Sector Unit; Human Development Unit; Engineering Unit and Environment; and the Water and Employment Generation Unit.

Most of the projects implemented or supported by PAPP are intentionally labor-intensive in order to help address the chronic levels of high unemployment and declining income levels among Palestinians. Also, wherever possible, PAPP relies on the expertise of private sector Palestinian firms rather than on expatriate consultancy firms in order to provide a positive financial and technical impact on a fragile Palestinian economy. *See also* **Palestine; United Nations**

UNITED NATIONS DISENGAGEMENT OBSERVER FORCE (UNDOF). Syria (q.v.) had launched an attack in October 1973 on Israeli military units stationed on the Golan Heights, which had been seized from Syria during the 1967 Arab-Israeli War. The attack was coordinated with the Egyptian forces, which crossed the Suez Canal to attack Israeli positions. Initially, the attacks were successful but were soon reversed as Israel (q.v.) counterattacked. A cease-fire was arranged by the United Nations (q.v.) and peacekeepers from the United Nations Truce Supervision Organization (UNTSO) (q.v.) moved to the cease-fire area and established observation posts.

In May 1974, an agreement, brokered by the United States, was concluded with both sides signing an Agreement on Disengagement, which also called for a neutral peacekeeping operation to oversee the cease-fire. The agreement was endorsed by the United Nations (q.v.) and UNDOF was set up to supervise the cease-fire, the redeployment of military forces, and the establishment of a buffer zone between the belligerents. The core of UNDOF was drawn from the United Nations Emergency Force II (q.v.), with two battalions of troops being transferred to join with the personnel from UNTSO.

The UNDOF force operates a series of observation posts and mobile patrols from within the buffer zone, also known as the Area of Separation, and the UNTSO observers within the force verify the number of forces and weapons deployed by both sides in the adjoining Area of Limitation.

UNITED NATIONS ECONOMIC AND SOCIAL COMMISSION FOR WESTERN ASIA (ESCWA). The United Nations Economic and Social Commission for Western Asia has its headquarters in Beirut, Lebanon (q.v.). It was established by the United Nations in 1973 and began operations in 1974 as the United Nations Economic and Social Office in Beirut (UNESOB), changing to its present name in 1985. The organization forms a link with the UN Economic and Social Council and has a membership of 13 Arab states. Its main objective is to pro-

pose policies and actions to support development, economic cooperation, and integration in Western Asia, working together with relevant
national, regional, and international bodies. ESCWA also undertakes or
sponsors the collection, analysis, evaluation, and publication of statistical and technical information and conducts economic, social, and development studies at the regional or subregional level. The commission
further provides consultancy services for the member states in the fields
of economic and social development, organizes scientific conferences,
seminars, and training courses, and oversees the implementation of
regional and subregional projects.

ESCWA is a multidisciplinary body, working with other specialized agencies of the UN to achieve development within a framework of
regional cooperation and avoid conflict. The commission holds ministerial sessions every other year at a time determined by members of the
commission. The commission is run by an executive secretary, at the
level of under secretary-general, assisted by a deputy executive secretary. The commission has an extensive publications program among
which are; *Population Bulletin, Survey of Economic and Social Developments in the ESCWA Countries, Preliminary Overview of Economic
Development in the ESCWA Region, Review of Science and Technology
in ESCWA Countries, Agriculture Review in ESCWA Countries, Review
of Industry in ESCWA Countries, Review of Transport in ESCWA
Countries, Bulletin on Vital Statistics in the ESCWA Region, National
Accounts Studies of ESCWA Region,* and *Statistical Abstract of ESCWA
Member States.*

UNITED NATIONS EMERGENCY FORCE I (UNEFI). The United
Nations Emergency Force I was a peacekeeping operation established
during the Suez Crisis in 1956 following the Israeli (q.v.), British, and
French invasion of Egypt (q.v.). The peacekeeping force was authorized
on 5 November 1956 and was drawn from member states excluding the
five permanent members of the Security Council and parties with an
interest in the conflict. The presence of the peacekeeping force required
the consent of all the parties and was only authorized to use force in
self-defense. The force of 6,000 troops was deployed in mid-November
and negotiations began for the withdrawal of the occupation forces. A
phased withdrawal was negotiated and the British and French troop
withdrawal was completed by 22 December, but the Israeli withdrawal
was not completed until March 1957.

UNEF remained on the Egyptian-Israeli border following the
withdrawal with a base at Sharm al-Shaykh, which controlled access to

the Gulf of Aqaba. By 1967, the force had been reduced in size to some 3,400 troops. In May 1967, tension rose again in the area and President Gamal Abdul Nasser (q.v.) requested the withdrawal of UNEFI, which took place on 18 May 1967 and was followed three weeks later by another Arab-Israeli war.

UNITED NATIONS EMERGENCY FORCE II (UNEFII). In October 1973, Egypt and Syria (qq.v.) launched coordinated attacks on Israel (q.v.) with Egypt crossing the Suez Canal and overwhelming observation posts manned by United Nations Truce Supervision Organization (UNTSO) (q.v.) positions. However, Israel launched a successful counterattack, which trapped the Egyptian army on the east bank of the Suez Canal and created a bridgehead to the west bank of the canal. At this point, the Soviet Union was threatening to intervene to protect Egypt and this led to the United Nations Security Council considering the issue on 24 October 1973. On the following day, the Security Council called for an immediate cease-fire, and asked the Secretary-General to increase the number of UNTSO observers and to establish a United Nations Emergency Force based on UNEFI.

The United Nations (q.v.) estimated that a force of some 7,000 troops was needed and eight countries contributed to the force. UNEFII troops were deployed to the front lines between the Egyptians and the Israelis and also worked with the International Red Cross to provide humanitarian aid to the trapped Egyptian forces. A disengagement was negotiated in January 1974 and UNEFII supervised the withdrawal of Israeli forces, with UNTSO surveying and demarcating the buffer zones. The Egyptian-Israeli peace treaty of March 1979 called for continued observation of the border area by peacekeeping forces and both sides wanted UNEFII to assume this role. However, the Palestine Liberation Organization (q.v.), the Soviet Union, and other Arab states objected, which led to the creation of the Multinational Force and Observers (q.v.). The United Nations allowed the mandate for UNEFII to lapse on 24 July 1979 and the force withdrew, leaving the UNTSO observers in place. Elements of UNEFII were detached in June 1974 to form the basis of the United Nations Disengagement Observer Force (q.v.).

UNITED NATIONS GUARD CONTINGENT IN IRAQ (UNGCI). The United Nations established the United Nations Guard Contingent in Iraq to replace allied soldiers who had been protecting the Kurds (q.v.) in northern Iraq (q.v.) following the 1991 Gulf War (q.v.). The force was designed to provide limited security for the United Nations (q.v.) suboffices and Humanitarian Centers program to provide aid to the Kurds. The size of UNGCI was limited to 500 soldiers with no more than 150 assigned to any region under United Nations protection. The troops were authorized only to carry side arms provided by the Iraqi government. The first guards arrived on 19 May 1991 and were at full strength by July 1991. The UNCGI was drawn from 35 countries with its main headquarters in Baghdad. The mission included providing protection to individuals involved in giving humanitarian aid to the Kurds as well as to United Nations property and buildings.

UNITED NATIONS INTERIM FORCE IN LEBANON (UNIFIL). Israel invaded Lebanon (qq.v.) in March 1978 with 20,000 troops to aid the expansion of a security zone in southern Lebanon controlled by its client Major Sa'd Haddad. The Lebanese government was not able to defend its territory against constant Israeli incursions and to separate the Israeli forces in south Lebanon from the Palestine Liberation Organization (q.v.) forces and those of the Lebanese National Movement. The United Nations (q.v.) responded by sending 6,000 troops to maintain order in south Lebanon and northern Israel.

The presence of UNIFIL did not end the fighting and it was largely ignored by the heavily armed groups operating in the region. It became largely dedicated to the provision of services and humanitarian relief in the areas under its control. Israel resisted efforts to include the so-called security zone in southern Lebanon in the area covered by the mandate and totally ignored the presence of UNIFIL when it invaded Lebanon in 1982. The composition of UNIFIL has varied since 1978; the force has recorded some 200 fatalities due to combat and accidents and has suffered from attacks by both Christian and Muslim militia in the area.

UNITED NATIONS IRAN-IRAQ MILITARY OBSERVER GROUP (UNIIMOG). The Iraq-Iran War (q.v.) broke out in 1980; attempts by the United Nations (q.v.) to broker a peace were unsuccessful over a number of years. However, in 1984 the two states agreed to a limited United Nations presence on their territories and in June of that year one team went to Baghdad and the other to Tehran. The teams consisted only of three observers each to oversee compliance with a call to cease attacks on the civilian populations. The teams were detached from the United Nations Truce Supervision Organization (q.v.).

In 1988, Iraq and Iran agreed to a cease-fire and the United Nations Security Council approved the fielding of UNIIMOG to monitor the cease-fire with the mandate being approved on 9 August 1988. The peacekeeping force was also charged with: investigating alleged violations of the cease-fire; restoring the situation when a violation occurred; preventing changes in the status quo prior to the withdrawal of all belligerent forces to internationally agreed boundaries; supervising and verifying the withdrawals; and overseeing the exchange of prisoners. The United Nations maintained a headquarters in each capital with observers deployed on either side of the cease-fire line, but UNIIMOG forces were not allowed to cross the line, except for limited liaison meetings. The force comprised 350 observers drawn from 26 member states, but the number was reduced after Iraq came to an accommodation with Iran after the Gulf War (q.v.). The force on the Iraqi side of the cease-fire line had relative freedom of movement but the Iranians placed greater restrictions due to their mistrust of foreign military personnel. By the end of 1990 the cease-fire line had developed into a one-kilometer neutral zone, and UNIIMOG was withdrawn shortly afterwards following successful negotiations between Iraq and Iran.

UNITED NATIONS IRAQ-KUWAIT MILITARY OBSERVER MISSION (UNIKOM). After the cease-fire in the 1991 Gulf War (q.v.), a United Nations Military Observer Group of 320 military personnel from 35 countries was established to monitor the agreement. This was in line with UN Security Council Resolution 687 (q.v.) of 3 April 1991. UNIKOM's mandate was to monitor the Khor Abdullah waterway and a demilitarized zone extending some nine kilometers into Iraq and 5 kilometers into Kuwait, based on the agreed 1963 boundaries, and to deter violations of the boundary and observe hostile, or potentially hostile actions. A new international frontier was demarcated, at the expense of Iraq, by a UN committee in 1993 and Iraq accepted this in November 1994, with UNIKOM effectively functioning within the new boundaries.

UNITED NATIONS MISSION FOR THE REFERENDUM IN WESTERN SAHARA (MINURSO). This peacekeeping and observer mission was established in response to the 6 September 1991 cease-fire agreed between Morocco and Polisario in the Western Sahara (q.v.). MINURSO was charged with holding a referendum to determine whether the population wished to be incorporated into Morocco or to be independent. In order to achieve this, MINURSO was also charged with the compilation of a register of people eligible to vote and a team of 40 UN police were attached to the force to supervise registration. However, by 1996 the task had not been achieved and voter registration was suspended due to the inability of Morocco and Polisario to settle their differences on the issue. The size of MINURSO was cut by 20 percent and almost all of the police withdrawn. A further attempt was initiated in December 1999 and the mandate extended until May 2000.

UNITED NATIONS OBSERVATION GROUP IN LEBANON (UNOGIL). In 1958, President Camille Chamoun, a Christian Maronite, sought to extend his presidency beyond the legally allowable one term, which resulted in an armed uprising among the Muslim minority. The Lebanese government accused the United Arab Republic (UAR) (q.v.) of supplying weapons to the Muslims and complained that Syria (q.v.) was sending armed personnel into Lebanon (q.v.). The Arab League (q.v.) attempted to resolve the problem, but failed. On 11 June 1958, the United Nations (q.v.) resolved to send a neutral observer mission to be named *UNOGIL*. The group was charged with observation of the border with Syria to determine if armed personnel or weapons were crossing the frontier but had no mandate to halt any illegal movement across the frontier. Operations were carried out by mobile patrols, fixed observation posts, and air patrols by helicopters and light aircraft. Initially, UNOGIL personnel were detached from the United Nations Truce Supervision Organization (q.v.) and began to take up their duties on 12 June 1958. The first detachment consisted of 100 personnel but this was increased to 591 observers following American and British intervention in the Lebanese crisis. Elections for a new president helped to defuse the situation, relations with the UAR improved, and American and British troops were withdrawn. The United Nations accepted that the mandate was now complete and UNOGIL was withdrawn with the last observers leaving on 9 December 1958.

UNITED NATIONS RELIEF AND WORKS AGENCY FOR PALESTINE (UNWRA). This organization took over from the United Nations Relief for Palestinian Refugees in 1949 in order to fulfill the United Nations (q.v.) resolution providing for care of Palestinians who had lost their homes and means of livelihood during the 1948-1949 Arab-Israeli War. This meant that UNRWA had to deal with 914,221 Palestinians, of whom some 50,000 qualified for relief. This task was magnified by the 1967 Arab-Israeli War when another 335,000 Palestinians were displaced from the West Bank and Gaza, of whom 193,600 were eligible for UNRWA support. Funding for UNRWA is by voluntary contributions from member states of the United Nations and its mandate is reviewed on a regular basis. UNRWA provides camps, food, clothing, schools, vocational training, and health clinics, often working in cooperation with other agencies. Facilities are provided in the Gaza Strip, Jordan, Lebanon, Syria (qq.v.), and the West Bank, with some 3,416,447 refugees registered for relief. *See also* **Palestine**

UNITED NATIONS RELIEF FOR PALESTINIAN REFUGEES (UNRPR). The United Nations Relief for Palestinian Refugees was set up in the aftermath of the 1948 Arab-Israeli War to provide relief to the displaced Palestinians. It was succeeded in December 1949 by the United Nations Relief and Works Agency for Palestine (q.v.). *See also* **Palestine**

UNITED NATIONS SECURITY COUNCIL RESOLUTION 598. Adopted unanimously on 20 July 1987 the 10-clause resolution was adopted in order to try to put into operation an immediate cease-fire between Iraq and Iran (qq.v.), which had been at war since 1980. The resolution required verification of the cease-fire by United Nations (q.v.) observers, the release of prisoners of war, and agreement by both parties to mediation in order to resolve the causes of the conflict. *See also* **Iraq-Iran War 1980-1988**

UNITED NATIONS SECURITY COUNCIL RESOLUTION 688. Adopted on 3 April 1991 by 12 votes to one (Cuba) with two abstentions (Ecuador and Yemen), the 34-clause resolution recalled all 13 previous resolutions relating to the Iraqi invasion of Kuwait (q.v.). In addition, this resolution required Iraq (q.v.) to accept the destruction, removal, or rendering harmless of all chemical and biological weapons, including research, development and manufacturing facilities, and ballistic missiles with a range in excess of 150 kilometers. The resolution further required the return of all Kuwaiti property seized by Iraq, the establishment of an Iraqi-funded compensation fund, and the repatriation of all Kuwaiti and third-country nationals still in Iraq. It also reinforced the economic embargo against Iraq but excluded foodstuffs and medicine from the resolution. The resolution also required Iraq to confirm that it would not commit or support any acts of international terrorism. *See also* **United Nations Special Commission on Iraq (UN-SCOM)**

UNITED NATIONS SPECIAL COMMISSION ON IRAQ (UN-SCOM). According to the terms of paragraph 9 of UN Security Council Resolution 687 (q.v.) adopted on 3 April 1991, the secretary-general appointed a Special Commission to carry out on-site inspection of Iraq's (q.v.) biological, chemical, and missile facilities, and to cooperate with the International Atomic Energy Authority regarding on-site inspection of Iraq's nuclear capabilities and in setting up a monitoring system to verify Iraq's continued compliance of its undertakings in these areas. The UN Special Commission was headed by Rolfe Ekeus, a Swedish national. After Iraq had submitted previously withheld documents following top-level defections in 1995, UNSCOM revised its earlier report on Iraqi compliance with Resolution 687 and Resolution 715 on monitoring. UNSCOM had some 100 on-site inspectors, but the whole process has been subject to a series of crises between the inspectors and the Iraqi regime over access to suspect sites, documentation, etc. This led to bombing of Iraq by U.S. and British aircraft in December 1998 following an adverse report on compliance by UNSCOM to the UN secretary- general.

UNITED NATIONS SPECIAL COMMITTEE ON PALESTINE (UNSCOP). The United Nations Special Committee on Palestine was established by the General Assembly on 15 May 1947 to investigate all of the problems relating to Palestine (q.v.) and to report back by 1 September 1947. The UNSCOP report was submitted on 31 August 1947 and it unanimously recommended termination of the British mandate by 1 August 1948. Palestine was then to obtain independence following a transitional period supervised by the United Nations (q.v.) and guaranteed protection for the holy places. A majority plan was submitted by members of the committee recommending the partition of Palestine into an Arab state, a Jewish state, and Jerusalem (q.v.) administered by an international regime with the states being linked by an economic union. A minority report was submitted arguing for a federal system of government with two federated states, one Arab and one Jewish, with Jerusalem as the federal capital. The majority plan was adopted by the General Assembly on 29 November 1947. *See also* Israel

UNITED NATIONS SUSTAINABLE DEVELOPMENT NETWORKING PROGRAM (UNSDNP). This program has been established as part of the United Nations Development Program (UNDP) and is concerned with facilitating widespread use of the Internet as a means of promoting sustainable development in a systematic manner and at a relatively low cost. The UNSDNP operates at a country level, launching and supporting local Internet sites, and building national capacities and knowledge resources. In the Middle East, 12 countries were participating in the program, but at various stages, with Morocco, Lebanon (qq.v.), Tunisia, and the Palestine National Authority (q.v.) being operational as of December 1999. Jordan (q.v.) was almost operational and feasibility studies had been completed with Algeria, Egypt, and Syria (qq.v.). The remainder of the 12 countries, Iraq, Kuwait, Libya, and the United Arab Emirates (qq.v.), were only at the stage of preliminary negotiations as of December 1999.

UNITED NATIONS TRUCE SUPERVISION ORGANIZATION (UNTSO). The United Nations Truce Supervision Organization was formed to oversee the truce arrangements between the Arab states and Israel (q.v.) and became effective on 11 June 1948. Unarmed observers were sent to Egypt and Palestine (qq.v.) but hostilities continued and an armistice was only agreed between Israel and Egypt, Jordan, Lebanon, and Syria (qq.v.) in 1949. UNTSO observers were stationed along the four armistice lines and even remained in the region during the 1956 Suez crisis when they were supplemented by the United Nations Emergency Force (q.v.). UNTSO was also involved in demarcating the cease-fire lines between Syria and Israel following the 1967 Arab-Israeli War and provided observers along the Suez Canal. UNTSO observers have also been involved in the United Nations Interim Force in Lebanon (q.v.). The maximum strength of UNTSO was 572 in 1948 but has now been reduced to under 300 observers with its headquarters in Jerusalem (q.v.). Since 1948, 22 UNTSO observers have been killed in the various operations.

UNITED NATIONS YEMEN OBSERVATION MISSION (UNYOM). In December 1961, Yemen (q.v.) had withdrawn from a federation with Egypt (q.v.) and faced a civil war situation with a coup against the royal government in September 1962. A new revolutionary government was backed by Egypt (q.v.) and recognized by the Soviet Union, and civil war ensued. Egypt despatched a large military force to support the new government, while the royalists were supported by Saudi Arabia (q.v.). The deployment of a peacekeeping force was recommended by King Hussein of Jordan (qq.v.) and Yemen, Saudi Arabia, and Egypt agreed to accept the terms of a United Nations (q.v.) brokered settlement. The agreement was that Saudi Arabia would end its aid to the royalists and would not allow its forces to operate from their territory and, in return, Egypt would withdraw its troops from Yemen. The United Nations then established a demilitarized zone of 32 kilometers on either side of the

Saudi-Yemeni border and sent an observer force to patrol the area.

The United Nations mandated UNYOM on 11 June 1963. The force was drawn from the United Nations Truce Supervisory Organization and the United Nations Emergency Force I (qq.v.), and its maximum strength was 189 personnel. UNYOM conducted ground and air patrols of the demilitarized zone and set up checkpoints on roads and tracks that crossed the zone. The mandate of UNYOM was restricted to observation of the demilitarized zone and did not extend to the border between Yemen and the British-dominated South Arabian Federation or the undemarcated frontier between Yemen and Saudi Arabia. As a result, the royalist forces continued to receive arms from areas outside of the mandate, and Egypt did not totally withdraw troops from the area. The observer force was funded jointly by Saudi Arabia and Egypt. In August 1964, Saudi Arabia withdrew funding, which led Egypt to agree to the termination of the peacekeeping operation. The operation was ended on 4 September 1964 and the two sides in Yemen resolved their differences following the withdrawal of UNYOM.

UNITED STATES AGENCY FOR INTERNATIONAL DEVELOPMENT: WEST BANK AND GAZA MISSION (USAID-WBG). The United States Aid Program for the West Bank and Gaza is a central element of the U.S. government's role in the Palestinian-Israeli peace process and is part of a $375 million aid package to be distributed between 1996-2000. The program focuses on three strategic areas: expanding economic opportunities for Palestinians; increasing access to and more efficient use of scarce water; and encouraging the establishment of a functioning and accountable system of democratic governance.

In terms of the economy the major problems have been the dependence on Israel (q.v.) for access to markets for labor and goods, reliance on small enterprises, and the absence of a modern legal framework governing business transactions. The aid program of USAID-WBG has been directed at promoting the Gaza Industrial Estate, technical support for the development of markets, and the provision of loans to aid small businesses, the majority of which have gone to female entrepreneurs.

The aid program is also addressing the critical shortage and economic use of water and assisting in the implementation of the water resources articles of the Palestinian-Israeli agreements. Palestinian per capita water consumption is well below the minimum standards set by the World Health Organization and only 25 percent of households are connected to sewage networks. Assistance has been given to the Palestinian National Authority to develop a long-term planning framework, to develop new water supplies, and to improve water distribution systems. The program is also working on innovative projects to optimize water allocation, which include conservation and loss prevention, nonconventional sources, reuse and recharge, and aquifer protection.

In terms of governance USAID-WBG has been assisting the Palestinian National Authority and the Palestinian Legislative Council to build essential institutions, especially a vibrant civil society and a professional legislative body. The program also supported the 1996 elections through the provision of monitors and the mounting of voter education sessions. The program has also established a Citizen's Rights Center and is aiding the Palestinian Legislative Council with basic infrastructure and management systems in order to meet its legislative, oversight, and constituency relations roles. The priorities for year 2000 activities are in programs concerned with public outreach. *See also* **Palestine**

UTAIBA, JUHEIMAN IBN SAIF, AL- (1939-1980). Juheima ibn Saif al-Utaiba was born in Sajir in Qasin Province, the grandson of an *Ikhwan* (q.v.) militant who died in 1929 in the struggle against Abdul Aziz Al-Saud. At age 18, he joined the National Guard in which he served until 1972, becoming increasingly opposed to the presence of non-Muslim Westerners in Saudi Arabia (q.v.), including the National Guard. He enrolled at the Islamic University of Medina and concluded that the Saudi regime had deviated from the true path of Islam (q.v.), leading to his expulsion from the university in 1974.

Utaiba returned to Qasim province and began to preach the Wahhabi (q.v.) doctrine, setting up a number of cells in Bedouin settlements. In 1976, he moved with his followers to Riyadh, from where he attacked the Saudi family for deviation from the *Sharia* (q.v.), greed and corruption, abuse of the legal system, and socialization with atheists and unbelievers. In 1978, Utaiba and 98 of his followers were arrested, but released after the Council of Ulama ruled that their ideas were not treasonable.

Utaiba became a clandestine preacher and developed the concept of a Mahdi, or Messiah, which he had linked to traditional Wahhabi doctrines, according his brother-in-law, Muhammad ibn Abdulla al-Qahtani, a former student of the Islamic University of Riyadh, the status of Mahdi. This appealed to his followers as a concept because of the widely held ideal that a renewer of the faith appeared once every

Islamic century, and one was due to appear on 1 November 1979.

Utaiba's followers had concealed large deposits of arms in cellars and retreats of the Grand Mosque complex at Mecca (q.v.). On the Islamic New Year's eve, hundreds of Utaiba's supporters converged on the Grand Mosque with the objective of taking King Khalid al-Saud hostage, as he was expected to join the faithful at prayer, but he was not present. Despite this, Utaiba and his followers took over the Grand Mosque with Utaiba preaching a sermon condemning the Saudi regime and introducing al-Qahtani as the Mahdi. The occupation lasted two weeks and it took thousands of Saudi and Pakistani troops to regain the complex with 117 of Utaiba's followers being killed in the action, including al-Qahtani. Utaiba was one of 67 arrested who were decapitated in January 1980.

W

WAHHABISM. *Wahhabism* is an Islamic doctrine developed by Muhammad ibn Abd al-Wahhab (1703-1792), a native of the Nejd, which was a stronghold of the Hanbali Code (q.v.) of Islamic jurisprudence. The name was actually coined by opponents of the doctrines as Wahhab's followers called themselves *Muwahhidun* (Unitarians). Abd al-Wahhab condemned the medieval superstitions that had collected around the teachings of Islam (q.v.), favored reasoned interpretation of the *Sharia* (q.v.), and opposed the codification of the *Sharia* into a comprehensive system of jurisprudence. He was also opposed to the cult of saints who were often used by believers to intercede on their behalf with Allah, and his followers resorted to destroying the tombs of saints.

Wahhab made attendance at public prayers obligatory and banned the use of minarets in the building of mosques. He later entered into an alliance with the followers of Muhammad ibn Saud, who became ruler of the Nejd in 1745 and founded the House of Saud, to mount a campaign against adultery, corruption, and idolatry. Using the *Hadith* (q.v.) as an authority, they banned music, dancing, and poetry, an integral part of Arab life, and prohibited the use of silk, gold, ornaments, and jewelry.

The Wahhabis regarded themselves as true believers and launched a jihad (q.v.) against all others whom they regarded as apostates. In 1802, the Wahhabis attacked Korbala, a holy city of the Shi'i (q.v.), and under Saud ibn Abdul Aziz (ruled 1803-1814) Wahhabi rule spread to the Iraqi and Syrian borders, and also included the Hedjaz, which included the holy cities of Mecca (q.v.) and Medina. The Governor of Egypt (q.v.), Muhammad Ali, was instructed by the Ottoman Sultan to quell the movement resulting in the defeat and death of Abdullah ibn Saud (ruled 1814-1818).

The power of the Sauds waxed and waned until 1891, when they were finally expelled from the region of Riyadh. However, under Abdul Aziz ibn Abdul Rahman al-Saud, Wahhabism rose again in the Arabian Peninsula. The creed of Wahhabism was propagated using military and state power and the *Ikhwan* (q.v.), brethren or brotherhood, was fostered for this purpose. The Wahhabis considered themselves the truly guided Islamic community, and in 1902 began a campaign against polytheists, unbelievers, and hypocrites (believers whose behavior was considered non-Islamic). They also labelled any deviation from the *Sharia* as innovation and therefore, un-Islamic. The *Ikhwan* succeeded in regaining Diraiya and the Riyadh region in 1902 and a period of consolidation followed before the capture of the Hasa region in 1913, the Asir region in 1920, and the Hedjaz in 1924, thus creating the present-day state of Saudi Arabia (q.v.).

The sect lost some of its former militancy once the oil wealth began to flow in the 1930s but Saudi Arabia still remains a fundamentalist state. Wahhabism has followers in Central Asia, Pakistan, and India.

WESTERN SAHARA. The conflict in Western Sahara arose before Spain's withdrawal from the territory on 26 February 1976, as resistance to the Spanish presence had begun in 1906 and continued until put down by French forces, acting with Spain, in 1934. Morocco (q.v.) had laid claim to the north of the Western Sahara in 1956, and this was followed by Mauritania laying claim to the south. It was not until 1960 that a real Western Sahara political movement emerged and began to campaign for independence from Spain. The independence movement was banned on 17 June 1970.

In 1973, the Saharawi liberation movement, Polisario, was formed to wage a guerrilla war against Spain, while Morocco officially laid claim to the northern part of the territory. The following year saw a census of the population to determine eligibility to vote in a referendum to be organized by the United Nations (UN) (q.v.) and the International Court of Justice was asked to adjudicate on the claims to territory. On 16 October 1975, the court issued a judgment determining that neither Mauritania nor Morocco should have sovereignty over the Western Sahara.

Morocco responded by organizing a march of 35,000 people on the same day to reflect popular support for its cause, and on 31 October, Moroccan forces entered the northern territory. On 14 November 1975, a secret meeting was held in Madrid and an accord signed by Spain, Mauritania, and Morocco dividing the territory into two, with Morocco being given the northern two-thirds and the remainder being given to Mauritania. On 27 February 1976, Polisario formed the Saharawi Democratic Republic and established a government in exile. This government has been recognized by a number of African states and in 1984 was accepted into membership of the Organization of African Unity (q.v.).

Resistance from Polisario within Western Sahara continued such that by 1979 Mauritania had abandoned its claim to the south and signed a peace agreement that recognized the rights of the people to self-determination. However, Morocco responded by moving to occupy the south of the country and established administrative control over the whole of Western Sahara. As a consequence, sporadic guerrilla warfare continued until a cease-fire was agreed upon in 1989.

A settlement plan was negotiated which was to be administered by the United Nations, and a peacekeeping force, the Mission for the Referendum in Western Sahara (MINURSO) (q.v.), was despatched in September 1991 to organize a referendum to determine whether the population wished to be integrated into Morocco or to be independent. The mission was also charged with the compilation of a list of eligible voters, but this has been fraught with difficulty and both sides charge the other with violations of the cease-fire and corruption in voter registration.

In May 1996, the UN Security Council voted to reduce the size of the force by 20 percent and to withdraw almost all of the UN police who were assisting with voter registration. At the same time, voter registration was suspended by the UN due to the inability of Morocco and Polisario to resolve their differences over the issue. The situation was deadlocked with both sides accusing the other of damaging the process and of atrocities and human rights violations.

On 2 December 1999, the mandate for MINURSO was extended until May 2000 and an accord concluded between Morocco and the United Nations giving official status to the mission. In addition, the accord provides for the return of Saharawi refugees who have been admitted as voters in the referendum as well as their immediate families in accordance with the UN settlement plan.

WOMEN. *See* MUSLIM WOMEN'S LEAGUE; UNITED NATIONS DEVELOPMENT FUND FOR WOMEN; WORLD COUNCIL OF MUSLIM WOMEN FOUNDATION

WORLD ASSOCIATION OF MUSLIM YOUTH (WAMY). It was founded in 1972 by a group of concerned Muslims from around the world, with its headquarters in Riyadh, Saudi Arabia (q.v.), and with a host office in the United States at Falls Church, Virginia. The mission of the WAMY is to:

- serve the true Islamic ideology
- consolidate the factors of ideological unity and the strengthening of the Islamic fraternal relationship among Muslim youth
- crystallize and support the constructive role of youth and students in the development of an Islamic society
- assist Islamic youth organizations throughout the world by coordination of their activities and assistance with their projects

The WAMY is dependent upon donors and donations from well-wishers to pursue its activities and one major activity is the awarding of scholarships to outstanding Muslim students.

WORLD COUNCIL OF ISLAMIC CALL. *See* ISLAMIC CALL SOCIETY

WORLD COUNCIL OF MUSLIM WOMEN FOUNDATION. The World Council of Muslim Women Foundation was founded in 1993 in Edmonton, Canada, as a global nonprofit organization dedicated to the education and safety of all women and a peaceful world environment. The main objectives of the organization are to:

- create global awareness among Muslim women of their rights, responsibilities, and roles in society
- promote education toward a global environment of peace and safety
- promote education of the rights of women throughout the world
- promote and encourage mutual respect between Muslim women and women of other faiths
- promote interfaith education on a global basis
- acknowledge with respect the differences among Muslim women
- cooperate on a global basis with all women who share the vision of

a world wherein women's rights will be reaffirmed.

The foundation organizes seminars on a global basis to provide a forum for Muslim women and participates in conferences and seminars organized by other women's organizations which focus on women's rights and equality issues. The foundation works through other networks to promote its activities, including, among others, the Ismaili Community, the Aga Khan Foundation, the International Federation of University Women, and the International Council of Women.

WORLD ISLAMIC CALL SOCIETY. *See* **ISLAMIC CALL SOCIETY**

WORLD MUSLIM CONGRESS (WMC). This is the oldest Muslim organization. It was founded in Mecca, Saudi Arabia (qq.v.), in 1926, but did not come into operation until 1931 following the Second International Islamic Conference held in Jerusalem. It has consultative status with the Economic and Social Commission (ECOSOC) of the United Nations (q.v.), the United Nations High Commission for Refugees (UNHCR), and observer status with the Organization of the Islamic Conference (OIC) (q.v.)

The WMC is a nonpolitical organization believing in the universal brotherhood of mankind without discrimination. It also strives for interfaith dialogue with the objective of creating mutual tolerance among the followers of different religions. The congress is run by a president, vice president, and executive committee, all of whom are elected at the WMC's International Conference, normally serving for a five-year period.

It publishes *The Muslim World* (weekly) and a series of pamphlets on various topics, such as the situation in Chechnya, world Muslim minorities, and the problems of Kashmir.

Y

YEMEN. The Republic of Yemen was created on 22 May 1990 as a result of a merger between the Yemen Arab Republic (YAR), also known as North Yemen, and the People's Democratic Republic of Yemen (PDRY), also known as *South Yemen*. The new constitution had been endorsed by the two states in 1981, but not approved by referendum until May 1991.

The two states had evolved separately prior to this time with the YAR under the sovereignty of the Ottoman Empire (q.v.), though in reality, largely autonomous. At the beginning of the twentieth century the YAR was ruled by Imam Yahya Hamid al-Din (1869-1948). The country became independent following the collapse of the Ottoman Empire after World War I, but soon became embroiled in a conflict with Saudi Arabia (q.v.) over Hadeida port and part of the Asir Province of Saudi Arabia; this conflict was not resolved until 1934.

In February 1948, an abortive coup took place and the Imam (q.v.) was killed to be succeeded by his son, Ahmad ibn Yaha, whose ambition was to create a Greater Yemen. This was frustrated because of the British Protectorate of Aden. In 1956, Yaha signed a mutual defense pact with Egypt (q.v.) and formed a loose link in 1958 with the United Arab Republic (UAR) (q.v.), known as the *Union of Arab States*, which ceased with the collapse of the UAR in 1961. The Imam died in September 1962 and a military coup led to the outbreak of civil war between royalists, supported by Saudi Arabia (q.v.), and republicans, supported by Egypt (q.v.).

The civil war saw royalist gains and the republicans were further weakened by the withdrawal of Egyptian forces due to the 1967 Arab-Israeli War. However, the civil war continued until 1970, and a government based on a presidential council and a nominated consultative council emerged. The regime was still unstable with the deposing or assassination of leaders until June 1978, when Ali Abdullah Salih assumed power, appointing Abdul Karim Iryani as premier to placate the leftist opposition. In October 1981, a 1,000-member General People's Congress (GPC) was established, partly by indirect elections and partly by appointment. In December 1981, Iryani signed an agreement with the PDRY on unity.

A period of stability ensued and the economy was aided by an increase in oil production in 1984. Salih continued to retain friendly relations with Saudi Arabia, periodically renewed the 1981 unity agreement with the PDRY, and joined the Arab Cooperation Council (ACC) (q.v.).

At the turn of the twentieth century, Great Britain ruled Aden through a governor attached to the India Office, and the Aden Protectorate of 23 provinces through local rulers. Attempts by the YAR to annex parts of the Aden Protectorate were resisted by Great Britain, which introduced a nominated legislative assembly into Aden Colony in 1947. In 1962, Great Britain tried to create the Federation of South Arabia by joining the Colony and the Protectorate, but this was opposed by the National Liberation Front of South Yemen (NLF), which achieved power in 1967 after an armed struggle, leading to the creation of the People's Republic of South Yemen.

Internal struggles within the NLF led to the hardliners coming to the fore in June 1969. In 1978, fighting broke out in Aden, which the president lost and the Yemen Socialist Party (YSP) was formed. However, conflict ensued between the new Chairman of the Presidential Council, Abdul Fatta Ismail, and his ally Ali Nasser Muhammad, resulting in the enforced resignation of Ismail in April 1908 and his exile to Moscow. Ismail returned in 1985 following mediation by Moscow and was given a position within the YSP, but without power, and the compromise broke down with renewed fighting in January 1986. Although Ismail lost his life, the radical faction won and Ali Salim al-Badyh emerged as leader of the YSP. The presidency went to a technocrat, Haidar al-Attas, resulting in al-Baydh being the real power broker and he began to moderate his radical stance by introducing political and economic reform, particularly to counter a reduction in aid from Moscow from $400 million in 1988 to $50 million in 1989. These changes were sufficient to begin the drive for unification with the Yemen Arab Republic, which occurred on 22 May 1990.

After unification, Salih became president and al-Baydh vice president of the Republic of Yemen with the five-member Presidential Council consisting of three North Yemeni and two South Yemeni leaders. However, the two parts of the new state retained separate armed forces and broadcasting facilities. A number of new political parties also emerged, with the most important being the Islamic Yemeni Islah Group (YIG).

The economy of the new state was in a weak position and was placed under greater stress with the expulsion of 850,000 Yemeni workers by Saudi Arabia in August 1990. This was due to Yemen's refusal to join Saudi Arabia in the coalition against Iraq (q.v.) and its refusal in the United Nations Security Council to back UN Resolution 678 (q.v.) authorizing the use of "all necessary means" to expel Iraq from Kuwait (q.v.). In early January 1991, Yemen put forward a peace plan designed to prevent the Gulf War of 1991 (q.v.), but this failed to achieve support.

In May 1991, a referendum endorsed the new constitution but the promised general election, based on universal suffrage, did not take place until April 1993. The GPC won over 40 percent of the 301 seats, followed by the YIG and the YSP. However, al-Baydh objected to the YIG being incorporated into the coalition government and left Sanaa for Aden in August 1993, accusing the president of delaying progress on unification.

As part of the process of unification, control over the respective sections of the armed forces remained with the president and vice president, though some were posted away from their home region as a gesture toward unification. On 27 April 1994, northern forces attacked southern forces based at Dhamar and Amran in the former North Yemen and the south was forced onto the defensive, both militarily and politically. All efforts by the Arab League (q.v.), Egypt, and the United Nations failed to bring about a cease-fire as President Salih stuck to his slogan of "unity or death." On 27 May 1994, al-Baydh declared the south to be independent and renamed it the Democratic Republic of Yemen (DRY) placing his pro-Saudi vice president in charge of defending Aden while he retreated to Mukalla, 600 kilometers east of Aden.

The DRY tried to obtain international recognition but even its backer, Saudi Arabia, refused and concentrated instead on trying to arrange a cease-fire through the United Nations. President Salih insisted that this was purely an internal affair and, although the southerners put up strong resistance, the cutting off of Aden's water and electricity supplies made its fall inevitable. Northern troops also took Mukalla, and al-Baydh and his close followers fled to Saudi Arabia. The conflict ended on 4 July 1994 and cost some 10,000 fatalities and in excess of 25,000 casualties.

The victory meant the consolidation of power by President Salih, the GPC, and the concept of Yemeni unity. In the 1997 legislative election, the GPC won a landside victory and no longer had to govern as a coalition, as the YSP had boycotted the election.

Z

ZAIDIS. The Zaidis are a Shi'i (q.v.) Muslim sect which is least in conflict with Sunni (q.v.) Muslims as they do not believe in the infallibility of the Imams (q.v.). They share the first four Imams of the Shi'i, but then deviate, following a line through Zaid, son of Muhammad ibn al-Hanafiya and half-brother of Imam Hussein ibn Ali. According to the Zaidi beliefs any descendant of Ali can become Imam as long as he can demonstrate his ability to rule according to the *Sharia* (q.v.). Zaidi communities existed in northern Iran and Yemen (q.v.), and in North Yemen the Zaidi state established by Imam Yahya ibn Hussein al-Rassi lasted, with some breaks, until 1962.

ZAKAT. This is one of the five principal obligations, or pillars, of Islam, and is an almsgiving that must be observed by all Muslims who have reached majority age, and who possess a certain amount of personal wealth. *Zakat* has traditionally been construed as an annual tax on all property, currency, commercial assets, livestock, and agricultural produce, to be paid for the benefit of the poor and others with financial needs. It has also been used to support cultural, educational, and religious projects or institutions. In former times, the collection of the tax was the responsibility of the state but, in the present day, it is left for individuals to organize their own almsgiving. A special *zakat* collection is made in the mosques at the end of Ramadan to provide for the post-Ramadan celebrations of the needy.

Selected Bibliography

Introduction

This selected bibliography is a classified collection of major writings on Arab and Islamic organizations, primarily in the English language. Little published material exists on the organizations themselves except for annual reports and journal articles, and thus a great deal of the material centers on the states themselves and the politics, economics, and societies of the region.

The reader who requires a comprehensive survey is referred to the bibliographies listed below. Although now dated, the work by Derek Hopwood and Diana Grimwood-Jones (1972) *Middle East and Islam: A Bibliographical Introduction* is an extremely useful guide to sources on Islam. In terms of the 1990-1991 Gulf War, the reader is recommended to refer to Andrew Orgill (1995) *The 1990-91 Gulf War, Crisis, Conflict and Aftermath,* and for Arab countries, the series of bibliographies produced by Clio Press as part of the World Bibliographical Series.

Research scholars will find excellent collections at the Middle East Institute in Washington, D.C., and at the University of Texas at Austin and other academic institutions in the United States. The Arab Gulf States are catered for by the Arab Gulf Center at the University of Exeter, England, founded with support from the United Arab Emirates, and there are major collections at the University of Durham and St. Antony's College, Oxford. In terms of archival material, the India Office Library in the British Library is invaluable for the early history of the region, while the Public Record Office houses all the relevant official documents relating to British involvement in the Middle East, Africa, and colonies in Asia. Some of the official documents have been issued in the series published by Archive Editions and Cass, which are listed in the relevant section.

The reader interested in a general overview of the region is referred to William I. Cleveland (1994) *A History of the Modern Middle East,* and Albert Hourani, Philip S. Khoury, and Mary C. Wilson (1993) *The Modern Middle East.* In terms of regional stability, F. Gregory Gause III (1994) *Oil Monarchies: Domestic Security in the Gulf States* and Phebe Marr (1993) *Riding the Tiger: The Middle East Challenge after the Cold War* are of particular relevance. The extremely complex issue of border disputes and conflicts in the Arabian Gulf is well covered by Richard Schofield (1994) *Territorial Foundations of the Gulf States.*

As a result of the oil industry and its revenues, the economy of the region is important and has wider influences in the Islamic world due to the various Arab aid programs. The general economy is well represented by the literature and extremely good publications are Roberto Aliboni (1979) *Arab Industrialization and Economic Integration* and Roger Owen and Pamuk Sevket (1998) *A History of Middle East Economies in the Twentieth Century,* while the contemporary situation is catered for by Nemat Shaik (1998) *Prospects for Middle Eastern and North African Economies: From Boom to Bust and Back.*

The various political movements are also well served by the literature. In terms of the growth of Arab nationalism, the reader is referred to C. Ernest Dawn (1973) *From Ottomanism to Arabism: Essays on the Origins of Arab Nationalism,* and an excellent work for the beginner is Sylvia Haim (1962) *Arab Nationalism: An Anthology.* The concepts of Pan-Arabism and Arab Nationalism are dealt with by Tawfic E. Farah (1987) *Pan-Arabism and Arab Nationalism: The Continuing Debate.* A major political force in Iraq and Syria is the Ba'ath Party and John F. Devlin (1976) *The Ba'ath Party: A History from Its Origins to 1966* is a good introductory text, with the struggle between the parties in the two states excellently reviewed by Eberhard Kienle (1991) *Ba'ath Versus Ba'ath.*

Social structure in the Middle East is a complex area and an excellent collection of material is Augustus Richard Norton's two-volume text on *Civil Society in the Middle East* (1995 and 1996) and Hisham Sharibi (1998) *The Next Arab Decade: Alternative Futures.*

A large section of the bibliography is devoted to the country surveys, and the following selections represent good starting points for this area of study. For Bahrain the reader is referred to Jeffrey Nugent and Theodore H. Thomas (1985) *Bahrain and the Gulf.* Egypt's twentieth-century social and political changes are covered by Raymond Williams Baker (1978) *Egypt's Uncertain Revolution under Nasser and Sadat,* with the concept of fundamentalism dealt with by Barry Rubin (1990) *Islamic Fundamentalism in Egyptian Politics.* Iraq has been a significant player in the region, largely as a result of the Iraq-Iran War 1980-1988, the Gulf War 1990-1991 and the Kurdish question. For coverage of these aspects the following texts represent useful starting points: Abbas Alnasrawi (1994) *The Economy of Iraq: Oil, War, Destruction of Development and Prospects 1950-2010,* Gerard Chailand (1993) *A People without a Country: The Kurds and Kurdistan,* Phebe Marr (1985) *The Modern History of Iraq,* and Miron Rezun (1992) *Saddam Hussein's Gulf Wars: Ambivalent States in the Middle East.*

Israel is a significant presence in the region in its own right but also because of the Palestinian problem and the various Arab-Israeli wars. A good history for the general reader is Arnold Blumberg (1998) *The History of Israel,* while Israel's invasion of Lebanon is dealt with by Ze'ev Schiff and Ya'ari Ehud (1986) *Israel's Lebanon War* and Kirsten E. Schulze (1998) *Israel's Covert Diplomacy in Lebanon.* The question of Palestine has generated a mass of literature representing both sides of the issue and the question of international terrorism. A seminal study on the origins of the problem from a Palestinian viewpoint is Walid Khalidi (1984) *From Haven to Conquest: Readings in Zionism and the Palestine Problem until 1948,* with a more recent reference provided by Nafez Y. Nazzal and Laila A. Nazzal (1997) *Historical Dictionary of Palestine.* The role of the fundamentalists is well handled by Andrea Nusse (1998) *Muslim Palestine: The Ideology of Hamas.*

Jordan is also an important country in the region, largely because of its geographical position and the part that it has played over Palestine and in the peace process. In terms of its history, the reader is referred to Robert B. Satloff (1994) *From Abdullah to Hussein: Jordan in Transition,* and for Jordan's strategic position, Laurie A. Brand (1994) *Jordan's Inter-Arab Relations: The Political Economy of Alliance Making.* Kuwait is a small state but has significance because of her economy, the aid fund, and the 1990-1991 Gulf War. A good reference for the beginner is Jill Crystal (1992) *Kuwait: The Transformation of an Oil State* and for the contemporary position Anthony H. Cordesman (1997) *Kuwait: Recovery and Security after the Gulf War.*

Lebanon is important because of her internal politics, the Israeli invasion of 1982, and the impact of the fundamentalist Hamas movement backed by Iran. Nearly all of these facets are covered by William Harris (1997) *Faces of Lebanon: Sects, Wars and Global Extensions* and by Jonathan Randal *The Tragedy of Lebanon: Christian Warlords, Israeli Adventurers and American Bunglers.* Syria is linked with Lebanon as part of the concept of Greater Syria and involvement since the 1976 Lebanese civil wars. A good introductory reference is David Commins (1996) *Historical Dictionary of Syria.* Greater Syria is covered by Daniel Pipes (1990) *Greater Syria: The History of an Ambition* and the contemporary situation by Eberhard Kienle (1995) *Contemporary Syria: Liberalization between Cold War and Cold Peace.*

The Maghreb is important as an economic union with links to the Arab world and to Africa, with Islamic fundamentalism becoming a major factor in the area. The reader is referred to Francois Bugat and

William Dowell (1997) *The Islamic Movement in North Africa*, Graham Fuller (1996) *Algeria: The Next Fundamentalist State?* and Kenneth Perkins Le Gall (1997) *The Maghreb in Question: Essays in History and Historiography.*

The Arab Gulf States are important because of oil and Islam, particularly Saudi Arabia with the holy cities of Mecca and Medina. For the Sultanate of Oman a good introduction is provided by Ian Skeet (1992) *Oman: Politics and Development,* while the United Arab Emirates is covered in terms of its federal success by Malcolm Peck (1986) *The United Arab Emirates: A Venture in Unity.* Saudi Arabia has generated a large body of literature because of its economic and religious importance and a good comprehensive introductory work is Robert Lacey (1981) *The Kingdom: Arabia and the House of Saud* with a useful reference guide being J. E. Peterson (1993) *Historical Dictionary of Saudi Arabia.* Yemen is an example of successful unity and Robert D. Burrowes (1995) *Historical Dictionary of Yemen* is a good reference text, while the complex internal structure is covered by Paul K. Dresch (1989) *Tribes, Government and History in Yemen.*

Islam and Islamic fundamentalism are major factors in the concept of organizations in the Arab world and the wider Islamic community. The question of the Islamic resurgence is dealt with by Ibrahim M. Abu-Rabi (1996) *Intellectual Origins of Islamic Resurgence in the Modern Arab World.* A good reference work on fundamentalist movements is Ahmad S. Moussalli (1999) *Historical Dictionary of Islamic Fundamentalist Movements in the Arab World, Iran and Turkey,* together with Dilip Hiro (1989) *Holy Wars: The Rise of Islamic Fundamentalism.* An excellent study of the perception of fundamentalism as a threat outside of the Islamic community is J. Esposito (1992) *The Islamic Threat: Myth or Reality.*

Economic organizations are predominant in the Arab world and the Islamic community, largely because they are expressions of unity that are relatively easy to pursue. In terms of the Arab aid funds, the main publications are the annual reports of the various organizations. A major organization in the field is the Islamic Development Bank to which Saeed Ahmed Meenai (1989) *The Islamic Development Bank: A Case Study of Islamic Cooperation* is a good introduction. Among the regional bodies, the Gulf Cooperation Council is a significant organization operating at a variety of levels, and good introductions are provided by Erik R. Peterson (1988) *The Gulf Cooperation Council: Search for Unity in a Dynamic Region* and R. K. Ramazani *The Gulf Cooperation Council: Record and Analysis.* Another regional organization which impacts on the international arena is the Organization of Arab Petroleum Exporting Countries which is well introduced by Abdelkader Maachou (1982) *OAPEC: An International Organization for Economic Cooperation and an Instrument for Regional Integration.*

In Arab North Africa, the Union of the Arab Maghreb (UAM) has been an important development, and one of the best introductions to the problems it faces is William I. Zartmann "The Ups and Downs of Maghreb Unity" in Michael C. Hudson (1999) *Middle East Dilemma: The Politics and Economics of Arab Integration.* A major inter-regional organization is the Arab League, which is also an umbrella organization for a number of specialized agencies and presents a tangible expression of the drive for Arab unity. The two best works dealing with the organization are Robert W. McDonald (1965) *The League of Arab States: A Study in the Dynamics of Regional Cooperation* and Tawfig Y. Hasou (1989) *The Struggle for the Arab World: Egypt's Nasser and the Arab League.* Another umbrella organization designed to serve the wider Islamic community is the Organization of the Islamic Conference, and a useful introduction is provided by Noor Ahmed Baba "Organization of the Islamic Conference: Conceptual Framework and Institutional Structure" in *International Studies* 30, no. 1 (1993): 35-51.

The final sections of the selected bibliography deal with the concepts of regional security in an extremely volatile region. The first is the Iraq-Iran War (1980-1988), which has generated a large body of literature. An extremely readable account is provided by John Bulloch and Harvey Morris (1989) *The Gulf War: Its Origins, History and Consequences,* with a good analysis of the conflict provided by Majid Khadduri (1988) *The Gulf War: The Origins and Implications of the Iraq-Iran Conflict.* The second crisis is the 1990-1991 Gulf War brought about by Iraq's invasion of Kuwait. As might be expected of a conflict which became international in nature, involved the United Nations, split the Arab world, and is ongoing due to UN sanctions, there is a mass of literature covering all aspects of the conflict. General coverage of the conflict is provided by Amatzia Baram and Barry Rubin (1994) *Iraq's Road to War* and John Bulloch and Harvey Morris (1993) *Saddam's War: The Origins of the Kuwaiti Crisis and the International Response,* with a good reference text being Clayton R. Newell (1992) *The Historical Dictionary of the Persian Gulf War.*

The Internet is fast becoming a major source of information, with some of the organizations having their own Web sites. In terms of general sources with links to the Islamic community, *The Islamic*

Interlink at **www.ais.org** provides a good starting point, with a classified directory of sites dedicated to Islamic organizations and other relevant topics. A further major source for the Arab world is the Arab Net at **http://www.arab.net**, which has data on all the countries of the Arab world, a directory of relevant subjects, and a news site. It also has a facility within the section on each country to search links to other sites, including a number of official national sites. Academic institutions also provide similar facilities, with the University of Texas at Austin having a guide to Islamic resources on the Internet at **www.texas.edu/student/msa/links/**. This is obviously a fast-growing sector, which needs to be visited on a regular basis.

CONTENTS
Bibliographies
Official Documents
Periodicals
General References
Biographies
Economics: General
Politics: General
Society: General
Country Surveys
  Bahrain
  Egypt
  Iraq
  Israel
  Jordan
  Kuwait
  Lebanon
  Libya
  Maghreb
  Oman
  Palestine
  Qatar
  Saudi Arabia
  Syria
  United Arab Emirates
  Yemen

Islam
  Organizations

Abu Dhabi Fund for Arab Economic Development
Arab Cooperation Council
Arab Fund for Economic and Social Development
Arab League
Arab League Educational, Cultural, and Scientific Organization
Arab Monetary Fund
Gulf Cooperation Council
Islamic Development Bank
Kuwait Fund for Arab Economic Development
Organization of Arab Petroleum Exporting Countries
Organization of the Islamic Conference
Palestine Liberation Organization
Saudi Fund for Development
Union of the Arab Maghreb

Regional Security
  Iraq-Iran War
  Gulf War 1990-91 and Aftermath

BIBLIOGRAPHIES

Atiyeh, George N. *The Contemporary Middle East, 1948-1973, A Selective and Annotated Bibliography.* Boston, Mass.: G. K. Hall, 1975.

Clements, Frank A. *Kuwait: A Bibliography.* 2nd ed. Santa Barbara, Calif: Clio Press, 1996.

———. *Oman: A Bibliography.* 2nd ed. Santa Barbara, Calif.: Clio Press, 1994.

———. *United Arab Emirates: A Bibliography.* 2nd ed. Santa Barbara, Calif.: Clio Press, 1998.

Gardner, J. Anthony. *The Iraq-Iran War: A Bibliography.* London: Mansell, 1988.

Goodman, Sue A. *Persian Gulf War, 1990-91 (Desert Shield/Desert Storm).* Maxwell Air Force Base, Ala.: Air University Library, 1991.

Hopwood, Derek, and Diana Grimwood-Jones, eds. *Middle East and Islam: A Bibliographical Introduction.* Zug, Switzerland: Inter-Documentation Co., 1972.

Labaki, G. T. *The Lebanon Crisis (1975-1985): A Bibliography.* College Park: University of Maryland, Center for International Development and Conflict Management, 1986.

Lawless, R. I. *Libya*. Santa Barbara, Calif.: Clio Press, 1987.

McLachlan, K. S., and R.N. Schofield *A Bibliography of the Iran-Iraq Borderland*. London: Menas Press, 1987.

Mikdadi, Faysal. *Gamal Abdul Nasser: A Bibliography*. New York: Greenwood Press, 1991.

Orgill, Andrew. *The 1990-91 Gulf War: Crisis, Conflict and Aftermath: An Annotated Bibliography*. London: Mansell, 1995.

Otto, Ingebord, and Marianne Schmidt-Dumont, eds. *Der Golfkrieg (1990/91) Eine Auswahlbibliographie* [The Gulf War 1990/91: A Selected Bibliography]. Hamburg: Deutsches Ubersee-Institut, 1992.

Peterson, J. E. *Security in the Arabian Peninsula and Gulf States, 1973-1984*. Washington, D.C.: National Council on US-Arab Relations, 1985.

Reich, Bernard, and Sanford Silverburg. *U.S. Foreign Relations with the Middle East and North Africa*. Lanham, Md.: Scarecrow Press, 1999.

Sharif, Walid I. *Oil and Development in the Arab Gulf States: A Selected Annotated Bibliography*. London: Croom Helm, 1985.

Unwin, P. T. H. *Bahrain: A Bibliography*. Santa Barbara, Calif.: Clio Press, 1982.

―――. Qatar: A Bibliography. Santa Barbara, Calif.: Clio Press, 1982.

OFFICIAL DOCUMENTS

Ashtiany, Julia. *The Arabic Documents in the Archives of the British Political Agency Kuwait, 1904-1949*. London: India Office Library and Records, under the auspices of the British Academy Oriental Documents Committee, 1982.

Bailey, Ronald W., ed. *Records of Oman 1867-1960*. Farnham Common, England: Archive Editions, 1992.

Bidwell, Robin. "A Collection of Texts Dealing with the Sultanate of Muscat and Its International Relations 1790-1970." *Journal of Oman Studies* 6, no. 1 (1983): 21-33.

Burdett, A. L. P., ed. *Arab Dissident Movements 1905-1955*. Farnham Common, England: Archive Editions, 1996.

Copson, Raymond W. *Persian Gulf Conflict: Post-war Issues for Congress*. Congressional Research Service, Washington, D.C.: U.S. Government Printing Office, 1991.

Great Britain, Foreign Office. Confidential Reprint. *The Affairs of Arabia, 1905-1906.* 2 vols, edited by Robin Bidwell. London: Cass, 1971.

———. *The Affairs of Kuwait 1896-1905.* 2 vols, edited by Robin Bidwell. London: Cass, 1971.

Jarman, R. L., ed. *Political Diaries of Iraq 1917-1965.* Farnham Common, England: Archive Editions, 1998.

———. *Political Diaries of Jordan 1920-1965.* Farnham Common, England: Archive Editions, 1998.

———. *Political Diaries of the Levant: Lebanon and Syria 1920-1965.* Farnham Common, England: Archive Editions, 1998.

———. *Political Diaries of Saudi Arabia 1919-1965.* Farnham Common, England: Archive Editions, 1998.

———. *Political Diaries of the Persian Gulf 1904-1965.* Farnham Common, England: Archive Editions, 1998.

Lorimer, J. G. *Gazetteer of the Persian Gulf, Oman and Central Arabia.* Calcutta, India: Government Printing House, 1908-15. Reprint, Farnborough, England: Gregg International, 1970.

The Persian Gulf Administration Reports 1873-1957. Farnham Common, England: Archive Editions, 1986.

Schofield, Richard, ed. *Islands and Maritime Boundaries of the Gulf, 1798-1960.* London: Archive Editions, 1991.

Tuson, Penelope, and Emma Quick, eds. *Arabian Treaties 1600-1960.* Farnham Common, England: 1992.

Tuson, Penelope, and Joan C. Lancaster. *The Records of the British Residency and Agencies in the Persian Gulf.* London: India Office Library and Records, 1979.

PERIODICALS

Arab Gulf Journal. London: MD Research and Services. Biannual.

Asian Affairs (formerly *Journal of the Royal Central Asian Society*). London: Royal Society for Asian Affairs. 3 per annum.

Foreign Affairs. New York: Council on Foreign Relations. 5 per annum.

International Journal of Islamic and Arabic Studies. Bloomington, Ind.: International Institute of Islamic and Arabic Studies. Semi-annual.

International Journal of Middle East Studies. Cambridge, England; New York: Cambridge University Press. Quarterly.

Journal of Oman Studies. Muscat, Sultanate of Oman: Ministry of Information and Culture. Semi-annual.

The Middle East. London: IC Publications. Monthly.

Middle East Insight. Washington, D.C.: International Insight Inc. Bimonthly.

The Middle East Journal. Washington, D.C.: Middle East Institute. Quarterly.

Middle East Studies Association Bulletin. Tucson: University of Arizona, Middle East Studies Association. Semi-annual.

Muslim World. Hartford, Conn.: The Duncan Black Macdonald Center. Quarterly.

GENERAL REFERENCES

Abi-Aad, N., and Michael Grenon. *Instability and Conflict in the Middle East: People, Petroleum and Security Threats*. London: Macmillan; New York: St. Martin's Press, 1997.

Anscombe, Frederick F. *The Ottoman Gulf: The Creation of Kuwait, Saudi Arabia and Qatar*. New York:, Columbia University Press, 1997.

Barakat, Halim. *The Arab World: Society, Culture, State*. Berkeley, Calif.: University of California Press, 1993.

Cleveland, William L. *A History of the Modern Middle East*. Boulder, Colo.: Westview Press, 1994.

Cordesman, Anthony H. *Britain, Oman, Qatar and the UAE: Challenges of Security*. Boulder, Colo.: Westview Press, 1997.

———. *The Gulf and the Search for Strategic Stability*. Boulder, Colo.: Westview Press, 1984.

Corm, Georges. *Fragmentation of the Middle East: The Last Thirty Years*. London: Hutchinson, 1988.

Crystal, Jill. *Oil and Politics in the Gulf: Rulers and Merchants in Kuwait and Qatar*. Cambridge, England: Cambridge University Press, 1990.

Fisher, Sydney. *The Middle East: Vol. 2. From 1789*. London; New York: McGraw Hill, 1997.

Gause III, F. Gregory. *Oil Monarchies: Domestic Security Challenges in the Gulf States*. New York: Council on Foreign Relations Press, 1994.

Hourani, Albert. *A History of the Arab Peoples*. London: Faber, 1991.

Hourani, Albert, Philip S. Khoury, and Mary C. Wilson, eds. *The Modern Middle East*. London: I. B. Tauris, 1993.

Jawad, Haifaa A., ed. *The Middle East in the New World Order*. New York: St. Martin's Press, 1994.

Kemp, Geoffrey, and Robert E. Harkavy. *Strategic Geography and the Changing Middle East*. Washington, D.C.: Carnegie Endowment, 1997.

Mansfield, Peter. *A History of the Middle East*. London: Penguin, 1992.

Marr, Phebe. *Riding the Tiger: The Middle East Challenge after the Cold War*. Boulder, Colo.: Westview Press, 1993.

Middle East and North Africa. 1948-Annually. London: Europa Publications.

Mostyn, Trevor et al., eds. *The Cambridge Encyclopaedia of the Middle East*. Cambridge, England: Cambridge University Press, 1988.

Netton, Ian Richard, ed. *Arabia and the Gulf States: From Traditional Society to Modern States*. London: Croom Helm, 1986.

Peck, Malcolm C. *Historical Dictionary of the Gulf Arab States*. Lanham, Md.: Scarecrow Press, 1996.

Pridham, B. R., ed. *The Arab Gulf and the Arab World*. London: Croom Helm, 1988.

Schofield, Richard, ed. *Territorial Foundations of the Gulf States*. London: UCL Press, 1994.

Tschirigi, Dan, ed. *The Arab World Today*. Boulder, Colo.: Lynne Rienner, 1994.

Zahlan, Rosemarie Said. *The Making of the Modern Gulf States*. London: Unwin Hyman, 1989.

BIOGRAPHIES

Abdallah (King Abdallah of Jordan). *My Memoirs Completed*. London: Hutchinson, 1978.

Almana, Mohammed. *Arabia Unified: A Portrait of Ibn Saud*. Rev. ed. London: Hutchinson, 1982.

Bidwell, Robin. *Arabian Personalities of the Early Twentieth Century*. New York: Oleander Press, 1986.

Boutros-Ghali, Boutros. *Egypt's Road to Jerusalem: A Diplomat's Story of the Struggle for Peace in the Middle East*. New York: Random House, 1997.

Finklestone, Joseph. *Anwar Sadat: Visionary Who Dared*. London: Cass, 1996.

Hart, Alan. *Arafat: Terrorist or Peacemaker?* London: Sidgwick and Jackson, 1984.

Hussein, King. *Uneasy Lies the Head*. London: Heinemann, 1962.

Karsh, Efraim, and Inari Rautsi. *Saddam Hussein: A Political Biography*. New York: Free Press, 1991.

Kikhia, Mansour O. El-. *Libya's Qaddafi: The Politics of Contradiction*. Gainesville, Fla.: University Press of Florida, 1997.

Lunt, James. *Hussein of Jordan: A Political Biography*. London: Macmillan, 1989.

Mansfield, Peter. *Nasser*. London: Methuen, 1969.

Ma'oz, Moshe. *Asad: The Sphynx of Damascus*. London: Weidenfeld and Nicolson, 1988.

Matar, Fouad. *Saddam Hussein: A Biography*. London: Highlight Productions, 1990.

Mattar, Philip. *The Mufti of Jerusalem: Al-Hajj Amin Al-Husayni and the Palestinian National Movement*. New York: Columbia University Press, 1988.

McLoughlin, Leslie. *Ibn Saud: Founder of a Kingdom*. London: Macmillan, 1993.

Reich, Bernard, ed. *Political Leaders of the Contemporary Middle East and North Africa: A Biographical Dictionary*. Westport, Conn.: Greenwood Press, 1990.

Roded, Ruth. *Women in Islamic Biographical Collections: From Ibn Sa'd to Who's Who*. Boulder, Colo.: Lynne Reinner, 1993.

Seale, Patrick. *Asad of Syria: The Struggle for the Middle East*. Berkeley, Calif. : University of California Press, 1989.

Shimoni, Yaacov. *Biographical Dictionary of the Middle East*. New York: Facts on File, 1991.

Stephens, Robert. *Nasser: A Political Biography*. London: Penguin, 1971.

Sumaidi, Hussein. *Circle of Fear*. London: Brassey's, 1994.

Wallach, Janet, and John Wallach. *Arafat: In the Eyes of the Beholder*. New York: Carol Publishing Group, 1990.

Who's Who in the Arab World 1999-2000. Munich: K.G. Saur, 1998.

Wilson, Mary C. *King Abdallah of Jordan: A Political Biography*. Oxford, England: St. Antony's College, 1985.

ECONOMICS: GENERAL

Aarts, P. M. Tempel. "Economic Integration in the Middle East." *Japanese Institute of Middle Eastern Economics Review*, no. 31 (1995): 39-49.

Aliboni, Roberto, ed. *Arab Industrialisation and Economic Integration.* London: Croom Helm, 1979.

Amin, Galal. *The Modernization of Poverty: A Study in the Political Economy of Growth in Nine Arab Countries, 1945-1970.* Leiden, Netherlands: Brill, 1974.

Barkey, Henry J. *The Politics of Economic Reform in the Middle East.* New York: St. Martin's Press, 1992.

Beseisu, Fouad Hamdi. "Sub-Regional Economic Cooperation in the Arab Gulf." *Arab Gulf Journal* 1, no. 1 (1981): 45-64.

Chaudry, Kiran Aziz. *The Price of Wealth: Economies and Institutions in the Middle East.* Ithaca, N.Y.: Cornell University Press, 1997.

Erian, M. A. El-. "Middle Eastern Economics External Environment: What Lies Ahead?" *Middle East Policy* 4, no. 3 (1996): 137-46.

Ghonemy, M. Riad El-. *Affluence and Poverty in the Middle East.* London: Routledge, 1998.

Guazzone, Laura, ed. *The Middle East in Global Change: The Politics and Economics of Interdependence versus Fragmentation.* London: Macmillan, 1997.

Hollis, R., ed. *Oil and Regional Developments in the Gulf.* London: Royal Institute of International Affairs, 1998.

Karl, Terry Lynn. *The Paradox of Plenty: Oil Booms and Petro-States.* Berkeley, Calif.: University of California Press, 1997.

Kubursi, Atif A. *Oil: Industrialization and Development in the Arab Gulf States.* London: Croom Helm, 1984.

Lavy, Victor, and Eliezer Shaffer. *Foreign Aid and Economic Development in the Middle East: Egypt, Syria and Jordan.* New York: Praeger, 1991.

Makdisi, Samir A. "Arab Economic Co-operation." In *Arab Industrialisation and Economic Integration,* edited by Roberto Aliboni, 90-133. London: Croom Helm, 1979.

Mallakh, Ragaei El, Mihssen Kadhim, and Barry Poulson. *Capital Investment in the Middle East: The Use of Surplus Funds for Regional Development.* New York: Praeger, 1977.

Moore, C. H. "Islamic Banks and Competitive Politics in the Arab World and Turkey." *Middle East Journal* 44, no. 2 (1990): 234-55.

Musrey, Alfred G. *An Arab Common Market: A Study of Inter-Arab Trade Flows.* New York: Praeger, 1969.

Niblock, Tim, and Emma Murphy, eds. *Economic and Political Liberalization in the Middle East*. London: British Academic Press, 1993.

Owen, Roger, and Pamuk Sevket. *A History of Middle East Economies in the Twentieth Century*. London: I. B. Tauris, 1998.

Richards, A., and J. Waterbury, eds. *A Political Economy of the Middle East*. 2nd ed. Boulder, Colo.: Westview Press, 1996.

Saeed, Abdullah. "Islamic Banking in Practice: The Case of Faisal Islamic Bank of Egypt." *Journal of Arabic, Islamic and Middle Eastern Studies* 2, no. 1 (1995): 28-46.

Sayigh, Yusif A. "Arab Economic Integration: The Poor Harvest of the 1980s." In *Middle East Dilemma: The Politics and Economics of Arab Integration*, edited by Michael C. Hudson, 233-58. London; New York: I. B. Tauris, 1999.

———. *The Determinants of Arab Economic Development*. London: Croom Helm, 1978.

———. *The Economics of the Arab World: Development Since 1945*. London: Croom Helm, 1978.

Shafik, Nemat. *Economic Challenges Facing Middle East and North African Countries: Alternative Futures*. London: Macmillan, 1998.

———, *Prospects for Middle Eastern and North African Economies: From Boom to Bust and Back*. London: Macmillan, 1998.

Wilson, Rodney. *Economic Development in the Middle East*. London: Routledge, 1995.

——— ed. *Islamic Financial Markets*. London: Routledge, 1990.

Zurayk, Huda C., and Fadia Saadeh. "Women as Mobilizers of Human Resources in Arab Countries." In *Gender and Development in the Arab World: Women's Economic Participation; Patterns and Policies*, edited by Nabil F. Khoury and Valentine M. Moghadam, 35-48. London: Zed Books; Tokyo: United Nations University Press, 1995.

POLITICS: GENERAL

Abu Jaber, Kamel S. *The Arab Ba'th Socialist Party: History, Ideology and Organization*. Syracuse, N.Y.: Syracuse University Press, 1966.

Abukhalil, A. "A New Arab Ideology? The Rejuvenation of Arab Nationalism." *Middle East Journal* 46, no. 1 (1992): 76-96.

Ajami, Fouad. *The Arab Predicament: Arab Political Thought and Practice since 1967.* Rev. ed. Cambridge, England: Cambridge University Press, 1992.

Anderson, Lisa. "Absolutism and the Resilience of Monarchy in the Middle East." *Political Science Quarterly* 106, no. 1 (1991): 1-15.

Ayubi, Nazih H. *Over-stating the Arab State: Politics and Society in the Middle East.* London: I. B. Tauris, 1995.

Bromley, Simon. *Rethinking Middle East Politics: State Formation and Development.* London: Polity Press, 1994.

Brumberg, Daniel. "An Arab Path to Democracy." *Journal of Democracy* 1, no. 4 (1990): 120-25.

Crystal, Jill. "Authoritarianism and Its Adversaries in the Arab World." *World Politics* 46, no. 2 (1994): 262-89.

Davis, M. Jane, ed. *Politics and International Relations in the Middle East.* Aldershot, England: Elgar Press, 1995.

Dawn, C. Ernest. *From Ottomanism to Arabism: Essays on the Origins of Arab Nationalism.* Chicago: Robert E. Krieger, 1973.

Devlin, John F. *The Ba'th Party: A History from Its Origins to 1966.* Stanford, Calif.: Hoover Institution Press, 1976.

Eikelman, Dale F. "The Re-Imagination of the Middle East: Political and Academic Frontiers." *Middle East Studies Association Bulletin* 26, no. 1 (1992): 3-12.

Farah, Tawfic E., ed. *Pan-Arabism and Arab Nationalism: The Continuing Debate.* Boulder, Colo.: Westview Press, 1987.

———, and Yasumasa Kuroda. *Political Socialization in the Arab States.* Boulder, Colo.: Lynne Rienner, 1987.

Haddad, Mohammad. "The Rise of Arab Nationalism Reconsidered." *International Journal of Middle East Studies* 26, no. 2 (1994): 201-22.

Haim, Sylvia, ed. *Arab Nationalism: An Anthology.* Los Angeles, Calif.: University of California Press, 1962.

Harris, William, et al. *Challenges to Democracy in the Middle East.* Princeton, N.J.: Markus Wiener, 1997.

Hudson, Michael C. "State, Society and Legitimacy: An Essay on Arab Political Prospects in the 1990s." In *The Next Decade: Alternative Futures*, edited by Hisham Sherabi, 22-37. Boulder, Colo.: Westview Press, 1988.

Ibrahim, Saad Eddin. "Civil Society and Prospects for Democratization in the Arab World." In *Civil Society in the Middle East, Vol. 1,* edited by Augustus Richard Norton, 27-54. Leiden, Netherlands: Brill, 1995.

Jankowski, James, and Israel Gershoni, eds. *Rethinking Nationalism in the Arab Middle East*. New York: Columbia University Press, 1997.

Jillani, A. "Nasser, Saddam and Pan-Arabism." *Pakistan Horizon* 44, no. 2 (1992): 43-51.

Joffe, George. "Concepts of Sovereignty in the Gulf Region." In *Territorial Foundations of the Gulf States*, edited by Richard Schofield, 78-93. London: UCL Press, 1994.

Kedourie, Elie. *Arabic Political Memoirs and Other Studies*. London: Cass, 1974.

———. *Politics in the Middle East*. Oxford, England: Oxford University Press, 1992.

Kienle, Eberhard. *Ba'ath versus Ba'ath*. New York: St. Martin's Press, 1991.

Kramer, Martin. *Arab Awakening and Islamic Revival: The Politics of Ideas in the Middle East*. New Brunswick, N.J.: Transaction Books, 1996.

Long, David E., and Bernard Reich, eds. *The Government and Politics of the Middle East and North Africa*. Boulder, Colo.: Westview Press, 1995.

Luciani, Giacomo. *The Arab State*. London: Routledge, 1990.

Mackey, Sandra. *Passion and Politics: The Turbulent World of the Arabs*. New York; London: Dutton, 1992.

Ma'oz, Moshe, and Ilan Pappe, eds. *Middle Eastern Politics and Ideas: A History from Within*. New York: St. Martin's Press, 1998.

Mansour, Fawzy. *The Arab World: Nation, State and Democracy*. London: Zed Books; Tokyo: United Nations University Press, 1992.

Mirsky, Yehuda, and Matt Abrens. *Democracy in the Middle East: Defining the Challenge*. Washington, D.C.: The Washington Institute, 1993.

Mufti, Malik. *Sovereign Creations: Pan-Arabism and Political Order in Syria and Iraq*. Ithaca, N.Y.: Cornell University Press, 1996.

Muslih, Muhammad, and Augustus Richard Norton. *Political Tides in the Arab World*. New York: Foreign Policy Association, 1992.

Omar, Saleh. "Philosophical Origins of the Arab Ba'ath Party: The Work of Zaki al-Ansuzi." *Arab Studies Quarterly* 18, no. 2 (1996): 23-37.

Owen, Roger. *State Power and Politics in the Making of the Modern Middle East.* London: Routledge, 1992.

Peterson, J. E. *The Arab Gulf States: Steps towards Political Participation.* New York: Praeger, 1986.

Richards, Alan. "Economic Pressures for Accountable Governance in the Middle East and North Africa." In *Civil Society in the Middle East, Vol. 1,* edited by Augustus Richard Norton, 55-78. Leiden, Netherlands: Brill, 1995.

Salame, Ghassen, ed. *Democracy without Democrats? The Renewal of Politics in the Muslim World.* London: I. B. Tauris, 1994.

Satloff, Robert B. *The Politics of Change in the Middle East.* Boulder, Colo.: Westview Press, 1993.

Sayari, Sabri, ed. *Democratization in the Middle East: Trends and Prospects.* Washington, D.C.: National Academic Press, 1993.

Sharibi, H., ed. *Theory, Politics and the Arab World.* London: Routledge, 1990.

Tibi, Bassam. *Arab Nationalism: A Critical Enquiry.* London: New York, 1971.

Zubaida, Sami. *Islam, the People and the State: Political Ideas and Movements in the Middle East.* London: I. B. Tauris, 1994.

SOCIETY: GENERAL

Afshar, Haleh. *Women in the Middle East: Perceptions, Realities and Struggles for Liberation.* London: Macmillan, 1993.

Cantori, L. J. "Civil Society, Liberalism and the Corporatist Alternatives in the Middle East." *Middle East Studies Association Bulletin* 31, no. 1 (1997): 34-41.

Caton, Steven C. "Anthropological Theories of Tribe and State Formation in the Middle East: Ideology and the Semiotics of Power." In *Tribes and State Formation in the Middle East,* edited by Philip Koury and J. Kostiner, 74-108. Berkeley, Calif.: University of California Press, 1990.

Crystal, Jill. "Civil Society in the Arabian Gulf." In *Civil Society in the Middle East, Vol. 2,* edited by Augustus Richard Norton, 259-86. Leiden, Netherlands: Brill, 1996.

Denoueux, Guilan. *Urban Unrest in the Middle East: A Comparative Study of Informal Networks in Egypt, Iran and Lebanon.* Albany, N.Y.: State University of New York Press, 1993.

Eickelman, Dale F. "Changing Perceptions of State Authority: Morocco, Egypt and Oman." In *The Foundations of the Arab*

State, edited by Ghassan Salame, 177-204. London: Croom Helm, 1987.

Elmusa, S. S. "Faust without the Devil? The Interplay of Technology and Culture in Saudi Arabia." *Middle East Journal* 51, no. 3 (1997): 345-57.

Esman, Milton, and Itamar Rabinovich, eds. *Ethnicity and State in the Middle East*. Ithaca, N.Y.: Cornell University Press, 1988.

Farson, Samih, ed. *Arab Society: Continuity and Change*. London: Croom Helm, 1985.

———. "Class Structure and Social Change in the Arab World 1995." In *The Next Arab Decade: Alternative Futures*, edited by Hisham Sharibi, 221-38. Boulder, Colo.: Westview Press, 1998.

Gilbar, Gad G. *Population Dilemmas in the Middle East*. London: Cass, 1997.

Goldberg, Ellis. "Reading from Left to Right: The Social History of Egyptian Labor." In *The Social History of Labor in the Middle East*, edited by Ellis Jay Goldberg, 163-92. Boulder, Colo.: Westview Press, 1996.

———, Resat Kasaber, and Jock Migdal, eds. *Rules and Rights in the Middle East: Democracy, Law and Society*. Seattle: University of Washington Press, 1993.

Held, Colbert C. *Middle East Patterns: Places, People and Politics*. Boulder, Colo.: Westview Press, 1989.

Ibrahim, Saad Eddin. *The New Arab Social Order: A Study of the Social Impact of Oil Wealth*. Boulder, Colo.: Westview Press, 1982.

———, et al. *Society and State in the Arab World*. Amman, Jordan: The Arab Thought Forum, 1988.

Ismael, Tareq Y., and Jacqueline S. Ismael. "Civil Society in the Arab World: Historical Traces, Contemporary Visages."*Arab Studies Quarterly* 19, no. 1 (1997): 77-87.

Lewis, Norman. *Nomads and Settlers in Syria and Jordan, 1800-1980*. Cambridge, England: Cambridge University Press, 1987.

Lockman, Zackary, ed. *Workers and Working Classes in the Middle East: Struggles, Histories, Historiographies*. Albany, N.Y.: State University of New York Press, 1994.

Longuenesse, Elisabeth. "Labor in Syria: The Emergence of New Identities." In *The Social History of Labor in the Middle East*, edited by Ellis Jay Goldberg, 99-130. Boulder, Colo.: Westview Press, 1996.

Melikian, Levon. "Arab Socio-Political Impact on Gulf Life-Styles." In *The Arab Gulf and the Arab World*, edited by B. R. Pridham, 112-30. London: Croom Helm, 1988.

Naqeeb, Khaldoun al-. *Society and State in the Gulf and Arab Peninsula: A Different Perspective*. London: Routledge, 1990.

Norton, Augustus Richard, ed. *Civil Society in the Middle East, Vols. 1 and 2*. Leiden, Netherlands: Brill, 1995 and 1996.

Roded, Ruth, ed. *Women in Islam and the Middle East: A Reader*. London: I. B. Tauris, 1999.

Siddiqi, M. K. A. "The Structure of Society: The Islamic Concept." *Journal of Objective Studies* 6, no. 2 (1994): 1-10.

COUNTRY SURVEYS

BAHRAIN

Adamiyat, F. *Bahrain Islands: A Legal and Diplomatic Study of British-Iranian Controversy*. New York: Praeger, 1955.

Bahry, L. "The Opposition in Bahrain: A Bellwether for the Gulf." *Middle East Policy* 5, no. 2 (1997): 42-57.

Lawson, Fred H. *Bahrain: The Modernization of Autocracy*. Boulder, Colo.: Westview Press, 1989.

Looney, Robert E. *An Economic Assessment of Bahrain's Attempts at Industrial Diversification*. Safat, Kuwait: Industrial Bank of Kuwait, 1989.

Nugent, Jeffrey, and Theodore H. Thomas. *Bahrain and the Gulf*. London: Croom Helm, 1985.

Tajir, Mahdi Abdalla Al-. *Bahrain 1929-1945: Britain, the Shaikh and the Administration*. London: Croom Helm, 1987.

EGYPT

Abdallah, Ahmad. "Egypt's Islamists and the State." *Middle East Report*, no. 183 (July/Aug. 1993): 28-31.

Aftandilian, Gregory L. *Egypt's Bid for Arab Leadership: Implications for US Policy*. New York: Council on Foreign Relations, 1993.

Alterman, Jan B., ed. *Sadat and His Legacy: Egypt and the World, 1977-1998*. Washington, D.C.: Washington Institute for Near East Policy, 1998.

Ansari, H. "The Islamic Militants in the Politics of Egypt." *International Journal of Middle East Studies* 16, no. 1 (1984): 123-44.

Arabi, Q. Al-. "Egypt: Dialog between the Islamists and the Authorities Is Still Deadlocked." *Middle East Affairs* 3, no. 1-2 (1999): 194-201.

Ayalon, Ami. "Egypt's Political Order: Continuity and Challenges." In *The Politics of Change in the Middle East,* edited by Robert B. Satloff, 195-23. Boulder, Colo.: Westview Press, 1993.

Ayubi, Nazih N. *The State and Public Policies in Egypt since Sadat.* London: Ithaca Press, 1991.

Badravi, Malek. *Political Violence in Egypt, 1910-1925: Secret Societies, Plots and Assassinations.* London: Curzon Press, 1999.

Baker, Raymond Williams. *Egypt's Uncertain Revolution under Nasser and Sadat.* Cambridge, Mass.: Harvard University Press, 1978.

———. *Sadat and After: Struggles for Egypt's Political Soul.* Cambridge, Mass.: Harvard University Press, 1980.

Beattie, Kirk J. *Egypt during the Nasser Years: Ideology, Politics and Civil Society.* Boulder, Colo.: Westview Press, 1994.

Bianchi, Robert. *Unholy Corporatism: Associational Life in Twentieth Century Egypt.* Oxford, England: Oxford University Press, 1989.

Campagna, Joel. "From Accommodation to Confrontation: The Muslim Brotherhood in the Mubarak Years." *Journal of International Affairs* 41, no. 1 (1996): 278-304.

Eidelberg, Paul. *Sadat's Strategy.* Quebec: Dawn Books, 1979.

Fahmy, Ninette S. "The Performance of the Muslim Brotherhood in the Egyptian Syndicates: An Alternative Formula for Reform." *Middle East Journal* 52, no. 4 (1998): 551-62.

Fandy, Mamoun. "Egypt's Islamic Group: Regional Revenge?" *Middle East Journal* 48, no. 4 (1994): 607-26.

Gilsenan, Michael. "State and Popular Islam in Egypt." In *State and Ideology in the Middle East and Pakistan,* edited by Fred Halliday and Hamza Alavi, 167-90. London: Macmillan, 1988.

Goodson, Larry P., and Soha, Radwan. "Democratization in Egypt in the 1990s: Stagnant or Merely Stalled." *Arab Studies Quarterly* 19, no. 1 (1997): 1-21.

Gordon, Joel. *Nasser's Blessed Movement: Egypt's Free Officers and the July Revolution.* London: Oxford University Press, 1992.

Hahn, Peter L. "Discord or Partnership? British and American Policy toward Egypt 1942-56." In *Demise of the British Empire in the Middle East: Britain's Responses to Nationalist Movements, 1943-55,* edited by Michael J. Cohen and Martin Kolinsky, 162-84. London: Cass, 1998.

Harris, Lillian, ed. *Egypt: Internal Challenges and Regional Stability.* London: Routledge and Kegan Paul, 1988.

Heikal, M. *Nasser: The Cairo Documents.* London: New English Library, 1972.

Hinnebusch, Raymond A. *Egyptian Politics under Sadat: The Post-Populist Development of an Authoritarian Modernising State.* Cambridge, England: Cambridge University Press, 1985.

Ismail, S. "State-Society Relations in Egypt: Restructuring the Political." *Arab Studies Quarterly* 17, no. 3 (1995): 37-52.

Jankowski, James. "Egypt and Early Arab Nationalism, 1908-1922." In *The Origins of Arab Nationalism,* edited by Rashid Khalidi, 243-70. New York: Columbia University Press, 1991.

Kazarian, Elias G. *Islamic versus Traditional Banking: Financial Innovation in Egypt.* Boulder, Colo.: Westview Press, 1993.

Kepel, Gilles. *Muslim Extremism in Egypt: The Prophet and the Pharaoh.* Berkeley, Calif.: University of California Press, 1985.

Kerr, Malcolm H., and E. Sayed Yassin. *Rich States and Poor States in the Middle East: Egypt and the New Arab Order.* Boulder, Colo.: Westview Press; Cairo: American University Press, 1982.

Kienle, Eberhard. "More than a Response to Islamism: The Political Deliberalization of Egypt in the 1990s." *Middle East Journal* 52, no. 2 (1998): 219-39.

Lesch, David W. "Gamal Abd al-Nasser and an Example of Diplomatic Acumen." *Middle Eastern Studies* 31, no. 2 (1995): 362-74.

Makram-Ebeid, Mona. "Political Opposition in Egypt: Democratic Myth or Reality." *Middle East Journal* 43, no. 3 (1989): 423-36.

McDermott, Anthony. *Egypt from Nasser to Mubarak: A Flawed Revolution.* London: Croom Helm, 1988.

Meijer, Roel. *The Quest for Modernity: Secular Liberal and Left-Wing Political Thought in Egypt, 1945-1958.* London: Curzon Press, 1999.

Meitel, Yoram. "Egypt in the Gulf Crisis." In *Iraq's Road to War*, edited by Amatzia Baram and Barry Rubin, 191-204. New York: St. Martin's Press, 1993.

Morroe, Berger. *Islam in Egypt Today: Social and Political Aspects of Popular Religion*. Cambridge, England: Cambridge University Press, 1970.

Owen, Roger. "Socio-Economic Change and Political Mobilization: The Case of Egypt." In *Democracy without Democrats? The Renewal of Politics in the Muslim World*, edited by Ghassem Salame, 183-99. London: I. B. Tauris, 1994.

Podeh, E. "The Drift towards Neutrality: Egyptian Foreign Policy during the Early Nasserist Era 1952-55." *Middle Eastern Studies* 32, no. 1 (1996): 159-78.

Podeh, Richard B. "Egypt's Struggle against the Militant Muslim Groups." *Terrorism and Political Violence* 8, no. 2 (1996): 43-61.

Rubin, Barry. *Islamic Fundamentalism in Egyptian Politics*. New York: St. Martin's Press, 1990.

Satloff, Robert B. *Army and Politics in Mubarak's Egypt*. Policy Paper Number Ten: Washington, D.C.: The Washington Institute for Near East Policy, 1988.

Sayyid, Mustapha K. al-. "A Civil Society in Egypt?" *Middle East Journal* 47, no. 2 (1993): 228-42.

———. "The Rise and Fall of the United Arab Republic." In *Middle East Dilemma: The Politics and Economics of Arab Integration*, edited by Michael C. Hudson, 109-127. London; New York: I. B. Tauris, 1999.

Springborg, Robert. *Mubarak's Egypt: Fragmentation of the Political Order*. Boulder, Colo.: Kegan Paul International, 1987.

Sullivan, Denis. "Islam and Development in Egypt: Civil Society." In *Islam, Muslims and the Modern State: Case Studies of Muslims in Thirteen Countries*, edited by Hussin Mutalib and Taj Ul-Islam Hashmi, 211-31. New York: St. Martin's Press; London: Macmillan, 1994.

Tripp, Charles, ed. *Contemporary Egypt through Egyptian Eyes: Essays in Honour of P.J. Vatikiotis*. London: Routledge, 1993.

———. "Egypt 1945-52: The Uses of Disorder." In *Demise of the British Empire in the Middle East: Britain's Responses to Nationalist Movements, 1943-55*, edited by Michael J. Cohen and Martin Kolinsky, 112-41. London: Cass, 1998.

Utvik, B. O. "Filling the Vacant Throne of Nasser: The Economic Discourse of Egypt's Islamist Opposition." *Arab Studies Quarterly* 17, no. 4 (1995): 29-54.

Vatikiotis, P. J. *Nasser and His Generation.* New York: St. Martin's Press, 1978.

Wahba, Mourad M. *The Role of the State in the Egyptian Economy 1945-1981.* London: Ithaca Press, 1994.

Waterbury, John. *The Egypt of Nasser and Sadat: The Political Economy of Two Regimes.* Princeton, N.J.: Princeton University Press, 1983.

———. "The Soft State and the Open Door: Egypt's Experience with Economic Liberalization, 1974-1984." *Comparative Politics* 18, no. 1 (1985): 65-83.

Zaki, Moheb. *Civil Society and Democratization in Egypt, 1981-1995.* Cairo: Ibn Khaldun Center, 1995.

IRAQ

Abbas, A. *Saddam's Iraq—Revolution or Reaction.* London: Zed Books, 1986.

Abdalla, Abo Eslam A. *Saddam Hussein—The Roots and the Crimes.* Cairo: Bait Al-Hekma, 1990.

Abrahamian, Ervand. *Iraq between Two Revolutions.* Princeton, N. J.: Princeton University Press, 1982.

Adelman, Howard. "Humanitarian Intervention: The Case of the Kurds." *International Journal of Refugee Law* 4, no. 1 (1992): 4-38.

Alawi, Hassan Al-. *The Iraqi Shi'ite and the State 1914-1990.* London: Dar al-Zawra, 1990.

Alnasrawi, Abbas. *The Economy of Iraq: Oil, War, Destruction of Development and Prospects 1950-2010.* Westport, Conn.: Greenwood Press, 1994.

———. "Iraq: Economic Consequences of the 1991 Gulf War and Future Outlook." *Third World Quarterly* 13, no. 2 (1992): 335-52.

Axelgard, Frederick W. *Iraq in Transition.* Boulder, Colo.: Westview Press, 1986.

Baram, Amatzia. *Culture, History and Ideology in the Formation of Ba'thist Iraq 1968-1969.* London: Macmillan, 1991.

———. "The Future of Ba'thist Iraq: Power Structure, Challenges and Prospects." In *The Politics of Change in the Middle East,* edited by Robert B. Satloff, 31-62. Boulder, Colo.: Westview Press, 1993.

———. "Neo-Tribalism in Iraq: Saddam Hussein's Tribal Policies." *International Journal of Middle Eastern Studies* 29, no. 1 (1997): 1-31.

———. "Re-Inventing Nationalism in Ba'thi Iraq 1968-1994: Supra-Territorial and Territorial Identities and What Lies Below." *Interdisciplinary Journal of Middle Eastern Studies* 5 (Fall 1996): 29-56.

———. "The Ruling Political Elite in Ba'thi Iraq, 1968-1986: The Changing Features of a Collective Profile." *International Journal of Middle East Studies* 21, no. 4 (1989): 447-93.

Bengio, Ofra. "The Challenge to the Territorial Integrity of Iraq." *Survival* 39, no. 2 (1995): 74-94.

Bishku, M. "Iraq's Claim to Kuwait: A Historical Overview." *American Arab Affairs*, no. 37 (1991): 77-88.

Bulloch, John, and Harvey Morris. *No Friends but the Mountains: The Tragic History of the Kurds.* 2nd ed. London: Penguin, 1993.

Chailand, Gerard. *A People without a Country: The Kurds and Kurdistan.* 2nd ed. London: Zed Books, 1993.

Dann, Uriel. *Iraq under Qassem: A Political History.* New York: Praeger, 1969.

Eppel, Michael. "The Elite, the Effendiyya and the Growth of Nationalism and Pan-Arabism in Hashemite Iraq, 1921-1958." *International Journal of Middle Eastern Studies* 30, no. 2 (1998): 227-50.

———. *The Palestine Conflict in the History of Modern Iraq.* London: Cass, 1994.

Farouk-Sluglett, Marion, and Peter Sluglett. *Iraq since 1958: From Revolution to Dictatorship.* London: I. B. Tauris, 1990.

Fernea, Robert A., and William Robert Louis. *The Iraqi Revolution of 1958: The Old Social Classes Revisited.* London: I. B. Tauris, 1991.

Fuller, Graham E. "The Fate of the Kurds." *Foreign Affairs* 72, no. 2 (1993): 108-21.

———. *Iraq in the Next Decade: Will Iraq Survive until 2002?* Santa Monica, Calif.: Rand Corporation, 1993. (Rand Corporation Reports: N-3591-DAG)

Ghareeb, Edmund. *The Kurdish Question in Iraq.* Syracuse, N.Y.: Syracuse University Press, 1981.

Gunter, Michael M. "The Iraqi National Congress and the Future of the Iraqi Opposition." *Journal of South Asian and Middle East Studies* 19, no. 3 (1996): 1-20.

———. *The Kurds of Iraq: Tragedy and Hope*. New York: St. Martin's Press, 1992.

Haj, Samira. *The Making of Iraq 1900-1963*. Albany, N.Y.: State University of New York Press, 1997.

Halliday, Denis J. "The Impact of the UN Sanctions on the People of Iraq." *Journal of Palestine Studies* 28, no. 2 (1999): 29-37.

Heli, Walid Al-. *Human Rights in Iraq, 1968-1988*. London: Media Research, 1988.

Henderson, Simon. *Instant Empire: Saddam Hussein's Ambition for Iraq*. San Francisco: Mercury House, 1991.

Kazemzadeh, Masoud. "Thinking the Unthinkable: Solving the Problem of Saddam Hussein for Good." *Middle East Policy* 6, no. 1 (1998): 73-86.

Khadduri, Majid. *Independent Iraq, 1932-1958, a Study in Iraqi Politics*. London: Oxford University Press, 1960.

———. *Republican Iraq: A Study of Iraqi Politics since the Revolution of 1958*. London : Oxford University Press, 1969.

———. *Socialist Iraq: A Study in Iraqi Politics Since 1968*. Washington, D.C.: Middle East Institute, 1978.

Khafaji, Isam al-. *War As a Vehicle for the Rise and Demise of a State-Controlled Society: The Case of Ba'thist Iraq*. Amsterdam: University of Amsterdam, Middle East Papers, no. 4 (1995).

Khalil, Samir Al-. *Republic of Fear: The Inside Story of Saddam's Iraq*. Berkeley, Calif.: University of California Press; London: Hutchinson, 1989.

Kimball, Lorenzo Kent. *The Changing Pattern of Political Power in Iraq, 1958 to 1971*. New York: Robert Speller, 1972.

Longrigg, Stephen Hemsley. *Iraq from 1900-1950: A Political and Economic History*. London: Oxford University Press, under the auspices of the Royal Institute of International Affairs, 1953.

Lukitz, Liora. *Iraq: The Search for National Identity*. London: Cass, 1995.

Marr, Phebe. *The Modern History of Iraq*. Boulder, Colo.: Westview Press, 1985.

McDowell, David. *The Kurds*. London: Minority Rights Group, 1985.

Metz, Helen Chapin, ed. *Iraq: A Country Study*. Washington, D.C.: U.S. Department of the Army, 4th ed., 1990.

Middle East Watch. *Human Rights in Iraq.* New Haven, Conn.: Yale University Press, 1990.

Olson, Robert. "The Kurdish Question in the Aftermath of the Gulf War: Geopolitical and Geostrategic Changes in the Middle East." *Third World Quarterly* 13, no. 3 (1992): 475-99.

Podeh, Elie. *The Quest for Hegemony in the Arab World: The Struggle over the Baghdad Pact.* Leiden, Netherlands: Brill, 1995.

Rezun, Miron. *Saddam Hussein's Gulf Wars: Ambivalent States in the Middle East.* Westport, Conn.: Praeger, 1992.

Rozario, Paul. *Assessment of Iraq's Future after the Gulf War.* London: Gulf Centre for Strategic Studies, 1991.

Rubin, Barry. "Iraq and the PLO: Brother's Keepers, Losers Weepers." In *Iraq's Road to War*, edited by Amatzia Baram and Barry Rubin, 149-62. New York: St. Martin's Press, 1993.

Shabbr, Hassan. *Political Parties in Iraq from 1908 to 1958.* Beirut: Dar Al-Turath Al-Arabi, 1989.

Simon, R. S. *Iraq between the Two Wars.* New York: Columbia University Press, 1986.

Tripp, Charles. "The Gulf States and Iraq." *Survival* 34, no. 3 (1992): 43-61.

ISRAEL

Abu-Lughod, Ibrahim, and Ahmed Eqbal, eds. *The Invasion of Lebanon.* Washington, D.C.: Institute for Policy Studies, 1983.

Blumberg, Arnold. *The History of Israel.* Westport, Conn.: Greenwood Press, 1998.

Finkelstein, N. "The Real Meaning of the Wye River Memorandum." *Middle East Affairs*, 3, nos. 1-2 (1999): 79-96.

Levi-Faur, David. *Israel: The Dynamics of Change and Continuity.* London: Cass, 1999.

Lewis, Samuel W. "The United States and Israel: Evolution of an Unwritten Alliance." *Middle East Journal* 53, no. 3 (1999): 364-378.

Matar, Ibrahim. "Israeli Settlements in the West Bank and Gaza Strip."*Journal of Palestine Studies* 41, no. 1 (1981), 93-110.

Metzger, Jan. *This Land Is Our Land: The West Bank under Israeli Occupation.* London: Zed Books, 1983.

Neff, Donald. *Fifty Years of Israel.* Washington, D.C.: American Educational Trust, 1998.

Rejwan, Nissim. *Israel's Place in the Middle East*. Tampa, Fla.: University of Florida Press, 1990.

Schiff, Ze'ev, and Ehud Ya'ari. *Israel's Lebanon War*. London: Unwin, 1986.

Schulze, Kirsten E. *Israel's Covert Diplomacy in Lebanon*. London: Macmillan; New York: St. Martin's Press, 1998.

Sicker, Martin. *Pangs of the Messiah: The Troubled Birth of the Jewish State*. Westport, Conn.: Praeger, 2000.

Telhami, Shibley. "From Camp David to Wye: Changing Assumptions in Arab-Israeli Negotiations." *Middle East Journal* 53, no. 3 (1999): 379-92.

JORDAN

Adams, Linda S. "Political Liberalization in Jordan: An Analysis of the State's Relationship with the Muslim Brotherhood." *Journal of Church and State* 38, no. 3 (1996): 5-7-28.

Anderson, Betty B. "The State of Democracy in Jordan." *Critique*, no. 1 (1997): 55-76.

Aruri, Naseer. *Jordan: A Study in Political Development,1921-1965*. The Hague, Netherlands: Nijhoff, 1972.

Brand, Laurie A. "In the Beginning Was the State. . .: The Quest for Civil Society in Jordan." In *Civil Society in the Middle East, Vol. 1*, edited by August Richard Norton, 148-85. Leiden, Netherlands: Brill, 1995.

———. "The Effects of the Peace Process on Political Liberalization in Jordan." *Journal of Palestine Studies* 28, no. 2 (1999): 52-67.

———. *Jordan's Inter-Arab Relations: The Political Economy of Alliance Making*. New York: Columbia University Press, 1994.

Dann, Uriel. *King Hussein and the Challenge of Arab Radicalism: Jordan 1955-1967*. Oxford, England: Oxford University Press, 1989.

Garfinkle, Adam. *Israel and Jordan in the Shadow of War: Functional Ties and Futile Diplomacy in a Small Space*. New York: St. Martin's Press, 1992.

———. "The Nine Lives of Hashemite Jordan." In *The Politics of Change in the Middle East*, edited by Robert B. Satloff, 85-118. Boulder, Colo.: Westview Press, 1993.

Gubser, Peter. *Jordan: Crossroads of Middle Eastern Events*. London: Croom Helm; Boulder, Colo.: Westview Press, 1983.

———. "Jordan and Hussein." *Middle East Policy* 2, no. 2 (1993): 110-20.

Hinchcliffe, P. "Jordan's Relations with Her Neighbors: Victim of War or Casualty of Peace?" *Asian Affairs* 28, no. 3 (1997): 343-68.

Jureidini, Paul, and Robert McLaurin. *Jordan: The Impact of Social Change on the Role of the Tribes*. Washington, D.C.: Center for Strategic and International Studies and Praeger, 1984.

Khadar, Bichara, and Adnan Badran. *The Economic Development of Jordan*. London: Croom Helm, 1987.

Lowi, Miriam R. *Water and Power: The Politics of a Scarce Resource in the Jordan River Basin*. Cambridge, England: Cambridge University Press, 1995.

Lowrance, Sherry R. "After Beijing: Political Liberalization and the Women's Movement in Jordan." *Middle Eastern Studies* 34, no. 3 (1998): 83-102.

Meijer, R. "Jordan: The Precarious State." *Japanese Institute of Middle Eastern Economics* 10, no. 37 (1997): 69-86.

Milton-Edwards, B. "Façade Democracy and Jordan." *British Journal of Middle Eastern Studies* 20, no. 2 (1993): 181-203.

Nevo, Joseph. "Jordan's Relations with Iraq: Ally or Victim?" In *Iraq's Road to War*, edited by Amatzia Baram and Barry Rubin, p. 135-48. New York: St. Martin's Press, 1993.

Nowar, Ma'an Abu. *The History of the Hashemite Kingdom of Jordan: Vol. 1: The Creation and Development of Transjordan; 1920-1929*. London: Ithaca Press, 1989.

Robinson, Glenn E. "Can Islamists Be Democrats? The Case of Jordan." *Middle East Journal* 51, no. 3 (1977): 373-87.

———. "Defensive Democracy in Jordan." *International Journal of Middle Eastern Studies* 30, no. 3 (1998): 387-410.

Rogan, Eugene L., and Tariq Tell, eds. *Village Steppe and State: The Social Origin of Modern Jordan*. London: British Academic Press, 1994.

Roth, Katherine. "The Process of Democratization in Jordan." *Middle Eastern Studies* 30, no. 3 (1994): 530-57.

Salibi, Kamal S. *The Modern History of Jordan*. London: I. B. Tauris, 1993.

Sallukh, Bassel F. "State, Strength, Permeability, and Foreign Policy Behaviour: Jordan in Theoretical Perspective." *Arab Studies Quarterly* 18, no. 2 (1996): 39-65.

Satloff, Robert B. *From Abdullah to Hussein: Jordan in Transition*. Oxford, England: Oxford University Press, 1994.

————. *They Cannot Stop Our Tongues: Islamic Activism in Jordan.* Washington, D.C.: The Washington Institute for Near East Policy, 1988.

Shakhatreh, Hussein. "Determinants of Female Labour-Force Participation in Jordan." In *Gender and Development in the Arab World: Women's Economic Participation; Patterns and Policies*, edited by Nabil F. Khoury and Valentine M. Moghadam, 125-47. London: Zed Books; Tokyo: United Nations University Press, 1995.

Taraki, Lisa. "Jordanian Islamists and the Agenda for Women: Between Discourse and Practice." *Middle Eastern Studies* 32, no. 1 (1996): 140-58.

Wilson, Mary. *King Abdallah, Britain and the Making of Jordan.* Cambridge, England: Cambridge University Press, 1987.

Wilson, Rodney. *Politics and Economy in Jordan.* London: Routledge, 1991.

KUWAIT

Abu-Hakima, Ahmad Mustafa. *The Modern History of Kuwait, 1750-1965.* London: Luzac, 1983.

Ahmed, Ahmed A. "Kuwait's Public Commercial Investment in Arab Countries." *Middle Eastern Studies* 31, no. 2 (1995): 293-306.

Anthony, John D. "Special Report: Consultation and Consensus in Kuwait. The 18th GCC Summit." *Middle East Policy* 6, no. 1 (1998): 137-56.

Ashayeji, Abdullah. "Kuwait at the Crossroads: The Quest for Democratization." *Middle East Insight* 8, no. 5 (1992): 41-46.

Ashton, Nigel. "Britain and the Kuwait Crisis, 1961." *Diplomacy and Stagecraft* 9, no. 1 (1998): 163-81.

Assiri, Abdul-Reda. *Kuwait's Foreign Policy, City State in World Politics.* Boulder, Colo.: Westview Press, 1990.

Awano, H. "Kuwait Still Suffering After-Effects of Its October Crisis with Iraq." *Japanese Institute of Middle Eastern Economics Review*, no. 28 (1995): 31-40.

Cordesman, Anthony H. *Kuwait: Recovery and Security after the Gulf War.* Boulder, Colo.: Westview Press, 1997.

Crystal, Jill. *Kuwait: The Transformation of an Oil State.* Boulder, Colo.: Westview Press, 1992.

Dickson, H. R. P. *Kuwait and Her Neighbours.* London: Allen and Unwin, 1956.

Ebraheem, Hassan A. Al-. *Kuwait: A Political Study.* Kuwait: Al Qabas Printing Press, 1971.

———. *Kuwait and the Gulf: Small States and the International System.* Washington, D.C.: Center for Contemporary Arab Studies, Georgetown University; London: Croom Helm, 1984.

Finnie, David H. *Shifting Lines in the Sand: Kuwait's Elusive Frontier with Iraq.* Cambridge, Mass.: Harvard University Press, 1992.

Freeth, Zara, and Victor Winstone. *Kuwait: Prospect and Reality.* New York: Crone, Russak, 1972.

Ghabra, Shafeeq. "Balancing State and Society: The Islamic Movement in Kuwait." *Middle East Policy* 5, no. 2 (1997): 58-72.

———. "The Institutions and Arab Political Development: The Case of Kuwait." *Al-Mustaqbal al-Arabi,* no. 229 (1998): 3-45.

Hicks, Neil, Ghonim al-Najjar. "The Utility of Tradition: Civil Society in Kuwait." In *Civil Society in the Middle East,* Vol. 1, edited by Augustus Richard Norton, 186-213. Leiden, Netherlands: Brill, 1995.

Humaidhi, Bader Al-. "The Role of the Arab Gulf States in International Development Assistance." In *The Arab Gulf States and Japan Prospects for Cooperation,* edited by Walid Sharif. London: Croom Helm.

Ismael, Jacqueline. *Kuwait: Dependency and Class in a Rentier State.* Gainesville, Fla.: University Press of Florida, 1993.

Joyce, Miriam. "Kuwait and the Dynamics of Socio-economic Change." *Middle East Journal* 51, no. 3 (1997): 358-72.

———. "Kuwait: Elections and Issues of Democratization in a Middle Eastern State." *Digest of Middle East Studies* 7, no. 1 (1993): 1-17.

———. *Kuwait, 1945-1996: An Anglo-American Perspective.* London: Cass, 1998.

———. "Preserving the Sheikhdom: London, Washington, Iraq and Kuwait, 1958-1961." *Middle Eastern Studies* 31, no. 2 (1991): 281-92.

Khawajkie, M. "Kuwait and the Economic Integration of Arabian Gulf Countries." *Journal of the Gulf and Arabian Peninsula Studies* 3, no. 9 (1977): 9-30.

Kostiner, Joseph. "Kuwait: Confusing Friend and Foe." In *Iraq's Road to War,* edited by Amatzia Baram and Barry Rubin, p. 105-16. New York: St. Martin's Press, 1993.

Kuwait: Statehood and Boundaries. Mansouria, Kuwait: Centre for Research and Studies on Kuwait, n.d.

Lienhardt, Peter. *Disorientations: A Society in Flux: Kuwait in the 1950s*. Reading, England: Ithaca Press, 1993.

Longva, Ank Nga. *Walls Built on Sand: Migration, Exclusion and Society in Kuwait*. Boulder, Colo.: Westview Press, 1996.

Mallakh, Ragaei El, and Jacob Atta. *The Absorptive Capacity of Kuwait*. Lexington, Mass: Lexington Books, 1981.

Mesa, L. "Kuwait: Post-war Political Scenario." *Revista de Africa y Medio Oriente* 4, no. 2 (1992): 93-113.

Quaid, Hassan. *History of Kuwait*. Doha, Qatar: Dar Asharq, 1990.

Rahman, H. "Kuwaiti Ownership of Warba and Bubiyan Islands." *Middle Eastern Studies* 29, no. 2 (1993): 292-306.

Rumaihi, Mohammed al-. "Kuwaiti-American Relations: A Case of Mismanagement." *American-Arab Affairs*, no. 9 (1984): 77-80.

Russell, Sharon, et al. "Kuwait's Migration Policy since the Gulf Crisis." *International Journal of Middle Eastern Studies* 26, no. 4 (1994): 569-87.

Sabah, Y. F. Al-. *The Oil Economy of Kuwait*. London: Kegan Paul International, 1980.

Salih, K. "Kuwait's Parliamentary Elections 1963-1985: An Appraisal." *Journal of South Asia and Middle Eastern Studies* 16, no. 2 (1992): 17-40.

Shaab, Abdul-Reda Asirir. *The Government and Politics of Kuwait: Principles and Practices*. Kuwait: Al Watan Printing Press, 1996.

Tetreault, Mary Ann. "Civil Society in Kuwait: Protected Spaces and Women's Rights." *Middle East Journal* 47, no. 2 (1993): 275-91.

———. "Patterns of Culture and Democratization in Kuwait." *Studies in Comparative International Development* 30, no. 2 (1995): 26-64.

Tetreault, Mary Ann, and Mughni, Haya al-. "Gender, Citizenship and Nationalism in Kuwait." *British Journal of Middle Eastern Studies* 22, nos. 1-2 (1995): 64-80.

A Victory Turned Sour: Human Rights in Kuwait Since Liberation. Washington, D.C.: Middle East Watch, 1991.

Yahya, Mohammed Abdulrahman Al-. *Kuwait: Fall and Rebirth*. London: Kegan Paul International, 1993.

LEBANON

Abu-Hamad, Aziz. "Communal Strife in Lebanon: Ancient Animosities or State Intervention." *Journal of International Affairs* 49, no. 1 (1998): 231-54.

Abu Khalil, Asad. *Historical Dictionary of Lebanon.* Lanham, Md.: Scarecrow Press, 1998.

————. "The Study of Political Parties in the Arab World: The Case of Lebanon." *Journal of Asian and African Affairs* (Fall 1993): 49-64.

Abul-Husn, L. *The Lebanese Conflict: Looking Inward.* London: Lynne Rienner, 1998.

Agwani, M. S., ed. *The Lebanese Crisis 1958: A Documentary Record.* New York: Asia Publishing House, 1965.

Ahmed, Kaleem. "Asad's Policy in Lebanon." *Journal of the West Asian Studies Society,* nos. 3-4 (1987/88): 132-41.

Ajami, Fouad. *The Vanished Imam: Musa al Sadr and the Shia of Lebanon.* Ithaca, N.Y: Cornell University Press, 1986.

Avi-Ron, Reuven. *The Syrian Involvement in Lebanon since 1945.* Boulder, Colo.: Westview Press, 1991.

Barakat, H. *Towards a Viable Lebanon.* London: Croom Helm, 1987.

Besson, Yves. "UNRWA and Its Role in Lebanon." *Journal of Refugee Studies* 10, no. 3 (1997): 321-48.

Chamie, J. "Religious Groups in Lebanon: A Descriptive Investigation." *International Journal of Middle East Studies* 11, no. 2 (1983): 175-87.

Cobban, Helen. *The Making of Modern Lebanon.* London: Hutchinson, 1985.

Cooke. M. "Reimaging Lebanon." *South Atlantic Quarterly* 94, no. 4 (1995): 1075-1102.

Entelis, John P. *Pluralism and Party Transformation in Lebanon: al-Kata'ib 1936-1970.* Leiden, Netherlands: Brill, 1974.

Gilmour, David. *Lebanon: The Fractured Country.* Rev. ed. London: Sphere Books, 1984.

Gilsenan, Michael. *Lords of the Lebanese Marches: Violence and Narrative in an Arab Society.* Berkeley, Calif.: University of California Press, 1996.

Gordon, David C. *Lebanon: The Fragmented Nation.* London: Croom Helm, 1983.

Haley, Edward P, and Lewis W. Snyder, eds. *Lebanon in Crisis: Participants and Issues.* Syracuse, N.Y.: Syracuse University Press, 1979.

Hamdon, Kamal. "Will Lebanon Lose Its Economic Role in Its Arabic Environment." *Al-Tariq*, no. 1 (1994): 37-47.

Hanf, Theodor. *Coexistence in Wartime Lebanon: Decline of a State and Birth of a Nation.* London: I. B. Tauris and Center for Lebanese Studies, 1993.

Harris, William. *Faces of Lebanon: Sects, Wars and Global Extensions.* Princeton, N.J.: Markus Wiener, 1997.

Hobeika, Louis G. "Key Issues in the Reconstruction of the Lebanon." *Middle East Insight* 9, no. 2 (1993): 29-37.

Hollis, Rosemary, and Nadim Shehadi, eds. *Lebanon on Hold: Implications for Middle East Peace.* London: Royal Institute of International Affairs and Centre for Lebanese Studies, 1996.

Hoss, Salim el-. "Lebanon in the New World Order." *Middle East Insight* 9, no. 2 (1993): 23-28.

Hudson, M. C. *The Precarious Republic: Political Modernization in Lebanon.* New York: Random House, 1968.

Izzedin, Naijla Abu. *The Druzes: A New Study of Their History, Faith and Society.* Leiden, Netherlands: Brill, 1984.

Jureidimi, P. A. "Lebanon and the Peace Process: The Case for Greater Realism." *Perceptions* 1, no. 4 (1996/97): 17-29.

Khalidi, Walid. *Conflict and Violence in Lebanon: Confrontation in the Middle East.* Cambridge, Mass.: Harvard University Press, 1979.

Khashan, Hilal. "The Developmental Programs of Islamic Fundamentalist Groups in Lebanon As a Source of Popular Legitimisation." *Hamdard Islamicus* 18, no. 1 (1995): 51-71.

———. "Lebanon 1996 Controversial Parliamentary Elections." *Journal of South Asian and Middle East Studies* 20, no. 4 (1997): 24-49.

Khazen, Farid El-. "Lebanon's Communal Elite-Mass Politics: The Institutionalization of Disintegration." *Beirut Review*, no. 3 (1992): 53-82.

Malia, Joseph. *The Document of National Understanding: A Commentary.* Oxford, England: Centre for Lebanese Studies, 1992.

Malik, H. C. "Is There Still a Lebanon." *Middle East Quarterly* 4, no. 4 (1997): 17-23.

Nassar, Jamal R. "Sectarian Political Cultures: The Case of Lebanon." *Muslim World* 85, nos. 3-4 (1995): 246-65.

Nehma, M. G. "Lebanon: Open Area for Regional Feuds." *Journal of Third World Studies* 12, no. 1 (1995): 120-50.

Odeh, B. J. *Lebanon: Dynamics of Conflict.* London: Zed Books, 1985.

Olmert, Yossi. "A False Dilemma? Syria and Lebanon's Independence during the Mandatory Period." *Middle Eastern Studies* 32, no. 3 (1996): 41-73.

Parker, Richard B. "Kawkaba and the South Lebanon Imbroglio: A Personal Recollection, 1977-1978." *Middle East Journal* 50, no. 4 (1996): 547-58.

Petran, Tabitha. *The Struggle over Lebanon.* New York: Monthly Review Press, 1987.

Rabinovich, Itamar. *The War for Lebanon 1970-1983.* Ithaca, N.Y.: Cornell University Press, 1984.

Randal, Jonathan. *The Tragedy of Lebanon: Christian Warlords, Israeli Adventurers and American Bunglers,* Rev. ed. London: Hogarth Press, 1990.

Reinkowski, Maurus. "National Identity in Lebanon since 1990." *Orient* 38, no. 3 (1997): 493-515.

Saadeh, Sofia Antoun. *The Social Structure of Lebanon: Democracy or Servitude.* Beirut: Editions Dar An-Nahar, 1993.

Salem, Elie A. "A Decade of Challenges: Lebanon, 1982-1992." *Beirut Review,* no. 3 (1992): 17-37.

———. *Modernization without Revolution: Lebanon's Experience.* Bloomington, Ind.: Indiana University Press, 1973.

Salem, Paul. "The Wounded Republic: Lebanon's Struggle for Recovery." *Arab Studies Quarterly* 16, no. 4 (1994): 47-53.

Salibi, Kamal. S. *Crossroads to Civil War: Lebanon 1958-1976.* Delmar, N.Y.: Caravan, 1976.

———. *A House of Many Mansions: The History of Lebanon Reconsidered.* Berkeley, Calif.: University of California Press, 1989.

Samii, Abbas William. "The Shah's Lebanon Policy: The Role of SAVAK." *Middle Eastern Studies* 33, no. 1 (1997): 66-91.

Schiff, Ze'ev, and Ehud Ya'ari. *Israel's Lebanon War.* New York: Simon and Schuster, 1984.

Schulze, Kirsten E. *Israel's Covert Diplomacy in Lebanon.* London: Macmillan, 1998.

Shehardi, Nadim, and Dana Haffar, eds. *Lebanon: A History of Conflict and Consensus*. London: I. B. Tauris and Center for Lebanese Studies, 1988.

Sirreyh, Hussein. *Lebanon: Dimensions of Conflict*. London: International Institute for Strategic Studies, 1989. (Adelphi Papers No. 243)

———. "Lebanon in Search of a Viable Settlement." *Israel Affairs* 4, no. 2 (1977): 112-29.

Suleiman, Michael W. *Political Parties in Lebanon: The Challenge of a Fragmented Political Culture*. Ithaca, N.Y.: Cornell University Press, 1967.

Tanter, Raymond. *Who's Who at the Helm? Lessons of Lebanon*. Boulder, Colo.: Westview Press, 1990.

Traboulsi, Fawaz. "The Formation of a Political Strategy after the War in Lebanon." *Ab'ad*, no. 6 (1997): 29-92.

Usher, Graham. "Hizballah, Syria and the Lebanese Elections." *Journal of Palestine Studies* 26, no. 2 (1997): 59-67.

LIBYA

Ahmida, Ali Abdullatif. *The Making of Modern Libya: State Formation, Colonization and Resistance 1830-1932*. Albany, N.Y.: State University of New York Press, 1994.

Anderson, Lisa. "The Development of Nationalist Sentiment in Libya, 1908-1922." In *The Origins of Arab Nationalism*, edited by Rashid Khalidi et al., 225-42. New York: Columbia University Press, 1991.

Davis, Brian L. *Qaddafi, Terrorism and the Origins of the US Attack on Libya*. New York: Praeger, 1990.

Davis, John. *Libyan Politics: Tribe and Revolution*. London: I. B. Tauris, 1987; Berkeley, Calif.: University of California Press, 1988.

Elwarfally, M. G. *Imagery and Ideology in US Policy towards Libya 1969-82*. Pittsburgh, Penna.: Pittsburgh University Press, 1988.

Obeidi, Amal. *Political Culture in Libya*. London: Curzon Press, 1999.

St. John, Ronald Bruso. *Historical Dictionary of Libya*. 3rd ed. Lanham, Md.: Scarecrow Press, 1998.

———. *Qaddafi's World Design: Libyan Foreign Policy 1969-87*. London: Saqi Books, 1987.

Simons, Geoff. *Libya: The Struggle for Survival.* New York: St. Martin's Press, 1996.

Vandevalle, Dirk, ed. *Qadhafi's Libya, 1969-1994.* New York: St. Martin's Press, 1995.

MAGHREB

Abun-Nasr, J. *A History of the Maghreb.* London: Cambridge University Press, 1975.

Addi, L. "Algeria's Army. Algeria's Agony." *Foreign Affairs* 77, no. 4 (1998): 44-53.

———. "Algeria's Democracy: Between the Islamists and the Elite." *MERIP-Middle East Report* 22, no. 2 (1992): 36-38.

Ahnaf, M. Al-. "Tunisie-Un Debat sur les Rapports Etat/Religion." *Maghreb Machrek*, no. 126 (1989): 93-108.

Anderson, L. "Obligation and Accountability: Islamic Politics in North Africa." *Daedalus* 120, no. 3 (1991): 93-112.

Bahavjoub, A. "The Impact of the Gulf War on the Maghreb." *Journal of the Society for Moroccan Studies,* no. 2 (1922): 41-46.

Bissan, J. "Le Sahara dans le Développement des Etats Maghrebins." *Maghreb-Machrek*, no. 134 (1991): 3-27.

Blin, L. "Algérie-Les Elites Politiques." *Les Cahiers de l'Orient,* nos. 25-26 (1992): 237-59.

Burgat, François, and William Dowell. *The Islamic Movement in North Africa.* Austin, Tex.: Texas University Press, 1997.

Cassarino, Jean-Pierre. "The EU-Tunisian Association Agreement and Tunisia's Structural Reform Program." *Middle East Journal* 53, no. 1 (1999): 59-74.

Celik, Zeynep C. *Urban Forms and Colonial Confrontations: Algiers under French Rule.* Berkeley, Calif.: University of California Press, 1996.

Clancy-Smith, Julia A. *Rebel and Saint: Muslim Notables, Popular Protest, Colonial Encounters (Algeria and Tunisia 1800-1904).* Berkeley, Calif.: University of California Press, 1994.

Dervis, Kemal, and Nemat Shafik. "The Middle East and North Africa: A Tale of Two Futures." *Middle East Journal* 52, no. 4 (1998): 505-16.

Driss, R. "The Arab Maghreb Union." *Etudes Internationales,* no. 41 (1991): 218-26.

Entelis, John P. *Culture and Counterculture in Moroccan Politics.* Lanham, Md.: University Press of America, 1996.

————, and Phillip C. Naylor. *State and Society in Algeria.* Boulder, Colo.: Westview Press, 1992.

Fuller, Graham. *Algeria: The Next Fundamentalist State?* Santa Monica, Calif.: Rand, 1996.

Galal, Salma. "Women and Development in the Maghreb Countries." In *Gender and Development in the Arab World: Women's Economic Participation; Patterns and Policies,* edited by Nabil F. Khoury and Valentine M. Moghadam, 49-70. London: Zed Books; Tokyo: United Nations University Press, 1995.

Heradstveit, Daniel. *Political Islam in Algeria.* Oslo: Norwegian Institute of International Affairs, 1997.

Hermassi, Mohamed Abdelbaki. *Leadership and National Development in North Africa: A Comparative Study.* Berkeley, Calif.: University of California Press, 1970.

————. *Society and State in the Arab Maghreb.* Beirut: Center for Arab Unity Studies, 1987.

————. "Socio-Economic Change and Political Implications: The Maghreb." In *Democracy without Democrats? The Renewal of Politics in the Muslim World,* edited by Ghassem Salame, 227-42. London: I. B. Tauris, 1994.

Hopwood, Derek. *Habib Bourguiba of Tunisia: The Tragedy of Longevity.* New York: St. Martin's Press, 1992.

Kenz, Ali El-. *Algerian Reflections on Arab Crises,* translated by Robert W. Stookey. Austin, Tex.: Center for Middle Eastern Studies, distributed by University of Texas Press, 1991.

Khadir, Bichara. *Le Grand Maghreb et L'Europe: Enjeux et Perspectives.* Paris: Editions Publisud, 1992.

————. *Les Investissements de la CEE dans les Pays du Maghreb: Bilan et Perspective.* Louvain-la-Neuve, Belgium: Centre d'Etudes et de Recherches sur le Monde Arabe Contemporain, 1991.

Kodmani–Darwish, Bassma. *Maghreb: Les Années de Transition.* Paris: Masson, 1990.

Layachi, Azzedine. *Civil Society and Democratization in Morocco.* Cairo: Ibn Khaldun Center, 1995.

————, and A. Haireche. "National Development and Political Protest: Islamists in the Maghreb Countries." *Arab Studies Quarterly* 14, nos. 2-3 (1992): 69-92.

Le Gall, Kenneth Perkins. *The Maghrib in Question: Essays in History and Historiography*. Austin, Tex.: University of Texas Press, 1997.

Lewis, V. "Algeria: The Failed Revolution." *Mediterranean Quarterly* 3, no. 4 (1992): 66-74.

Maddy-Weitzmann, Bruce. "Conflict and Conflict Management in the Western Sahara: Is the Endgame Near?" *Middle East Journal* 45, no. 4 (1991): 594-607.

Malley, Robert. *The Call from Algeria: Third Worldism, Revolution and the Turn to Islam*. Berkeley, Calif.: University of California Press, 1996.

Mortimer, Robert. "Algeria: The Clash between Islam, Democracy and the Military." *Current History*, no. 570 (1993): 37-41.

———. "Islam and Multiparty Politics in Algeria." *Middle East Journal* 45, no. 4 (1991): 575-93.

Pazzanita, Anthony G. "From Boumedienne to Bejedid: The Algerian Regime in Transition." *Journal of South Asian and Middle Eastern Studies* 15, no. 4 (1992): 51-71.

———. "Political Transition in Mauritania: Problems and Prospects." *Middle East Journal* 53, no. 1 (1999): 44-58.

———, and Toug Hodges. *Historical Dictionary of Western Sahara*. Lanham, Md.: Scarecrow Press, 1998.

Perkins, Kenneth J. *Historical Dictionary of Tunisia*. 2nd ed. Lanham, Md.: Scarecrow Press, 1997.

Roosers, Claude. *Le Conflit du Sahara Occidental: Bibliographie, Documents, Chronologie*. Louvain-la-Neuve, Belgium: Centre d'Etudes et de Recherches sur le Monde Arabe Contemporain, 1991.

Ruedy, John. *Modern Algeria: The Origins and Development of a Nation*. Bloomington, Ind.: Indiana University Press, 1992.

Schilder, Kees. *Popular Islam in Tunisia: A Regional Cult Analysis*. Leiden, Netherlands: African Studies Center, 1990.

Shahin, E. E. *Political Ascent: Contemporary Islamic Movements in North Africa*. Boulder, Colo.: Westview Press, 1997.

Stone, Martin. *The Agony of Algeria*. New York: Columbia University Press, 1997.

Tessler, M. "Anger and Governance in the Arab World: Lessons from the Maghreb and Implications for the West." *Jerusalem Journal of International Relations* 13, no. 3 (1991): 7-33.

Vandewalle, Dirk, ed. *North Africa: Development and Reform in a Changing Global Economy.* New York: St. Martin's Press, 1996.

White, Gregory. "The Advent of Electoral Democracy in Morocco's Constitutional Monarchy? The Referendum of 1996." *Middle East Journal* 51, no. 3 (1997): 389-404.

Zartman, I. William. *Government and Politics in Northern Africa.* London: Methuen, 1963.

———. *Tunisia: The Political Economy of Reform.* Boulder, Colo.: Westview Press, 1991.

———, and William Mark Habeeb, eds. *Polity and Society in Contemporary North Africa.* Boulder, Colo.: Westview Press, 1993.

Zures, S. "Algeria, the Maghreb Union, and the Western Sahara Stalemate." *Arab Studies Quarterly* 47, no. 3 (1995): 23-36.

OMAN

Allen, Calvin H. *Oman: The Modernization of the Sultanate.* Boulder, Colo.: Westview Press, 1987.

Eikelman, Dale F. "Kings and People: Oman's State Consultative Council." *Middle East Journal* 38, no. 1 (1984): 51-71.

Graz, Liesl. *The Omanis: Sentinels of the Gulf.* London: Longman, 1982.

Haj, Abdullah Juma al-. "The Politics of Participation in the Gulf Cooperation Council States: The Omani Consultative Council." *Middle East Journal* 50, no. 4 (1996): 559-72.

Joyce, Miriam. *The Sultanate of Oman: A Twentieth Century History.* Westport, Conn.: Praeger, 1995.

———. "Washington and Treaty-Making with the Sultan of Muscat and Oman." *Middle Eastern Studies* 30, no. 1 (1994): 145-54.

Kechichian, Joseph A. *Oman and the World.* Santa Monica, Calif.: Rand, 1995.

Kelly, J. B. "A Prevalence of Furies: Tribes, Politics, and Religion in Oman and Trucial Oman." In *The Arabian Peninsula: Society and Politics*, edited by Derek Hopwood, 107-44. London: Allen and Unwin, 1972.

Maamiry, Ahmed Hamoud Al-. *Oman and East Africa.* 2nd rev. ed. New Delhi: Lancer Publishers, 1980.

O'Reilly, M. J. "Omanibalancing: Oman Confronts an Uncertain Future." *Middle East Journal* 52, no. 1 (1998): 70-84.

Peterson, J. E. *Oman in the Twentieth Century: Political Foundations of an Emerging State*. London: Croom Helm, 1978.

Pridham, B. R. "Oman: Change or Continuity?" In *Arabia and the Gulf: From Traditional Society to Modern States*, edited by Ian Richard Netton, p. 132-55. London: Croom Helm, 1986.

————, ed. *Oman: Economic, Social and Strategic Developments*. London: Croom Helm, 1986.

Riphenburg, Carol J. *Oman: Political Development in a Changing World*. Westport, Conn.: Praeger, 1998.

Risso, Patricia. *Oman and Muscat: An Early Modern History*. London: Croom Helm, 1986.

Skeet, Ian. *Oman: Politics and Development*. London: Macmillan, 1992.

Sohl, Raghid El-. *Oman and the South Eastern Shore of Arabia*. London: Garnet, 1997.

Townsend, John. *Oman: The Making of the Modern State*. London: Croom Helm, 1977.

Wikan, Unni. *Behind the Veil in Arabia: Women in Oman*. Baltimore, Md.: Johns Hopkins University Press, 1982.

Wilkinson, John C. *The Imamate Tradition of Oman*. Cambridge, England: Cambridge University Press, 1987.

————. "The Origins of the Omani State" In *The Arabian Peninsula: Society and Politics*, edited by Derek Hopwood, 67-88. London: Allen and Unwin, 1972.

Yousef, Mohamad bin Musa al-. *Oil and the Transformation of Oman, 1970-1995*. London: Stacey International, 1995.

PALESTINE

Abboushi, W. F. *The Unmaking of Palestine*. Boulder, Colo.: Lynne Rienner, 1985.

Abu-Lughod, Ibrahim, ed. *The Transformation of Palestine: Essays on the Origin and Development of the Arab-Israeli Conflict*. Evanston, Ill.: Northwestern University Press, 1987.

Boullata, Kamal, ed. *Palestine Today*. Washington, D.C.: Palestine Center for the Study of Nonviolence, 1990.

Chomsky, Noam. *The Fateful Triangle: The U.S., Israel and the Palestinians*. Boston: South End Press, 1984.

Farsoun, Samih K. *Palestine and the Palestinians*. Boulder, Colo.: Westview Press, 1997.

Friedman, Robert O. *The Middle East and the Peace Process: The Impact of the Oslo Accords.* Tampa, Fla.: University of Florida Press, 1998.

Geddes, Charles L., ed. *A Documentary History of the Arab-Israeli Conflict.* New York: Praeger, 1991.

Gilmour, David. *Dispossessed: The Ordeal of the Palestinians.* London: Sidgwick and Jackson, 1980.

Hadawi, Sami. *Bitter Harvest: A Modern History of Palestine.* New York: Olive Branch Press, 1991.

Khalidi, Walid. *Palestine Reborn.* London: I. B. Tauris, 1992.

————, ed. *From Haven to Conquest: Readings in Zionism and the Palestine Problem until 1948.* Washington, D.C.: Institute for Palestine Studies, 1984.

Muslih, Muhhamad Y. *The Origins of Palestinian Nationalism.* New York: Columbia University Press, 1988.

Nazzal, Nafez Y., and Laila A. Nazzal. *Historical Dictionary of Palestine.* Lanham, Md.: Scarecrow Press, 1997.

Nusse, Andrea. *Muslim Palestine: The Ideology of Hamas.* Amsterdam, Netherlands: Harwood Academic, 1998.

Said, Edward W. *The Question of Palestine.* Rev. ed. London: Vintage, 1992.

Sayigh, Rosemary. *Too Many Enemies: The Palestinian Experience in Lebanon.* London: Zed Books, 1994.

Sicker, Martin. *Reshaping Palestine: From Muhhamad Ali to the British Mandate, 1831-1922.* Westport, Conn.: Praeger, 1999.

Taraki, Lisa, ed. *Palestinian Society in the West Bank and the Gaza Strip.* Acre, Israel: Dar Al-Aswar, 1990.

QATAR

Abu Nab, Ibrahim. *Qatar: A Story of State Building.* Doha, Qatar: Al Noor Publishing, 1977.

————. *Economic and Social Infrastructure in Qatar.* Doha, Qatar: Al Noor Publishing, 1984.

Graham, Helga. *Arabian Time Machine: Self-portrait of an Oil State.* London: Heinemann, 1978.

Key, Kerim K. *The State of Qatar: An Economic and Commercial Survey.* Washington, D.C.: K. Key Publications, 1976.

Looney, Robert E. *Structural Impediments to Industrialization in Qatar.* Safat, Kuwait: Industrial Bank of Kuwait, 1990.

Mallakh, Ragaei El-. *Qatar: Development of an Oil Economy*. London: Croom Helm, 1979.

Namzel, A. Niza. "Qatar: The Duality of the Legal System." *Middle Eastern Studies* 30, no. 1 (1994): 79-90.

Zahlan, Rosemarie Said. *The Creation of Qatar*. New York: Barnes and Noble, 1979.

SAUDI ARABIA

Abir, Mordechai. *Saudi Arabia: Government, Society and the Gulf Crisis*. London: Routledge, 1993.

————. *Saudi Arabia in the Oil Era: Regime and Elites; Conflict and Collaboration*. London: Croom Helm, 1987.

Aburish, Said K. *The Rise, Corruption and Coming Fall of the House of Saud*. London: Bloomsbury Publishing, 1994.

Albens, Henry H. *Saudi Arabia: Technocrats in a Traditional Society*. New York: Peter Lang, 1989.

Anderson, Irvine H. *Aramco, the United States and Saudi Arabia: A Study of the Dynamics of Foreign Oil Policy, 1933-1950*. Princeton, N.J.: Princeton University Press, 1981.

Azmeh, Aziz al-. "Wahhabite Polity." In *Arabia and the Gulf: From Traditional Society to Modern States*, edited by Ian Richard Netton, 75-90. London: Croom Helm, 1986.

Beling, Willard A., ed. *King Faisal and the Modernization of Saudi Arabia*. London: Croom Helm, 1980.

Bligh, Alexander. "The Interplay between Opposition Activity in Saudi Arabia and Recent Trends in the Arab World." In *The Arabian Peninsula: Zone of Ferment*, edited by Robert W. Stookey, 65-78. Stanford, Calif.: Hoover Institution Press, 1984.

————. "The Saudi Religious Elite ('Ulama) as Participant in the Political System of the Kingdom." *International Journal of Middle East Studies* 17, no.1 (1985): 37-50.

Corancez, Alexandre Olivier de. *The History of the Wahhabis from Their Origin until the End of 1809*. Reading, England: Garnet Publishing, 1995.

Cordesman, Anthony H. *Saudi Arabia: Guarding the Desert Kingdom*. Boulder, Colo.: Westview Press, 1997.

————. *Western Strategic Interests in Saudi Arabia*. London: Croom Helm, 1987.

Dawisha, Adeed. "Internal Values and External Threats: The Making of Saudi Foreign Policy." *Orbis*, 23, no. 1 (1979): 129-43.

Dekmejian, R. Hrair. "The Rise of Political Islamism in Saudi Arabia." *Middle East Journal* 48, no. 4 (1994): 627-44.

———. "Saudi Arabia's Consultative Council." *Middle East Journal* 52, no. 2 (1998): 204-18.

Farsy, Fouad al-. *Modernity and Tradition: The Saudi Equation.* London: Kegan Paul International, 1990.

Gause, F. Gregory. *Saudi-Yemeni Relations: Domestic Structures and Foreign Influence.* New York: Columbia University Press, 1990.

Goldberg, Jacob. *The Foreign Policy of Saudi Arabia: The Formative Years, 1902-1918.* Cambridge, Mass.: Harvard University Press, 1986.

Golub, David B. *When Oil and Politics Mix: Saudi Oil Policy, 1973-1985.* Cambridge, Mass.: Harvard Center for Middle Eastern Studies, 1985.

Habib, J. S. *Ibn Saud's Warriors of Islam: The Ikhwan of Najd and Their Role in the Creation of the Saudi Kingdom, 1910-1930.* Leiden, Netherlands: Brill, 1978.

Helms, Christine Moss. *The Cohesion of Saudi Arabia: Evolution of Political Identity.* Baltimore, Md.: Johns Hopkins University Press, 1981.

Holden, David, and Richard Johns. *The House of Saud: The Rise and Rule of the Most Powerful Dynasty in the Arab World.* London: Sidgwick and Jackson; New York: Holt and Reinhart, 1981.

Kostiner, Joseph. "State, Islam and Opposition in Saudi Arabia: The Post-Desert Storm Phase." *Terrorism and Political Violence* 8, no. 2 (1996): 43-61.

Lacey, Robert. *The Kingdom: Arabia and the House of Saud.* London: Hutchinson; New York: Harcourt, Brace Jovanovich, 1981.

Looney, Robert E. *Economic Development in Saudi Arabia: Consequences of the Oil Price Decline.* Greenwich, Conn.: JAI Press, 1990.

McLachlan, Keith. "Saudi Arabia: Political and Social Evolution." In *Arabia and the Gulf: From Traditional Society to Modern States*, edited by Ian Richard Netton, 91-106. London: Croom Helm, 1986.

Mallakh, Ragaei El. *Saudi Arabia: Rush to Development.* Baltimore, Md.: Johns Hopkins University Press, 1982.

Nakleh, Emile A. "Regime Stability and Change in the Gulf: The Case of Saudi Arabia." In *The Politics of Change in the Middle*

East, edited by Robert B. Satloff, 119-44. Boulder, Colo.: Westview Press, 1993.

Namay, R. "Constitutional Reform: A Systemization of Saudi Politics." *Journal of South Asian and Middle Eastern Studies* 16, no. 3 (1993): 43-88.

Nehme, Michael G. "Saudi Development Plans between Capitalist and Islamic Values." *Middle Eastern Studies* 30, no. 3 (1994): 632-45.

———. "The Shifting Sands of Political Participation in Saudi Arabia." *Orient* 36, no. 1 (1995): 45-60.

Nevo, Joseph. "Religion and National Identity in Saudi Arabia." *Middle Eastern Studies* 34, no. 3 (1998), 34-53.

Ochsenwald, William. "Saudi Arabia and the Islamic Revival." *International Journal of Middle East Studies* 13, no. 3 (1981): 271-86.

Peterson, J. E. *Historical Dictionary of Saudi Arabia*. Metuchen, N.J.: Scarecrow Press, 1993.

Philby, H. St. John. *Arabia of the Wahhabis*. London: Constable, 1928.

Quahtani, Fahd. *Conflict within Al-Saud: A Study in the Political System and the Foundation of the State*. London: Al-Safa Publications, 1988.

———. "God, King and Nation: The Rhetoric of Politics in Saudi Arabia in the 1990s." *Middle East Journal* 50, no. 3 (1996): 359-71.

Rasheed, Madawai al-, and L. al-Rasheed. "The Politics of Encapsulation: Saudi Policy towards Tribal and Religious Opposition." *Middle Eastern Studies* 32, no. 1 (1996): 96-119.

Rashid, Ibrahim, ed. *Documents on the History of Saudi Arabia, Vol. 1: The Unification of Central Arabia under Ibn Saud, 1909-1925*. Salisbury, N.C.: Documentary Publications, 1976.

Rentz, George. "Wahhabism and Saudi Arabia." In *The Arabian Peninsula: Society and Politics*, edited by Derek Hopwood, p. 54-66. London: Allen and Unwin, 1972.

Safran, Nadav. *Saudi Arabia: The Ceaseless Quest for Security*: Cambridge, Mass.: Harvard University Press, 1985.

Salameh, Ghassane. "Political Power and the Saudi State." *MERIP Reports*, no. 91 (1980): 5-22.

Shaw, John A., and David E. Long. *Saudi Arabian Modernization: The Impact of Change on Stability*. New York: Praeger, 1982.

Troeller, Gary. *The Birth of Saudi Arabia: Britain and the Rise of the House of Saud*. London: Cass, 1976.

Turner, Louis, and James Bedmore. "Saudi Arabia: The Power of the Purse Strings." *International Affairs* (London) 54, no. 3 (1978): 405-20.

Yassini, Ayman Al-. *Religion and State in the Kingdom of Saudi Arabia.* Boulder, Colo.: Westview Press, 1985.

SYRIA

Ahsan, S. A. "Economic Policy and Class Structure in Syria: 1958-80." *International Journal of Middle East Studies* 16, no. 2 (1984): 301-23.

Batatu, Hanna. "Syria's Muslim Brethren." In *State and Ideology in the Middle East and Pakistan,* edited by Fred Halliday and Hamza Alavi, 112-32. London: Macmillan, 1988.

Bey, Salman Mardam. *Syria's Quest for Independence 1939-1945.* London: Ithaca Press, 1994.

Commins, David. *Historical Dictionary of Syria.* Lanham, Md.: Scarecrow Press, 1996.

Drysdale, Alasdair. "The Succession Question in Syria." *Middle East Journal* 39, no. 2 (1985): 246-57.

―――, and Raymond A. Hinnesbusch. *Syria and the Middle East Peace Process.* New York: Council on Foreign Relations, 1991.

Ehteshami, Anoushiravan. "Defense and Security Politics of Syria in a Changing Regional Environment." *International Relations* 13, no. 1 (1996): 49-67.

Faksh, M. "Asad's Western Turn: Implications for Syria." *Middle East Policy* 2, no. 3 (1993): 49-61.

Farah, Caesar F. "Religion, Ethnicity and Conflict in the Syrian Region." *Arab Historical Review for Ottoman Studies,* nos. 15-16 (1997): 135-47.

Galvin, James. "The Social Origins of Popular Nationalism in Syria: Evidence for a New Framework." *International Journal of Middle Eastern Studies* 26, no. 4 (1994): 645-61.

Harik, Judith. "Syrian Foreign Policy and State Resistance Dynamics in Lebanon." *Studies in Conflict and Terrorism* 20, no. 3 (1997): 249-66.

Harris, William. "The Crisis of Democracy in Twentieth-Century Syria and Lebanon." *Interdisciplinary Journal of Middle Eastern Studies* 5 (Fall 1996): 1-28.

Hill, Fiona E. "Reverse Orientalism?: Tribe and Nation in Syria." *Journal of Arabic, Islamic and Middle Eastern Studies* 1, no. 2 (1994): 59-75.

Hinnebusch, Raymond A. "Asad's Syria and the New World Order: The Struggle for Regime Survival." *Middle East Policy* 2, no. 1 (1993): 1-4.

———. *Authoritarian Power and State Transformation in Ba'thist Syria: Army, Party and Peasant*. Boulder, Colo.: Westview Press, 1990.

———. "Change Held in Abeyance: Durability and Vulnerability in Asad's Syria." *UCLA Journal of International Law and Foreign Affairs* 2 (Fall/Winter 1998): 171-83.

———. "State and Civil Society in Syria." *Middle East Journal* 47, no. 2 (1993): 241-57.

Hopwood, Derek. *Syria 1945-1986: Politics and Society*. London: Unwin Hyman, 1987.

Hourani, Albert. *Syria and Lebanon: A Political Essay*. London: Oxford University Press, 1946.

Kelidar, Abbas. "Religion and State in Syria." *Asian Affairs* 61, no. 1 (1974): 16-22.

Khoury, Philip S. *Syria and the French Mandate: The Politics of Arab Nationalism, 1920-1945*. Princeton, N.J.: Princeton University Press, 1982.

———. *Urban Notables and Arab Nationalism: The Politics of Damascus 1860-1920*. Cambridge, England: Cambridge University Press, 1983.

Kienle, Eberhard. *Contemporary Syria: Liberalization between Cold War and Cold Peace*. London: British Academic Press, 1995.

Knudsen, Erik L. "Hafiz al-Asad, Islamic Fundamentalism and the Syrian State: An Analysis of Fundamentalist Opposition to the Ba'thist-Alawite Political/Military Complex." *Current World Leaders* 37, no. 2 (1994): 71-85.

Lawson, Fred H. "Domestic Transformation and Foreign Steadfastness in Contemporary Syria." *Middle East Journal* 48, no. 1 (1996): 47-64.

Leesch, David W. *Syria and the United States: Eisenhower's Cold War in the Middle East*. Boulder, Colo.: Westview Press, 1992.

Longrigg, Stephen Hemsley. *Syria and Lebanon under French Mandate*. London: Oxford University Press, 1958.

Maoz, Moshe. *Syria and Israel: From War to Peace-Making*. Oxford, England: Oxford University Press, 1995.

————, and Avner Yani, eds. *Syria under Assad: Domestic Constraints and Regional Risks.* London: Croom Helm, 1986.

Muslih, Muhammad. "Dateline Damascus: Asad Is Ready." *Foreign Policy,* no. 96 (1994): 145-63.

Perthos, Volker. *The Political Economy of Syria under Asad.* London: I. B. Tauris, 1995.

Pipes, Daniel. *Damascus Courts the West: Syrian Politics 1989-1991.* Policy Paper No. Twenty-Six. Washington, D.C.: The Washington Institute for Near East Policy, 1991.

————. *Greater Syria: The History of an Ambition.* Oxford, England: Oxford University Press, 1990.

Rabinovich, Itamar. "Stability and Change in Syria." In *The Politics of Change in the Middle East,* edited by Robert B. Satloff, 11-29. Boulder, Colo.: Westview Press, 1993.

————. *Syria under the Ba'th 1963-1966: The Army-Party Symbiosis.* Jerusalem: Israel Universities Press, 1972.

Rathmell, Andrew. *Secret War in the Middle East: The Covert Struggle for Syria, 1949-1961.* London: I. B. Tauris, 1995.

Robinson, L. "Rentierism and Foreign Policy in Syria." *Arab Studies Journal* 4, no. 1 (1996): 34-54.

Russell, Malcolm B. *The First Modern Arab State: Syria under Faysal, 1918-1920.* Minneapolis, Minn.: Bibliotheca Islamica, 1985.

Sadsowski, Yahya. "Baathist Ethics and the Spirit of State Capitulation." In *Ideology and Power in the Middle East,* edited by P. J. Chelkowski and R. J. Praeger, 160-86. Durham, N.C.: Duke University Press, 1988.

Seale, Patrick. "Asad's Regional Strategy and the Challenge from Netanyahu." *Journal of Palestine Studies* 26, no. 1 (1996): 27-41.

————. *The Struggle for Syria: A Study in Post-war Arab Politics 1945-1958.* London: Oxford University Press, 1965.

Sorenson, David S. "National Security and Political Succession in Syria." *Mediterranean Quarterly* 9, no. 1 (1998): 69-91.

Tauber, Wliezer. *The Formation of Modern Syria and Iraq.* London: Cass, 1995.

Torrey, Gordon H. *Syrian Politics and the Military, 1945-1958.* Columbus, Ohio: Ohio State University Press, 1964.

Van Dam, Nikolaos. *The Struggle for Power in Syria: Sectarianism, Regionalism and Tribalism in Politics, 1961-1980.* 2nd ed. London: Croom Helm, 1981.

Zisser, Eyal. "The Succession Struggle in Damascus." *Middle East Quarterly* 2, no. 3 (1995): 57-64.

Zuwiyya-Yamak, L. *The Syrian Socialist Nationalist Party: An Ideological Analysis.* Cambridge, Mass.: Harvard University Press, 1966.

UNITED ARAB EMIRATES

Abdullah, Muhammad Morsy. *The United Arab Emirates: A Modern History.* London: Croom Helm; New York: Barnes and Noble, 1978.

Alkim, Hassan Hamdan. *The Foreign Policy of the UAE.* London: Saqi Books, 1989.

Formen, Werner. *Phoenix Rising: The United Arab Emirates; Past, Present and Future.* London: Harvill, 1996.

Ghareeb, Edmund, and Ibrahim Al Abed. *Perspectives on the United Arab Emirates.* London: Trident Press, 1997.

Hear-Bey, Frauke. *From Trucial States to United Arab Emirates.* London: Longman, 1982.

———. "The United Arab Emirates: A Quarter Century of Federation." In *Middle East Dilemma: The Politics and Economics of Arab Integration,* edited by Michael C. Hudson, 128-49. London: I. B. Tauris, 1999.

Hinchcliffe, Doreen. "Women and the Law in the United Arab Emirates." In *The Arabian Gulf: From Traditional Society to Modern States,* edited by Ian Richard Netton, 238-44. London: Croom Helm, 1986.

Khalifa, Ali Mohammed. *The United Arab Emirates: Unity in Fragmentation.* London: Croom Helm; Boulder, Colo.: Westview Press, 1979.

Koury, Enver. *The United Arab Emirates: Its Political System and Politics.* Hyattsville, Md.: Institute of Middle Eastern and North African Affairs, 1980.

Peck, Malcolm C. *The United Arab Emirates: A Venture in Unity.* Boulder, Colo.: Westview Press; London: Croom Helm, 1986.

Rugh, W. A. "The United Arab Emirates: What Are the Sources of Its Stability." *Middle East Policy* 5, no. 3 (1997): 14-24.

Shahin, A. R. Al-. "Federal Executive Power in UAE: Hindrances and Solutions." *Journal of the Gulf and Arabian Peninsula* 20, no. 79 (1995): 43-88.

Taryam, R. O. *The Establishment of the United Arab Emirates, 1980-85*. London: Croom Helm, 1987.

Zahlan, Rosemary Said. *The Origins of the United Arab Emirates*. London: Macmillan, 1978.

YEMEN

Adams, Michael. "One Yemen or Two?" In *The Arabian Gulf: From Traditional Society to Modern States*, edited by Ian Richard Netton, 120-31. London: Croom Helm, 1986.

Bidwell, Robin. *The Two Yemens*. London: Longman; Boulder, Colo.: Westview Press, 1983.

Burrowes, Robert D. *Historical Dictionary of Yemen*. Lanham, Md.: Scarecrow Press. 1995.

———. "Prelude to Unification: The Yemen Arab Republic, 1962-1990." *International Journal of Middle Eastern Studies* 23, no. 4 (1991): 483-506.

———. *The Yemen Arab Republic: The Politics of Development, 1962-1986*. Boulder, Colo.: Westview Press, 1987.

———. "The Yemen Arab Republic's Legacy and Yemeni Unification." *Arab Studies Quarterly* 14, no. 4 (1992): 41-68.

Carapico, Sheila. "The Economic Dimension of Yemeni Unity." *MERIP Middle East Report* 23, no. 5 (1993): 9-14.

———. "Elections and Mass Politics in Yemen." *Middle East Report*, no. 185 (Nov./Dec. 1993): 2-6.

———. "Yemen between Civility and Civil War." In *Civil Society in the Middle East, Vol. 2*, edited by Augustus Richard Norton, 287-316. Leiden, Netherlands: Brill, 1996.

Detalle, R. "The Yemeni Elections Up Close." *MERIP Middle East Report* 23, no. 6 (1993): 8-12.

Dresch, Paul K. *Tribes, Government and History in Yemen*. Oxford, England: Clarendon Press, 1989.

———, and K. B. Haykel. "Stereotypes and Political Styles: Islamists and Tribesfolk in Yemen." *International Journal of Middle East Studies* 27, no. 4 (1995): 405-31.

Dunbar, Charles. "The Unification of Yemen: Process, Politics and Prospects." *Middle East Journal* 46, no. 3 (1992): 456-76.

Gray, Matthew. "Electoral Politics and the 1997 Elections in Yemen." *Journal of South Asian and Middle East Studies* 21, no. 3 (1999): 31-47.

Halliday, Fred. *Revolution and Foreign Policy: The Case of South Yemen 1967-1987*. Cambridge, England: Cambridge University Press, 1990.

———. "The Yemens: Conflict and Coexistence." *The World Today* 40, no. 809 (1984): 355-62.

Hartmann, R. "Yemeni Exodus from Saudi Arabia: The Gulf Conflict and the Ceasing of the Workers' Emigration." *Journal of South Asia and Middle East Studies* 19, no. 2 (1995): 38-52.

Joffe, E. G. H., et al., eds. *Yemen Today: Crisis and Solutions*. London: Caravel Press, 1967.

Katz, M. "Yemeni Unity and Saudi Security." *Middle East Policy* 1, no. 1 (1992): 117-35.

Kostiner, Joseph. *The Struggle for South Yemen*. London: Croom Helm, 1984.

Mundy, Martha. *Domestic Government: Kinship, Community and Polity in North Yemen*. London: I. B. Tauris, 1995.

Peterson, J. E. *Conflict in the Yemens and Superpower Involvement*. Washington, D.C.: Georgetown University, Center for Contemporary Arab Studies 1981.

———. "The Yemen Arab Republic and the Politics of Balance." *Asian Affairs* 68, pt. 3 (1981): 254-66.

Pridham, B. R., ed. *Contemporary Yemen: Politics and Historical Background*. London: Croom Helm, 1984.

Saidi, Muhammad Ahmed al-. *The Cooperative Movement of Yemen and Issues of Regional Development*. New York: Professors World Peace Academy, 1993.

Stookey, Robert W. "Yemen: Revolution versus Tradition." In *The Arabian Peninsula: Zone of Ferment*, edited by Robert W. Stookey, 79-108. Stanford, Calif.: Hoover Institution Press, 1984.

Suwaidi, Jamal S. al-, ed. *The Yemeni War of 1994: Causes and Consequences*. Abu Dhabi: Emirates Center for Strategic Studies and Research, 1996.

Wenner, Manfred W. *The Yemen Arab Republic: Development and Change in an Ancient Land*. Boulder, Colo.: Westview Press, 1991.

Zabarah, Mohammed Ahmad. *Yemen: Traditionalism vs. Modernity*. New York: Praeger, 1982.

ISLAM

Abu-Rabi, Ibrahim M. *Intellectual Origins of Islamic Resurgence in the Modern Arab World.* Albany, N.Y.: State University of New York Press, 1996.

Ahmed, A. *Postmodernism and Islam.* London: Routledge, 1992.

Arkoun, Mohammed. *Rethinking Islam: Common Questions, Uncommon Answers.* Boulder, Colo.: Westview Press, 1994.

Awass, Omer. "Secular Nationalism and Islam in the 20th Century Muslim World." *Hamdard Islamicus* 19, no. 4 (1996): 91-116.

Awda, Nicholas. *Women in Islam: An Anthology from the Qur'an and Hadith.* London: Curzon Press, 1999.

Ayubi, Nazih. *Political Islam: Religion and Politics in the Arab World.* London: Routledge, 1991.

Bari, Z. "Islamic Revival in the Gulf: An Overview." *International Studies* 31, no. 1 (1994): 49-68.

Burgat, Francois, and William Dowell. *The Islamist Movement in North Africa.* Austin, Tex.: University of Texas Press, 1993.

Choueiri, Youssef M. *Islamic Fundamentalism.* Boston, Mass.: Twayne Publishers, 1990.

Dalacoura, Katerina. *Islam, Liberalism and Human Rights.* London: Ithaca Press, 1998.

Davidson, Lawrence. *Islamic Fundamentalism.* Westport, Conn.: Greenwood Press, 1998.

Enayat, H. *Modern Islamic Political Thought.* London: Macmillan, 1982.

Entelis, J. P. "Political Islam." *Middle East Studies Association Bulletin* 30, no. 2 (1996): 165-69.

Esposito, J. *Islam and Politics.* Syracuse, N.J.: Syracuse University Press, 1991.

———. *Islam: The Straight Path.* 2nd ed. London: Oxford University Press, 1991.

———. *The Islamic Threat: Myth or Reality.* London: Oxford University Press, 1992.

Ghadbian, Najib. *Democratization and the Islamist Challenge in the Arab World.* Boulder, Colo.: Westview Press, 1987.

Hajjar, Sami G. "Political Violence in Islam: Fundamentalism and Jihad." *Small Weapons and Insurgencies* 6, no. 3 (1995): 329-56.

Halliday, Fred. *Islam and the Myth of Confrontation: Religion and Politics in the Middle East.* London: I. B. Tauris, 1996.

Hamdi, Mohamed Elhachmi. *The Politicisation of Islam: A Case Study of Tunisia.* Boulder, Colo.: Westview Press, 1998.

Hermassi, Mohamed Abdelbaki. "Islam, Democracy and the Challenge of Political Change." In *Democracy in the Middle East: Defining the Challenge,* edited by Yehuda Mirsky and Matt Abrens, 41-52. Washington, D.C.: The Washington Institute, 1993.

Hiro, Dilip. *Holy Wars: The Rise of Islamic Fundamentalism.* London: Routledge, 1989.

Hunter, Shireen T., ed. *The Politics of Islamic Revivalism: Diversity and Unity.* Washington, D.C.: Center for Strategic and International Studies, 1988.

Huntington, Samuel P. "Clash of Civilizations." *Foreign Affairs* 72, no. 3 (1993): 22-49.

Jansen, Johannes J. G. *The Dual Nature of Islamic Fundamentalism.* London: Hurst, 1990.

Jerichow, Anders, and J. B. Simonsen, eds. *Islam in a Changing World.* London: Curzon Press, 1997.

Kamali, M. "Characteristics of the Islamic State." *Islamic Studies* 32, no. 1 (1993): 17-40.

Khuri, Fuad I. *Imams and Emirs: State, Religion and Sects in Islam.* London: Saqi Books, 1990.

Kramer, Martin, ed. *The Islamism Debate.* Tel Aviv: Tel Aviv University Press, 1997.

Kucukcan, T. "The Nature of Islamic Resurgence in Near and Middle Eastern Muslim Societies." *Hamdard Islamicus* 14, no. 2 (1991): 65-104.

Kurodo, Toshio, and Richard I. Lawless, eds. *Nature of the Islamic Community.* Toyko: Keiso Shobo, 1991.

Landau, J. M. *The Politics of Pan-Islam: Ideology and Organization.* Oxford, England: Oxford University Press, 1990.

Lapidus, Ira M. "State and Religion in Islamic Societies." *Past and Present,* no. 151 (1996): 3-27.

Lewis, Bernard. *Islam and the West.* London: Oxford University Press, 1993.

Mayer, Anne E. *Islam and Human Rights: Tradition and Politics.* Boulder, Colo.: Westview Press, 1991.

Mitchell, R. P. *The Society of the Muslim Brothers.* Oxford, England: Oxford University Press, 1969.

Moassally, Ahmad S. *Historical Dictionary of Islamic Fundamentalist Movements in the Arab World, Iran and Turkey*. Lanham, Md.: Scarecrow Press, 1999.

Munson, Henry Jr. *Islam and Revolution in the Middle East*. New Haven, Conn.: Yale University Press, 1988.

Mutalib, Hussin, and Taj ul-Islam Hashmi, eds. *Islam, Muslims and the Modern State: Case-Studies of Muslims in Thirteen Countries*. New York: St. Martin's Press; London: Macmillan, 1994.

Piscatori, James, ed. *Islamic Fundamentalism and the Gulf Crisis*. Chicago, Ill.,: American Academy of Arts and Sciences, 1991.

Roy, Oliver. *The Failure of Political Islam*. London: I. B. Tauris, 1994.

Sivan, Emmanuel, and Menachen Friedman, eds. *Religious Radicalism and Politics in the Middle East*. Albany, N.Y.: State University of New York Press, 1990.

Tessler, M., and J. Jesse. "Gender and Support for Islamist Movements: Evidence from Egypt, Kuwait and Palestine." *Muslim World* 86, no. 2 (1996): 200-28.

Tibi, Bassam. *The Challenge of Fundamentalism: Political Islam and New World Disorder*. Berkeley, Calif.: University of California Press, 1998.

Voll, John Obert. *Islam, Continuity and Change in the Modern World*. 2nd ed. Syracuse, N.Y.: Syracuse University Press, 1994.

ORGANIZATIONS

ABU DHABI FUND FOR ARAB ECONOMIC DEVELOPMENT

Annual Report. Abu Dhabi: Abu Dhabi Fund for Arab Economic Development, 1972- annual.

Mallakh, Ragaei, and Mihssen Kadhim. "Arab Institutionalized Development Aid: An Evaluation." *Middle East Journal* 30, no. 4 (1976): 471-84.

Nowais, Nasser Al. "The Experience of the Abu Dhabi Fund in the Aid Process." *Arab Gulf Journal* 4, no. 1 (1984): 7-17.

Porter, R. S. "Gulf Aid and Investment in the Arab World." In *The Arab Gulf and the Arab World*, edited by B. R. Pridham, 189-213. London: Croom Helm, 1988.

"UAE: Falling Oil Revenues Will Hit Aid." *Middle East Economic Digest* 27, no. 10 (March 1983): 60-63.

ARAB COOPERATION COUNCIL

Owen, Roger. "Inter-Arab Economic Relations during the Twentieth Century: World Market vs. Regional Market." In *Middle East Dilemma: The Politics and Economics of Arab Integration*, edited by Michael C. Hudson, 217-32. London: I. B. Tauris, 1999.

Ryan, Curtis R. "Jordan and the Rise and Fall of the Arab Cooperation Council." *Middle East Journal* 52, no. 3 (1998): 386-401.

ARAB FUND FOR ECONOMIC AND SOCIAL DEVELOPMENT

Alkazaz, A. "The Arab Fund for Economic and Social Development." *Orient* 17, no. 4 (1976): 85-108.

"AFESD Plans Major Expansion in Lending Activities for 1976." *Middle East Economic Survey* (Beirut) 19, no. 16 (1976): 1-8.

Demir, S. *Arab Development Funds in the Middle East*. London; New York: Pergamon, 1979.

Imady, Mohammed. "The Prospects of Economic Growth in the 1980s: Energy As a Source of Wealth for the Middle East." *OAPEC News Bulletin*, no. 5 (Dec. 1979): 17-28.

Montodene, Piers. "Arab Money for China to Bypass IMF." *Eight Days* 3, no. 38 (26 Sept. 1981): 4-5.

ARAB LEAGUE

"Arab League and Africa." *African Development* 9, no. 7 (1995): 1-15, maps.

Ansari, Mohammad Iqbal. *The Arab League, 1945-1955*. Aligarh, India: Bligarh Muslim University, Institute of Islamic Studies, 1968.

Aronson, Geoffrey. "The Arab Boycott and Its Dirty Little Secret!" *Middle East Insight* 10, no. 1 (1993): 21-24.

Ayari, Chedly. "What Future for Cooperation." *Africa Report*, no. 27 (May/June 1982): 42-48.

Azedo, Mario J. "The Organization of African Unity and Afro-Arab Cooperation." *Africa Today* 35, nos. 3-4 (1988): 68-80.

Aziz, Mohammed Abdulaziz. "The Origins and Birth of the Arab League." *Revue Egyptienne de Droit International*, no. 11 (1955): 39-58.

Azzam, Abd al-Rahman. "The Arab League and World Unity." In *Arab Nationalism: An Anthology*, edited by Sylvia G. Haim, 154-171. 2nd ed. Berkeley, Calif.: University of California Press, 1976.

Chill, D. S. *The Arab Boycott of Israel: Economic Aggression and World Reaction*. New York: Praeger, 1976.

Feiler, G. *From Boycott to Economic Cooperation: The Political Economy of the Arab Boycott of Israel*. London: Cass, 1998.

Boutros-Ghali, Boutros. "The Arab League 1945-1955." *International Conciliation*, no. 498 (1955): 387-448. (Carnegie Endowment for International Peace)

Gomaa, Ahmed M. *The Foundation of the League of Arab States: Wartime Diplomacy and Inter-Arab Politics 1941 to 1945*. London: Longman, 1977.

Hasou, Tawfig Y. *The Struggle for the Arab World, Egypt's Nasser and the Arab League*. London: Kegan Paul International, 1985.

Hassouna, Hussein A. *The League of Arab States and Regional Disputes: A Study of Middle East Conflicts*. New York: Oceana Publications; Leiden, Netherlands: A. W. Sijthoff, 1975.

Kaikati, J. G. "The Challenge of the Arab Boycott." *Sloan Management Review* 18, no. 2 (1977): 83-101.

Khadduri, Majid. "Towards Arab Union: The League of Arab States." *American Political Review*, no. 40 (1946): 90-100.

Khalil, Muhammad. *The Arab States and the Arab League: A Documentary Record, Vol. 1. Constitutional Developments*. Beirut: Khayats, 1962.

Maddy-Weitzman, Bruce. "Chafing at the Bit: King Abdallah and the Arab League." In *The Hashemites in the Modern Arab World: Essays in Honour of the Late Professor Uriel Dann*, edited by Aher Susser and Aryeh Shmuelevitz, 183-97. London: Cass, 1995.

McDonald, Robert W. *The League of Arab States: A Study in the Dynamics of Regional Organization*. Princeton, N.J.: Princeton University Press, 1965.

Messoud, Samih. "Coordination between Arab League Institutions and Arab Organizations: Problems and Scope." *Oil and Arab Cooperation* 8, no. 2 (1982): 91-112.

Olusala, Ojo. "The Relationship between the Organization of African Unity and the League of Arab States." *African Spectrum* 16 (1981): 20-25.

Saito, D. "Relaxation of the Arab Boycott of Israel and Progress in Japan-Israel Economic Relations." *Japanese Institute of Middle Eastern Economics* 10, no. 37 (1997): 5-19.

Solafy, Ali. *The League of Arab States: Role and Objectives.* Washington, D.C.: Arab Information Center, 1989.

Thornhill, Michael. "Britain and the Politics of the Arab League, 1943-50." In *Demise of the British Empire in the Middle East: Britain's Responses to Nationalist Movements, 1943-55*, edited by Michael J. Cohen and Martin Kolinsky, 41-63. London: Cass, 1998.

ARAB LEAGUE EDUCATIONAL, CULTURAL, AND SCIENTIFIC ORGANIZATION

Ali, Syed Iftehar. "Arab League Educational, Cultural and Scientific Organization and Its Contribution to Middle East Libraries." *International Library Review* 17, no. 1 (1985): 67-75.

Alkhras, Mahmud el-. "ALECSO and Special Library Collections in the Arab Countries." *UNESCO Journal of Information Science, Librarianship and Archive Administration*, no. 3 (Jan./March 1981): 55-59.

Messadi, Mahmoud. "The Financing of Cultural Activities in Arab Countries." *Cultures* 7, no. 3 (1980): 19-30.

Osman, Abdel Moneim Mohamed. "Comparative Education and Sociological Thought in the Arab Region, with Special Reference to the Work of ALECSO." *International Review of Education* 27, no. 4 (1982): 483-95.

ARAB MONETARY FUND

"AMF Considers New Facility." *Mideast Markets* 11, no. 1 (1984): 7-8.

"AMF to Call Up Outstanding Subscription." *Middle East Economic Survey*, no. 29 (4 May 1981): 7-8.

"Arab Funds to Promote Inter-Arab Trade." *Middle East Economic Survey*, 27, no. 28 (April 1984): 61-62.

"Arab Monetary Fund Meeting Stresses Economic Integration." *An-Nahar Arab Report and Memo* 5, no. 17 (April 1981): 18-19.

Arab Monetary Fund: Structure and Activities, 1977-1983. Abu Dhabi: Arab Monetary Fund, 1984.

Bailey, Robert. "Arab Monetary Fund Provides Multilateral Regional Finance." *IHT Special Supplement on Arab Banking and Finance* (Nov. 1980): 1-9.

Haseeb, Khair El Dir, and Samir Makdisi, eds. *Arab Monetary Integration: Issues and Perspectives*. London: Croom Helm, 1981.

Haskin, Jwad M. "Economic Imbalances in the Arab World." *Arab Gulf* 2, no. 2 (1982): 13-24.

Iskander, M., et al. "Arab Financial Institutions and Capital Markets." *Euromoney* (March 1976), Supplement, 1-47.

Karamali, Bachir A. "The Arab Monetary Fund: Foundation, Activities and Objectives." *Syrie et Monde Arabe* 32 (1986): 46-50 (In French).

Peterson, Erik A. "Interview with Ghabash Saeed Ahmad." *American Arab Affairs*, no. 4 (Spring 1983): 81-86.

Truell, Peter, and Susannah Tarbush. "Gulf States Wary of Monetary Union." *Middle East*, no. 85 (Nov. 1981): 64-65.

GULF COOPERATION COUNCIL

Abdulla, Abdul Khaleq. "The Gulf Cooperation Council: Nature, Origin and Process." In *Middle East Dilemma: The Politics and Economics of Arab Integration*, edited by Michael C. Hudson, 150-70. London: I. B. Tauris, 1999.

Allen, R., et al. "Gulf Cooperation: Theory or Practice?" *Middle East Economic Digest* 27, no. 43 (1983): 14-23.

Amin, Sayed Hassan. *Political and Strategic Issues in the Persian Arab Gulf*. Glasgow, Scotland: Royston, 1984.

Anthony, John Duke. "The Gulf Cooperation Council." *Journal of South Asian and Middle Eastern Studies* 5, no. 4 (1982): 3-18.

———. "The Gulf Cooperation Council." *International Journal* (Canada) 41, no. 2 (1986): 383-401.

Ashaal, Abdullah Al-. "International Relations in the Framework of the Gulf Cooperation Council." *Majallat Dirasat al-Khalif* 10, no. 37 (1984): 61-90.

Christie, John, and Joseph Wright Twiman. "Moderation and Stability in the Gulf." *American Arab Affairs*, no. 18 (Autumn 1986): 1032.

Cordesman, Anthony H. "Military Strategy and Regional Security in the Gulf: The Options for the West and the Moderate Gulf States." In *Oman, Economic, Social and Strategic*

Developments, edited by B. R. Pridham, 209-48. London: Croom Helm, 1986.

Fairservice, Ian, and Chuck Grieve, eds. *Arabian Profiles: The Arab Gulf Cooperation Council*. Dubai: Motivate Publishing, 1991.

Girgis, Moris, and Nizzar Al-Rabei. "Towards a Unified Regional Industrial Strategy." *Journal of the Gulf and Arabian Peninsula Studies* 13, no. 50 (1987): 207-34.

Hameed, Mazher A. *Arabia Imperilled: The Security Imperatives of the Arab Gulf States*. Washington, D.C.: Middle East Assessment Group; London: Croom Helm, 1986.

Hunter, Shireen, ed. *Gulf Cooperation Council: Problems and Prospects*. Washington, D.C.: Center for Strategic and International Studies, Georgetown University, 1984.

Jha, Ajay N. "Gulf Cooperation Council: An Economic Grouping or Security Alliance." *Asian Profile* (Hong Kong) 14, no. 4 (1986): 361-72.

Kechichian, Joseph A. "The Gulf Cooperation Council: Search for Unity." *Third World Quarterly* 7, no. 4 (1985): 853-81.

Kundi, Mansoor Akbar. "Security Integration under the Gulf Cooperation Council." *Pakistan Horizon* 42, no. 1 (1989): 93-99.

Kuwaiz, Abdullah Fahed Al-. "Economic Integration of the GCC: Challenges, Achievements and Future Outlook." *American Arab Affairs*, no. 19 (Winter 1986): 28-37.

Moyuddin, Badr I. "Industrialization of the Arab Gulf." *Journal of Arab Affairs* 4 (Spring 1985): 47-66.

Nafeesi, Abdullah Fahed Al-. "Gulf Cooperation Council: The Political and Strategic Framework." *Arab Gulf* 15, no. 1 (1983): 573-84.

Nakleh, Emile A. *The Gulf Cooperation Council: Policies, Problems and Prospects*. New York: Praeger, 1986.

———. "Political Stability in the Gulf Cooperation Council States: Challenges and Prospects." *Middle East Insight* 6 (Winter 1989): 40-46.

Peterson, Erik R. *The Gulf Cooperation Council: Search for Unity in a Dynamic Region*. Boulder, Colo.: Westview Press, 1988.

Peterson, J. E. *Defending Arabia*. New York: St. Martin's Press; London: Croom Helm, 1986.

Ramazani, R. K. *The Gulf Cooperation Council: Record and Analysis*. Charlottesville, Va.: University Press of Virginia, 1988.

Rizki, Hasan Askari. "Gulf Cooperation Council." *Pakistan Horizon* 35, no. 2 (1982): 29-38.

Sandwick, John A., ed. *The Gulf Cooperation Council: Modernization and Stability in an Interdependent World.* Boulder, Colo.: Westview Press, 1987.

Sullivan, Dennis J. "The Gulf Cooperation Council: Regional Security or Collective Defense?" *Journal of South Asian and Middle Eastern Studies* 12, no. 4 (1989): 39-56.

Troxler, Nancy C. "The Gulf Cooperation Council: The Emergence of an Institution." *Millennium Journal of International Studies* 16, no. 1 (1987): 3-6.

Watson, W. "Economic Prospects for the Gulf Cooperation Council." *Journal of Energy and Development* 17, no. 2 (1992): 173-207.

Winckler, Onn. "The Immigration Policy of the Gulf Cooperation Council States." *Middle Eastern Studies* 33, no. 3 (1997): 480-93.

ISLAMIC DEVELOPMENT BANK

Abdus-Shahid, Talib Siraaj. "Interest, Usury and the Islamic Development Bank: Alternative Non-interest Financing." *Law and Policy International Business* 16, no. 4 (1984): 1095-1137.

Agreement Establishing the Islamic Development Bank. Riyadh, Saudi Arabia: Ministry of Finance, 1974.

Hammour, M. "Privatization in IDB Member Countries." *Journal of Economic Cooperation among Islamic Countries* 18, no. 102 (1997): 167-200.

"IDB Finances Islamic Economics." *Middle East Economic Digest Special Report* (Nov. 1981): 2-22.

"Implications of the Uruguay Round Agreements for the Activities of the Islamic Development Bank." *Journal of Economic Cooperation among Islamic Countries* 16, nos. 1-2 (1995): 179-99.

Meenai, Saeed Ahmed. "The Islamic Development Bank Grows Fast." *Crown Agents Quarterly Review* (Summer 1979): 6-9.

―――. *The Islamic Development Bank: A Case Study of Islamic Cooperation.* London: Kegan Paul International, 1989.

KUWAIT FUND FOR ARAB ECONOMIC DEVELOPMENT

Basic Information. Kuwait: Research Division KFAED, 1974- irregular.

Demir, Soliman. *The Kuwait Fund and the Political Economy of Arab Regional Development.* New York: Praeger, 1976.

El Mallakh, Ragaei. *Economic Development and Regional Cooperation: Kuwait.* Chicago: University of Chicago Press, 1988.

Hamad, Abd al-Latif al-. *Financing Arab Economic Development: The Experience of the Kuwait Fund.* Kuwait: KFAED, 1972.

Kuwait Fund for Arab Economic Development: Annual Report. Kuwait: KFAED, 1972-.

"Kuwait: The Strategy of Investment." *Syrie et Monde Arabe,* 28, no. 336 (Jan. 1982): 21-57 (In French).

"Kuwait's Role in International Development Finance: With a Special Reference to Kuwait Fund for Arab Economic Development." *Search Journal for Arabic and Islamic Studies* 4, nos. 1-2 (1983): 61-72.

———. "Economic Development through Cooperation: The Kuwait Fund." *Middle East Journal* 18, no. 4 (1964): 408-20.

Moubarak, Walid E. "The Kuwait Fund in the Context of Arab and Third World Politics." *Middle East Journal* 41, no. 4 (1987): 538-52.

Stephens, Robert. *The Arab's New Frontier.* 3rd ed. London: Temple Smith, 1976.

Wahhab, Mahmud Abd al-. "The Kuwait Fund for Development: A Quarter Century of Donating and Giving." *Al Arabi* (Feb. 1987): 69-75 (In Arabic).

———. "On a Bridge between the Arabs and Africa." *Al-Arabi* (Sept. 1985): 132-51 (In Arabic).

ORGANIZATION OF ARAB PETROLEUM EXPORTING COUNTRIES

Ahrari, Mohammed. "OAPEC and 'Authoritative' Allocation of Oil: An Analysis of the Arab Oil Embargo." *Studies in Comparative International Development* 14, no. 1 (1979): 9-21.

Ali, R. *Oil and Power: Political Dynamics in the Middle East.* London: Pinter, 1987.

Attiga, Ali. *The Arabs and the Oil Crisis: 1973-1986.* Kuwait: OAPEC, 1987.

Carriero, Libero. "Technology and International Relations: Considerations on the Industrial Development of the OAPEC

Countries." *Annals of International Studies* (Switzerland), no. 13 (1983-84): 141-56.

Khaduri, Walid. "Oil, International Relations and Arab Interests." *Al-Mustaqbal al-'Arabi* 4, no. 27 (May 1981): 68-80 (In Arabic).

Maachou, Abdelkader. *OAPEC: An International Organization for Economic Cooperation and an Instrument for Regional Integration.* Paris: Berger-Levrault, 1982.

Mallakh, Ragaei El. "The Organization of the Arab Petroleum Exporting Countries: Objectives and Potential." vol. 2, (1977): p. 399-415, *Annual Reviews* (Palo Alto, California).

Mingst, Karen A. "Regional Sectorial Economic Integration: The Case of OAPEC." *Journal of Common Market Studies* 16, no. 2 (1977): 95-113.

"The OAPEC Sponsored Countries." *Arab Oil and Gas* 10, no. 223 (Jan. 1981): 16-21.

"OPEC Heading Specialized Arab Organizations." *Arab Economist* 8, no. 137 (1981): 39-42.

"Progress Report of OAPEC Joint Venture Companies." *Arab Economist* 14, no. 148 (Jan. 1982): 38-41.

Sankari, Farouk A. "The Character and Impact of Arab Oil Embargoes." In *Arab Oil: Impact on the Arab Countries and Global Implications*, edited by Naiem A. Sherbiny and Mark A. Tessler, 265-78. New York: Praeger, 1976.

Shavi, Khali al-. "Certain Features of the Organization of Arab Petroleum Exporting Countries (OAPEC)." *OAPEC Bulletin* 8, no. 1 (Jan. 1982): 16-20.

Sherbiny, Naiem, and Mark A. Tessler. *Arab Oil: Impact on the Arab Countries and Global Implications.* New York: Praeger, 1976.

Tetreault, Mary Ann. *The Organization of Arab Petroleum Exporting Countries: History, Policies and Prospects.* Westport, Conn.: Greenwood Press, 1981.

Tomeh, George. "OAPEC: Its Growing Role in Arab and World Affairs." *Journal of Energy and Development* 3 (Autumn 1987): 26-36.

"Trade and Industry: The Case for Downstream Development of OAPEC Countries: The Arab Petroleum Research Center." *Arab Oil and Gas* 10, no. 230 (1981): 36-40.

ORGANIZATION OF THE ISLAMIC CONFERENCE

Azhari, R. N. "The Organization of the Islamic Conference: Positive and Negative Grounds for Future Activities." *Iranian Journal of International Affairs* 9, no. 3 (1997): 341-70.

Baba, N. "Nasser's Pan-Arab Radicalism and the Saudi Drive for Islamic Solidarity: A Response for Security." *India Quarterly* 48, nos. 1-2 (1992): 1-22.

Baba, Noor Ahmed. "Organization of the Islamic Conference: Conceptual Framework and Institutional Structure." *International Studies* 30, no. 1 (1993): 35-51.

Cakmal, M. "Food Security in the OIC Countries." *Journal of Economic Cooperation among Islamic Countries* 11, nos. 3-4 (1990), 93-109.

Choudhury, M. "Islamic Development Cooperation: Issues and Problems." *Journal of Economic Cooperation among Islamic Countries* 11, nos. 3-4 (1990): 111-30.

Cindoruk, S. "Economic Cooperation Among OIC Countries and the Islamic Common Market." *Journal of Economic Cooperation among Islamic Countries* 13, nos. 1-2 (1992): 1-18.

———. "Economic Problems of the Least Developed and Land-Locked OIC Countries." *Journal of Economic Cooperation among Islamic Countries* 12, nos. 3-4 (1991): 25-57.

Gurler, O. "Food Production, Trade and Consumption in the OIC Countries." *Journal of Economic Cooperation among Islamic Countries* 17, nos. 3-4 (1996): 41-86.

Hadri, A. H. "Privatization in OIC Member Countries." *Journal of Economic Cooperation among Islamic Countries* 18, nos. 1-2 (1997): 149-66.

Hamou, E. A. "The Least Developed OIC Countries: Have They Lost the Case for Development?" *Journal of Economic Cooperation among Islamic Countries* 18, no. 4 (1997): 77-142.

———. "Implications of the Uruguay Round Agreements on the Commodity Trade of OIC Countries: A Preliminary Assessment." *Journal of Economic Cooperation among Islamic Countries* 16, nos. 1-2 (1995): 1-110.

Kamaruddin, A. R. "OIC Information Systems Network: Information Highway for OIC Member Countries." *Journal of Economic Cooperation among Islamic Countries* 17, nos. 1-2 (1996): 61-86.

Kilcer, S. "A Preliminary Survey of the Housing Section in OIC Countries." *Journal of Economic Cooperation among Islamic Countries* 17, nos. 3-4 (1996): 87-129.

Krommonacker, R. J. "Implications of the Uruguay Round on Foreign Trade of Member Countries of the Organization of Islamic Conference." *Journal of Economic Cooperation among Islamic Countries* 16, nos. 3-4 (1995): 43-61.

Singh, D. "India and the OIC (Organization of Islamic Conference)." *India Quarterly* 50, no. 4 (1994): 15-34.

Zeinelabdin, A. "Stock Markets in Selected OIC Countries." *Journal of Economic Cooperation among Islamic Countries* 12, nos. 3-4 (1991): 51-74.

PALESTINE LIBERATION ORGANIZATION

Amos, John W. *Palestinian Resistance: Organization of a Nationalist Movement.* New York: Pergamon Press, 1980.

Andoni, Lomis. "The PLO at the Crossroad." *Journal of Palestine Studies* 81, no. 1 (1991): 54-65.

Becker, Jillian. *The PLO: The Rise and Fall of the Palestine Liberation Organization.* New York: St. Martin's Press, 1984.

Cobban, Helena. *The Palestinian Liberation Organization: People, Power and Politics.* New York: Columbia University Press, 1984.

Dobson, Christopher. *Black September: Its Short, Violent History.* London: Macmillan, 1974.

Freedman, Robert O., ed. *The Intifada: Its Impact on Israel, the Arab World and the Superpowers.* Miami, Fla.: Florida International University Press, 1991.

Gresch, Alain. *The PLO: The Struggle Within: Towards an Independent Palestinian State.* London: Zed Books, 1988.

Hilal, Jamil. "PLO Institutions: The Challenge Ahead." *Journal of Palestine Studies* 89, no. 1 (1993): 46-60.

Livingstone, Neil C., and David Halevy. *Inside the PLO: Covert Units, Secret Funds, and the War against Israel and the United States.* New York: William Morrow, 1990.

Lockman, Zachary, and Joel Beinin, eds. *Intifada: The Palestinian Uprising against Israeli Occupation.* London: I. B. Tauris, 1990.

Marshall, Phil. *Intifada: Zionism, Imperialism and Palestinian Resistance.* London: Bookmarks, 1989.

Nasser, Jamal R. *The Palestine Liberation Organization: From Armed Struggle to the Declaration of Independence.* London: Eurospan, 1992.

O'Ballance, Edgar. *The Palestinian Intifada.* London: Macmillan, 1998.

Rayyes, Riad El-, and Dunia Nahas. *Guerrillas for Palestine.* London: Croom Helm, 1976.

Sayigh, Yazzid. *Armed Struggle and the Search for State: The Palestinian National Movement, 1949-1993.* Oxford: Clarendon Press, 1997.

SAUDI FUND FOR DEVELOPMENT

"Expansion of Activities of the Saudi Development Fund." *OAPEC News Bulletin* 4, no. 4 (1978): 19-24.

Presley, John R. "Trade and Foreign Aid: The Saudi Experience (1978-81)." *Arab Gulf Journal* 3, no. 1 (1983): 61-73.

UNION OF THE ARAB MAGHREB

Aghrout, Ahmad. "The Food Deficits Problem in the Arab Maghreb Union: Present State and Future Perspectives." *British Journal of Middle Eastern Studies* 19, no. 1 (1992): 54-67.

———, and Keith Sutton. "Regional Economic Union in the Maghreb." *Journal of Modern African Studies* 28, no. 1 (1990): 115-40.

Driss, R. "The Arab Maghreb Union." *Etudes Internationales* 41 (1991): 218-26.

Ghonemy, M. Riad El-. *Land, Food and Development in North Africa.* Boulder, Colo.: Westview Press, 1993.

Nabli, M. K. "Trade Liberalization in the Maghreb Countries in the Context of the Free Trade Agreement with Europe in a Cooperative Perspective." *Journal of Economic Cooperation among Islamic Countries* 18, no. 4 (1997): 1-22.

Sutton, Keith. "Political Association and Maghreb Economic Development." *Journal of Modern African Studies* 10, no. 2 (1972): 191-201.

Wright, Stephen. "Maghreb 1984-A Region Divided." In *Africa Contemporary Record, 1984-85,* 89-94. New York: Holmes and Meier, 1986.

Zartmann, I. William. "The Ups and Downs of Maghreb Unity." In *Middle East Dilemma: The Politics and Economics of Arab*

Integration, edited by Michael C. Hudson, 171-86. London: I. B. Tauris, 1999.

REGIONAL SECURITY

IRAQ-IRAN WAR

Abdulghani, Jasim. *Iran and Iraq: The Years of Crisis*. London: Croom Helm, 1988.

Ali, Mehrunnisa. "The Impact of the Iraq-Iran War." *Pakistan Horizon* 33, no. 4 (1980): 21-34.

Amin, Sated Hosan. "The Iran-Iraq Conflict: Legal Implications." *The International and Comparative Law Quarterly* 31, no. 1 (1982): 167-88.

Axelgard, Frederick W. *A New Iraq? The Gulf War and Implications for US Policy*. New York: Praeger, 1988.

Azhary, M. S. El-, ed. *The Iran-Iraq War: An Historical, Economic and Political Analysis*. London: Croom Helm; New York: St. Martin's Press, 1984.

Bulloch, John, and Harvey Morris. *The Gulf War: Its Origins, History and Consequences*. London: Methuen, 1989.

Chubin, Shahram, and Charles Tripp. *Iraq and Iran at War*. London: I. B. Tauris, 1988.

Dekker, I. F., and Harry H. G. Post. *The Gulf War of 1980-1988: The Iran-Iraq War in International Legal Perspective*. Dordrecht, Netherlands: Nijhoff, 1992.

Dessouki, Ali E. Hilal. *The Iran-Iraq War: Issues of Conflict and Prospects for Settlement*. Princeton, N.J.: Princeton University, Center for International Studies, 1981.

Grummon, Stephen R. *The Iraq-Iran War: Islam Embattled*. New York: Praeger with the Center for Strategic and International Studies, Georgetown University, 1982.

Ismael, Tareq. *Iraq and Iran: The Roots of Conflict*. Syracuse, N.Y.: Syracuse University Press, 1982.

Joyner, Christopher C., ed. *The Persian Gulf War: Lessons for Strategy, Law and Diplomacy*. Westport, Conn.: Greenwood Press, 1990.

Karsh, Efraim. "Geopolitical Determinism: The Origins of the Iran-Iraq War." *Middle East Journal* 44, no. 2 (1990): 256-68.

———. *The Iraq-Iran War: Impact and Implications*. London: Macmillan, 1989.

Khadduri, Majid. *The Gulf War: The Origins and Implications of the Iraq-Iran Conflict.* New York: Oxford University Press, 1988.

King, Ralph. *The Iran-Iraq War: The Political Implications.* London: International Institute for Strategic Studies, 1987. (Adelphi Paper 219)

Malek, Mohammed H., ed. *International Mediation and the Gulf War.* Glasgow, Scotland: Royston, 1991.

Nonneman, Gerd. *Iraq, the Gulf States and the War: A Changing Relationship, 1980-86 and Beyond.* London: Ithaca Press, 1986.

Olson, William J. "The Iran-Iraq War and the Future of the Persian Gulf." *Military Review* 64, no. 2 (1984): 17-29.

Rajaee, Farhang, ed. *The Iran-Iraq War: The Politics of Aggression.* Gainesville, Fla.: University Press of Florida, 1993.

Rezun, Miron. *Saddam Hussein's Gulf Wars: Ambivalent Stakes in the Middle East.* Westport, Conn.: Praeger, 1992.

Sterner, Michael. "The Iran-Iraq War." *Foreign Affairs* 63, no. 1 (1984): 128-43.

Tahir-Kheli, Shirin, and Shaheen Ayubi, eds. *The Iran-Iraq War: Oil Weapons, New Conflicts.* New York: Praeger, 1983.

Workman, W. T. *The Social Origins of the Iraq-Iran War.* Boulder, Colo.: Lynne Rienner, 1994.

GULF WAR 1990-91 AND AFTERMATH

Algosaibi, Ghazi A. *The Gulf Crisis: An Attempt to Understand.* London: Kegan Paul International, 1993.

Ali, Omar. *Crisis in the Arabian Gulf: An Independent Iraqi View.* Westport, Conn.: Praeger, 1993.

Amos, Deborah. *Lines in the Sand: Desert Storm and the Remaking of the Arab World.* New York: Simon and Schuster, 1992.

Baram, Amatzia, and Barry Rubin, eds. *Iraq's Road to War.* London: Macmillan, 1994.

Bresheeth, Haim, and Nira Yuval-Davis, eds. *The Gulf War and the New World Order.* London: Zed Books, 1991.

Brittain, Victoria, ed. *The Gulf between Us: The Gulf War and Beyond.* London: Virago, 1991.

Bulloch, John. *United Nations Demarcation of the Iraq-Kuwait Border: Dangerous Precedent, Regional Time Bomb or Contribution to Middle East Peace.* London: Gulf Centre for Strategic Studies, 1993.

————, and Harvey Morris. *Saddam's War: The Origins of the Kuwaiti Crisis and the International Response.* London: Faber, 1993.

Cainkar, Louise. "The Gulf War: Sanctions and the Lives of Iraqi Women." *Arab Studies Quarterly* 15, no. 2 (1993): 15-51.

————. *The Iraqi Aggression on Kuwait: The Truth and the Tragedy.* Kuwait: Center for Research and Studies on Kuwait, 1994.

Clawson, Patrick. "Iraq's Economy and International Sanctions." In *Iraq's Road to War*, edited by Amatzia Baram and Barry Rubin. New York: St. Martin's Press, 1993.

Darwich, Adel, and Gregory Alexander. *Unholy Babylon: The Secret History of Saddam's War.* New York: St. Martin's Press, 1991.

Dowty, Alan. "Sanctioning Iraq: The Limits of the New World Order." *Washington Quarterly* 17, no. 3 (1994): 179-202.

Ebert, Barbara Gregory. "The Gulf War and Its Aftermath: An Assessment of Evolving Arab Responses." *Middle East Policy* 1, no. 4 (1992): 77-95.

Ehteshami, Anoushiravan, Gerd Nonneman, and Charles Tripp. *War and Peace in the Gulf: Domestic Politics and Regional Relations into the 1990s.* Reading, England: Ithaca Press, 1991.

Freedman, Lawrence, and Efraim Karsh. *The Gulf Conflict: Diplomacy and War in the New World Order 1990-91.* London: Faber, 1993.

Heikal, Mohamed. *Illusions of Triumph: An Arab View of the Gulf War.* London: HarperCollins, 1992.

Helms, Robert F, and Robert H. Dorff. *The Persian Gulf Crisis: Power in the Post-Cold War World.* Westport, Conn.: Praeger, 1993.

Jabbar, Falih al-Jabbar. "The Gulf War and Ideology: The Double-Edged Sword of Islam." In *The Gulf War and the New World Order*, edited by Haim Bresheeth and Nira Yuval-Davis, 211-17. London: Zed Books, 1991.

Kaikobad, K. H. *The Shatt Al-Arab Boundary Question: A Legal Appraisal.* Oxford, England: Oxford University Press, 1988.

Khadduri, Majid, and Edmund Ghareeb. *War in the Gulf 1990-91: The Iraq-Kuwait Conflict and Its Implications.* Oxford, England: Oxford University Press, 1997.

Lauterpacht, E., ed. *The Kuwait Crisis: Basic Documents.* Cambridge, England: Grotius, 1991.

Maddy-Weitzman, Bruce, and Joseph Kostiner. "From Jedda to Cairo: The Failure of Arab Mediation in the Gulf Crisis." *Diplomacy and Statecraft* 7, no. 2 (1996): 466-92.

Mendelson, Maurice, and Susan Hulton. "Iraq's Claim to Sovereignty over Kuwait." In *Territorial Foundations of the Gulf States*, edited by Richard Schofield, 117-52. London: UCL Press, 1994.

Miller, Judith, and Laurie Mylroie. *Saddam Hussein and the Crisis in the Gulf.* New York: Times Books, 1990.

Munro, Alan. *An Arabian Affair: The Gulf War from Saudi Arabia.* London: Brassey's 1996.

Mylroie, Laurie. "Why Saddam Hussein Invaded Kuwait." *Orbis* 37, no. 1 (1993): 123-34.

Newell, Clayton R. *The Historical Dictionary of the Persian Gulf War, 1990-1991.* Lanham, Md.: Scarecrow Press, 1998.

Record, Jeffrey. *Hollow Victory: A Contrary View of the Gulf War.* Washington, D.C.: Brassey's, 1993.

Renshon, Stanley A., ed. *The Political Psychology of the Gulf War: Leaders, Publics and the Process of Conflict.* Pittsburgh, Pa.: University of Pittsburgh Press, 1993.

Rouchdy, Malak S. "Egypt's Speculations in the Gulf Crisis: The Government's Policies and the Opposition Movements." In *The Gulf War and the New World Order*, edited by Haim Bresheeth and Nira Yuval-Davis, 70-77. London: Zed Books, 1991.

Schofield, Richard. *Kuwait and Iraq: Historical Claims and Territorial Disputes.* London: Royal Institute of International Affairs, 1991.

———. "The Kuwaiti Islands of Warbah and Bubiyan, and Iraqi Access." In *Territorial Foundations of the Gulf States*, edited by Richard Schofield, 153-75. London: UCL Press, 1994.

Sciolino, Elaine. *The Outlaw State: Saddam Hussein's Quest for Power and the Gulf Crisis.* New York: Wiley, 1991.

Seddon, David. "Politics and the Gulf Crisis: Government and Popular Responses in the Maghreb." In *The Gulf War and the New World Order*, edited by Haim Bresheeth, and Nira Yuval-Davis, 104-15. London: Zed Books, 1991.

Sifri, M. L., and Christopher Carf, eds. *The Gulf War Reader: History, Documents, Opinions.* New York: Times Books, 1991.

Vaux, Kenneth L. *Ethics and the Gulf War: Religion, Rhetoric and Righteousness.* Boulder, Colo.: Westview Press, 1992.

About the Author

Frank A. Clements is Director of Information Services at the College of St. Mark and St. John, Plymouth, England, where he also lectures on the Middle East. He has worked as a consultant in the Arab world in Jordan and Tunisia, in Belize for the World Bank and in Swaziland for the U.K. Department for International Development. He is a Fellow of the British Society for Middle Eastern Studies and has published books on Arab Nationalism, Arab Regional Organizations, the Israeli Secret Services, Kuwait, Oman, Saudi Arabia, and the United Arab Emirates. He also abstracts a number of Middle East and Muslim journals for Historical Abstracts.